Y0-CAE-711

DATE DUE

DEC 1 0 1993			
NOV 2 1 1993			
DEC 1 7 1993			
NOV 2 1 1994			
GAYLORD			PRINTED IN U.S.A.

SOCIALISM REVISED AND MODERNIZED

SOCIALISM REVISED AND MODERNIZED

THE CASE FOR PRAGMATIC MARKET SOCIALISM

James A. Yunker

PRAEGER

New York
Westport, Connecticut
London

Copyright Acknowledgments

The author and publisher are grateful to the following for allowing the use of excerpts from:

Marx, Karl. *Das Kapital*, 3rd ed. 1967. Trans. Samuel Moore and Edward Aveling. International Publishers: NY. Copyright © International Publishers.

Mises, Ludwig. *Socialism: An Economic and Sociological Analysis*, revised English edition. Yale University Press: CT. Copyright © Jonathan Cape Limited: London.

Library of Congress Cataloging-in-Publication Data

Yunker, James A.
    Socialism revised and modernized : the case for pragmatic market socialism / James A. Yunker.
        p.   cm.
    Includes bibliographical references and indexes.
    ISBN 0-275-94134-5 (alk. paper)
    1. Socialism.   2. Marxian economics.   3. Mixed economy.
    I. Title.
    HX73.Y89   1992
    335.43'4—dc20   91-33764

British Library Cataloguing in Publication Data is available.

Copyright © 1992 by James A. Yunker

Library of Congress Catalog Card Number: 91-33764
ISBN: 0-275-94134-5

First published in 1992

Praeger Publishers, One Madison Avenue, New York, NY 10010
An imprint of Greenwood Publishing Group, Inc.

Printed in the United States of America

The paper used in this book complies with the
Permanent Paper Standard issued by the National
Information Standards Organization (Z39.48-1984).

10 9 8 7 6 5 4 3 2 1

To the Memory of

Oskar Lange
(1904-1965)

socialist, economist, and pioneer
in the reconciliation of
conflicting ideologies

CONTENTS

TABLES AND FIGURES

TABLES

FIGURES

PREFACE

During the winter of 1961-1962, I was a freshman economics major at Fordham University in the Bronx. For no particular reason, I happened to read C. Wright Mills's *The Power Elite*. This book had a decisive catalytic impact on my thinking, attitudes, and judgments. Within six months, I had firmly concluded that the various well-known and widely accepted economic, political, and moral justifications for contemporary capitalism, justifications which I had hitherto accepted without question, were almost assuredly devoid of legitimacy. These justifications were almost assuredly invalid because of the availability of various democratic market socialist alternatives to capitalism. Within two years, after additional study of economics and related matters, I had settled upon the "pragmatic" form of democratic market socialism as the most satisfactory of these alternatives. In my senior year at Fordham (1964-1965), I received the annual economics essay award for a paper which sketched out and briefly evaluated the plan of pragmatic market socialism which is the subject of this book.

More than twenty-five years have intervened between that initial awakening and the writing of *Socialism Revised and Modernized*. A large proportion of my time and energy during this period has been devoted to the study of the pragmatic market socialist alternative, and to what I have come to think of as "capitalist apologetics" in the light of that alternative. My dissertation at Northwestern University, completed in 1971, was on a topic in market socialism, and a substantial proportion of my subsequent published writing between 1974 and the present time has centered specifically on pragmatic market socialism. Although I have had the opportunity, through a number of articles in professional periodicals, of presenting a large proportion of the case for pragmatic market socialism, I have always recognized the need for a substantial book on the subject. Not only are there severe length constraints on professionally oriented articles, but in each particular article the author must maintain a very tight and narrow focus on one specific problem or issue. According to the proverb, if you look too closely at the trees, you will lose sight of the forest.

I first commenced serious work on a book on pragmatic market socialism in the early 1980s, and devoted the better part of the decade to it. The idea was to produce a comprehensive and yet reasonably detailed analysis of the potential performance of a pragmatic market socialist alternative to contemporary capitalism. Unfortunately, the length of the final manuscript (over 1,300 pages of typescript) was such as to preclude publication, at least for the time being. The present book was written over the 1990-1991 academic year. It is almost as comprehensive as its unpublished predecessor but is rather less detailed. Its relatively brief gestation is accounted for by the fact that much of its analysis and argumentation is based directly on the earlier book. Any reader who concludes that many topics need further development is certainly correct. It is my sincere hope that this book will provide the impetus to a great deal of additional study and writing, both on my part and on the part of others.

Although this book is addressed in the first instance to my colleagues in the profession of economics, it will be readily appreciated that it is hardly a conventional academic contribution. If implemented, pragmatic market socialism would affect every adult citizen directly in the pocketbook: According to the argument, the great majority would be favorably affected. Therefore the subject is potentially of interest to almost everyone on grounds of basic financial self-interest. Beyond that, it is maintained herein that highly unequal distribution of unearned property return, as under contemporary capitalism, constitutes a moral liability on the social system. Therefore social dividend distribution of property return, as discussed herein, would represent a moral advance. The combination of financial and ethical considerations, not to mention vital political considerations (in particular, would or would not pragmatic market socialism constitute a threat to political democracy and human freedom?), lends a high degree of breadth and interest to the contents of this book. Thus it is hoped that the book will be read and studied by many individuals who are not professional economists.

Socialism is first and foremost an economic concept rather than a political or philosophical concept. Any serious case for socialism must therefore take careful account of various relevant economic factors and considerations. Contemporary economics has become sufficiently mathematized that the majority of economists are instinctively skeptical of wholly nonmathematical analyses of important policy questions. Therefore it is essential that some of the more central arguments herein be developed mathematically. An effort has been made to accommodate readers from outside economics by placing the more technical material in an appendix at the end of the book. Nonmathematical readers should not be intimidated or deterred by this material. The fact of the matter is that the mathematical analysis *does not* resolve the central questions. In the end, it merely points up the ambiguity of mainstream economic theory on these central questions. Economists may or may not find the mathematical analysis to be of indirect assistance in arriving at their own personal judgments. But noneconomists may easily arrive at their own judgments without reference to the mathematical analysis, and they are certainly encouraged to do so. The bulk of the information, analysis, and evaluation contained in this book is unencumbered by mathematics, and it may be readily understood by any reasonably well informed person, even though that person may possess only a rudimentary acquaintance with economics and/or mathematics.

There are a great many individuals to whom I owe a debt of gratitude in the development of this book. In mentioning a few people here, I do not mean to slight the input of a great many others over the years. Professor Karl de Schweinitz, my dissertation adviser at Northwestern University, instilled in me a respect for scholarly inquiry which I had hitherto lacked. During my long career at Western Illinois University, several economics faculty members have been unusually supportive, in particular Norman Walzer and Richard Hattwick. A number of important scholars have provided useful commentary and criticism: in particular Abram Bergson, Howard Sherman, Charles Lindblom, and Leland Stauber.

I also wish to express my thanks to the numerous anonymous referees who over the years have recommended the publication of my papers on pragmatic market socialism, and to the editors who accepted these recommendations. The fact that these articles address ideological issues, and moreover that they arrive at decidedly unconventional conclusions on these issues, has always rendered them vulnerable to charges that they represent "unscientific" thinking which has no place in the scholarly literature. Under the circumstances, a referee or an editor with excessive concern for his or her professional standing might be tempted to reject my work as the safest course of action; one is unlikely to experience criticism for work *not* published.

I am especially indebted to James R. Dunton, Editor-in-Chief of Praeger Publishers, for his decision to publish this book. I am also very grateful to several staff members at Praeger for their assistance in the preparation of the manuscript for publication.

1

A New Perspective
on Socialism

A. SOCIALISM IN THE TWENTY-FIRST CENTURY?

An objective observer of human affairs might well conclude, in these waning years of the twentieth century, that socialism is either dead or at least moribund. Everywhere in the world, it appears that ideas, institutions, and policies which have traditionally been associated with socialism are in retreat. Deregulation of business enterprise and reduction of the progressivity of the tax system have been public policy in the United States throughout the Reagan and Bush administrations. Privatization of a large proportion of the nationalized industry sector has been carried out by the Conservative government in the United Kingdom. Welfare programs and benefits have been trimmed in both the United States and the United Kingdom, as well as in many other nations. In the People's Republic of China, the responsibility system in agriculture has supplanted the collective farm. Even in what was once the world's leading bastion of old-fashioned, hard-core socialism, the Soviet Union, the first steps are now being taken not only toward the dismantling of the entire central planning system, but also toward the actual privatization of the preponderance of state-owned industrial enterprise.

Even allowing for journalistic exaggeration of these transitions in the popular media, the existing trend is nothing short of dramatic. Should the trend persist for a few more decades, it seems evident that socialism will be genuinely dead, or at least that it will have been so drastically eviscerated and redefined as to be unrecognizable to Karl Marx and the other great intellectual contributors to the socialist movement. Would such an outcome be a benefit to mankind? Were the hundreds of millions of human individuals, who over the course of nearly 200 years have found inspiration in socialism, entirely misguided and deluded? Is the basic concept of socialism, in whatever form or variety which ever has been or which ever might be undertaken, so inherently flawed and impractical that any and all such undertakings must inevitably undermine and depreciate human wel- fare? Certainly in our self-righteously capitalistic United States of the present day, the overwhelming majority of the population, of whatever occupation and social stratum, would respond to these queries emphatically in the affirmative. But even in many nations without such long-standing, intensely ingrained prejudice against socialism, large and increasing majorities would concur with this response.

In full recognition that this argument opposes the contemporary tide of opinion throughout the world, this book will argue that whatever the actual outcome may be, the concept of socialism *ought not* to disappear from human affairs. It will argue that there is indeed a core of genuine value in the socialist concept, and that this core might be realized, in the United States and elsewhere, by an economic system designated herein "pragmatic market socialism." It is both a strength and a weakness of the pragmatic market socialist proposal that this socialist economic system has never been imple- mented anywhere in the real world. The strength lies in the fact that the system has been explicitly designed to avoid the defects of past socialist experiments, particularly those in the Communist nations. Thus the usual litany of arguments against socialism cannot sensibly be applied to the pragmatic market socialist proposal. The weakness lies in the fact that any untried proposal is vulnerable to the objection, however unthinking and unjustified, that it represents merely a utopian pipe dream devoid of any meaningful bearing on real-world human society. This book will state the case for pragmatic market socialism; it will then be up to the readers to decide whether that case is sensible or utopian.

It is important to understand that although pragmatic market socialism is indubitably an authentic variety of socialism according to the currently reigning dictionary definition of "socialism," the proposal itself is very precise and very limited, and has little or nothing in common with a great many popular conceptions of socialism. For example, socialism is often defined as a "planned economy." But as the name pragmatic *market* socialism suggests, this proposal envisions a market economy at least as free and unrestrained as the contemporary economic system in the United States. Again, socialism is often defined as the "welfare state." But the fact is that the pragmatic market socialist proposal is entirely neutral on the question of the proper limits on welfare programs and benefits. For example, welfare programs and benefits in the United States might be further restricted under pragmatic market socialism, and the economy would remain no more and no less "pragmatic market socialist" than it would be if such programs and benefits were maintained at their present level. There are a number of such important dichotomies between conventional interpretations of socialism and the pragmatic market socialist proposal, and these dichotomies will be further developed in the course of the discussion.

The core of the pragmatic market socialist proposal is for no more and no less than public ownership of all large, established business corporations. Such corporations in the United States are exemplified by such household names as General Motors, International Business Machines, American Telephone and Telegraph, and AMOCO. These names are mentioned merely for purposes of illustration. There are hundreds and possibly thousands of large, established corporations in the United States which are not household names. Under pragmatic market socialism all such corporations would be publicly owned.

The purpose of public ownership of such corporations would definitely *not* be to implement any form of central planning or direct control, such as has been exercised over industrial enterprises in the Soviet Union by Gosplan and the other bureaucracies of the Soviet central planning system, or such as is envisioned in various proposals in the West for "national planning." Rather, pragmatic market socialism envisions business enterprises operating just as independently and autonomously as they do under market capitalism. Moreover, the purpose of public ownership would not be to replace profit maximization as the chief motivation of business enterprise with some more broadly defined social objective. Rather, pragmatic market socialism envisions business enterprises pursuing profits just as intensively as they do under market capitalism. Finally, the purpose of public ownership would not be to suppress "wasteful competition" among business enterprises. Rather, the pragmatic market socialist proposal is based on the judgment that on the whole, competition is a healthy force in the economy. Pragmatic market socialism envisions at least as much competition among business enterprises as prevails under market capitalism. It is therefore anticipated that the bankruptcy rate among publicly owned business enterprises would be at least as high as it is among large, established corporations in the market capitalist economy.

What, then, *is* the intended purpose of public ownership under pragmatic market socialism? It would be primarily to achieve a greater degree of equality in the distribution of capital property return produced by the business activity of large, established corporations. The pragmatic market socialist proposal is based on the judgment that under modern industrial and institutional conditions, capital property income is unearned by its recipients, and therefore its highly unequal distribution represents a moral liability on the existing capitalist socioeconomic system.

In the United States, as well as in the other non-Communist nations of the world, capital property return is very unequally distributed among the population. Capital property return paid out by business enterprises, financial intermediaries, and government agencies is received by households as various components of capital property income, primarily dividends and interest. Another important component of property income consists of capital gains realized on sales of stocks and bonds. These forms of income are sharply differentiated from labor income (wages and salaries). Whereas no working person can fail to recognize that labor income is earned in a very direct and obvious manner, questions might certainly be raised about property income. It *seems* to accrue to its recipients without any apparent expenditure of effort on their part. Karl Marx formalized the proposition of unearned capital property income in terms of the surplus labor theory of exploitation. It will be argued herein that capital property income is more accurately described as "rentier income" than as "surplus labor." But whether capital property income is considered rentier income or surplus labor, it remains equally unearned. Of course the characterization of capital property income as unearned is extremely controversial, and in one sense the entire argument of this book is that this characterization, despite widespread current opinion to the contrary, is fundamentally accurate. But aside from the *nature* of capital property income, we must consider its *distribution*.

After all, if the distribution of capital property income were sufficiently equal, or at least sufficiently fair in appearance, then whether this income is unearned would be moot. Therefore we must ask: In an industrially advanced capitalist nation such as the United States, to whom does the substantial aggregate of capital property income go? No doubt a tiny fraction of capital property income does go to the proverbial "impoverished widows and orphans" of capitalistic folklore. And no doubt a considerably larger fraction goes to deserving, hardworking members of the great middle class of farmers, skilled workers, supervisors, executives, and professionals for which the United States is justly renowned. But a very substantial proportion of capital property income is pocketed by a very different category of people. In this book the working definition of "capitalist" is an individual who possesses sufficient financial capital wealth (primarily stocks and bonds) that the capital property income derived from this wealth is adequate *by itself* to support at least a comfortable lifestyle. In other words, a "capitalist" is a person who is *not obliged* to seek and retain employment as a means of obtaining a livelihood. Such individuals are extremely rare in modern society (and indeed were equally so in all past societies). Nevertheless, they account for a very substantial proportion, probably upward of 50 percent, of the total capital property income received by individual households in a modern capitalist nation.

When we examine the population of capitalists, whom do we find? According to the standard contention of capitalist apologetics, we find mostly elderly retirees and/or successful entrepreneurs. It will be argued herein that the available evidence casts serious doubt on this contention, and that in fact the available evidence strongly suggests that among the population of capitalists we will find mostly inheritors and/or unusually lucky speculators in financial capital markets. Clearly retirees and entrepreneurs are a far more deserving class of people than are inheritors and speculators. To the extent that the capitalist class is envisioned as composed principally of retirees and entrepreneurs, it will be less objectionable that apparently unearned property income sources such as dividends, interest, and capital gains are very unequally distributed. For if this vision of the capitalist class is accepted, then even if capital property income is unearned by the *current effort* of the recipient, it can be viewed as a legitimate earned reward to the *past effort* of the recipient: as a return to a lifetime of hard work (in the case of the retiree), or as a return to the social contribution of founding a new business enterprise (in the case of the successful entrepreneur).

The trouble with this benign perception of affairs is that it is sufficiently false as to be seriously misleading. If one looks beyond the selective and heavily biased evidence offered by the business press (*Fortune, Forbes, Business Week*, etc.) to the serious socioeconomic evidence on the nature and determinants of capital wealth distribution, quite a different perception of reality emerges. It would appear that only a very small fraction of the total amount of capital property return is received by worthy, deserving, middle-class retirees: These people are mostly supported by various types of pension income, which is quite distinct from dividends, interest, and capital gains. It would further appear that only a very small fraction of the total amount of capital property income is received by individuals who have, at any point in their lives, founded a successful business enterprise. In fact, it seems clear that the large majority of capital property income is received rather by individuals who were, at some point in their lives, the beneficiaries of inheritances and/or random luck. It seems inescapable that nearly all substantial capital fortunes were initially based on some kind of inheritance. As for the really large capital fortunes, almost always the initial inheritance was at some point greatly augmented by lucky speculation in the financial capital markets (as opposed to the creation of new business enterprise).

The significance of this is that there is no economic or ethical legitimacy in the highly unequal distribution of capital property income currently witnessed in advanced capitalist nations such as the United States, the

United Kingdom, and many others. The distribution of capital property income under contemporary capitalism is economically unnecessary and morally inequitable. Some individuals might perceive "economic necessity" and "moral equity" as separate questions. They might be inclined to argue that although the distribution of capital income under contemporary capitalism is sufficiently unequal as to be morally inequitable, it remains economically necessary—not because property income is principally a reward to entrepreneurship or other worthy forms of endeavor, but rather because no viable socialist alternative to capitalism exists. In other words, highly unequal distribution of property income is a "necessary evil"—as clearly demonstrated by the lackluster economic performance of socialism in the Soviet Union, and by many other compelling examples of the inefficiency and ineffectiveness of public ownership and/or control of economic enterprise.

The case for pragmatic market socialism presented in this book, on the contrary, is founded on the proposition that "economic necessity" and "moral equity" are inextricably linked. It is based on the proposition that contemporary capitalism *is* morally inequitable *because* it is economically unnecessary. That is to say, a "necessary evil" is not an evil, and we should not describe highly unequal distribution of capital property income as morally inequitable if it is in fact economically necessary. This book will endeavor to show that contemporary capitalism is not economically necessary by setting forth and evaluating a clearly defined socialist alternative: the pragmatic market socialist economic system. It will argue that the pragmatic market socialist economic system would be at least as economically efficient as the contemporary capitalist economic system, both in the short term and in the long term. At the same time it would enable a far more equal and equitable distribution of capital property return than is currently witnessed under capitalism. Pragmatic market socialism represents a viable alternative to capitalism, and the availability of this alternative refutes allegations of the economic necessity of the capitalistic status quo.

As already mentioned, the core of the pragmatic market socialist proposal is public ownership of large, established corporations. Capital property return (dividends, interest, etc.) paid out by these publicly owned corporations would be received by a national government ownership agency tentatively designated the Bureau of Public Ownership (BPO). The BPO would retain no more than 5 percent of the property return it receives for administrative expenses and incentive payments to its agents. It would distribute the bulk of property return (95 percent or more) to the general population in the form of social dividend income. Each person's entitlement to social dividend income would be proportional to his or her personally earned labor income (wages and salaries) or (if retired) pension income. For the overwhelming majority of the population, this manner of distributing capital property income produced by large, established corporations will be financially advantageous. It will be argued in Chapter 7 that available statistical evidence supports the expectation that in the United States, assuming no efficiency losses elsewhere in the economic system as a result of replacing capitalism with pragmatic market socialism, well over 90 percent of the population would receive more social dividend income on an annual basis under pragmatic market socialism than they currently receive capital property income under capitalism. This is a profoundly significant fact, especially if it can be demonstrated that there are very meager and unpersuasive grounds for anticipating efficiency losses elsewhere in the economic system under pragmatic market socialism relative to contemporary capitalism. Such a demonstration is the central intention of this book.

The dominant purpose of public ownership of large, established corporations under pragmatic market socialism would be simply to effect a more equal distribution of the capital property return produced by these corporations. Therefore, no significant changes are intended with respect to the environment, incentives, and behavior of these corporations. They would continue to function in a competitive economic marketplace, and would be subjected to the same opportunities and threats (including the threat of bankruptcy) that exist under capitalism. In its relations with corporation executives, the Bureau of Public Ownership would endeavor to simulate the role of the private capital owners under capitalism. The BPO agent assigned to a particular corporation would in important respects be akin to that corporation's board of directors under capitalism. The operative incentive applied to corporation executives would be to maximize the long-term rate of profitability achieved by their corporations, and in pursuing this objective they would enjoy essentially the same latitude and be subject to essentially the same accountability as under capitalism. Quite literally, upon a transition to pragmatic market socialism, the high business executives of large, established corporations could be given the following simple instruction: "Continue doing exactly what you have been doing under the capitalist economic system."

Needless to emphasize, socialists have traditionally been extremely dubious of the pursuit of profits by business enterprises, and no doubt many conventionally minded socialists would become apoplectic at the thought that under socialism the pursuit of profits would remain the central goal of the publicly owned business enterprises. It must be recognized that logically there are two very distinct reasons why high profitability in the business enterprise sector might be considered bad. First, there is the image of the profits going into the bulging pockets of undeserving, plutocratic capitalists. However relevant this image might be under contemporary capitalism, it would be entirely irrelevant under pragmatic market socialism. Under the latter system, high profits in the publicly owned business enterprise sector would translate into a large social dividend fund—and that fund would be fairly and (relative to capitalism) equally distributed among individuals in proportion to earned labor income.

Second, there is the possibility that profit maximization, in and of itself, might be economically unhealthy. Modern economics distinguishes two primary circumstances under which profit maximization is socially inefficient: imperfect competition and external effects. The overwhelming consensus among modern Western economists is that these two circumstances are *not* sufficiently prevalent in the real-world economy as to overturn the proposition that on the whole, profit maximization in the corporate business enterprise sector is an economically efficient and socially beneficial incentive. The pragmatic market socialist proposal is based squarely upon this consensus.

And however foreign the notion of profit maximization might seem to conventional socialists, the position taken here is that the logical purposive core of socialism pertains to the *distribution* of capital property return, and not to its level or economic purpose in the allocation of scarce capital resources. More precisely, a high level of capital property return (i.e., profits) signifies a high level of efficiency in the allocation of scarce capital resources. Inequity then emerges under the contemporary capitalist economic system in the distribution of capital property return in proportion to financial wealth. But this inequity is curable through social dividend distribution of capital property return under pragmatic market socialism—without any alteration in the means by which capital property return is generated by the business enterprise sector. If efficiency is to be maintained, the problem of highly unequal distribution of capital property return must be handled through alteration of the distribution mechanism and not through alteration of incentives in the business enterprise sector.

Through its reliance on market mechanisms and profit maximization among publicly owned business enterprises, the pragmatic market socialist proposal is rendered immune (in a logical sense at least) to several well-known and highly influential objections to socialism. The proposal does not entail the establishment of a bureaucratic central planning system, as in the Soviet Union. It does not involve the substitution of social goals for commercial motives, as in the traditional nationalized industry. But this is not to imply the nonexistence of logically consistent and reasonably plausible objections to pragmatic market socialism. Such objections obviously exist, and this study will endeavor to respond to them and to establish the point that despite these objections, the weight of the available evidence generally comes down in favor of pragmatic market socialism and against contemporary capitalism.

To some extent the argument will be developed in terms of the institutional proposal itself, in the belief that a proper understanding of the actual proposal will dissolve some problems. For example, the concept of socialism has often been criticized on the basis of allegedly inadequate incentives to entrepreneurship. This criticism is based on the very small kernel of truth in the proposition that capital property income under capitalism represents a return to private entrepreneurship. Although large, established corporations dominate economic life under contemporary capitalism, at any given time there are obvious examples of the important catalytic effect of private entrepreneurship in the economy. The recent rise of the microcomputer industry provides a dramatic case in point. The present ubiquity of microcomputers in American professional work would not have been achieved without the standardization imposed by the entry of IBM into the field in 1981. But IBM's action was prompted by the earlier success of private entrepreneurs such as Steve Jobs, founder of Apple Computer. Although Jobs is hardly representative of the "typical capitalist" under modern capitalism, no doubt there are a few capitalists who fit that image.

Chief among the means by which it is intended that genuine private entrepreneurship be preserved and enhanced under pragmatic market socialism is the exclusion of entrepreneurial firms from public ownership. The reader may have noticed that the pragmatic market socialist proposal is for the public ownership of *large and established* business corporations. Both of these modifiers, "large" and "established," are significant. What is commonly considered "small business" in the modern economy (small retail trade, family farms, professional proprietorships and partnerships, etc.) would be excluded from public ownership. So also would be all entrepreneurial firms, of whatever scale. An entrepreneurial firm is defined as a firm in which the founder-owner is still active in day-to-day management as the chief executive officer. Typically under capitalism when the entrepreneur tires of the management role, he sells his ownership share to a large, existing corporation, which operates the firm as a subsidiary. This pattern would be maintained under pragmatic market socialism, with the only difference being that the "large, existing corporation" to which the entrepreneur's ownership share would be sold would in all likelihood be a publicly owned corporation operating under the overall authority of the Bureau of the Public Ownership. Thus the personal and financial incentives to entrepreneurship should be virtually the same under pragmatic market socialism as they are under capitalism. Clearly, any part of property return which represents a genuine return to entrepreneurship would not be available under pragmatic market socialism for the social dividend fund. However, the numerically small deduction from the fund thus entailed would be amply justified on the basis of the economic value of genuine entrepreneurship. Thus the "weak entrepreneurial motives" argument loses all or most of its force when applied to the pragmatic market socialist proposal.

Another important issue is whether the Bureau of Public Ownership could successfully simulate the class of private owners under capitalism, and generate as high a level of competitive pursuit of profit as is witnessed under contemporary capitalism. To some extent this problem is addressed in the institutional proposal offered for the BPO, with particular emphasis on the "BPO agent." And to some extent the problem is addressed by means of a careful consideration, involving theoretical modeling as well as empirical evidence, of the "capital management" issue.

Although the economic contribution of the capitalist class is often described in capitalist apologetics in quasi-mystical terms such as "enterprise," the essence of the matter may be described in more prosaic and neutral-sounding terminology as "capital management." Capital management refers to the various exertions of the capital owner, in the form of corporate supervision, investment analysis, entrepreneurship, and so on, in the interest of augmenting the rate of financial return on his or her personally owned capital wealth. It might be proposed that the amount of capital management effort expended is directly proportional to the amount of property return received by the expender. If the class of capital owners which receives 100 percent of capital return under capitalism is replaced under pragmatic market socialism by a Bureau of Public Ownership which receives only 5 percent of capital return (the rest being disbursed to the general population through a social dividend fund), then the amount of capital management effort expended under pragmatic market socialism might be only 5 percent of what it currently is under capitalism. The result could easily be a disastrous decline in the rationality of capital allocation and overall economic efficiency.

The capital management issue is taken herein as the basis for the most logical, sensible, and plausible objection to be made against pragmatic market socialism. Much of the following discussion represents an effort to refute this objection by both direct and indirect argument and evidence. But there are other important objections to be offered against pragmatic market socialism. It could be alleged that owing to the absence of interest payments to private households under pragmatic market socialism, private saving would be lower than under capitalism, and that this situation might curtail the investment funds which society has available to maintain and expand the capital stock. It could be alleged that the expected lifetime distribution of capital property income is not nearly as unequal as the distribution of *current* capital wealth would seem to indicate (this is a formal statement of what might be termed the "people's capitalism thesis"). It could be alleged that the combination of economic and political power implied by public ownership of large, established corporations under pragmatic market socialism would represent a threat to our democratic institutions and practices. These and other objections to pragmatic market socialism will be carefully examined.

Although the verdict eventually reached herein on the various possible objections is that they do not constitute adequate grounds for rejecting the pragmatic market socialist alternative, it is certainly not alleged that the case for pragmatic market socialism is so logically and empirically overpowering that there is no rational, legitimate basis for qualms and reservations. The currently available evidence, ranging from the speculations of contemporary economic theory to the history of socialism in the Soviet Union and elsewhere, is in the final analysis insufficient to reach a definitive verdict on the potential performance of pragmatic market socialism relative to contemporary capitalism. It is explicitly and openly conceded that in practice, pragmatic market socialism might prove defective and disappointing. Therefore its implementation in an advanced capitalist economy such as that of the United States or the United Kingdom must clearly be regarded as *tentative and experimental.* There must be clear and explicit recognition of the possibility that the system will be discarded and capitalism reestablished if, after a reasonable trial period (somewhere between ten and twenty years), the economic and/or political performance of pragmatic market socialism is deemed unsatisfactory. Thus the argument being put forward in this book is not (strictly speaking) that pragmatic market socialism *will* perform better than contemporary capitalism, but merely that there is a *sufficiently high probability* that pragmatic market socialism will perform better than contemporary capitalism to merit an *experimental* venture with the system.

Realism dictates not only that it be admitted that the superiority of pragmatic market socialism over contemporary capitalism is itself uncertain, but also that even if the new economic system does prove itself superior, the *degree* of realized improvement in the overall quality of life would in all probability be far short of dramatic. No promises can be made that pragmatic market socialism would, in and of itself, lead to utopian conditions, an earthly paradise, or anything of that nature. Some recently

published theoretical work by the author (Yunker, 1991) describes numerical simulations of capitalist and pragmatic market socialist versions of a
simple computable general equilibrium economic model. This type of
approach is routinely applied by economists to evaluate various economic
and social policy issues. The benchmark simulation (Yunker, 1991; Table
4) shows a net gain in social welfare of 2.55 percent as between pragmatic
market socialism and capitalism. One must be realistic about the limited
value of such exercises in the evaluation of real-world policy questions. At
best, such simulations provide very indirect and imperfect insights. However, it may be said that a social welfare gain of 2.55 percent is certainly not
drastically inconsistent with the impression one might gain from an informal
and impressionistic consideration of the potential performance of pragmatic
market socialism relative to capitalism. The simulation results described in
the author's theoretical work seem about right, and they underscore the
limited claims being made herein as to the potential benefits to be expected
from pragmatic market socialism.

Clearly, the case being made for pragmatic market socialism is a very
cautious and conservative case. It is conceded both that the benefits are
uncertain and that even if benefits are indeed realized, they would probably
be modest. But it is hoped that what the case thereby loses in force it gains
in credibility and believability. In the perspective of history it seems evident
that many proponents of socialism in the past, from Karl Marx onward,
overstated the case for socialism. Their thunderous denunciations of
capitalism have suggested nothing less than that capitalism represents hell
on earth—from which the logical inference may be drawn that the abolition
of capitalism will produce paradise on earth. If the numerous trials and
tribulations visited upon the populations of the Communist nations
throughout the twentieth century have established just one fact, it is that the
abolition of capitalism will not by itself necessarily yield any benefits to
humanity. History has sternly emphasized the lesson that if chaos and
retrogression are to be avoided, the socialist successor to the capitalist
economic system must be carefully thought out prior to undertaking the
transition. Therefore, the reader will find in this book very little in the way
of rhetorical chastisement of the capitalist economic system, but much in
the way of careful and detailed specification of a pragmatic market socialist
alternative, together with a properly conservative analysis of the potential
advantages of this alternative. The objective is not so much a forcefully
stated argument for pragmatic market socialism as it is a carefully stated
argument for it.

It will become clear, in the course of this argument, that there is a
tremendous amount of overlap between the proposed pragmatic market

socialist economic system and the capitalist economic system of the present day. The differences between the two are sufficient to mark a clear and undeniable distinction between socialism and capitalism; nevertheless, in the larger scheme of economic mechanisms and human affairs, the differences are so minor as to be almost negligible. Among the perceptions which underpin the pragmatic market socialist proposal is that the level of economic efficiency and social welfare in the advanced capitalist nations (the United States, the nations of Western Europe, and so on) is extraordinarily high, relative to any time or place in human history. Attached to this is the perception that the economic and social performance of socialism as it has been practiced in the Communist nations of the world has been deeply disappointing and extremely sobering. The pragmatic market socialist proposal has been carefully developed to preserve the perceived advantages of Western capitalism and to avoid the perceived disadvantages of Eastern socialism.

The high degree of similarity and overlap between contemporary capitalism and pragmatic market socialism constitutes both a strength and a weakness of the proposal. The weakness is that dramatic improvements are unlikely—because the two systems are too much alike. The strength is that for the same reason serious disadvantages of pragmatic market socialism are equally unlikely, and the conventional critique of socialism, on which is founded the predominantly negative opinion in the West of socialism as a general concept, is very nebulous and speculative when applied to pragmatic market socialism.

The overlap and similarity between contemporary capitalism and the pragmatic market socialist proposal bring into sharper focus another very significant aspect of the proposal. This proposal is not nearly as opposed to the contemporary world trend as it might at first seem. The common interpretation of this trend is that it represents a retreat of socialism on all fronts. But in fact most of the transitions represent a retreat of the principle of *state intervention in social and economic outcomes*. In other words, the transitions represent a resurgence of the classical laissez-faire principle associated with early-nineteenth-century industrial capitalism.

But there is no logical conflict between the laissez-faire principle, as commonly understood, and the pragmatic market socialist principle being put forward in this book. It would be perfectly possible under a pragmatic market socialist economic system, as envisioned in this study, to have even a lower degree of state intervention in social and economic outcomes than is presently observed in the capitalistic United States, which prides itself on maintaining a much higher standard of individual autonomy than is commonly achieved elsewhere in the world. For example, under pragmatic market socialism the Food and Drug Administration, the Environmental Protection Agency, and dozens of other regulatory agencies could be abolished, the United States Post Office could be managed on purely commercial lines, the progressive individual income tax could be abolished and replaced by a regressive poll tax—and the economy would be no less pragmatic market socialist in nature than it had been before. Lest misunderstanding arise, the examples just mentioned are certainly not being recommended. The point is merely that pragmatic market socialism, per se, would be entirely neutral toward them.

Therefore, in fact, most of the transitions which are occurring throughout the world do *not* involve a retreat of socialism per se, according to the strict dictionary definition of "socialism." This dictionary definition is merely that there be public ownership of the capital means of production. The purposes of public ownership might be very general and extensive—as they have been, for example, under Soviet socialism. Or they might be very precise and limited—as they would probably be in a hypothetical pragmatic market socialist United States of the future. Therefore the implementation of pragmatic market socialism in nations such as the United States would not constitute the drastic reversal of the contemporary world trend in social policy that might initially be thought. A perception of direct conflict between the existing trend and the pragmatic market socialist proposal results from an imperfect understanding of both the logical essence of socialism and the precise nature of the pragmatic market socialist proposal. In fairness, it must be admitted that the widespread prevalence of such misunderstanding at the present time is as much the fault of past proponents of socialism as of its opponents.

As the twentieth century draws to a close, many individuals of conservative propensities are confidently proclaiming the death of socialism. Such proclamations are premature. Socialism may have a future in the twenty-first century. But such a future is likely to come about only if a more precise and accurate understanding can be achieved of the logical essence of socialism as public ownership of the capital means of production. The pragmatic market socialist proposal represents an effort to extract from this logical essence a realistic and practical policy proposal for the improvement of the existing socioeconomic system. No doubt this proposal does in fact represent a drastic revision of socialism as commonly understood. However, such a revision is long overdue, and it represents a much-needed modernization of socialism if socialism is to remain relevant to the contemporary world.

Therefore no apologies are made for this revision, and if the proposal is not to the taste of many self-professed socialists in the contemporary

Western world, so much the worse. Quite frankly, this book is not addressed primarily to those individuals in the non-Communist world who consider themselves advocates of socialism. Rather, it is addressed primarily to those individuals in the non-Communist world who today consider themselves opponents of socialism—or at least highly skeptical of socialism. In the final analysis, it is the judgment of this latter group of people which will determine whether socialism has a future in the twenty-first century.

B. OUTLINE AND SYNOPSIS

This study is concerned with a very difficult and complex question: the potential economic and political performance of a hypothetical, untried socialist alternative to the existing capitalist status quo. To aggravate matters, the question is extremely controversial and subject to strong ideological preconceptions. The role of intuitive judgment in "counterfactual analysis" obviously is extremely important. Nevertheless, the aspiration is to minimize intuitive judgment as much as possible in favor of logical reasoning and empirical evidence. In spite of the author's best efforts, the resultant discussion will no doubt seem excessively diffuse and superficial in some locations and excessively precise and elaborate in others. Obviously, much appeal must be made to the reader's toleration and forbearance.

It is hoped that some of the strain on the reader's attention, concentration, and patience can be eased by providing at this point a brief narrative outline of the remainder of the book. This outline will list the chapter and section titles, and provide brief statements of the purposes and arguments of each. Each reader will have a personal judgment on the relative importance of various aspects of the discussion; this outline should therefore be helpful for reference purposes.

Chapter 2: The Pragmatic Market Socialist Proposal. Traditional advocacies of socialism, from that of Karl Marx onward, have been heavy on destructive criticism of the capitalist status quo and light on constructive formulation of a sensible and appealing socialist alternative to that status quo. Whatever the drawbacks of the present advocacy of socialism, at least it does not share this decisive weakness. Nowhere in this book will the reader find direct criticism of capitalism. And the proposed socialist alternative to capitalism is carefully specified at the outset. Chapter 2 describes the pragmatic market socialist proposal in as much detail as is reasonably practicable, given the inevitable space constraints, and given certain irreducible uncertainties in planning for the future. The remainder of the book does not constitute direct criticism of capitalism; rather, it is primarily a series of responses to a number of diverse arguments that pragmatic market socialism would not represent an improvement over contemporary capitalism.

2A. Transition and Compensation. The significance of "socialization" in terms of the pragmatic market socialist proposal is outlined. The basic intention is to abolish the distribution of property return generated by large-scale, established productive activity in the business and government sectors in proportion to the financial assets of private households. Private households may possess any amount of financial assets (i.e., money, savings, wealth), but there would be no interest or other forms of property return on such financial asset accumulations. Certain exceptions to this rule include compounded interest paid into pension fund accumulations, and inflation-compensating interest paid by banks and other savings depositories.

A tentative compensation plan is described. While it is intended that there be full compensation of the base value of investment assets purchased directly from saving out of personal labor income, compensation may not cover the full appreciated value of investment assets or the full base plus appreciated value of investment assets purchased from inheritances rather than from personal labor income. All compensation paid for surrendered investment assets of private individuals would be in the form of cash especially created by the central banking system. The potential inflation problem of such an undertaking is assessed, and it is concluded that, contrary to an understandable first impression, inflation would probably not be a serious problem.

Private ownership of small-scale and/or entrepreneurial business enterprise would definitely be retained, although such businesses would be subject to a capital use tax designed to appropriate most of the purely rental return to capital ownership. Certain other possible exceptions to public ownership are briefly described and discussed.

2B. The Social Dividend. Property return generated by large-scale, established productive activity in the business and government sectors would, under pragmatic market socialism, be distributed to private individuals in proportion to their earned labor income. The social dividend income of each individual would be a fixed percentage of his or her wage and salary income. The question of what this fixed percentage is likely to be in practice is addressed. The possibility of a merit principle and/or a lottery principle for the distribution of a small fraction of the social dividend is briefly considered.

2C. The Bureau of Public Ownership. The Bureau of Public Ownership (BPO) would take over the positive function fulfilled by the class of private capital owners under capitalism: enforcing a competitive, profit-seeking motivation on the corporation executives who direct the large-scale established business sector. A fairly detailed institutional proposal is described for the accomplishment of this objective by means of a central BPO office supplemented by a dispersed corps of quasi-autonomous "BPO agents." The BPO would retain a small percentage, on the order of 5 percent, of the property return it receives, to cover its expenses, leaving approximately 95 percent of total property return available for social dividend distribution. An effort is made to clarify relationships among the national government, the BPO directorship, the BPO central office, BPO agents, and corporation executives.

2D. Auxiliary Proposals. The basic intentions of pragmatic market socialism would be fully achieved via the BPO and social dividend distribution of property return. This section goes on to describe and briefly evaluate some additional possibilities which are not part of the core proposal. The most important of these has to do with enhancing the dynamic performance of the economy by establishing two new national government agencies, the National Investment Banking System (NIBS) and the National Entrepreneurial Investment Board (NEIB). These agencies would be independent of the BPO and would supplement, rather than supplant, the business capital investment activity already conducted by existing business enterprises and financial intermediaries under BPO ownership. Also considered are a proposal for a modest amount of business enterprise disaggregation in order to improve competition, and a proposal for drastic simplification of the tax system to a single value-added tax to be paid by business enterprises.

2E. Pragmatic Market Socialism in Perspective. This section considers the pragmatic market socialist proposal in historical perspective. The nature and purposes of socialism, as perceived by Karl Marx and by the nineteenth-century revisionist socialists, are discussed. It is concluded that although certain of these purposes have been rendered irrelevant in the modern world, the purpose of rectifying the injustice of highly unequal distribution of unearned property return remains relevant. The significance of the Soviet socialist experience is assessed. The intellectual history of the market socialist concept, from Oskar Lange's contribution in the 1930s through the present day, is briefly summarized. Various alternatives to the pragmatic concept of market socialism are discussed, including the original Langian marginal cost pricing proposal, the "service" market socialism concept, and cooperative market socialism. Finally, the notion of achieving the purposes of pragmatic market socialism by virtually confiscatory taxation of property income is considered but dismissed, primarily on the basis that such a plan would lead to inadequate social accountability of the corporate executive elite.

Chapter 3: Pragmatic Market Socialism: Pro and Con

3A. Benefits of Pragmatic Market Socialism. This section commences with a disclaimer of utopianism—a disclaimer made necessary by the ill-considered claims and promises issued by numerous overenthusiastic past proponents of socialism. The present study concentrates on a relatively short list of relatively plausible benefits. The most important argument concerns the beneficial effect of greater equality in the distribution of unearned property return. While the case for pragmatic market socialism places the greatest emphasis on the proposition that the proposed system would not be less efficient than the contemporary capitalist system (so that the equity gain would not be offset by an efficiency loss), at least two important and reasonably plausible arguments may be offered that pragmatic market socialism would be *more* efficient than contemporary capitalism. The first is that the distribution of social dividend income as a wage and salary supplement might increase labor (presuming an upward-sloping supply curve of labor), and the second is that the concentration of corporate ownership power within the Bureau of Public Ownership might counteract possible adverse effects on the incentives to effort of corporation executives stemming from the "separation of ownership and control." Finally, more speculative benefits of a transition to socialism are touched upon briefly, including a potential improvement in the quality of political democracy and a potential amelioration of the international conflict situation. Although such considerations go well beyond the economic focus of this book, they are certainly relevant to one's overall judgment on the pragmatic market socialist proposal.

3B. Capitalist Apologetics: An Appreciation. Capitalist apologetics arose in the nineteenth century in response to the socialist challenge. Most of their further development in the twentieth has consisted of criticism of communistic socialism in the Soviet Union and elsewhere. Perhaps because many intellectuals believe that an existing status quo, such as the capitalist, requires no defense, rather little in the way of serious, systematic, and rigorous defense of capitalism is to be found in the published literature. Nevertheless, the various propositions of capitalist apologetics seem to be remarkably well entrenched in the minds of both the general population and the intellectual elite. The strength of certain preconceptions in this area is such that there is a marked tendency to apply them unthinkingly to pragmatic market socialism even though this particular variety of socialism has been explicitly differentiated from other forms of socialism to which such preconceptions might be more appropriate (Soviet socialism, British nation-alized industries, etc.). This amounts to begging the question and constitutes an unanswerable, albeit invalid, argument against pragmatic market socialism. The remainder of the book endeavors to extract from the overall body of capitalist apologetics that subset which might legitimately apply to pragmatic market socialism, for purposes of clarification and analysis.

3C. **Objections to Pragmatic Market Socialism**. This section outlines the five main themes in the body of opinion which asserts the economic and ethical legitimacy of the contemporary capitalist system which might legitimately apply to pragmatic market socialism. The single most important objection to contemporary capitalism implied by the pragmatic market socialist proposal is that contemporary capitalism perpetuates the inequity of a highly unequal distribution of a substantial flow of unearned property return. The first three themes in capitalist apologetics deny that property income is unearned. The "return to capital management" justification proposes that individual capital owners earn the property income they receive by virtue of their active social contributions in the management and supervision of an existing stock of capital, both physical and financial. The "return to saving" justification proposes that individual capital owners earn the property return they receive by virtue of their passive social contributions in providing saving resources through which the capital stock is expanded. Still another justification proposes that individual capital owners earn the property return they receive by their active social contributions, in the form of risk-taking, entrepreneurship, innovation, and so on, to the dynamic progress of the economy. The fourth theme, the "people's capitalism thesis," asserts that the distribution of capital wealth and income—in expected lifetime terms (versus current terms)—is *not* excessively unequal. The fifth and final theme stresses noneconomic justifications for capitalism, the best-known of which is the proposition that capitalism is more compatible with political democracy than is socialism. Each of these defenses of capitalism is considered in sequence in Chapters 4 through 8. This section concludes with an argument that a number of "additional problems of socialism" which are not explicitly addressed in the following discussion (for example: bureaucracy, information, property rights, public choice) are either reworkings of objections to other forms of socialism than the pragmatic, rewordings of the objections dealt with in the following, or merely obstructionist quibbles unsupported by meaningful theoretical or empirical evidence.

Chapter 4: The Capital Management Issue

4A. **Introduction and Overview**. As industrial production has matured in Western Europe, the United States, and elsewhere in the world throughout the nineteenth and twentieth centuries, an increasingly strong perception has emerged that capital ownership, in and of itself, is unproductive, and that, consequently, capital property income is unearned income. This perception, the basis of the monumental critique of capitalism formulated by Karl Marx in the latter nineteenth century, continues to possess strong intuitive appeal based on the universal experience of mankind. No one seriously questions that labor income in the form of wages and salaries is a legitimate recompense for the stressful personal exertion involved in labor, whether it be primarily mental or physical. But capital property income, in the form of dividends, interest, capital gains, and so forth, *seems* to accrue without benefit of any serious effort or contribution on the part of the recipient. Ex post facto, capitalist apologetics has developed several justifications for capital property income, but their very multiplicity may suggest that none of them is actually valid. Of these, "capital management," in various forms and guises, is probably the most plausible. However, thoughtful consideration of the basic characteristics of contemporary real-world industrial capitalism suggests that capital, whether physical or financial, obtains its value from the efforts of labor across a wide range from unskilled manual labor to high-level corporate executive activity. This section informally summarizes a number of significant pieces of evidence, ranging from the fact that most capitalists apparently work at ordinary jobs and professions to the separation of ownership and control, which together suggest the unearned nature of capital property income.

4B. Surplus Value versus Unearned Income. This section reviews and criticizes the surplus labor value theory of Karl Marx as a basis for the proposition that capital property income is unearned. It is pointed out that Marx formulated this theory prior to the development of modern neoclassical economics, and that quite possibly had neoclassical economic theory emerged a little earlier, he would have incorporated it into his critique of capitalism. There is no necessary conflict between the marginal productivity of capital theory of neoclassical economics and the socialist proposition of unearned capital property income, so long as the physical separation between capital (whether physical or financial) and the capital owner is acknowledged and appreciated. The marginal productivity contribution to production is made almost entirely by capital itself, and only vestigially through the capital management effort of the capital owner. This interpretation emerges naturally as a generalization and extension of the well-known differential land-rent theory of David Ricardo, which has been widely accepted within Western economics since the early nineteenth century.

4C. Theoretical Analysis of Capital Management. This section develops a theoretical model of the "representative capital manager" as an adaptation of the standard textbook model of the labor-leisure decision of the individual household. Using the model, it is formally demonstrated that the validity or invalidity of the capital management defense of capitalism cannot be unambiguously determined on the basis of currently accepted neoclassical economic theory. Both the pro-capitalist and the pro-socialist positions are within the wide realm of possibility allowed by the theory. Special emphasis is placed on one particular pro-socialist response to the pro-capitalist proposition that the reduction of the "retention coefficient" as between capitalism and pragmatic market socialism would significantly reduce capital management effort: This is the proposition that the relationship between capital management effort and return on capital is "plateau-shaped" and that beyond very tiny levels of capital management effort, there is little or no additional payoff to capital management effort in terms of a higher rate of return on capital.

4D. Circumstantial Evidence from the Real World. The preceding section suggests that the basic question of relative effort of the representative capital manager as between capitalism and pragmatic market socialism cannot be answered unambiguously on the basis of theoretical analysis. Thus the question must be assessed using available empirical evidence. However, the available empirical evidence is for the most part casually empirical rather than formally statistical in nature, is indirectly rather than directly relevant to the main issue, and as such is far from conclusive. In the end, the judgment made on the issue by any particular person will be strongly influenced by subjective and often intuitive opinions based on personal knowledge and experience of the world. With this proviso in mind, brief surveys are provided of four specific areas of empirical evidence bearing on the capital management issue: (1) the separation of ownership and control; (2) institutional investors and capital markets; (3) public enterprise in non-Communist nations; (4) economic production in Communist nations.

Chief conclusions drawn from these surveys are the following: The separation of ownership and control casts severe doubt on the proposition that capital property income is earned by capital management in the form of corporate management and/or supervision; while the practical realities of institutional investors in modern capital markets cast severe doubt on the proposition that capital property income is earned by capital management in the form of investment analysis. Public enterprises in non-Communist nations, as well as the economies of the Communist nations themselves (at least until the very recent past), have demonstrated reasonable levels of economic performance in the complete absence of the alleged capital management contributions of private capital owners. These relatively successful cases of noncapitalist economic production cast severe doubt on the proposition that capital owners make a necessary and significant contribution to economic production. Although substantial efficiency shortfalls may certainly be perceived in both cases, the important reasons for these shortfalls cited by professional analysts (e.g., social objectives rather than commercial objectives under public enterprise, central planning rather than a market economy under traditional Soviet Communism, etc.) would not apply to pragmatic market socialism (since publicly owned enterprises would be primarily profit-maximizers, since there would be no effort at Soviet-style central planning, etc.).

Chapter 5: The Saving Issue

5A. Introduction and Overview. A traditional objection to socialism, dating back to the "abstinence" theory of Nassau Senior in the early nineteenth century, is that the termination under socialism of interest and other property return payments on financial wealth will drastically reduce the incentives to private saving, leading either to economic ruin through capital starvation or at least to heavy-handed social intervention in the saving-investment process. This objection has the salient advantage over the capital management objection that it is not intuitively falsified by the common experience of mankind, for each and every experienced individual in society is personally conscious of the "sacrifices of saving." But the fact that there are important reasons for private household saving other than "to take advantage of the interest rate" (e.g., provision for old age, increased security and flexibility, augmented future consumption) suggests that there are indeed sufficient alternative rewards to private saving for interest and other forms of property income to be neither morally nor economically necessary.

5B. Theoretical Analysis of Private Saving. This section reviews the well-known two-period model of private household saving. This model demonstrates the possibility that the income effect of an interest rate change could dominate the substitution effect, so that the termination of interest payments on private savings accumulations under pragmatic market socialism could actually lead to a higher level of private household saving than currently occurs under capitalism. Another important point brought to light by the theoretical analysis is that higher household saving could also come about under pragmatic market socialism because most households would have a higher income out of which to save (since for most households the new social dividend income would exceed the old capital property income). It is emphasized that these are merely theoretical possibilities, and that the results obtained from the analysis are basically ambiguous on the question of interest. Consideration of more recent and elaborate theoretical and empirical economic work on saving does not suggest any important diminution in the basically agnostic conclusions to be drawn from modern economics about the potential effect on the private household saving rate of the termination of interest income on private household savings accumulations under pragmatic market socialism.

5C. Public and Private Saving. In the judgment of the leading economic eminence of the twentieth century, John Maynard Keynes, the interest rate has a negligible effect on private saving. The first two sections of Chapter 5 have argued that there are no worthwhile grounds, either of a common-sensical, theoretical, or empirical nature, for assuming that this judgment is incorrect. However, it is also clear that there are no compelling reasons for assuming that the judgment is correct. It follows that there may be a need under pragmatic market socialism for a new flow of social saving to compensate for the diminished flow of private saving. This final section of Chapter 5 argues that, even on efficiency grounds, no convincing case can be made that social intervention in the determination of the aggregate saving rate would be significantly suboptimal.

Chapter 6: Investment, Growth, and Entrepreneurship

6A. Insights of the Austrian School. For more than a century, members of the Austrian school of institutional economics have made important contributions to the body of capitalist apologetics. During the latter part of the twentieth century, a very widespread opinion has arisen, particularly within the neoconservative school of thought, that the great twentieth century Austrian school luminaries Ludwig von Mises and Friedrich von Hayek have, in their volumninous writings, dealt the basic concept of socialism an intellectually crippling blow. Specifically, they have demonstrated that although socialism might conceivably achieve a respectable level of *static* economic efficiency in the short run, its *dynamic* efficiency in the long run would be abysmal, owing to the logical and/or the practical impossibility of maintaining adequate incentives, under public ownership, to innovation, entrepreneurship, discovery, and/or other aspects of that vital rivalrous process on which economic and social progress is founded.

It is argued here that within the voluminous writings of Mises, Hayek, and other members of or sympathizers with the Austrian school, there is extremely little which is directly relevant to the pragmatic market socialist proposal. However, one may indeed directly ascertain a potential Austrian school critique of pragmatic market socialism on the basis of a six-page passage pertaining to the "artificial market" in Mises's book *Socialism: An Economic and Sociological Analysis* (1951, pp. 137-142). It would appear from his sketchy characterization of the "artificial market" that it embodies the fundamental notion of pragmatic market socialism. Careful consideration of Mises's argument reveals it as little more than a loose rendering, in appropriately "dynamic" trappings, of the capital management objection to pragmatic market socialism considered in Chapter 4. The weakness of Mises's argument can be readily perceived by anyone who recognizes and appreciates the significance of the important and active role of institutional investors in modern capital markets.

6B. The Investment Mechanism. In an effort to partially dispel the cloud of quasi-mystical confusion with which the Austrian school (among others) has managed to obscure and obfuscate the issue of the potential dynamic performance of socialism, this section reviews and amplifies various aspects of capital investment and dynamic evolution within a potential pragmatic market socialist economy. Topics range from the allowance of private ownership of entrepreneurial firms to the two proposed dynamically oriented government agencies: the National Investment Banking System (NIBS) and the National Entrepreneurial Investment Board (NEIB). The thrust of the discussion is that a pragmatic market socialist economy would be no more prone to dynamic problems, relative to contemporary capitalism, than to static problems.

6C. The Level of Investment. The preceding section argued that the *disposition* of capital investment funds under pragmatic market socialism would be at least as efficient and effective as it is under capitalism. This section argues that the *level* of capital investment funds under pragmatic market socialism might well be *higher* than it is under capitalism, owing to the emphasis in the incentive structure of the NIBS and the NEIB on the profitability of "new" capital rather than of "total" capital. Consequently, the economy could experience an appreciably higher long-term rate of economic expansion under pragmatic market socialism.

Chapter 7: People's Capitalism

7A. Introduction and Overview. The implicit message of the extremely successful "people's capitalism" component of capitalist apologetics is that whether capital property income is or is not earned in some more or less theoretical sense is actually irrelevant, because of the likelihood that worthwhile individuals (energetic, bold, productive, etc.) will in fact obtain a fair share of capital property return. This section provides an overview of the principal variations on the people's capitalism theme found in both popular and professional literature. It is argued that the strong persuasive power of people's capitalism derives principally from its clever appeal to three major human weaknesses: ignorance, greed, and pride.

7B. Who Would Benefit from the Social Dividend? On the basis of the 1963 Federal Reserve Board survey on capital wealthholding in the United States, it is estimated that approximately 94 percent of U.S. households would receive more current social dividend income on an annual basis under pragmatic market socialism than they currently receive capital property income under capitalism. This is the salient consequence of the extreme inequality in capital wealth distribution under contemporary capitalism.

7C. The Minor Role of Life Cycle Saving. The allegation that the extreme inequality in capital wealth distribution is importantly attributable to life cycle saving is refuted by further data. Among these further data are additional indications from the Federal Reserve Board survey, which show that the inequality in capital wealthholding within each age bracket of the U.S. population is only marginally less than that within the entire population, and that even among the most elderly U.S. population group, a strong majority would be benefited from social dividend distribution of capital property return.

7D. Determinants of Capital Wealth Mobility. Inheritance and random variation are considered as contributory factors to age-independent capital wealth inequality. This consideration suggests that the great majority of the 6 percent of the population that would not benefit from social dividend distribution of property return are in this situation not by virtue of personal merit but by virtue of inheritance and/or good luck. The personal merit theory of great capital wealth achieved through entrepreneurship, inventions, hard work, and so on, is supported only by the extremely selective and atypical "rags to riches" stories offered by the popular business press. The more serious socioeconomic evidence, for example, that obtained from the probate court research of Harbury in the United Kingdom and Menchik in the United States, indicates a very strong influence of inheritance on wealthholding. The additional strong impact of random chance is suggested both by impressionistic consideration of the real world and by the generally realistic results produced by random chance models of wealth accumulation and distribution.

Chapter 8: Capitalism and Democracy

8A. Capitalism: Bulwark of Democracy? In his influential tract *The Road to Serfdom* (1944), Friedrich von Hayek provided an important statement of the argument that socialism, through its combination of economic and political power, tends to weaken and eventually annihilate the principles of personal freedom and political democracy. A sharper and better-focused statement of the argument is found in Milton Friedman's *Capitalism and Freedom* (1963). The empirical basis of the argument is the historical pattern of oligarchic control by the Communist Party in the Soviet Union and elsewhere in the Communist world. It is argued here that the strong centralization of power long observed in the Communist nations has been the result of the workings of history and not of the inherent propensities of public ownership of capital. In Russia, for example, there was no important democratic tradition prior to the Bolshevik Revolution of 1917, and in the decades following the Revolution, Communist Party rule was maintained because of the natural stresses induced by drastic social and economic transitions, and also because of the threat of invasion or intervention by a hostile capitalist world.

8B. Prospects for Democratic Socialism. Attempted use of the public ownership authority under pragmatic market socialism to consolidate the power of the incumbent political party would of course be strictly forbidden by statute. Two important factors in the practical enforcement of this statutory proscription are considered in this section. The first would be the autonomy of much of the media of mass communications under pragmatic market socialism. Newspapers, news magazines, press services, radio and television networks and stations, and like media, would not fall under BPO authority but would instead be operated as labor-managed (i.e., cooperative) business enterprises. The possibility of an automatic subsidy system, to reduce the dependence of these media on advertising placed by publicly owned business enterprises, is also considered. The second factor is the potency of the democratic tradition within such nations as the United States and the nations of Western Europe, nations for which the pragmatic market socialist proposal is originally and primarily intended. This tradition has more or less immunized these nations against military coups (at least at the present moment in world history) despite the fact that there is no tangible defense against such coups. The same conditions which preclude a military takeover of the United States at the present time would also preclude an "economic takeover" by the incumbent political party in a potential pragmatic market socialist United States of the future. This section concludes with a brief argument that under pragmatic market socialism, the political system in the United States and other such nations would be somewhat more genuinely democratic than it is under contemporary capitalism. The replacement of capitalism by pragmatic market socialism would eliminate the excessive influence in social decision-making of an unduly conservative class of wealthy capitalists.

Chapter 9: Capitalism and History

9A. Possibilities for Ideological Harmonization. Since the late 1940s, the human race has confronted the nightmarish possibility of a ruinous nuclear World War III fought between alliances of Communist and non-Communist nations. An important contributory factor to this terrible risk has been the ideological confrontation between communism and its alternatives. In turn, an important contributory factor to this ideological confrontation has been the opposition between socialism and capitalism. The implementation of pragmatic market socialism in the important Western

non-Communist nations would almost certainly have a significant beneficial effect on the international conflict situation. The possibility of genuine
and permanent rapprochement, as manifested by a major, long-term program of disarmament, would be significantly enhanced. Thus, in addition
to the "internal" benefits which have been the major focus of this study,
pragmatic market socialism offers the possibility of an "external" benefit
of potentially tremendous proportions.

9B. Reform Movements in the Communist Nations. Among the important objections against the argument put forward in the previous section
is that whatever possibility for ideological harmonization may once have
resided in pragmatic market socialism is no longer relevant. The ideological
battle between communism and noncommunism is now over, and communism has been totally defeated. In due course, we may expect the Soviet
Union and the other Communist countries to reestablish market capitalism
and adopt authentically democratic systems of political governance. This
objection, unfortunately, is still somewhat premature. The "end of ideology" has been periodically proclaimed in the past, and despite these
proclamations serious ideological conflict persisted. Although progress
toward arms control and disarmament has been greatly accelerated in recent
years, we should not ignore the fact that a tremendous arsenal of nuclear
weapons still stands at the ready. We can be confident of the "end of
ideology" only when a nuclear World War III involving the United States
and the Soviet Union is not only militarily but also psychologically impossible. At this point in time, there is still enough intensity left in the
ideological conflict to pose a serious problem. It is proposed that true
ideological convergence on a common pattern of democratic market
socialism is a more promising scenario of future development than is the
ideological capitulation (by the Communist nations) scenario being promul-
gated today by conservative analysts of the international situation.

Chapter 10: Prospects for Change?

10A. A Proposal for Action. Some general guidelines are proposed for
the implementation of pragmatic market socialism through the democratic
process. A campaign to implement pragmatic market socialism must be
centered on a very precise and limited proposal, embodied in a piece of
national legislation tentatively titled "An Act for Economic Justice." It must
be a very calm, unhurried, and low-key campaign, conducted mainly
through dissemination of rational, nonthreatening information and argumentation. Great emphasis must be placed on the point that what is being
proposed is merely an *experimental* implementation of pragmatic market
socialism. The organizational focus might be a special purpose pressure
group tentatively designated the Pragmatic Progress Society.

10B. What Are the Chances? At the present point in world history, it must be conceded that the chances for the successful implementation of pragmatic market socialism in the major Western capitalist nations, or indeed, anywhere in the world, appear to be decidedly bleak. However, the project is not wholly impossible. The case for pragmatic market socialism is strong, and most opposition to pragmatic market socialism stems from imperfect understanding of the proposal rather than from informed judgment. There is a tremendous amount of untapped moral energy running throughout humanity in the present era, particularly in the wealthy nations. After a prolonged bout with cynicism and pessimism, the populations of these nations may be ready for a return to idealism and optimism—particularly if that idealism and optimism can be mobilized in a rational, sensible, and worthy cause. Under the circumstances, it would be an abrogation of the finer qualities of our human nature to abstain from commitment and action merely on grounds that such commitment and action *may* prove futile.

2

THE PRAGMATIC MARKET
SOCIALIST PROPOSAL

A. TRANSITION AND COMPENSATION

Pragmatic market socialism envisions a society purged of the unjust phenomenon of very large personal capital fortunes based primarily on inheritance and accumulation of capital property income. At the same time this society would incorporate a market economy whose day-to-day functioning would virtually duplicate that of the present capitalist economy. The intention may be described as a "socialist analogue" to contemporary market capitalism. Essential elements of such an analogue will be outlined in this chapter.

The implementation of pragmatic market socialism would require the transfer of those legal rights to capital property income (such as contained in stock and bond instruments) which are currently owned by private households under capitalism, to a national government public ownership agency, tentatively designated the Bureau of Public Ownership (BPO). Capital ownership rights held by corporations and other organizations would be unaffected. Also, private ownership of small business firms and entrepreneurial business firms would be retained. "Socialization," in the sense implied by the pragmatic market socialist proposal, may be defined as the termination of the present distribution of privately owned property rights to future property return flows reflecting the productivity of the nonhuman factors of production (capital and natural resources) utilized in large-scale, established productive activity. Such a termination is justified on the basis that the present distribution of such rights not only is extremely unequal, but also does not accurately reflect the respective contributions to economic production which have been and are being made by the various members of society.[1]

Realizing this objective would require the surrender to public ownership of privately owned, income-producing investment assets such as corporate stocks and bonds, as well as government bonds and notes. Government securities are included with private business securities because the same process which generates unearned income on business securities also generates unearned income on government securities. International capital ownership relations would be involved in the socialization process: Domestic private households would surrender income-producing ownership claims issued by foreign business firms and government agencies to the BPO, and domestic business firms and government agencies would direct to the BPO property income payments previously directed to foreign private households. Also required would be the termination of real interest payments on other financial assets, such as bank time deposits. Generally speaking, the object would be to eliminate the receipt of unearned income flows by private households on the basis of ownership of financial assets, in whatever form. The elimination of private household ownership of salable income-earning financial assets would at the same time eliminate the receipt of capital gains income by private households.

It is important to recognize that the transitions described do not amount to a proscription on privately owned "wealth" in general, but merely to a proscription on privately owned *capital wealth*. Thus under pragmatic market socialism, a wealthy individual could own mansions and estates, yachts and private jets, Rolls Royce automobiles and Rembrandt paintings, and maintain savings accounts in the tens of millions of dollars. But such an individual could not receive property income in the form of dividends on corporate securities, real interest on savings accounts, and so on. In other words, pragmatic market socialism does not imply the termination of luxurious lifestyles—it merely implies the termination of the financing of luxurious lifestyles on the basis of unearned capital property income.

Most general rules admit of some exceptions, and certain exceptions to the general proscription on private household receipt of capital property income would obviously exist under pragmatic market socialism. Small businesses and entrepreneurial businesses have been mentioned above, and they will be further discussed toward the end of this section. In addition, there are at least two reasonable exceptions to the general principle of abolition of interest payments on financial assets. First, banks and other savings associations should be required to pay a rate of compound interest on savings deposits equal to the current rate of inflation. This would be for the purpose of maintaining the real value of savings accumulations against inflationary decay. This is an "apparent" rather than an "actual" exception to the above-described intention of socialism because a nominal rate of interest equal to the rate of inflation implies a zero real interest rate.

Second, financial intermediaries such as insurance companies and pension funds holding private savings accumulations intended for the provision of retirement income would pay a competitively determined compound interest rate into these accumulations. This would maintain the present situation with respect to retirement income, and would reduce the current saving rate required of private households to achieve any given retirement income goal. As such contractual retirement income payments are terminated upon the death of the beneficiary, or of his or her spouse, they do not involve permanent, transferable property income rights, and thus the allowance for compound interest in the accumulation of retirement income rights would not be inconsistent with the intention of socialism.

With regard to compensation for surrendered investment assets, particularly great care would be exercised to avoid the expropriation of any asset accumulations derived directly from the personal labor income of the owner. On the other hand, it would not be regarded as morally obligatory to compensate fully that value of investment assets representing appreciation since initial acquisition out of labor income, or representing initial plus appreciated value of inheritances. As larger capital wealthholdings almost invariably involve some combination of inheritance and appreciation, the percentage of capital wealth compensated would decline with the wealth level. However, the compensation schedule would be sufficiently liberal to avoid imposing undue material hardship on individuals previously dependent mostly on property income. The objective of avoiding any expropriation of labor income accumulations would be facilitated by a provision for full compensation of all small-to-medium capital asset accumulations, up to perhaps $1 million in value, even though in fact many such accumulations would represent primarily appreciated value, frequently on an inherited asset base. Beyond $1 million, a declining fraction of capital wealth would be compensated, with the proviso that full compensation would be paid for all capital wealth derived directly from the owner's personal labor income (or that of a spouse). The burden of proof, however, would be placed on those very wealthy capitalists claiming to have derived their capital wealth entirely from their own personal labor income.

Although various nationalizations of privately owned business in the past are commonly thought of as having represented "socialization," the fact is that most of these endeavors were entirely unrelated to socialization as envisioned by the pragmatic market socialist proposal. First, these nationalizations were carried out in order to supplant straightforward commercial motivations in the affected firms with broader, socially determined objectives. In contrast, pragmatic market socialism envisions the continuation of profit maximization as the standard motivation in the publicly owned business enterprise sector. Second, equalization of the distribution of unearned capital property return was not an important consideration in traditional nationalizations, whereas it is the central consideration in pragmatic market socialism. Therefore, traditional nationalizations have usually been accompanied by compensation plans involving the replacement of corporate stocks and bonds with national government bonds. But as mentioned above, interest on government bonds is no less unearned than interest on corporate bonds. Thus compensation paid for privately owned capital assets as part of the implementation of pragmatic market socialism clearly could not be in the form of interest-bearing government bonds.

All compensation for surrendered investment assets would be paid in cash especially created for the purpose by the central banking system. At first glance, this suggests the possibility of a giant inflation. But in fact any inflationary propensity would be minor. Small-to-medium capital wealth accumulations mostly represent stores of value, so that their conversion to cash should not augment the propensity to immediate consumption. Large capital wealth accumulations, on the other hand, represent sources of significant property income to their owners. Although under socialism financial asset accumulations would no longer be sources of property income for their owners, the conversion of compensation cash into immediate consumption would be greatly constrained by a significant wealth effect. As only a part of large capital wealth accumulations would be compensated, the value of cash compensation would be considerably less than the prior value of the surrendered assets. Moreover, compensation cash would not yield a future property return. Wealthy capitalists accustomed to spending large amounts on consumption in the expectation of large future flows of property income may well be obliged to reduce their current consumption, lest spending out of compensation cash hoards rapidly deplete them and leave their owners in serious financial straits. In sum, while it is clear that large-scale cash creation by the national government *in the absence of the envisioned capital wealth transfer* would be highly inflationary, this should not be allowed to create a naive expectation of serious inflation resulting from the potential transition under consideration here.

Two types of business enterprise would definitely remain in private ownership under pragmatic market socialism: small business and entrepreneurial business. However, all privately owned businesses would be subject to a "capital use" tax, payable to the Bureau of Public Ownership, and designed to appropriate most of the purely rental component of their profits. The capital use tax would be approximately equal to the average rate of profit on business physical capital in the economy, and would be assessed on the net value of such capital owned by the firm. Employees of privately owned firms would be eligible for social dividend income, to be paid out of capital use tax proceeds. The exception to social ownership with respect to small business is motivated mainly by the heavy administrative burden that would be imposed on the BPO if it were responsible for evaluating the profit performance of the managers of the hundreds of thousands of small business enterprises in a large, modern economy. The exception with respect to entrepreneurial business is motivated by the possibility that private entrepreneurial endeavor might play a significant positive role in the dynamic performance of the economy.

While it is evident that the great majority of product and process innovations are undertaken by established firms in the modern economy, there have been many instances in the history of modern capitalism of an apparently beneficial catalytic impact of private entrepreneurial activity. It is intended that entrepreneurial activity be encouraged under pragmatic market socialism via the National Investment Banking System (NIBS) and the National Entrepreneurial Investment Board (NEIB), described below (Chapter 2, Section D, and Chapter 6, Section C). But some analysts might be skeptical of such "institutionalized" entrepreneurial activity. While it is quite possible that the significance of private entrepreneurial activity is exaggerated to the point of mythology in capitalist apologetics, there is sufficient plausibility that this activity is indeed important to merit an exception to the general principle of social ownership of business enterprise.

Therefore, publicly owned financial intermediaries would not merely be allowed but would be actively encouraged to lend financial capital to entrepreneurial business enterprises founded by private individuals. So long as the founder-owner remains personally active as the chief executive of an entrepreneurial firm, it would remain privately owned no matter how large and successful it becomes. The transition to public ownership would normally occur when the founder-owner voluntarily departs from the management of the firm following upon its sale to an established publicly owned firm. This is already the typical pattern under capitalism: A founder-owner builds up an entrepreneurial enterprise, then realizes its capitalized value as personal gain by selling it to an established firm. As this standard pattern of private entrepreneurship would be duplicated under pragmatic market socialism, there is little reason to expect pragmatic market socialism to be significantly less favored by private entrepreneurship than is the contemporary capitalist economy.

Possible other exceptions to public ownership by the BPO include nonprofit organizations and cooperative firms (i.e., labor-managed firms)— subject to the provisions that such firms do not make property income payments to passive private outside owners, and that they be subject to the standard capital use tax. In fact, the basic pragmatic market socialist proposal does incorporate the provision that much of the media of communication (publishing houses, radio and television networks, etc.) would definitely be exempted from BPO ownership on political grounds. As discussed in Chapter 8, Section B, these firms would operate under the cooperative principle in order to forestall any possibilities that they could be utilized by the incumbent political party in the national government to hamper and suppress political dissent and opposition.

B. THE SOCIAL DIVIDEND

Under pragmatic market socialism, the Bureau of Public Ownership would receive property income on those investment assets currently owned by private households under capitalism. Such investment assets include primarily stocks and bonds issued by business enterprises, and bonds and notes issued by government agencies. In addition, the BPO would receive the proceeds from the capital use tax on privately owned small and entrepreneurial businesses. Contractual arrangements for interest income and repayment of principal would be enforced by the BPO through the same legal channels currently utilized under capitalism. As for the profits of publicly owned business enterprises, the division of these between dividends paid to the BPO (and other outside owners, such as financial intermediaries), and retained earnings, would remain at the discretion of the executives of each corporation. The BPO would take over the formal legal powers vested in stock instruments, but in contrast with the situation under capitalism, in which the board of directors of each corporation may in principle issue detailed instructions to the executives regarding production, pricing, disposition of after-tax profits, and so on, the BPO's powers would be strictly confined to supervision of top executive remuneration and evaluation of top executives in terms of summary measures of corporate performance. Thus the amount of property return it received in each period would not be directly controllable by the BPO.

The statutory articles under which it would be established would require the BPO to disburse the large majority of the property return it receives to the general public as social dividend income. The benchmark figure cited herein is a minimum of 95 percent social dividend distribution, implying a maximum 5 percent retention percentage by the BPO. Quite possibly it would not be necessary to have the BPO retain this large a percentage of the property return in order to accomplish its economic purpose. In arguing for a hypothetical alternative as inherently controversial as pragmatic market socialism, it is wise to err on the side of conservatism.

It is essential that the net property return, after deducting BPO expenses, not be "plowed into" general public expenditures, and that the benefit of public ownership of capital be realized in the form of lower taxes on the public. For pragmatic market socialism to be politically feasible, it must be possible for each citizen to compare a direct and tangible social dividend income supplement against whatever direct and tangible property income supplement has been lost through the abolition of capitalism. Furthermore, it will improve the quality of social decision-making if each citizen can make a tangible distinction between the personal benefit flowing from public ownership of the nonhuman factors utilized in large-scale production, such a benefit taking the form of social dividend income, and the cost of public goods and services in the form of tax obligations.

Current labor income (wages and salaries) would be the dominant basis for distribution of the social dividend fund. That is, employed individuals would receive social dividend income in proportion to their earned labor income. Retirees would receive social dividend in proportion to pensions and other contractual retirement benefits. Whereas under capitalism, property return is distributed to individuals in proportion to their personally owned accumulations of financial assets, under pragmatic market socialism, this return would be distributed to individuals in proportion to their personally earned labor incomes.

Admirers of capitalism continually dwell on the point that under socialism, deserving people would no longer receive interest income and other forms of property income. Thus is engendered a sense of profound loss and deprivation. In arguing the case for pragmatic market socialism, therefore, it is vitally important to place heavy emphasis on the fact that under this particular socialist proposal, the loss to the private household of capital property income would be directly counterbalanced by the gain of social dividend income. At the present time, people tend to regard it as a serious liability of socialism that it would deprive them of property income—without considering the fact that the present-day capitalist system (relative to the pragmatic market socialist alternative) is depriving them of social dividend income.

It will be argued below (Chapter 7, Section B) that for about 94 percent of the United States population, the amount of social dividend income which capitalism is presently denying them is greater than the amount of capital property income which pragmatic market socialism would deny them. This is, of course, only an estimate. But regardless of the exact figure, it is fairly clear from the available evidence on capital wealth distribution that unless pragmatic market socialism were to be more or less drastically inefficient relative to capitalism, the great majority of the population would receive more social dividend income than they currently receive capital property income. If ever the practical implications of this reality are finally recognized and comprehended by the general public, the continuation of the present capitalistic status quo may well be called into serious political question.

The administrative costs of social dividend disbursement could probably be kept to a modest level by having the BPO make aggregate distributions to business enterprises and government agencies. Each enterprise and agency would receive an amount proportional to its wage and salary bill, and would be responsible for distributing an amount to each individual employee proportional to that employee's labor remuneration. Retired persons living on pension or equivalent income would receive social dividend income through BPO distributions to financial intermediaries. A number of additional policy questions concerning the social dividend will be left for future consideration. Examples include whether social dividend income should be received by the disabled and the unemployed, the self-employed, and nonremunerated workers such as married homemakers.

There are two crucial numerical questions with respect to the social dividend under pragmatic market socialism: (1) What percentage of his or her labor income would the individual citizen receive in the form of social dividend income? (2) What part of the population would receive more social dividend income than they currently receive capital property income? As mentioned above, the second question is addressed carefully in Chapter 7, Section B. The first question is briefly considered in the following paragraph.

An extravagant upper estimate of the social dividend percentage would be national income less wage and salary income, as a percentage of wage and salary income. This would give a figure in excess of 20 percent. Of course, such a figure would be a gross over-estimate. To cite one consideration out of several, only about 25 percent of the corporate profits figure in national income accounting is actually distributed as dividends; the rest goes to taxes and retained earnings. A relatively conservative estimate made by the present author of the amount of property return that would have been available in 1972 in the United States for social dividend distribution, represented 6.75 percent of the "compensation of employees" figure in the national income accounts (Yunker, 1977). Taking practically every reasonable deduction into account, the social dividend percentage would almost certainly be a minimum of 5 percent, and it might well be substantially higher. Even taking the minimum 5 percent figure, for most individuals 5 percent of their present labor income in social dividend income would not represent a trifling or negligible amount of money.

An important allegation of capitalist apologetics is that capital property income, in whatever amounts received by private individuals, reflects the recipients' personal contributions to society. It is argued herein that the dominant role of inheritance and random variation under contemporary capitalism in generating the present highly unequal distribution of the stock of capital wealth (and consequently of the flow of capital property income) makes a mockery of this contention. However, it has become ingrained in the public mind that an important positive function of property income is to reward the social contributions of individuals. An effort might be made under pragmatic market socialism to inject a measure of reality into this perception by means of earmarking a very small percentage of the social dividend fund, certainly not to exceed 10 percent, for merit awards. Such awards would be bestowed on individuals who have made, in the judgment of disinterested committees, outstanding contributions in science, culture, and other areas of human endeavor. They would be in the form of a substantial assured annuity, sufficient to support at least a comfortable lifestyle, to continue for the lifetime of the recipient.

Another allegation of capitalist apologetics cites what might be termed the "inspirational" role of property return. The existence of property return, so it could be argued, enables every person in society to dream about the possibility of someday being liberated from the onerous necessity to per-form daily labor by means of accumulating a sufficient amount of capital wealth to live on the property income produced by the accumulation. It may or may not be admitted that without benefit of inheritances and/or extraor-dinary good luck, such dreams are very rarely fulfilled. But even if it is admitted, it may nevertheless be maintained that even that tiny and vestigial hope of "living off the interest" which capitalism extends to the noninheritor is a very fine and worthwhile thing which would necessarily be abrogated by socialism.

The recent popularity in the United States of state lotteries featuring substantial long-term income awards suggests a solution to the problem (presuming it is a problem). The solution would be a BPO lottery featuring substantial lifetime income awards, in which chances would be purchased by means of individuals' voluntarily authorizing the withholding of whatever proportion they wish of the social dividend payment to which they are entitled on the basis of their labor income. In contrast with state lotteries, the BPO lottery would not be considered a revenue source: The only deduction from the prize fund represented by duly authorized withheld social dividend would be for the administrative costs of the lottery. Thus, if

38   SOCIALISM REVISED AND MODERNIZED

it should be true that a considerable number of people derive significant
comfort from the thought that extraordinary good luck might someday
liberate them forever from the need to work for a living, such people could
be as happy under pragmatic market socialism as they are under capitalism.

C. THE BUREAU OF PUBLIC OWNERSHIP

According to basic economic theory, the critical consequence of private
ownership of business enterprises is that these enterprises are guided in their
activities by a profit maximization incentive. This incentive in turn con-
duces to a high level of efficiency in the operations through which business
enterprises transform productive factors such as labor, machinery, and raw
materials into finished goods and services. In the case of business
enterprises which are financial intermediaries (banks, savings institutions,
insurance companies, pension funds, etc.), the profit maximization incentive guarantees the efficient allocation of financial capital among private
households borrowing for consumption purposes, business firms borrowing
for capital investment purposes, and government agencies borrowing to
create social infrastructure and to cover other public expenditures.

Private ownership of business enterprise is thus primarily defensible on
grounds that the profit incentive thus imposed on business enterprises
promotes economic efficiency. From an economic point of view, therefore,
the principal positive function of the class of private capital owners is to
enforce a strong profit maximization incentive among the corps of executives responsible for the day-to-day management of the large corporate
enterprises which dominate contemporary economic life. The mission of
the Bureau of Public Ownership (BPO) would be to duplicate this positive
role: to enforce upon the executives who manage the publicly owned
business corporations a strong profit motivation. The fact that the proposed
BPO is not a purely passive agency which would simply collect and disburse
property income indicates that it is accepted that capital owners do—or at
least may—make some positive social contribution which needs to be
maintained. However, under contemporary capitalism society pays the class
of private capital owners far more than is necessary to elicit this positive
contribution.

The exact organizational details that would best accomplish the goal of
maintaining a strong profit motivation within the publicly owned business
enterprise sector at a reasonable cost to society are a matter for careful
thought and study—both prior to and after a potential implementation of
pragmatic market socialism. However, some tentative general guidelines

must obviously be provided here. To begin with, the organization and procedures of a potential federal government BPO are sketched very briefly. This is followed by a lengthier evaluative amplification of these proposals.

The Bureau of Public Ownership would establish performance criteria according to which each corporation president would be evaluated for purposes of remuneration and retention. This applies alike to industrial corporations, mercantile corporations, transportation corporations, financial intermediary corporations, and so on. These performance criteria would be strongly dependent upon the current property return produced by the corporation, including profits and interest payments, but some weight might also be attached to indicators of long-term profit potential, such as sales growth, innovations, and cost reductions. Principles of remuneration for top corporation executives would be proposed by the corporation executives themselves, subject to approval by the BPO. Remuneration would be strongly dependent on profitability, but so also—possibly even more significantly from the point of view of the effort incentives of the top executives—would be job retention. Presidents of corporations exhibiting sufficiently deficient performance would be subject to dismissal. As dismissal of a corporation president would be a drastic action, the conditions under which this event would occur would be carefully prescribed, along lines indicated in the following.

It is envisioned that the Bureau of Public Ownership would be a two-tiered agency. The first tier would be a central office located in the national capital. One responsibility of the central office would be to collect property return from the publicly owned business corporations and disburse social dividend payments to the working population. Another responsibility would be to collect an array of statistical information from the corporations that could be used to estimate corporate performance functions. From such performance functions the expected performance of any given corporation could be estimated, along with a confidence interval around that performance level. A numerical rule would then be specified according to which: (1) if a given corporation's actual performance, relative to its expected performance, is above a certain critical upper level, then the corporation president *must not* be dismissed; while (2) if a given corporation's relative performance is below a critical lower level, then the corporation president *must* be dismissed. Between the upper and lower critical levels of relative performance, retention or dismissal would be principally at the discretion of that corporation's BPO agent.

The second tier of the BPO would consist of a corps of BPO agents. Unlike the first-tier central office, the second tier would be physically decentralized into perhaps 200-300 local offices, each office comprising a group of 10-15 agents. Unlike the employees of the central office, BPO agents would not be permanent employees. Rather, they would be selected at random from a roster of qualified personnel ("qualified" being defined in terms of considerable experience in business enterprise management) for a standard period of service, perhaps five to seven years. Only extraordinarily successful agents would be tapped for service beyond the standard term. Each BPO agent would be assigned several corporations, and his or her remuneration would consist mostly of a small percentage of the property return generated by the corporations within his or her sphere of responsibility and paid by these corporations to the BPO central office. To reduce propensities to concentrate solely on current property return, the BPO agent would continue to receive a diminishing percentage of these corporations' property return payments to the BPO for several years after leaving the position. The responsibilities and retention percentages of BPO agents would be calibrated to make these positions highly remunerative—but not extravagantly so.

While the BPO agent would be strictly prohibited from issuing any specific operating instructions (or even advice) to the corporations within the agent's sphere of responsibility, the agent's assignment would be careful study of the performance of these corporations. To facilitate this assignment, the BPO agent would enjoy unrestricted access to the accounting records and other documentation of the corporation. When the performance of a given corporation falls within the discretionary range described above, it would be the corporation's BPO agent who would dominate the decision on whether the corporation president is to stay or go. It is envisioned that a decision to dismiss would be subject to review by the members of the local BPO office involved, and also by an appeals board in the central office. But a very large majority of a review board would have to dissent from a dismissal decision in order for it to be revoked, and the expectation is that only rarely would such a decision in fact be revoked. Most probably the successor to a dismissed corporation president would be selected by a committee composed of executives of the corporation and, once installed, would be guaranteed a tenure of perhaps two to three years in order to have a fair opportunity to affect the corporation's performance.

This completes a nutshell summary of the BPO. Now let us review some of these details, and add additional details, in the context of an evaluative commentary on the proposed BPO agency. It has been prescribed that the Bureau of Public Ownership would be a national government agency. Ever since the development of a nondemocratic socialist society in the Soviet Union, followed by several other Communist nations, opponents of socialism have warned against the perils to democracy of combining economic and political power within the national government. While the perils may be exaggerated by these opponents, some attention certainly needs to be paid to this issue. In addition, there is the customary economic efficiency argument to be made in favor of decentralization of economic decision-making power. Consequently, the charter of the BPO would formally limit the authority of the national government over the BPO, and the authority of the BPO over business enterprises.

However, as is well recognized in the administrative literature, there is a tradeoff between the principle of decentralization and the principle of accountability. The natural implication of public ownership of business enterprise is that the general public should benefit from business enterprise: that business enterprise should be conducted efficiently, productively, and profitably. In order for this to be the case, there must be an effective mechanism by which the general public can enforce its interest in efficiency, productivity, and profitability on the executives of large-scale business corporations. Owing to the domination of economic activity by large corporations in the modern economy, these executives have become the crucial catalysts in the whole economic process. Their incentives to effort must be strong if the economic process is to be successful. The two institutional levels through which the general public would maintain these incentives to effort under pragmatic market socialism would be the national government and the BPO, which together might be regarded as the "board of directors" through which the general public (the "stockholders") enforces its interests on the corporation executives ("management" in the usual business administration parlance). If the considerations of decentralization and the avoidance of totalitarianism become too exaggerated, the result would be inadequate incentives to effort among the corps of corporation executives, causing indiscipline, slackness, inefficiency, stagnation, and decay. The proposals offered here represent an effort to achieve a satisfactory balance between decentralization and accountability.

The decentralization objective would be recognized in the principle that neither the national government acting through the BPO, nor the BPO itself, may issue any instructions, recommendations, advice, or guidelines to corporation executives regarding the microeconomic decision variables of business enterprise. These variables would include: production levels, prices, marketing expenditures, hiring and firing of employees, borrowing, profit retention (retained earnings), and capital investment projects. The penalty for disregarding this injunction would be impeachment of the national government official, dismissal of the BPO administrator or employee, and perhaps harsh legal sanctions.

The accountability objective would be recognized in the principle that the remuneration and retention of corporation executives would be at the discretion of BPO personnel, and further that the remuneration and retention of the top BPO administrators would be at the discretion of national government officials. The plan of remuneration utilized for the executives of each corporation would be drawn up by the executives themselves, but it could be vetoed by BPO personnel. Perhaps even more important than this power would be the power of dismissal. Quite possibly, this power should be confined to the highest executive of each corporation: its president (or CEO: chief executive officer). Should the profit performance of a given corporation be inadequate, the chief executive of the corporation could be dismissed by the BPO. A somewhat analogous situation would hold with respect to national government officials and the top BPO administrators, although there would undoubtedly be some differences in specific detail.

Skeptics will no doubt assert that the accountability principle would overwhelm the decentralization principle in practice: BPO personnel would issue detailed instructions on production levels and other matters which, although formally illegal, would nevertheless be obeyed by corporation executives under the threat of dismissal. The following points may be offered against this speculation. First, BPO personnel would have no reason to take an interest in the microeconomic decision variables of business enterprises, as their personal material interest would be confined to bottom-line profitability. Second, the BPO would be statutorily confined to a relatively small scale that would militate against microeconomic intervention. There would probably be at least five to ten publicly owned corporations per professional-level BPO employee, so that it would be difficult for any one BPO employee to learn sufficient detail about any one corporation's activities to become tempted to overrule the decisions made by its executives. Finally—and possibly most important—the discretionary power of the BPO to dismiss any given corporation executive would not be unrestricted. The nature of this discretionary power may be elaborated as follows.

It is proposed that there be a department within the national office of the Bureau of Public Ownership concerned with the econometric estimation of expected profit rate functions, based on statistical data provided by the publicly owned firms. Such functions would relate the current profit rate of firms to a number of observable environmental determinants, such as factor cost trends, overall market growth or decline, number of competitors, and so on. Also included would be variables known to have an adverse effect on current profitability but a favorable effect on future profitability: examples might include research and development expenditures, indicators of product and process innovations, and market share trend. Such functions could be estimated for various industries, size and age ranges, product categories, and so on. On the basis of these functions, an expected rate of current profitability for any particular firm would be estimated as a weighted average of expected rates obtained from the various functions (for industry, size, etc.). In addition, the standard deviation of the profit rate would be estimated.

Two critical profit rates could then be numerically determined for each corporation. The higher of these would represent a profit rate such that if the corporation were achieving that rate or higher, its chief executive *must not* be dismissed by the BPO under any circumstances. Such a rate might be, for example, one-half of a standard deviation under the expected rate, since this indicates that there is not a statistically significant shortfall between actual profit rate and expected profit rate. The lower of the two critical rates would represent a profit rate such that if a particular corporation were achieving that rate or lower, its chief executive *must* be dismissed by the BPO without further question. Such a rate might be two standard deviations below the expected rate, implying a statistically significant shortfall in the profit rate. Such a provision would of course render a large proportion of chief executives in a given year immune from the possibility of dismissal, and thus immune from illegal threats of dismissal should they fail to heed microeconomic orders from BPO personnel.

While it is envisioned that BPO personnel and corporation presidents would maintain arm's length relations with one another, an adversarial stance is neither required nor desirable. In line with this, the BPO agent would be an essential part of the BPO structure. The agent's principal role would be to make the decision regarding retention versus dismissal for chief executives whose corporations' profit rates fall into the gray area between the two critical profit rates described above. Each BPO agent would be assigned several corporations, and his or her sole source of income would be a small percentage of the property income paid by these corporations to the BPO. In contrast to long-term clerical, professional, and administrative BPO personnel, the agents would be short-term employees with considerable prior experience as middle-to-upper-level business executives. A roster of mostly middle-aged business executives would be maintained, many of whom would not be too far from retirement age, and potential new BPO agents would be selected at random from it. Those selected would be given the opportunity of serving five to seven years as BPO agents. During these terms, the central office of the BPO would not be allowed to dismiss an agent for anything short of criminal activity, or gross and provable negligence of duty. The average achieved rate of remuneration for BPO agents would be sufficiently generous to make this an attractive opportunity for most of those tapped. Thus the key decision on retention versus dismissal of corporation executives whose profit performance has been subpar would be made not by the "government bureaucrats" of anti-socialist rhetoric, but by quasi-autonomous individuals with long prior experience as business enterprise managers—individuals who presumably would be both knowledgeable about business management and sympathetic to business managers.

Another purpose is served by the "agent" aspect of BPO organization: the purpose of maintaining a competitive profit-seeking motivation in the business enterprise sector. It would probably be cost-efficient to centralize most of the clerical, statistical, and administrative functions of the BPO in the national capital. With the aid of computers, it should be possible to keep the number of central office employees to a few thousand. At least as numerous as permanent central office employees would be the agents recruited from business enterprise management. However, in contrast with the concentrated central office BPO employees, the BPO agents would be highly dispersed among hundreds of BPO offices located in towns and cities across the nation. Each local office would consist of 10 to 15 agents, plus clerical and secretarial support. The BPO agents in any one local office would be prohibited from having any contact with agents in other local offices. Also, the corporate responsibilities of the agents in any one local office would be in relatively noncompetitive industries.

These arrangements would be designed to support the strict injunction against any efforts by BPO personnel to organize, foster, or encourage collusive behavior among competitive publicly owned corporations. Such efforts would constitute violations of existing antitrust laws in the United States, and it is envisioned that these laws would be strictly enforced on both BPO central office personnel and agents. The objective of pragmatic market socialism would be to achieve at least as much competition in the business sector as currently exists under capitalism. Thus the key power of discretionary dismissal of corporation executives would reside not in the central office of the BPO, but rather with the highly dispersed agents. In addition, a reasonable amount of monitoring of the activity of individual agents would be undertaken to curtail any temptations to encourage collusion. Such monitoring would maintain a sufficient probability of apprehension—when taken in conjunction with the stringent penalties should a violation be uncovered—to keep such activity to a minimum.

A well-known proposition from capitalist apologetics denies the possibility of meaningful competition among business enterprises under socialism because all firms would fall under the same public ownership aegis. A related proposition is that business inefficiency would be necessarily subsidized under socialism because it would be politically impossible to allow inefficient firms to become bankrupt and cease operations. It must certainly be conceded that such assertions could be based on numerous traditional advocacies of socialism, whose authors have decried the "anarchy of the market" under capitalism and who have perceived in bankruptcies merely one more proof of "wasteful competition" under capitalism. However, the pragmatic market socialist proposal is clearly based upon a very different viewpoint regarding competition and bankruptcies. Competition is viewed as a positive force in the economy, and the possibility of bankruptcy is regarded as providing necessary discipline toward the end of efficiency.

The argument may no doubt be proposed that competition is "logically impossible" under any form of socialism (including pragmatic market socialism) owing to public ownership of all firms. But such an argument is based upon an invalid presumption of monolithic uniformity of purpose and complete centralization of authority (the "military model") within the public ownership agency. The BPO described above would almost certainly be consistent with a high level of business competition. Even now there are many illustrations from the real world of the possibility of substantial competition between individuals and organizations which are "united" under the same formal authority. One thinks of rivalry between different subsidiaries of a conglomerate corporation, of interservice rivalry among various branches of the military, of competition among employees of the same corporation for promotions, of competition among sports teams which are part of the same league, of competition among students who are members of the same professor's class. The level of observed competition is not so much determined by the existence or nonexistence of formal overall authorities, as by the incentive systems confronting the individuals involved in the process. Under the BPO proposal set forth herein, high executives of publicly owned corporations would have just as much incentive to compete with one another as do the high executives of privately owned corporations in the contemporary capitalist economy.

The BPO envisioned by pragmatic market socialism is clearly based on the conventional consensus in orthodox Western economics that on the whole, profit maximization by business enterprises possesses highly desirable efficiency properties. It is certainly possible to dispute this consensus, and many socialist writers in the past have done so, but such disputes lead into a spacious and foggy speculative realm which is merely shrugged off—not to say scorned—by the great majority of contemporary Western economists. It is not a realm which will be entered in this book—because there is no need to enter it. Even the most conventionally minded economists will concede that the pursuit of profits by business enterprises can have some adverse side effects, and that it is legitimate for society to try to control some of these by means of business regulation. Thus in the United States, there are numerous regulatory agencies: the Food and Drug Administration, the Federal Trade Commission, the Environmental Protection Agency, and so on and so forth. These agencies would continue to operate under pragmatic market socialism in the same way and for the same purposes they currently have under market capitalism.[2] The pragmatic market socialist proposal is entirely independent of and neutral toward questions regarding the appropriate extent of business regulation by the national government and other levels of government.

A more relevant concern, in terms of the potential economic performance of pragmatic market socialism relative to contemporary capitalism, is the following basic question: Would the Bureau of Public Ownership under pragmatic market socialism be able to establish as intense a profit motivation among the corporation executives as currently exists under capitalism, given that it would be required to distribute to the general public as social dividend income the overwhelming preponderance (95 percent or more) of the property return produced by the corporations? Under capitalism, the totality of this income is paid to private owners in proportion to their personal ownership of physical and financial capital assets. Under pragmatic market socialism, the two tiers of the BPO, comprising the corps of agents and the central office personnel, would together retain only 5 percent or less of this income to cover the incentive payments to the agents and the administrative expenses of the central office. Could the BPO, given this limitation, be as effective as the private owners in establishing the desired profit incentive in the business enterprise sector? In other words, could society obtain the same efficiency properties as exist under capitalism, at a much lower direct administrative cost? This critical question will be addressed at various appropriate locations below, particularly in Chapter 4 ("The Capital Management Issue").

D. AUXILIARY PROPOSALS

Throughout modern history, advocacies of socialism have normally incorporated numerous further recommendations for the improvement of society beyond socialism—as defined strictly in the sense of public ownership of capital and other nonhuman factors of production. Therefore it is in line with tradition that the present advocacy of socialism presents a few such recommendations. This section, however, will be confined to very brief discussions of only three auxiliary proposals of particular relevance to the issue of economic performance. Although in a strict sense this section constitutes a digression from the topic of pragmatic market socialism, it may serve a useful purpose in helping to crystallize the reader's intuitive comprehension of the specific socialist proposal under consideration.

The concept of socialism has become encrusted, over the decades since the time of Karl Marx, with many implications and connotations which are not logical consequences of the basic socialist concept, which involves no more and no less than public ownership of nonhuman factors used in large-scale production. Central planning, one-party oligarchy, redistribution of labor income, and paternalistic welfarism are just a few examples of social institutions and policies which are invalidly identified with "socialism" by a great many people. Even professional social scientists are not wholly immune from such misunderstandings. The core proposal of pragmatic market socialism consists of the Bureau of Public Ownership and social dividend distribution of capital property return. This core proposal would achieve no more than and no less than the basic socialist concept. But that this form of socialism would be very different from numerous other so-called socialist proposals of the past—proposals whose unattractiveness has been demonstrated by history—will be made clearer by briefly considering some auxiliary proposals stemming from the same philosophy and worldview that motivate the core proposal.

Business Capital Investment. Capitalist apologetics has traditionally expressed the gravest concerns regarding the potential fate of capital investment and economic growth under socialism. One of these concerns is that owing to the termination of interest and other property return payments on private household savings accumulations under socialism, the supply of saving will dry up and society will confront a stagnant and decaying capital stock. Another concern is that if "government bureaucrats" are involved in the investment process rather than "entrepreneurs," capital investment funds will be allocated among competing uses in such a politically biased and/or haphazard manner that the dynamic performance of the economy will plummet to abysmal depths. These concerns will be addressed below, primarily in Chapters 5 ("The Saving Issue") and 6 ("Investment, Growth, and Entrepreneurship"). The verdict reached on these concerns is that they do not constitute sufficient grounds for the rejection of the pragmatic market socialist alternative. The fact is that the pragmatic market socialist proposal is based on a very full and profound awareness of the critical importance of capital investment in a modern industrial economy.

At this point, two specific manifestations of this awareness will be very briefly described as auxiliary proposals to the core proposal for the Bureau of Public Ownership and social dividend distribution of capital property return. The role of these proposals in the overall case for pragmatic market socialism will be examined at appropriate points in later chapters. First, it is proposed that a new category of national government expenditure be created: business capital investment. The annual appropriation for this purpose would go through the usual budgetary process. Whether that appropriation would be large or small would depend primarily on two factors: (1) the level of private household saving attained under pragmatic market socialism; (2) the democratically determined judgment of the citizen body as to how much business capital investment is appropriate.

Second, it is proposed that two new national government agencies be created—independent of the BPO—for the disposition of this budgetary appropriation into the business sector: (1) The National Investment Banking System (NIBS); and (2) the National Entrepreneurial Investment Board (NEIB). These two agencies would supplement—not replace—the investment activity carried on by firms under BPO ownership. BPO-owned firms would include nonfinancial corporations that "lend" investment funds to themselves via retained earnings, and financial intermediary corporations such as banks, insurance companies, pension funds, and so on, which lend investment funds to, and purchase securities from, other business corporations. However, the NIBS and the NEIB would be slightly different from standard financial intermediaries, and through these differences (as explained below in Chapter 6, Section C) it is hoped that a somewhat higher long-term rate of business capital accumulation and economic growth might be achieved under pragmatic market socialism than that currently prevailing under capitalism.

What would distinguish the NIBS and the NEIB from the standard BPO-owned investment channels would be that while the performance evaluation of executives of firms in the standard channels would be implicitly oriented to the rate of property return produced on the entire accumulated stock of business capital, the performance evaluation of NIBS loan officers and NEIB agents would be explicitly oriented toward recent business capital investment. NIBS loan officers would be evaluated not on the basis of the success of all past loans they have made, but only on the basis of the success of their recent loans, say those made within the prior two or three years. The purpose of the NEIB is indicated by its name: to establish entrepreneurial firms. By its nature, an entrepreneurial firm has no interest in the rate of return achieved on the physical capital accumulations of existing firms. Therefore, evaluating the success of an agency in terms of the rate of property return produced by entrepreneurial firms established by the agency automatically implies performance evaluation in terms of recent capital investment. In addition to direct funding from the national government budget, the NIBS and the NEIB would rechannel all property return received on their loans and investments into business physical capital investment. The NIBS would operate exclusively on the supply side of capital investment, while the NEIB would operate on both demand and supply sides. In addition to its direct appropriations and retained earnings, the NEIB could solicit funding for entrepreneurial firms from ordinary financial intermediaries under BPO ownership.

Industrial Disaggregation. The pragmatic market socialist viewpoint takes over the mainstream economic judgment that competition among business enterprises is an extremely beneficial force. Imperfect competition is regarded as a malignancy which imperils this beneficial force. But as imperfect competition is profitable to individual firms, there is nevertheless a strong tendency toward it in the real world. The tendency is held in check both by the physical decentralization of firms and by the physical decentralization of the ownership interest. The physical decentralization of capital ownership under capitalism would be maintained under pragmatic market socialism by the dispersion, over several hundred local offices, of several thousand quasi-autonomous BPO agents who would exercise the critical authority to dismiss corporation presidents.

Another means of strengthening the competitive force within the business sector would be to carry out a program of industrial disaggregation along the structural lines which have long been recommended by many experts in industrial organization and antitrust policy.[3] The indications from a large body of research in industrial organization over the past few decades suggest strongly that a modest amount of disaggregation is unlikely to jeopardize either static economies of scale or dynamic technological progress. The failure of society to undertake such a disaggregation may be plausibly attributed to the political influence jointly exercised by wealthy capitalists and high corporation executives, both of which groups are unduly apprehensive that disaggregation would imperil a status quo that they personally find very agreeable. The inauguration of pragmatic market socialism might sufficiently reduce this political influence to enable a meaningful program of disaggregation.

Tax System Rationalization. The pragmatic market socialist viewpoint also takes over the orthodox economic judgment that the present tax system in nations such as the United States injects a great deal of distortion and irrationality into economic calculation. To a large extent, the efficiency losses which the present tax system inflicts on the economy are justified by reference to "equity advantages." Under pragmatic market socialism, an important equity advantage would be obtained independently of the tax system, through the BPO's appropriation of property return produced by large-scale productive enterprise, and its distribution to the population in the form of social dividend income proportional to earned labor income. There would no longer be any need to have a tax system which "offsets" the inequity of unequal distribution of unearned property return. This suggests the possibility of a fundamental revision of the tax system.

One such fundamental revision would be as follows. First, personal income taxation would be abolished, and all taxes would be levied on business enterprises. This in itself would greatly diminish the administrative costs of tax collection in industrialized nations where there are at least several dozen income-earning individuals for every business enterprise. Second, primary reliance would be placed on a simple, flat-rate value-added tax. By the common consensus of experts in public finance, such a tax would minimize the distortions introduced into economic calculation and processes by the existence of taxation.[4]

The abolition of progressive income taxation would eliminate the present penalization of high-income individuals, but this would be fully defensible under pragmatic market socialism because the phenomenon of high-income capitalists supporting lavish lifestyles by means of unearned capital property income derived from inherited capital fortunes would no longer exist. This abolition would also eliminate the favoring of low-income individuals through low taxation, but if it were deemed socially desirable, the favors could be restored through the provision of additional welfare benefits for which eligibility would be achieved through low income. In other words, the objective of welfare redistribution could be pursued on the expenditure side of government activity rather than on the revenue side. Any such redistribution ought, however, to be assessed in full recognition of the fact that the case for redistribution of labor income is far less substantial than the case for altering the distribution of property income currently prevailing under contemporary capitalism. Owing to the earned nature of labor income, the disincentive effects of labor income redistribution are likely to be substantial. It is important to emphasize that the pragmatic market socialist proposal, in itself, pertains exclusively to property income; it is inherently neutral on the question of the proper distribution of labor income.

E. PRAGMATIC MARKET SOCIALISM IN PERSPECTIVE

With the exception that capitalist owners would be replaced by the Bureau of Public Ownership in order that the distribution of capital property return be substantially equalized and made more equitable, pragmatic market socialism would endeavor in all other essential economic aspects to duplicate the workings of the market capitalist economy with which we are currently familiar. Practically all the fundamental characteristics of the capitalist market economy—competition among firms, personal autonomy of workers, price determination by supply and demand, financial incentives, consumer sovereignty, and so on—would be reproduced under pragmatic market socialism. A few examples of the many correspondences follow:

Corporation executives would have full autonomy, within currently existing taxation and regulation constraints, with respect to all the microeconomic decision variables of business enterprise: production and inventory levels, prices, marketing, research and development, product and process innovation, investment projects, retained earnings, borrowing from financial intermediaries, and so on. Bankruptcy would provide the natural demise of business enterprises unable to earn sufficient revenue to cover expenses, including interest expenses on past loans and bond issues. Entrepreneurial firms would be established as new subsidiaries of existing firms, by means of private entrepreneurial activity, as well as by national government agencies founded explicitly for the encouragement of entrepreneurial activity in the economy. Although both large-scale non-financial corporations and large-scale financial intermediaries such as insurance companies and pension funds would be publicly owned, they would continue to deal with one another in investment capital markets as separate, self-interested entities. Markets for financial capital assets would continue to operate in which the agents would be the various publicly owned business corporations. Although private individuals would be excluded from such markets, the markets would continue to function in much the same way they do now, since even at the present time transactions by private individuals account for only a relatively small fraction of the total transactions in such markets. "Takeovers" of a sort might continue to occur, in the form of sales by the BPO of ownership rights over certain corporations to other corporations. Labor unions would continue the role they play under capitalism, although it is to be hoped that because of the public disposition of most property return, labor relations would be somewhat more amicable and strike actions somewhat less frequent.

Needless to say, the correspondence between the envisioned institutions of pragmatic market socialism and those of contemporary market capitalism is much closer than that envisioned by most alternative concepts of socialism. The key distinction between pragmatic market socialism and other socialist prescriptions is that the former proceeds from the perception that the capitalist market economy, at least as it currently exists in advanced industrial nations such as the United States and the nations of Western

Europe, has achieved a very high level of productive efficiency, material prosperity, and social welfare. Thus there is great concern that the socialist objective of equalizing the distribution of property return and eliminating economic parasitism not be attained at a serious cost in terms of reduced productive efficiency. In contrast, other socialist proposals proceed from a much less favorable impression of the productive efficiency of capitalism. Indeed, for many of the authors of these proposals, the principal advantage of socialism is hardly that it will equalize the distribution of property return and eliminate economic parasitism, but rather that it will permit fundamental transformations in the operations of the economy that will significantly increase long-term productive efficiency.

Karl Marx's intellectually and politically potent critique of capitalism was founded on observation of the harsh early industrial capitalist economic system in Western Europe in the first half of the nineteenth century.[5] In stark contrast with the "bourgeois economists" who were at that time singing the praises of laissez-faire, Marx viewed the capitalist market system as one of anarchic greed running amok, the consequences of which included grinding poverty for the masses, recurrent business depressions, psychological alienation, and moral decay. As is well known, Marx devoted very little thought to the socialist cure for the capitalist disease. It seemed obvious to him that public ownership of the means of production would simultaneously eliminate surplus labor exploitation and the anarchy of the market. This was clearly enough to merit the transformation, and the fine details could be worked out after the revolution.

Although Marx devoted enormous effort in *Das Kapital* to arguing that capital property income represents surplus labor, and therefore the capitalist economic system is inherently exploitative, the fact is that he did not believe that capitalism would be abolished on this account. In Marx's view, it is not the moral impropriety of surplus labor exploitation that will bring the capitalist system down but its susceptibility to ever-worsening business depressions. But the available statistical data does not suggest worsening business depressions in the period prior to the Great Depression of the 1930s, nor does the abundant statistical evidence pertaining to the post-World War II period suggest worsening business depressions. It must be conceded that Marx's prognostications of total economic collapse came perilously close to realization in the Great Depression. But it now appears that the Great Depression was an isolated episode, and the Western economics profession is increasingly confident that the Keynesian anticyclical fiscal policy prescriptions that emerged from the catastrophe have rendered any repetition of it exceedingly unlikely.[6] Moreover, for at least 100 years in such advanced capitalist nations as the United States, there has been a gradual upward trend in the living standards of all segments of the population, including those of unskilled laborers, the oppressed proletariat of the Marxist worldview.

The empirical falsification of Marx's prediction of increasing economic misery, whether interpreted cyclically or secularly, has greatly diminished the credibility not merely of Marx's critique of capitalism but also of the socialist critique of capitalism in general. In light of this, it goes without saying that the pragmatic market socialist proposal cannot be reasonably grounded on aspirations toward improved anticyclical control of the economy or on the elimination of mass poverty in society. In the advanced capitalist nations, mass poverty does not exist, and the degree of anticyclical control seems reasonably adequate.

The dominance within the world socialist movement of the original Marxist vision was short-lived—the vision of social ownership of the nonhuman factors of production achieved through violent revolution. Even before the turn of the century, the great revisionist schism had diverted a large part of the socialist movement into the social democratic channel which has since become the dominant channel everywhere outside of the Communist nations. Violent revolution was abandoned in favor of peaceful democratic change, and public ownership of capital was shelved in favor of incrementalist reformism through business regulation, social insurance, progressive taxation, and so on.[7] Despite the designation of this program as "socialism" by both proponents and opponents of social democracy, the profound and continuing influence of Marx's thought is still manifested in the standard dictionary definition of "socialism" as public ownership of the capital means of production, rather than as a general program of various forms of state intervention in economic processes for purposes of improving social welfare.

Pragmatic market socialism is fully independent of and neutral toward the social democratic program. It is only through misunderstanding that opponents of social democratic "socialism" would consider it obligatory to oppose pragmatic market socialism. At the same time, proponents of social democratic "socialism" need not feel threatened by pragmatic market socialism. Indeed, social democrats ought to support pragmatic market socialism because it calls for public ownership of the capital means of production, and if they will recall the history of the world socialist movement, they will recall that public ownership of the capital means of production was abandoned by the founders of social democracy not on grounds that it was inherently undesirable but on grounds that it was politically impractical in the short run.

Pragmatic market socialism shares with social democracy an aspiration toward a fairer and more equitable distribution of welfare among the population. But in contrast with the varied and complex policy proposals of social democracy, it proposes merely a single straightforward reform: distribution of unearned property return generated by large-scale, established business enterprises as a social dividend supplement to labor income. Thus the varied and complex arguments which are used to support the varied and complex policy proposals of social democracy cannot be utilized in support of pragmatic market socialism.

While social democracy was gradually becoming dominant within the socialist movement almost everywhere in the world, historical events took an unexpected and dramatic turn when the original, unrepentant, hard-core Marxist viewpoint suddenly took control of an important nation-state. The Bolshevik Revolution of 1917 transformed the Russian empire, with its nascent capitalist society governed by an absolute monarchy, into the Soviet Union, in which unalloyed social ownership of the nonhuman factors of production was almost immediately combined with harsh internal dictatorship and complete international isolation. For Karl Marx, the salient practical advantage of socialism lay in the abolition of recurrent devastating business depressions. For Joseph Stalin, the specific means through which depressions would be eliminated and rapid economic growth assured was the implementation under socialism of a tight and highly comprehensive central planning system closely controlled by the national government. Thus emerged the centralized planning systems governing physical production and investment which became deeply institutionalized in the U.S.S.R. and several other Communist nations.[8]

In the nearly universal judgment of noncommunist authorities, the costs of these central planning systems far outweigh the benefits. Whatever gains are achieved from coordination are presumably swamped by the losses incurred through the very limited flexibility and responsiveness imposed at the individual enterprise level by the existence of the planning system.[9] The proponent of pragmatic market socialism shares this prevalent judgment, and is thus very much dedicated to the principle of virtually complete autonomy of the individual business enterprise. Government control of firms under pragmatic market socialism would be strictly confined to retention and remuneration of corporation presidents on the basis of objective success criteria including, predominantly, indicators of present and future profitability. Furthermore, it is expected that the quest for profits would bring the publicly owned business corporations into vigorous competition with one another. In the absence of extraordinary economies of scale, each product line would be provided by at least several different firms. Any BPO agents endeavoring to foster collusion between their respective corporations would be subject to severe legal sanctions.

All market socialist proposals, and not merely the pragmatic, stand in sharp opposition to central planning socialism as exemplified by the Soviet model. All of them envision a very high degree of decentralization of economic decision-making power, and all of them envision consumer sovereignty upheld by competition among business firms. What distinguishes the pragmatic market socialist proposal is the specification that profitability remain the basic success criterion of corporate economic activity—just as it is presumed to be under contemporary market capitalism. Several other well-known plans of market socialism propose fundamental revisions in the motivations of corporations. Among these are the Langian, service, and cooperative market socialist schemes.[10]

The notion of market socialism gained a foothold in Western economic thought owing to Oskar Lange (1904-1965), a Polish economist who worked at leading Western universities during the 1930s and 1940s before eventually returning to Poland. In the latter 1930s, Lange published a lengthy essay, "On the Economic Theory of Socialism," which endeavored to introduce the idea of market socialism to the economics profession as an explicit alternative to the only type of socialism then widely recognized: the centrally planned economic system emerging in the Soviet Union.[11] The impact of Lange's advocacy of market socialism was greatly augmented by his demonstrated expertise in contemporary mathematical neoclassical economic theory. Prior to Lange, most neoclassical economists tended to complacently dismiss socialist thought as the product of either ignorance or mental deficiency. These weaknesses manifestly did not apply to Oskar Lange. The Langian market socialist proposal became very well known within the economics profession largely as a result of Abram Bergson's 1948 essay "Socialist Economics," included in the *Survey of Contemporary Economics* sponsored by the American Economic Association. Bergson's lukewarm appraisal of the Langian plan of market socialism profoundly influenced subsequent thinking, as may be judged from the numerous treatments in comparative economic systems textbooks of market socialism which virtually paraphrase his discussion.[12]

Langian market socialism proposes that profit maximization be replaced by equalization of marginal cost to price as the basic guideline for the management of corporate enterprise. Although the rule is consistent with theoretical efficiency, few neoclassical economists believe that it constitutes a practical guide for modern corporate management.[13] Aside from the complexity of specifying the marginal cost of a particular product in a multiproduct firm, there is no easily observable success criterion by which an outside observer could readily ascertain that the rule was being satisfied.

The notion of universal imposition of marginal cost pricing as the sole guide for production conjures up visions of baffled corporation executives paralyzed into inactivity while the enterprises drift into a state of profound stagnation. The common consensus today is that Langian market socialism is at best a mildly interesting theoretical construct but is far too impractical to be taken seriously as a potential alternative to capitalism.

Service market socialism proposes that all or most firms in the economy become what is generally termed "nonprofit enterprises." An observable success criterion for nonprofit enterprise exists in the form of revenue. To a theoretical economist, revenue maximization (subject to a minimum profit constraint) is inferior to profit maximization because it involves average cost pricing rather than marginal cost pricing. Of course, this inferiority would necessarily exist only for firms which are perfectly competitive, and it is certainly arguable that perfect competition is not a sufficiently realistic model for much of the real-world business enterprise sector. Be that as it may, most neoclassical economists would be apprehensive that a general shift from profit maximization to nonprofit production would promote inefficiency and stagnation.

Cooperative market socialism (labor-management, self-management, producers' cooperation, etc.) proposes that the ownership of any given business enterprise be vested entirely and exclusively in its current employees. The motivation of corporations would thereby shift from profit maximization to employee welfare maximization. The potential economic implications of such a transformation have been intensively studied by many economic theoreticians since the mid-1960s.[14] It would seem that the majority of the contributors to this voluminous literature have been skeptical of cooperation. The theoretical models often highlight potential situations in which the performance of the cooperative is deficient in some sense relative to that of its "capitalist twin."[15] This skepticism probably has its roots in the commonplace observation that although the concept of producers' cooperation has been around since the inception of the socialist critique of capitalism in the early nineteenth century, cooperative firms have a rather poor track record of success in competition with standard capitalist firms in which all or most of the ownership rights reside in individuals outside the firm. Once again, the majority of neoclassical economists are apprehensive that a shift from profit maximization to employee welfare maximization would promote inefficiency and stagnation.[16]

While the pragmatic market socialist proposal is obviously very much influenced by these apprehensions, it should be mentioned that particularly with respect to service and cooperative market socialism, the theoretical and empirical cases against these departures from profit maximization are by no means compelling. One of the potential advantages of pragmatic market socialism, indeed, is that it might permit a certain amount of controlled experimentation with different corporation motivations. The results of such experimentation might bring to light desirable properties of alternatives to profit maximization which are not theoretically provable, or perhaps even perceptible, at the present limited stage of our knowledge.

The emphasis placed herein on the similarities between pragmatic market socialism and contemporary capitalism, together with the conventional wisdom among social democrats that public ownership of capital is "no longer relevant," may easily generate the thought that what is intended by pragmatic market socialism could be just as well attained by means of taxation and does not require public ownership of capital. Specifically, through the individual income tax system there could be confiscatory taxation (100 percent or nearly 100 percent) of all forms of property income, and the proceeds of this tax could then be distributed as a social dividend supplement to labor income. In this way, there would be no need for entanglements between a Bureau of Public Ownership and the business enterprise sector. Also, it could be a means of avoiding the "socialistic bugaboo" and thus of enhancing the possibility of actual implementation of the plan in the real world. This latter argument, although possibly well-intended, betrays a rather contemptuous view of public intelligence. Surely if pragmatic market socialism as described herein is in fact politically inconceivable, 100 percent taxation of property income would be no less so, and for the same reasons. Even if the word "socialism" were never utilized by proponents of the "100 percent taxation" plan, no doubt defenders of the capitalist status quo would make haste to apply the appellation, and no doubt the appellation would be accepted by the general public.

But a more positive reason for preferring the pragmatic market socialist proposal over 100 percent taxation is that the proposal would enable an adequate degree of social accountability of high corporation executives. The simple and straightforward relationships envisioned between the Bureau of Public Ownership and the publicly owned corporation executives can hardly be fairly described as "entanglements." At the same time, these relationships are necessary if society is to prevent the permanent ordination of the corporate executive elite as an excessively privileged, powerful, and uncontrolled force in society. At various points reference will be made to the separation of ownership and control, an extremely important and significant characteristic of modern capitalism. This separation is the single most important piece of empirical evidence indicating the unearned nature of capital property income (see Chapter 4, Section D).

Also as discussed below (Chapter 3, Section A), the separation phenomenon raises serious questions as to the adequacy of incentives to effort among top corporation executives under contemporary capitalism, and suggests the possibility that the Bureau of Public Ownership could exert stronger disciplinary control over these executives. If 100 percent taxation were to become a reality, the class of capital owners would no longer be relevant. They would have no financial incentive whatever to concern themselves with the property return being produced by corporations, and the pressures they currently exert toward the efficiency of the corporate executive elite (however effortless and/or inadequate these pressures might be) would disappear altogether. Thus the 100 percent taxation plan cannot be taken seriously by anyone who possesses proper appreciation of the implications of the separation of ownership and control which is manifestly present in the contemporary capitalist economy.

NOTES

1. Proponents and opponents alike customarily envision "socialism" in broader terms than these. In addition to public ownership of capital, socialism is frequently identified with central planning, business regulation, paternalistic welfarism, pure egalitarianism (i.e., as favorable to equalization of labor income as well as property income), and communalism (public ownership of personal consumption goods as well as the means of production). The identification of these various concepts with "socialism" is grounded in the complex intellectual and real-world history of socialism. The popular, professional, and polemical literature which traces this history is tremendous. The range of style and treatment is enormous, from popular surveys such as Edward Hyams (1974) through college textbooks such as Ben Aggar (1979) to scholarly works such as George D. H. Cole's five volumes (1953-1960) and Carl Landauer's two volumes (1960). There are also several documentary compilations available, such as those edited by Irving Howe (1976) and Emile Burns (1982). As the present work is not an analysis of historical socialist thought but rather a contemporary reformulation and advocacy of socialism, little reference will be made to the historical literature. However, study of that literature will affirm that the pragmatic market socialist proposal is fully compatible with the core of socialist philosophy as defined by Karl Marx and as still enshrined in the typical dictionary definition of socialism, exemplified by the following: "a political and economic theory and movement for the reform of society by the substitution of collective for individual ownership of capital and property" (*Universal English Dictionary*).

2. The nature and purpose of direct public intervention in the market capitalist economy is treated in such textbooks and treatises as those by Clair Wilcox (1960), Dudley Pegrum (1965), Alfred Kahn (1970), Elizabeth Bailey (1973), and William Shepherd (1985). Influential skeptical evaluations of regulation include those of George Stigler (1971), Richard Posner (1974), and Sam Peltzman (1976). These

were important inputs into the deregulatory trend of the 1980s. An illustrative reference on deregulation is Elizabeth Bailey, David R. Graham and Daniel P. Kaplan (1985). If pragmatic market socialism were to be implemented, little or nothing of the economic policy analysis dealt with in this type of literature would have to be rethought.

3. Joe S. Bain, whose substantial and influential textbook on industrial economics was published in 1959, explicitly endorsed a structural approach to antitrust which would result in appreciable disaggregation within American in- dustry (Bain, 1959, esp. pp. 607-610), and cited Carl Kaysen and Donald Turner's 1959 proposals on antitrust policy as a desirable policy direction. Bain's successor as the author of the single most influential textbook in the field, Frederick M. Scherer, continued to explicitly endorse disaggregation. Scherer's text was first published in 1970, and by the time of the second edition, published in 1980, he was still asserting that "a considerable amount of fragmentation could take place without appreciably impairing industrial efficiency" (Scherer, 1980, p. 542). This statement was immediately followed by a lengthy passage of disclaimer revolving around the idea that fragmentation is not *necessarily* beneficial even in highly concentrated industries. The disclaimer may have been influenced by increasing public and professional skepticism during the 1970s toward disaggregation in particular and antitrust in general, as reflected by the assaults on antitrust of Richard Posner (1976) and Robert Bork (1978). By the 1980s, standard textbooks in the field had adopted a strictly neutral stance on the desirability of disaggregation. For example, in discussing the evaporation of structurally based antitrust enforcement efforts during the Reagan era, Douglas F. Greer (1984) commented mildly (p. 203): "Whether these developments take us too far in condoning monopolization is a much debated question."

4. A selection of textbook statements on the theoretical efficiency of value-added taxation follows: Leif Johansen (1965, p. 271): "If various goods pass through the same number of sales stages, and if the structure of trade margins is the same for all goods, a value-added tax will not result in any distortion of the relative prices." Bernard Herber (1975, p. 307): "A VAT of the consumption variety would impose an identical tax rate on all economic goods, thus not interfering with the relative price relationships between different economic goods." John Due and Ann Fried- laender (1977, p. 392): "The value-added tax produces no economic distortions or loss of efficiency if properly designed." In the United States, the value-added tax has been mostly discussed not as the potential principal source of government tax revenue but as a possible candidate for replacing the corporate income tax. In 1972, the Tax Institute of America put out a special issue of *Tax Policy* devoted to the value-added tax (Vol. 39 (10-12): 1-138, October-December 1972). In the same year the Government Printing Office published a transcript of the hearings on the value-added tax before the Joint Economic Committee of the 92nd Congress, 2nd session. A somewhat more recent evaluation of value-added taxation is that of Cedric Sanford (1981).

5. Karl Marx's central role in the codification of the socialist critique of capitalism is acknowledged by a vast literature, ranging from adulatory to denun-

ciatory. Marx was a multifaceted thinker, but obviously it is his economic theory which is most relevant to our present purpose. Some illustrative references on Marx's economic theory, from a variety of viewpoints, are the following: Joan Robinson (1942); Paul Sweezy (1942); Ronald Meek (1956); Robert Freedman (1962); Ernest Mandel (1970); Murray Wolfson (1968); Michio Morishima (1973); Paul Samuelson (1971); Meghnad Desai (1979); Ben Fine and Laurence Harris (1979); Geoffrey Kay (1979); John Roemer (1981, 1982, 1986, 1988). In addition, Marxist economics is invariably covered in books dealing with the history of economic thought. Some examples include: Robert Lekachman (1959, Chapter 9); Overton Taylor (1960, Chapter 11); John Fred Bell (1967, Chapter 15); Ingrid Rima (1978, Chapter 9); Mark Blaug (1985, Chapter 7).

6. Two authoritative quotes indicative of the post-Keynesian confidence in the avoidability of catastrophic business depressions under modern capitalism are provided by Paul Samuelson and Martin Bronfenbrenner. Samuelson (1959, pp. 183-184): "And beyond this knowledge of the facts of the case there is a calculated confidence in our ability to battle this scourge of depression... While it would be rash to say that the business cycle has been banished from American life, it would be foolish to overlook the changed betting odds with respect to the likelihood of sustained deflations such as occurred during the 1830s, the 1870s, the 1890s and the 1930s." Bronfenbrenner (1969, p. viii): "Certain important threads of agreement ran through the discussion... It was generally agreed that another catastrophe of the 1929-33 type is, if not impossible, conceivable only by an extraordinary combination of erroneous policies."

7. Founded in the "revisionism" of Eduard Bernstein (*Evolutionary Socialism*, 1899) and other late-nineteenth-century socialists, the social democratic interpretation of socialism is particularly strong in Western Europe, and although "socialists" in this tradition often rise to the highest government offices (e.g., Mitterand's tenure as the president of France), the fundamental economic privileges of capitalists in these nations are not seriously molested. As a consequence, Soviet ideologues have dismissed social democracy as ineffectual "reformist opportunism" which is content to grovel at the foot of capitalism's table in the forlorn hope of securing a few pitiful scraps for the oppressed proletarian masses.

In Great Britain, social democratic thinking perhaps reached its intellectual apogee in the work of such illustrious members of the Fabian Society as George Bernard Shaw, H. G. Wells, and Beatrice and Sidney Webb. More recent expressions of the tradition include C. A. R. Crosland's *The Future of Socialism* (1963) and Alec Nove's *The Economics of Feasible Socialism* (1983). In the United States, social democracy was unsuccessfully pursued throughout the first half of the twentieth century by the Socialist Party under the leadership of Eugene Debs and Norman Thomas. Probably the most highly regarded figure currently associated with this tradition is Michael Harrington, whose *The Other America: Poverty in the United States* (1962) was an important milestone in the development of the U.S. welfare system from the 1930s through the 1970s. In *The Twilight of Capitalism* (1980), Harrington attributes most serious social problems in the contemporary United States to the widespread ignorance and/or dismissal of Marxist social theory. Important figures in the allied area of "radical economics" in academia are Howard Sherman (1972) and Samuel Bowles and Herbert Gintis (1973, 1986).

8. A few examples of the numerous treatises and textbooks on the Soviet economy include Alec Nove (1961); Peter Wiles (1962); Nicholas Spulber (1962); Abram Bergson (1964); Edward Ames (1965); Michael Kaser (1970); Morris Bornstein and Daniel Fusfeld (1974); David Dyker (1976); Paul Gregory and Robert Stuart (1981); Padma Desai (1987); and Edward Hewett (1988). There are also a number of anthologies of translations of writings by Soviet economists: Myron Sharpe (1966); Murray Yanowitch (1969); Martin Cave et al (1982); and Anthony Jones (1989). In comparative economic systems textbooks the centrally planned socialist economy of the U.S.S.R. is almost always the single most intensively examined subject. Examples of such texts include Richard Carson (1973); Egon Neuberger and William Duffy (1976); Allan Gruchy (1977); Wayne Leeman (1977); Vaclav Holesovsky (1977); Peter Wiles (1977); Andrew Zimbalist and Howard Sherman (1984); Gary Pickersgill and Joyce Pickersgill (1985); Morris Bornstein (1985); John Elliott (1985); Paul Gregory and Robert Stuart (1985); Martin Schnitzer (1987); H. Stephen Gardner (1988).

9. It should be noted that although Soviet-style central planning is almost universally judged inefficient by Western observers, this judgment is based on nothing more exalted than casual empiricism, possibly colored by ideological distaste for socialism. Planning is not inefficient in a general sense—as will be attested by any business planner working for a large, privately owned corporation in the West. It is clear from a priori logic that there exists some happy medium along the centralization/decentralization (or planning/laissez-faire) spectrum. The problem is to find this happy medium. As this particular problem is probably insolvable in some comprehensive, global sense, the more relevant problem is to try to determine whether some specific planning institution or procedure (such as the Soviet Gosplan organization) is socially beneficial (moves society closer to the optimal point on the spectrum) or socially detrimental (moves society farther away from the optimal point). Several economists have made contributions, mostly of a mathematical nature, to the theory of planning: Jan Tinbergen (1954); Leonid Hurwicz (1969, 1982); David Conn (1977); Geoffrey Heal (1973, 1982); and John Bennett (1989). The work that has been done in the area is certainly impressive, but owing to the complex nature of the problem, it is probably fair to say that we are still a very long way from convincing applications of these ideas and theories to practical matters—such as, for example, the Gosplan planning organization in the U.S.S.R.

10. The four concepts of market socialism included here (Langian, service, cooperative, and pragmatic) were first discussed by the author in a 1975 survey article in *Annals of Public and Cooperative Economy*. That article, although concise, goes into more in the way of technical economic details than does the discussion provided here. These four concepts of market socialism are by no means the only possibilities. For example, since the 1975 survey article, Leland Stauber has contributed two articles and a book on what might be termed the "regional ownership" concept of market socialism. Stauber introduced his plan in two articles

published in the mid-1970s: the first in *Polity* (1975) and the second in the *Journal of Comparative Economics* (1977). The 1977 *JCE* article elicited comments by Wayne Leeman and Susan Rose-Ackerman which were published in the March 1978 issue of the *JCE*. Stauber's response to these comments was published in the December 1978 issue of the *JCE*. More recently, Stauber has provided a book-length study (1987) which reexamines the regional ownership market socialist proposal in light of a detailed historical and institutional study of the post-war Austrian economy. In some ways, regional ownership market socialism would be even more similar to contemporary real-world capitalism than the pragmatic market socialist proposal, and it would avoid possible threats to political democracy from overcentralization of economic power. Its principal drawback would be inadequate accountability of corporation executives. The critical comments at the end of this section on the notion of "socialism through taxation" also apply to some extent to regional ownership market socialism.

11. The immediate impetus to Oskar Lange's famous essay "On the Economic Theory of Socialism" was the publication in 1935 of *Collectivist Economic Planning*, edited by Friedrich von Hayek, a collection of papers which took a very skeptical view of the likelihood of efficient economic production under socialism. At that time Lange was a young academic émigré from Poland whose sophisticated contributions to economic theory were highly regarded by some important figures in the English economics establishment. Lange's response to Hayek's collection took the form of a two-part article, published in the October 1936 and February 1937 issues of the *Review of Economic Studies*. Shortly after its initial appearance, Lange's essay was published in book form by the University of Minnesota Press (1938). The book, also titled *On the Economic Theory of Socialism*, contained additional contributions by Benjamin Lippincott (listed as editor) and Fred M. Taylor, whose 1928 presidential address to the American Economic Association to some extent foreshadowed Lange's proposal. The 1938 edition was reprinted in paperback form by McGraw-Hill in 1964.

Following his famous essay, Lange returned to mainstream work on economic theory and econometrics, in which he made further notable contributions before returning to Poland after the Communist takeover. In post-World War II Poland, Lange's research and writing were severely constrained by the imported Soviet central planning orthodoxy, and such contributions as *Problems of Political Economy of Socialism* (1959) did little to enhance Lange's reputation as an economist in the West. The same may be said of Lange's rather fatuous little contribution, "The Computer and the Market" (published posthumously), to Maurice Dobb's festschrift volume, edited by C. H. Feinstein (1967). Despite this, Lange still commanded sufficient respect among mainstream Western economists that his passing rated an obituary in no less a journal than *Econometrica* (Walter Fisher, 1966).

12. The significance of Lange's contribution may be gauged from the fact that almost all college textbooks for courses in comparative economic systems contain at least several pages of explicit discussion of the concept of "market socialism," covering at a minimum the seminal contribution of Oskar Lange. A list of several

representative textbooks, chronologically ordered by date of publication, follows: George Halm (1960, Part 5 "The Economic Theory of Liberal Socialism"); Richard Carson (1973, Chapter 19 "Traditional Market Socialism: Structure and Functioning"); Egon Neuberger and William Duffy (1976, Chapter 8 "The Plan and the Market: The Models of Oskar Lange"); Allan Gruchy (1977, Chapter 13 section "The Decentralized, Market-Oriented Communist Economy"); Wayne Leeman (1977, Part II "Market Socialism"); Vaclav Holesovsky (1977, Chapter 6 section "The Lange Model"); Andrew Zimbalist and Howard Sherman (1984, Chapter 14 "The Theory of Market Socialism"); Gary Pickersgill and Joyce Pickersgill (1985, Part V "The Market Socialist Economy"); Morris Bornstein (1985, Part III "Socialist Market Economy"); John Elliott (1985, Chapter 15 "The Economic Theory of Decentralized Socialism"); Paul Gregory and Robert Stuart (1985, Chapter 5 section "Market Socialism: Theoretical Foundations"); H. Stephen Gardner (1988, Chapter 10 section "Lange's Theory of Market Socialism").

Although there has never developed a flourishing professional journal literature on the Langian proposal such as has developed on the pure theory of the cooperative, commentaries or analyses more or less closely focused on the original Lange proposal continue to appear sporadically. Some examples include Freidrich Hayek (1940); Abram Bergson (1967); James Yunker (1971, 1973); Paul Craig Roberts (1971); Nicholas Spulber (1972); George Feiwel (1972); Egon Neuberger (1973); Evsey Domar (1974); Deborah Milenkovitch (1984); and John Bennett (1985). Much more abundant is the literature which has been tangentially affected by Lange. Some studies in the pure theory of welfare economics or public enterprise economics have appropriated Langian nomenclature: Abba Lerner's 1944 treatise on welfare economics falls into this category. And many contributions to the "economics of socialism" published since the latter 1930s, while not particularly oriented to Lange, nevertheless manifest some of his influence, more or less, as the case may be. Examples include Henry Dickinson (1939); Burnham Beckwith (1949, 1974, 1978); Trygve Hoff (1949); and Henry Smith (1962). In much of the literature in which Lange appears, his core marginal cost pricing proposal is a rather incidental element in discussions that envision "socialism" in far more extensive and comprehensive terms than those envisioned in either Lange's essay or the present work on pragmatic market socialism.

13. The marginal cost pricing efficiency principle is generally considered to have been established in the 1930s by the definitive contributions of Harold Hotelling (1938, 1939). However, these contributions just codified the principle, which in fact goes back to a much earlier date. For example, Lange's "On the Economic Theory of Socialism," in which the principle is applied to a socialist economy, appeared well before Hotelling's articles. The notion of using marginal cost pricing as a guideline for public enterprises is as old as the principle itself. But from its inception, it would seem, the principle has never been taken too seriously by economic theoreticians. For example, as early as 1949, Nancy Ruggles could provide a substantial survey of hypothetical objections to marginal cost pricing from the realm of economic theory. An indirect assault on the relevance of the principle is contained in the abundant second-best literature which shows that the

true efficiency rule becomes much more complicated than $MC = p$ if various market imperfections or other constraints exist (e.g., William Baumol and David Bradford, 1970). Other difficulties are suggested by the following questions: (1) What is the marginal cost of any one product of a multiproduct firm? (2) How should marginal cost be evaluated for a firm which confronts variable demand and fluctuating production (the peak-load problem)? As a result of the many complexities and imponderable factors, only rarely are attempts made in the real world to implement theoretically optimum pricing and production in publicly owned enterprises. The attempt along these lines made by the French is probably the single most important example (see J. R. Nelson, 1964). For a review of the relatively limited impact of the marginal cost pricing concept in United States public utility pricing, see Leonard Weiss (1981).

14. Benjamin Ward initiated the technical literature on the economic theory of the cooperative with a simple model of employee income-maximization in a 1958 *American Economic Review* article, a model later developed in Chapter 8 of Ward's 1967 textbook on socialist economic theory. The revelation that the basic notion of a cooperative was reasonably amenable to the standard mathematical tools of neoclassical economic theory inspired an increasing wave of work. Early contributions include Amartya Sen (1966); Evsey Domar (1966); Walter Oi and Elizabeth Clayton (1968); and James Meade (1972). By the late 1970s the technical literature had become sufficiently extensive to support a major survey article by Alfred Steinherr (1978) in the *Annals of Public and Cooperative Economy*. In 1983 Frederick Pryor provided an even more ambitious survey article in the same journal. The literature continued to flourish throughout the 1980s. It would seem, for example, that in recent years from 10 to 20 percent of the articles published in the *Journal of Comparative Economics* have to do with the economic theory of the cooperative firm. Aside from the pure theory of the cooperative, there is a substantial professional literature that evaluates cooperative production from both theoretical and empirical standpoints, especially in the light of the large-scale experiment in self-management undertaken in Yugoslavia. A few examples from the growing number of book-length studies of this type include Deborah Milenkovitch (1971); Howard Wachtel (1973); Ellen Comisso (1979); Norman Ireland (1982); Saul Estrin (1983); and Stephen Sacks (1983).

15. The predisposition toward finding hypothetical deficiencies in the performance of the cooperative firm relative to its capitalist twin has been present right from the inception of the technical literature. In his seminal work on the theory of the cooperative, Benjamin Ward emphasized the finding of an upward-sloping (or "perverse") supply curve of output. That is, in his labor dividend maximizing model, Ward found that the comparative statics effect of price on output is negative: as output price increases, the supply of output decreases. A downward-sloping supply curve of output in turn suggests problems with respect to both the existence and the stability of the supply-demand equilibrium for the product produced by the cooperative.

16. There are some notable exceptions to the rule of generally negative evaluations of cooperative enterprise by Western economists. Jaroslav Vanek has provided

a comprehensive and elaborate statement of the case for cooperative production in terms of contemporary economic theory. Starting with a sketch of the argument published in the *American Economic Review* in 1969, he then elaborated the argument in a major treatise published in 1970. The 1970 treatise was followed by a popular exposition (1971) and a compilation of articles (1977). Vanek is not alone in having provided a professionally sound and vigorously argued case for the cooperative principle addressed especially to the United States population: David Schweickart's 1980 book provides another excellent example of American pro-cooperative thinking.

3

PRAGMATIC MARKET SOCIALISM: PRO AND CON

A. BENEFITS OF PRAGMATIC MARKET SOCIALISM

The great socialist movement which arose and gathered momentum in the nineteenth century had as its basic purpose the elimination of extremes of wealth and poverty in society. Such extremes were generally viewed by socialists as proceeding from an exploitative process compounded by a cyclical process. These processes manifested the "anarchy of the market," an anarchy which becomes particularly obvious and onerous during the deepest troughs of the recurrent business depressions generated by the capitalist economic system. After coalescing briefly around the monumental intellectual codification of Karl Marx, the socialist movement quickly diverged, toward the close of the nineteenth century, into two principal channels. Orthodox Marxist socialists believed that the only escape route from capitalism lay through a violent revolution which would totally abolish private ownership of capital property and establish some sort of comprehensive economic planning. Revisionist (or social democratic) socialists believed that the basic socialist objective could be achieved, without benefit of violent revolution, total abolition of capital property, or comprehensive economic planning, by means of a judicious program of state intervention in the various forms of social insurance, business regulation, progressive taxation, nationalization of key industries, selective economic planning, and so on.

Although a perception of the inherent inequity of private ownership of capital property in the capitalist system has been a ubiquitous thread running through virtually all socialist critiques of capitalism, it has not so much been the inequity itself as its larger economic and social ramifications that has concerned the formulators of these critiques. Nearly all socialists have agreed that the inequity generates intolerable extremes of wealth and poverty, and intolerable business depressions. But there has also been an almost irresistible tendency among past proponents of socialism to go beyond these specific complaints, and to perceive in capitalism the roots of numerous additional social ills and evils. Some of these proponents have dwelt upon these alleged additional liabilities of capitalism with such enthusiasm and conviction as to suggest that any possible direct economic benefits of socialism, such as the equalization of capital property income, are actually very minor issues. Although the intention may have been to gather support for socialism from every possible quarter, in the light of history it appears that these ill-considered charges against capitalism may have seriously weakened the socialist cause by suggesting that its adherents were mostly harebrained enthusiasts driven by utopian fantasies.

Clearly pragmatic market socialism, as developed herein, is a very precise and conservative formulation of socialism, and its purposes and objectives are correspondingly precise and conservative. Certainly there is a significant overlap between these purposes and objectives and those historically associated with the socialist movement. But although quite significant, the overlap is limited, and it is important that it be properly understood. In contrast with almost all past advocacies of socialism, this advocacy of pragmatic market socialism is primarily motivated by the objective of eliminating the inequity, which is inherent in the private ownership of capital property under modern industrial conditions, of highly unequal distribution of unearned capital property return. It is this inequity itself, and not its perceived larger social and economic consequences, which is perceived as the salient and decisive difficulty with contemporary capitalism.

The core pragmatic market socialist proposal consists of BPO ownership of large, established corporations and the distribution of the property return produced by these corporations as a social dividend supplement to labor income. This proposal would accomplish a substantial equalization of unearned capital property return, and in so doing it would somewhat increase the overall equality of income distribution and somewhat reduce the observed extremes of wealth and poverty in society. But note the emphasis on the adverb "somewhat." No dramatic changes can be promised regarding these matters on the basis of the core pragmatic market socialist proposal. Nor would the core proposal address what to Karl Marx was the fatal defect of capitalism: business depressions. But the fact is that the severe nineteenth-century problems in these areas have already been solved within the context of twentieth-century capitalism in the industrially advanced nations. Within the United States, the nations of Western Europe, and elsewhere in the world, existing extremes of wealth and poverty are not "intolerable," nor are business depressions. *However*, twentieth-century capitalism does fully share with nineteenth-century capitalism one critical defect: highly unequal distribution of unearned capital property return. It is argued herein that there are no countervailing justifications for this defect in terms of static efficiency, dynamic performance, political considerations, or anything else. Therefore this defect, and this defect alone, suffices to justify the abolition of the principle of private ownership of capital property which defines capitalism.

Certainly an alteration in the fundamental capital ownership principle would have a number of additional ramifications. But past advocates of socialism have been overoptimistic concerning these ramifications. Public ownership of capital will not of itself totally abrogate extremes of poverty and wealth, totally suppress the "anarchy of the market," totally eliminate business depressions. Neither will it necessarily have any significant beneficial effect on recognized social problems, even those which are apparently aggravated by adverse economic conditions: problems such as alienation, crime, drug abuse, racism, sexism, environmental degradation, militarism, and imperialism. Aside from the direct economic effects emphasized in the foregoing, any other potential benefits from socialism may be arranged on a scale, according to personal judgment, from most probable and important to least probable and important. Numerous advocates of socialism in the past have argued strongly for benefits that many, if not most, reasonable persons judge to be highly improbable.

These overenthusiastic advocates of socialism seem to have attributed to capitalism almost any social ill of which one might think. Alienation, crime, and drug abuse emerge as desperate responses to the grinding poverty imposed by capitalism on the masses—especially when the impoverished masses observe obscenely extravagant living standards among the plutocratic capitalist class. Greedy capitalists encourage racism and sexism in order to keep the price of labor low—particularly the price of unskilled labor provided by the oppressed. Greedy capitalists thoughtlessly destroy the environment in order to make large short-term profits. Territorial expansion and wars are promoted by capitalists desirous of gaining profitable colonial investment opportunities and/or of profitably selling arms.

All such arguments share the same fatal flaw: The problems they address were prevalent within civilization long before the rise of modern capitalism, and there is no compelling evidence to indicate that the problems were appreciably aggravated by the rise of modern capitalism. This is not to say that some of these problems are not more serious and dangerous now than they were in the past. Clearly war is a greater threat to humanity in the age of nuclear weapons than it was in the age of swords and spears. Clearly environmental degradation is a greater threat in a world containing several billion human beings than it was when the human population numbered only a few hundred million. Clearly alienation, crime, and drug abuse will be more of a problem when the bulk of the population lives in large, impersonal cities rather than in small towns and villages. But the reasons for aggravated social problems are bound up with the physical expansion of the human population, industrialization, urbanization, technological change, and such—they have little or nothing to do with the capitalist principle of private ownership of capital property in and of itself.

Owing to these kinds of arguments, socialists are frequently generically denigrated as utopians who naively expect that socialism will change human nature. This particular advocacy of socialism endeavors to avoid the taint of utopianism by focusing on a relatively small number of benefits at the top of the probable importance ranking. Moreover, it endeavors to avoid exaggerated rhetoric in the evaluation of these benefits. In contrast with a great many past advocacies of socialism, no allegations are made herein that socialism, in the form of pragmatic market socialism, would be very likely to achieve a substantial improvement over contemporary capitalism in terms of economic efficiency. As the pragmatic market socialist economy would parallel the contemporary capitalist economy in a great many respects, no strong argument can be made that the former would be more efficient. By the same token, of course, no strong argument can be made that the pragmatic market socialist economy would be less efficient than the con- temporary capitalist economy. Since it seems probable that the economic efficiency of the two systems would be at least roughly comparable, the equality (or equity) argument for socialism comes to the fore.

Economists have generally been willing to admit that the gross inequality in capital wealth ownership under capitalism constitutes a liability of the system, and that, all other things being equal, the greater equality in property income distribution that could be achieved under socialism would be socially desirable. But they have tended to add in the same breath that all other things would not be equal, because socialism would not be as efficient as capitalism. Their viewpoint on the issue has suggested that if the economic efficiency justification for capitalism could be neutralized to a reasonable degree of certainty, the preferability of socialism would be clearly established. The detailed analysis presented the following chapters, particularly in Chapters 4 ("The Capital Management Issue"), 5 ("The Saving Issue") and 6 ("Investment, Growth, and Entrepreneurship"), casts grave doubt on the allegation that property return is earned income under capitalism, and therefore that the alternative social dividend distribution principle for property return under pragmatic market socialism would lead to economic inefficiency.

As the general consensus in favor of economic equality (in the absence of offsetting efficiency disadvantages) is very strong, only a brief justification of it needs to be offered. The strongest economic argument for income equality resides in the principle of diminishing marginal utility of income, together with the presumption that individuals are probably fairly homogeneous with respect to their ability to extract utility from material consumption of goods purchasable with income.[1] On the basis of these presumptions, an income decline of a given amount will reduce the utility of a high-income person by a smaller amount than an income increase of the same amount will increase the utility of a low-income person. The principle of diminishing marginal utility of income, regarded as self-evident by such prominent economists as Edgeworth and Pigou, has more recently been supported indirectly by the discovery by John von Neumann and Oskar Morgenstern that a reasonable notion of "risk aversion" implies diminishing marginal utility of income.[2] That most individuals are risk averse is demonstrated by the importance of the insurance industry in modern economies.

A subsidiary argument for equality relies on the notion of external effects: There is a tendency for individuals to feel envious toward those with higher consumption standards, and concerned for those with lower consumption standards. Applying this concept to the real world suggests that wealthy capitalists might feel somewhat guilty and uncomfortable about their extravagant living standards, and that the rest of the population experiences a certain amount of envious resentment when they reflect on the extravagant living standards of wealthy capitalists (particularly if they recognize that these standards are more the result of inheritance and/or good luck in the capital asset market than they are the result of personal merit and social productivity).[3]

The pragmatic market socialist economy would achieve an appreciable gain in equality. The current distribution of property return in the United States reflects the distribution of capital wealth, the gross inequality of which is shown by a Gini coefficient of about 0.90 for the overall population (see Chapter 7, Section B below). In contrast, the Gini coefficient for the distribution of labor income in the U.S. population is only around 0.35. As property income would be distributed under pragmatic market socialism as social dividend income proportional to labor income, the Gini coefficient for this income flow would decline from, say, approximately 0.90 to 0.35. If property income accounts for about 20 percent of total income and labor income for about 80 percent, this would suggest a decline in the Gini coefficient for total income from approximately 0.46 to 0.35. This would surely be a significant and worthwhile gain.

The main emphasis in the discussion of the efficiency question in the following chapters will be on the proposition that pragmatic market socialism would not be less efficient than capitalism. However, it ought to be added that there are at least two nonnegligible reasons for speculating that the pragmatic market socialist economy would in fact prove to be more efficient than the contemporary capitalist economy. As indicated above, no argument is intended that pragmatic market socialism would be *highly likely to achieve a substantial improvement* over contemporary capitalism in terms of economic efficiency. However, a reasonable argument may certainly be made that pragmatic market socialism would be *somewhat likely to achieve a significant improvement* over contemporary capitalism in terms of economic efficiency.

The first reason depends on the notion of an upward-sloping supply curve of labor. It will be noted below (Chapter 4, Section C) that there is no strong justification, either in theory or in empirics, for presuming an upward-sloping supply curve of either capital management effort or labor. But let us suppose that there are upward-sloping supply curves of both types of human exertion. Critics may predict inefficiency under pragmatic market socialism on grounds that the altered distribution of capital property return would reduce the effective wage of capital management effort and thereby discourage capital management effort. But such critics will probably neglect to consider that the reduction in the effective wage of capital management effort would be compensated (under the pragmatic market socialist proposal in which property income would be paid as social dividend income to individuals on the basis of their earned labor income) by an increase in the effective wage of labor. If it is imagined that the decrease in the effective wage of capital management effort will decrease capital management effort, it should also be clear that the increase in the effective wage of labor will increase labor. The extensive literature on the equity-efficiency tradeoff with respect to social redistribution of labor income is in fact based on the assumption of an upward-sloping supply curve of labor, so that it can scarcely be asserted that conventional economic thinking does not allow this compensating advantage of pragmatic market socialism.[4]

The second reason pertains to the possibility that the incentives to effort of high corporation executives under contemporary capitalism may have been seriously weakened by the separation of ownership and control. The high dispersion of the ownership interest relative to the concentration of managerial power brought about by the advent of megacorporations in the modern economy, may well have significantly attenuated the accountability of high corporation executives to the ownership interest. Therefore, the concentration of the ownership interest under pragmatic market socialism in a small, activist BPO with an explicit, socially sanctioned mission of encouraging the profitability of business enterprise could certainly induce a higher level of professionalism and energy in the pursuit of profits by corporation executives. Owing to the critical economic role of this small corps of individuals in the megacorporate economy, this might in turn have a substantial beneficial impact on the overall efficiency and dynamism of the economy.[5]

There are at least four important components of the disciplinary system which enforces strong effort incentives upon corporation executives in a modern industrial economy: (1) the threat of financial insolvency and bankruptcy; (2) competition among firms for markets and profits; (3) pressure from lending institutions in the capital markets; and (4) pressure from boards of directors. It is intended that all four of these be just as relevant and effective under pragmatic market socialism as they are currently under capitalism. Publicly owned firms whose expenditures exceed revenues would be dissolved through the normal process of bankruptcy. There would be a multiplicity of publicly owned but self-interested manufacturing and service firms in competition with one another. Although private individuals would be excluded from capital markets, these markets would still provide an arena for active competition among publicly owned but self-interested financial intermediary firms. Under pragmatic market socialism, the role of the corporation's board of directors would be taken over by a BPO agent, who would be no less self-interested than the board of directors. And the BPO agent might be able to impose his or her own self-interest on the corporation management more effectively than does the board of directors under contemporary capitalism.

Consider the authority under capitalism of the board of directors. In principle, this authority is relatively unconstrained. The board of directors, for example, may legally issue specific instructions on pricing and production to corporation executives. It may legally dismiss the chief executive officer of the corporation even if the corporation is highly profitable and its affairs are in order. Although it has been stated that the authority of the Bureau of Public Ownership under pragmatic market socialism would be "analogous to" the authority of corporate boards of directors under capitalism, in fact there would be some important restrictions on its authority. Under pragmatic market socialism, the BPO—both its central office and its agents—would be legally prohibited from issuing any instructions to a corporation concerning its microeconomic business decision variables (hiring and firing of labor, production levels, prices, advertising, etc.). Moreover, assuming that relatively objective, quantitative measures of a corporation's performance were satisfactory, the BPO would be unable to dismiss the corporation's chief executive. These considerations might give rise to qualms that the authority of the BPO over corporation executives would be inferior to that of boards of directors under capitalism.

Such qualms would to a large extent be based on misapprehensions of the actual functioning of corporate governance under capitalism. While it is true that the formal authority of the board of directors under capitalism is formidable, its actual authority is usually very attenuated. In the first place, the members of the board normally represent only a very small fraction of the total outstanding voting stock. Second, the members of the board are normally nominated by the incumbent managers, whose tastes tend to run to outsiders with little knowledge of the business. Third, boards of directors meet very intermittently, and when they do meet, the agenda is prepared by representatives of management and the proceedings are conducted by representatives of management. The upshot of these considerations is that the board of directors very rarely presents a serious threat to the job security of the incumbent chief executive, even under relatively dismal corporate performance.[6]

Under pragmatic market socialism, in contrast, presuming corporate performance to be objectively inferior, the threat of dismissal of the chief executive would be considerably greater than it is under capitalism. The decision on dismissal would be dominated by one person, the corporation's BPO agent. This agent would devote full time to the evaluation of the corporations within his or her sphere of responsibility and, as an individual with considerable experience in business management, would be able to apply a discriminating judgment to the information acquired. This concentration of the social ownership interest in the hands of a single agent strongly suggests that in spite of the apparently attenuated legal authority of the BPO over corporation executives, in practice its authority over them would be more active and formidable in the critical matter of enforcing effort incentives than is the present authority of capital owners under capitalism.

Beyond this, the benefits of pragmatic market socialism are sufficiently nebulous and problematic to be worthy of only brief mention. One traditional speculation of socialists has been that the concentration of capital wealth under capitalism entails a parallel concentration of political power which diminishes the quality and legitimacy of the democratic process. In the absence of a wealthy elite principally dependent on property income (i.e., a capitalist class), the true social interest in regard to various difficult social policy problems might be more quickly and accurately perceived. This issue will be further examined in Chapter 8, Section B ("Prospects for

Democratic Socialism").

There is another matter of the greatest consequence in the contemporary age. Several decades ago the terrifying possibility emerged of a global nuclear war that could have a devastating and possibly fatal impact on human civilization. Among the impediments confronting efforts to reduce this threat, not the least has been the virulent ideological confrontation between the Communist and non-Communist nations. There are four central propositions in traditional Communist ideology with which non-Communists generally disagree: (1) that socialism is superior to capitalism; (2) that central planning is superior to market allocation; (3) that the one-party political system is superior to the multiparty system; (4) that international activism dedicated to the overthrow of capitalism is morally legitimate. A typical proponent of pragmatic market socialism would tend to be as unalterably opposed as the next non-Communist to propositions (2), (3), and (4). But at the same time this proponent would judge the Communist viewpoint to be essentially correct with respect to proposition (1): the preferability of socialism over capitalism. The implementation of pragmatic market socialism in the militarily powerful nations of the West, especially the United States, would remove an important contributory factor to the ideological conflict, and thus improve the odds of a peaceful and permanent resolution of the international conflict situation.

It is of course a matter of considerable uncertainty as to how important the socialism versus capitalism issue has been in exacerbating the international conflict between the Communist and non-Communist blocs. Many reputable historians, political scientists, and other social analysts will confidently assert that this issue is in fact a negligible consideration, as the Communist nations have merely utilized ideology as a pretense to legitimize their imperialistic ambitions. Moreover, in the judgment of these same analysts, recent developments within the Communist nations suggest strongly that in any event the ideological struggle is nearing its conclusion, that traditional, orthodox communism has been unconditionally defeated, and that within a few decades even the hard-core Communist nations of Russia and China will have fully embraced both democracy and capitalism.

It could be that the above judgments reflect both an inadequate appreciation of the seriousness of the ideological conflict between communism and noncommunism in the past, and an overoptimistic expectation that this conflict is now behind us. At this point we are still a good distance from an international situation in which the implementation of pragmatic market socialism in the non-Communist West clearly would have no beneficial effect whatsoever as far as the cause of world peace is concerned. This issue will be examined further in Chapter 9 ("Capitalism and History").

B. CAPITALIST APOLOGETICS: AN APPRECIATION

Several hundred years ago there was little or no criticism or complaint raised, either in Western Europe or anywhere else, against the various political and economic rights of the hereditary aristocracy. These rights were regarded by the aristocrats themselves, by the intelligentsia, and by the common people alike as part of the natural order of things, as having been either rationally or divinely ordained for the benefit of the human race. But for reasons that probably will never be completely understood, hereditary aristocracy came under assault in modern history. Partly by violent revolution and partly by peaceful evolution, the domination of society by hereditary aristocrats was gradually weakened and abolished. Their formerly sacred rights were first attenuated and ultimately abrogated. In many if not most nations in the contemporary world, absolute monarchy, and other forms of governance related to hereditary aristocracy, has been entirely supplanted by the institutions, attitudes, and practices of political democracy.

Certainly the downfall of the hereditary aristocracy could not have occurred in the absence of an increasing consensus among nonaristocrats that no rational basis existed for the political and economic rights of aristocrats: that the financial and social benefits they reaped in the exercise of these rights were unjustified and unearned. At one time, of course, aristocratic apologetics played an important role in human thinking. These apologetics endeavored to justify aristocratic rights, to argue that the benefits received by the aristocrats were indeed earned, either directly or indirectly. Some apologists alleged that the benefits were a direct recompense for wise governance or cultural contributions by the aristocratic class. Others alleged that the only alternative to the status quo was the horror of mob rule or demagogic tyranny, and that these benefits were therefore indirectly earned by the aristocratic class through its role in preserving order and civilization. Such arguments gradually lost out to the Enlightenment viewpoint that aristocratic rights had no legitimate foundation either in rationality or in morality, and that they were merely obsolete and unjust relics of an earlier, ruder period in human history. This viewpoint was in better accord with the commonsense intuition of the preponderance of humanity. Whatever may have been the case in the ancient and medieval periods, as the modern era developed, aristocratic rights did not *seem* to be earned in any sensible, understandable manner. The perception of them gradually changed from "natural rights" to "unjustified privileges."

Capitalist apologetics of today have a great deal in common with the aristocratic apologetics of yesterday—except, of course, that capitalist apologetics still generally dominate outside of the handful of Communist nations. Capitalist apologetics claims that the capital property income received by the capitalist class is legitimately earned, directly and/or indirectly. There is the same emphasis on the alleged positive contributions of the capitalist class (in the form of saving, entrepreneurship, enterprise, risk-taking, etc.) as there was on the alleged wise governance and cultural contributions of the aristocratic class. There is the admonition that the only alternative to the capitalistic status quo is Orwellian scarcity and despair— analogous to the earlier admonition that the only alternative to the aristocratic status quo was the horror of mob rule or demagogic tyranny. The various propositions of capitalist apologetics are at the present moment in history very firmly entrenched both in the popular mind and in professional thought. But the simple fact that a significant socialist movement has arisen in modern history suggests that these various propositions are not in complete accordance with the commonsense intuitions of humanity. Perhaps the day is approaching when common sense will emerge, the light of day will shine forth, and capitalist apologetics will encounter the same fate as did aristocratic apologetics.

Typical dictionary definitions of "capitalism" and "socialism" are relatively precise and limited. "Capitalism" is customarily defined as an economic system in which the capital means of production are predominantly privately owned and controlled, while "socialism" is customarily defined as an economic system in which the capital means of production are predominantly socially owned and controlled. Needless to emphasize, over nearly two centuries of socialist opposition to capitalism and capitalist reaction against socialism, both terms have accumulated a rich and emotionally potent set of connotations. To pro-socialists, capitalism represents a nightmarish world of slums and despair presided over by arrogant capitalist plutocrats. To pro-capitalists, socialism represents a nightmarish world of slums and despair presided over by soulless government bureaucrats.

In view of the strong emotions aroused by these concepts, it is perhaps not surprising that careful, impartial thinking about them is relatively rare. Considered as a totality, the socialist critique of capitalism may certainly be described as multifaceted, amorphous, and nebulous. And similarly, when considered as a totality, the response to that critique by defenders of capitalism is equally multifaceted, amorphous, and nebulous. But it is probably fair to say that there is nothing in the body of capitalist apologetics which compares in intellectual scope and vigor with the work of Karl Marx. Why is this the case? Is the work of Marx so riddled with logical and empirical error as to be unworthy of refutation? Or is the work so complete

and overpowering as to defy refutation? Or has the intellectual elite,
observing the persistence of capitalism (outside of a relatively small number
of Communist nations), merely presumed that the status quo requires no
defense?

Pro-capitalist, anti-socialist writing began appearing in the early
nineteenth century, well before the publication of Marx's magnum opus,
Das Kapital. Much of it was provided by individuals who would be utterly
forgotten today had they not appeared as references in Marx's work. Oddly
enough, most of the justifications of capitalism with which we will mainly
be concerned herein (the need to encourage capital management effort,
saving, entrepreneurship, etc.) appeared, in more or less vague and informal
terms, very early in the nineteenth century. These defensive ideas were
generated by the pure and basic definition of socialism as public ownership
of capital, in the years when socialist proposals were purely hypothetical.
Later on, well after the death of Marx, when "real-world socialism" began
to take shape, capitalist apologetics shifted to criticism of any and all
negative aspects or characteristics of these real-world manifestations of
socialism—whether or not these aspects or characteristics could sensibly
be associated with the basic public ownership of capital principle which
defines socialism.

Two specific real-world forms of socialism have served as inspiration
and targets for the defenders of capitalism: the communistic and the social
democratic. Communistic socialism became firmly established in Russia in
the aftermath of World War I, and it experienced major territorial expansion
in the aftermath of World War II. The early decades of the twentieth century
also saw several social democratic parties come to power in Western
European nations and elsewhere. As a result of the history of communistic
socialism, numerous severe defects have been attributed to socialism:
everything from bureaucratic strangulation of the economy by the central
planning system to bloody political purges and international adventurism.
Owing to the success of social democratic parties and policies in important
nations which remained basically capitalist (in terms of the private ownership of capital principle), social democratic socialism has not been decried
and dismissed by critics of socialism with the same uncompromising
hostility as that applied to communistic socialism. The tactic of capitalist
apologetics in the case of social democracy has been to identify as
"socialism" various potential reductio ad absurdum extensions of the social
democratic program which in actuality are entertained seriously by only a
tiny radical fringe within this movement. For example, confiscatory taxation
of all forms of property income might be described as "socialism."

At this point in the present study, the basic pragmatic market socialist proposal has been presented. The remainder of the study will endeavor to draw forth out of the multifaceted, amorphous, and nebulous body of capitalist apologetics the relatively small subset of ideas and propositions which might actually apply to pragmatic market socialism. These ideas and propositions will be subjected to analysis and criticism, and it will be left to the reader to determine whether they do or do not constitute an adequate basis for the preservation of the capitalist status quo.[7]

An extremely important contention which is implicit throughout the remainder of this book is that most of the "arguments against socialism" applied by capitalist apologetics to communistic socialism and social democratic socialism would not apply to pragmatic market socialism. It is implicitly maintained, for example, that the defects of central planning would not apply to pragmatic market socialism, nor would the defects of excessively progressive income taxation. It may be predicted with almost complete confidence that some critics of pragmatic market socialism will proclaim the complete impossibility of establishing in the real world a socialist economic system even remotely akin to that envisioned and proposed herein, and that any conceivable real-world socialist system would display some, most, or all of the defects of communistic socialism and social democratic socialism. Thus, claims will no doubt be made that, for example, it would be politically impossible for any government in power to allow a large, publicly owned corporation to become bankrupt, that national government officials would of political necessity become deeply immersed in business decision-making, that by the ineffable force of self-interest these officials would endeavor to utilize the public ownership authority to undermine the democratic process, and so on. Critics of pragmatic market socialism adopting this particular tactic will claim that the analysis and rebuttal of capitalist apologetics provided in this study are irrelevant and beside the point, because they completely overlook the "real problems of socialism" that have been demonstrated by the histories of real-world communistic socialism and social democratic socialism.

Any reasonably informed and objective individual can perceive that the pragmatic market socialist proposal constitutes a careful and sincere effort to avoid the perceived difficulties of communistic socialism and social democratic socialism. Criticism of the proposal that amounts to a flat, unadorned, dogmatic denial of its real-world practicality is nothing more than begging the question (which doubtless is easier to do than engaging in serious thought about the proposal), and should not be taken seriously. It is true that there is no logical response to be made to begging the question— apart from engaging in the same tactic. But one hopes that most readers of this work will recognize begging the question for what it is, and will appreciate why it would be fruitless and futile to incorporate into this work lengthy speculations on why, for example, unprofitable publicly owned business enterprises *would* be allowed to lapse into bankruptcy under pragmatic market socialism, or why government bureaucracies *would not* take over the economy under pragmatic market socialism.

It has to be appreciated that the pragmatic market socialist proposal represents a new departure for socialism, a fundamentally new interpretation and implementation of socialism. This novel interpretation and implementation of socialism will no doubt be unacceptable to many traditional socialists. This is of no concern, because of the demonstrated impotence of traditional socialist thought in the contemporary period. Predictions of the utter impracticality and impossibility of pragmatic market socialism betray both intellectual arrogance and inadequate appreciation of history. History has witnessed a remarkable amount of unforeseen social transition and evolution. It also seems that the processes of social change are accelerating in the modern era. Under the circumstances, careful and objective consideration of the pragmatic market socialist alternative should not be deterred by thoughtless, dogmatic pronouncements issued by inflexible and superficial mentalities.

C. OBJECTIONS TO PRAGMATIC MARKET SOCIALISM

What *sensible* objections might be offered by a defender of capitalism against the pragmatic market socialist alternative? These objections might conveniently be categorized as objections to the various components of the fundamental proposition motivating this proposal for pragmatic market socialism. It has been proposed in this work that the clearest and most important defect of the contemporary capitalist system is that it preserves and perpetuates the inequity of a very unequal distribution of unearned property return. The various lines of defense against this proposition may be categorized as follows. First, it may be held that property income is not unearned but, rather, that it is an earned return, earned either as a return to capital management effort, as a return to saving, or as a return to innovation, risk-taking, and entrepreneurship. Next, there is the argument that the distribution of capital property income—when properly interpreted—is not unduly unequal. This is the "people's capitalism thesis," which proposes to automatically eliminate possible inequity by eliminating inequality. It implicitly asserts the irrelevance of the earned versus unearned issue, in that relatively equal distribution by the economic marketplace of a certain return—even if unearned—cannot be objectionable. After the people's capitalism thesis, the last of the economic arguments for capitalism, the defense of capitalism tails off into various rather conjectural political, social, psychological, and philosophical propositions. No doubt the most important of the noneconomic arguments for capitalism is its alleged role in the protection and preservation of political democracy. Each of the following chapters will deal in sequence with a particular more or less separate and well-defined component of the body of capitalist apologetics.

Chapter 4 covers the capital management issue. In the judgment of the author, the capital management argument appears to be by far the most plausible argument against pragmatic market socialism. The commonplace opinion of the man in the street under contemporary capitalism is that socialism would fail because there "wouldn't be any incentives" and "nobody would bother to work very much." To the extent that this commonplace opinion might possess some relevance as far as the pragmatic market socialist plan proposed herein is concerned, its relevance lies in the possibility of economic inefficiency owing to the inadequacy of incentives to capital management effort.

Under contemporary capitalism, a large proportion of property return goes to those private individuals directly involved in managing the capital stock. Such "managers" include not only corporation executives and stockholders but also financial investors who guide the flow of new financial capital into the various available physical capital investments. Under pragmatic market socialism, only a small fraction of capital property return would be retained for the purpose of providing direct incentives to capital management effort; the great preponderance would be dispersed to the general public in the form of the social dividend. The salient question is whether this institutional shift would—as alleged by capitalist apologetics—significantly and adversely affect the diligence with which financial capital is allocated and physical capital is managed, and hence the overall efficiency and productivity of the economy. The response to this question will involve an extended discussion ranging from casual empiricism through a technical specification of the problem to diverse pieces of empirical evidence pertaining to such things as the separation of ownership and control, institutional investors, and the relative efficiency of noncapitalist production in nationalized industries and Communist nations. Although the capital management defense of capitalism is acknowledged to be logically consistent and reasonably plausible, it is argued that in the light of all relevant theoretical and empirical evidence, this defense ultimately fails to justify the capitalist economic system.

Chapter 5 covers the saving issue. This defense of capitalism proceeds from the assumption that people naturally prefer to consume now rather than later, and asserts that the role of property income is to overcome this potentially disastrous tendency by offering an inducement to postpone consumption. In the absence of the property income inducement to save, private saving would be drastically curtailed, as would capital investment, as such investment is drawn from the pool of available saving. Moreover, any attempt to replace private saving with public saving would probably generate serious dynamic inefficiency. This argument is examined in the light of both theoretical and empirical evidence, ranging from the intuitive motivations to save to economic theories of the effect of the rate of property return on current private saving. The main counterarguments to the saving defense of capitalism are summarized as follows: (1) the effect of the rate of property return on current private saving is theoretically indeterminate; (2) there are various empirical indications that if there is any positive effect of the rate of property return on private saving at all, it is likely to be very small; (3) in any event, if it does become necessary to add a social saving allocation to voluntary private saving, there is no good reason to believe that the total saving rate thus achieved would be any less socially desirable than the rate currently maintained under contemporary capitalism.

Chapter 6 covers investment, growth, and entrepreneurship. A familiar argument against socialism which is particularly associated with the Austrian school is that while conceivably a socialist economic system might maintain a reasonable degree of economic efficiency in the short term, its long-run economic performance would be disastrous because of inadequate incentives to such critical determinants of economic progress as innovation, risk-taking, and entrepreneurship. The argument is summarized in the proposition that while socialism may display static efficiency, it cannot sustain dynamic progressiveness—and in the long run it is dynamic progressiveness which determines economic and social welfare. It is argued herein that the logical essence of this argument devolves to a quasi-mystical rehashing, in suitably "dynamic" jargon, of the capital management issue dealt with in Chapter 4. If the obscurantist rhetoric in which the argument is customarily presented can be transcended, it is perceived that the active role of institutional investors in modern capital markets constitutes an effective rebuttal of the argument.

Chapter 7 covers people's capitalism. Although not directly concerned with the key economic efficiency issue, people's capitalism is nevertheless an extremely important component of the case against socialism—and is quite possibly the single most important component in a practical political sense. The people's capitalism approach tries to get as many people as possible to believe that even were socialism not to be less efficient than capitalism in terms of aggregate economic productivity, it would still be detrimental to their own personal welfare, because they are already—or soon will become, if capitalism persists—members of the capitalist class which socialism proposes to dispossess. The joint appeal thus made to greed and pride is very powerful and effective. It is therefore especially important to analyze this line of defense very closely. The available empirical evidence, ranging from statistical work on the importance of inheritance in wealthholding to computer simulations of the workings of chance in capital wealth accumulation, is on the whole decidedly inconsistent with the basic tenets of people's capitalism. It would appear that unless pragmatic market socialism turns out to be extremely inefficient relative to capitalism, the overwhelming majority of the population would have its overall income position improved through receipt of social dividend income rather than capital property income. This is true both in terms of current income and in terms of expected lifetime income.

Chapter 8 concerns capitalism and democracy. The most important of the noneconomic justifications for capitalism is the allegation that the overwhelming economic power possessed by the state under socialism would create conditions and pressures tending toward the extinction of genuine political democracy. This argument is rather speculative and conjectural (even though based on a crude empirical inference from the observed situation in the Communist nations), and so must be its rebuttal. We are not able to draw upon a substantial body of theoretical knowledge and empirical evidence relevant to the issue, as we may in the case of the economic arguments against socialism discussed in the previous four chapters. Nevertheless, the rebuttal to this argument against pragmatic market socialism, while less tangible than the other rebuttals, is no less sensible and effective. Probably its most important aspect consists of the observation that although military force offers a more direct and certain means of overthrowing democracy than would government ownership of business enterprises, in the great contemporary democracies military forces are not utilized for this purpose. It is clear that the power of tradition can preserve democracy indefinitely against what might appear to be, according to the "law of the jungle," very serious threats.

As this book is an advocacy of pragmatic market socialism, it is to be expected that all of the arguments against pragmatic market socialism considered in Chapters 4 through 8 will be found wanting. No doubt skeptics will deem the critique of capitalist apologetics offered in these chapters to be incomplete, inadequate, and fallacious. Conceivably these skeptics may be right. It has already been explicitly conceded that the available evidence in the form of logical propositions and empirical indications is inadequate to support an absolutely certain judgment on pragmatic market socialism—

either pro or con. Thus the proposal, to reiterate a key point, is for a *provisional and experimental* implementation of pragmatic market socialism, with the express intention of returning to capitalism should the pragmatic market socialist system perform inadequately in practice. However, having conceded the possibility of error, it is certainly fair to ask even those readers who are initially very skeptical to try to maintain as impartial an attitude as possible in their consideration of capitalist apologetics in light of the pragmatic market socialist alternative.

Admittedly the maintenance of the requisite level of impartiality will be difficult for especially skeptical readers. Once a person has formed a very strong judgment on a controversial question, it becomes very difficult for that person to take seriously opposing viewpoints on the matter, and to genuinely reconsider the issue. There emerges a very strong temptation to attribute opposing viewpoints either to mental incompetence or to simple ignorance. As the following chapters take up, examine (in the context of pragmatic market socialism), and ultimately reject a series of well-known arguments against socialism, an extremely skeptical reader might be strongly impelled to discount, reject, and ignore all this evidence and argumentation on grounds that none of it represents the heart of the matter insofar as the potential failings of pragmatic market socialism are concerned.

Although any reasonably fair-minded individual will recognize that the following five chapters cover a very substantial component of the case against pragmatic market socialism, it is also clear that numerous additional objections might be raised. Conceivably some of these additional objections may contain genuine merit. But the reader is asked to pause for reflection before concluding that the issues covered are beside the point and that the more serious objections to be made against pragmatic market socialism are being ignored. There are three important possibilities to be considered with respect to any particular additional objection which might come to mind. First, this objection might actually be to some other form of socialism which has been explicitly dissociated from pragmatic market socialism. Second, this additional objection might actually be a reformulation or rewording of an objection which is covered. Finally, this additional objection may be merely a nebulous, legalistic, or obstructionist quibble which is not explicitly dealt with herein owing to space constraints. This chapter will conclude with some brief examples of these kinds of objections.

It was mentioned above that with the emergence of "real-world socialism" in the twentieth century, most of the further development of capitalist apologetics has consisted of critiques of communistic socialism and social democratic socialism. Of the two, for obvious reasons communistic socialism has been the more bitterly assailed. Through communistic socialism, socialism as a general concept has been associated with a number of extremely negative conditions, the two most important of which are the absence of genuine political democracy and the bureaucratic strangulation of economic and social life. The issue of democracy is explicitly considered in Chapter 8, but there is no explicit consideration of the bureaucracy issue. Social democratic socialism is also associated with bureaucratic strangulation (although to a lesser extent), as well as with other problems: excessive egalitarianism, suffocating paternalism, and so on. The pragmatic market socialist proposal has been explicitly designed to avoid most of the perceived defects of real-world communistic and social democratic socialism. For example, one of the explicit provisions against bureaucratic strangulation is the specification that the Bureau of Public Ownership must not under any circumstances issue instructions to the managers of the publicly owned business enterprises concerning microeconomic decision variables: prices, production levels, investment projects, and so on. Furthermore, there is absolutely nothing in the proposal regarding such standard forms of state intervention in the economy as income taxation and direct regulation of business.

An exceptionally closed-minded critic may simply deny that the pragmatic market socialist system is possible in the real world. That is, despite the clearly and carefully stated intention to avoid, for example, bureaucratic strangulation, nevertheless bureaucratic strangulation would inevitably emerge. According to the argument, real-world experience (i.e., the history of communistic socialism in the Soviet Union and elsewhere, and/or the history of social democratic socialism in the Scandinavian countries and elsewhere) proves that socialism inevitably leads to bureaucratic strangulation, suffocating paternalism, and so on. The argument is basically that no new form of socialism is possible; that the defects of all past experiences with socialism must inevitably characterize all future experiences with socialism. Aside from citing the undeniable fact of social progress throughout history, there is really no response to be made to this kind of argument, since it is merely an attempt to beg the question. If one endeavors to pursue the question of exactly *why* bureaucratic strangulation is inevitable under socialism, chances are that the discussion will trail off into a morass of non sequiturs, circular reasoning, and rhetorical murk. Space constraints preclude extensive forays into such morass. Therefore very little attention can be paid to criticisms of pragmatic market socialism which are irrelevant—unless it is simply *assumed* that pragmatic market socialism must inevitably share the adverse characteristics of other forms of socialism from which it has been explicitly dissociated.

No detailed argumentation is provided herein that pragmatic market socialism would not in fact be prey to such problems as bureaucratic strangulation and suffocating paternalism because the institutional proposal is explicitly designed to avoid these problems. But let us turn now to brief discussions of three specific topics in contemporary economic theory in which a particularly closed-minded and determined critic might perceive objections to pragmatic market socialism: property rights theory, information theory, and principal-agent theory. It will be argued that insofar as there is any substance in property rights objections to pragmatic market socialism, this substance lies in the capital management issue, which is given careful consideration herein. In other words, property rights objections are simply reworkings of an objection which is covered. As for objections derived from information theory and principal-agent theory, these are examples of the third type of additional objection mentioned above: a superficial, off-the-cuff quibble, devoid of serious merit, which betrays the solidly impenetrable intellect of the proposer.

The various analytical models utilized in the following discussion to examine the potential economic performance of pragmatic market socialism are all drawn from more or less conventional, mainstream neoclassical economic theory. In general, the models suggest that the relative performance of the proposed system could be either superior or inferior to that of contemporary capitalism. In other words, the fundamental, axiomatic assumptions of neoclassical economic theory are not sufficient, in themselves, to predict the potential performance of pragmatic market socialism relative to capitalism. The potential performance question is therefore an empirical rather than a theoretical question. While a relatively open-minded individual with a proper appreciation of the limitations of contemporary economic theory might not find this conclusion particularly unexpected or upsetting, a less open-minded individual might be unwilling to accept the implication that contemporary economic theory is essentially neutral on whether pragmatic market socialism would be superior or inferior to capitalism. Such an individual might try to invoke some of the undeveloped and unintegrated ideas drifting around on the periphery of economic theory as definitive refutations of pragmatic market socialism. Since such refutations are not forthcoming from conventional neoclassical economic theory, that theory is deemed beside the point, on the conjecture that the real problems of pragmatic market socialism reside in other, newer areas of theory.

Any knowledgeable economist will readily, if not happily, acknowledge the numerous defects and limitations of neoclassical theory as a guide to economic reality. He or she will nevertheless stoutly maintain that neoclassical theory is a sufficiently accurate approximation to reality to provide many important insights into economic reality which cannot be obtained through informal, nonmathematical reasoning. The very fact that such peripheral topic areas in economic theory as property rights have not been significantly integrated into core theory might suggest that they also suffer from defects and limitations as guides to economic reality. Possibly the careful and systematic application of such outer branches of theory to the question of the potential relative performance of pragmatic market socialism would yield some additional insights not attainable using conventional neoclassical theory.[8] But to assume that "definitive" results would be obtained betrays excessive optimism regarding these outer branches. And to assume further that these "definitive" results would demonstrate compellingly that pragmatic market socialism would be inferior to capitalism betrays a mind that is not only closed but locked. Until such serious investigations are undertaken, the discussion must necessarily run along such informal and inconclusive lines as the following.

Although critics of socialism often cite its "abrogation" of property rights, it is more appropriate to think of the effect of socialization in terms of a "transfer" or "redistribution" of property rights.[9] Specifically, under pragmatic market socialism, the rights to property return earned by non-human factors of production would be transferred from the holders of financial capital to the earners of labor income: A given person's claim to the pool of property return would be proportional to his or her flow of labor income, rather than to his or her stock of financial wealth. Therefore the earners of labor income under pragmatic market socialism would have basically the same incentive to put pressure on those directly involved in the extraction of property return from nonhuman factors of production—the corporation executives—as do the owners of financial wealth under capitalism. The simplistic notion that under socialism there would be no incentive to anyone to operate capital efficiently because no one would receive property income is clearly invalid with respect to pragmatic market socialism. Social dividend is property income in another form. In practice, this means that in a democratic nation such as the United States, the elected representatives of the people in the legislative and the executive branches of government would take a keen interest in whether the Bureau of Public Ownership was doing its job effectively. For its part, the BPO would not be able to take refuge, as may some other government agencies and enterprises, behind fuzzy performance criteria. The dominant success criterion for the BPO is the amount of social dividend it distributes to the public, an objectively measurable quantity. Moreover, an objectively measurable benchmark exists: the amount of property return that capitalism was distributing to capital owners prior to the socialist transformation.

It might be argued, however, that the interest of the recipients of social dividend income under pragmatic market socialism would be too trivial and atomized for it to be translated into effective pressure on the corporation executives. That is, each person would receive only a tiny fraction of the overall social dividend, and the influence of any one person on political governance in a mass democracy is negligible. One difficulty with this argument is that apparently it already holds true under modern capitalism. A given stockholder or bondholder in a large corporation receives only a tiny fraction of that corporation's property return disbursements, and the influence of any one stockholder or bondholder on the operation of the corporation by its management is negligible. Obviously this existing situation is not hobbling the productive efficiency of capitalism. Nor is there any strong reason for expecting it to hobble the productive efficiency of pragmatic market socialism—particularly when one reflects on the activist policy envisioned for the BPO in enforcing a strong incentive to produce property return on the corporation executives.

Now as a matter of fact, in the model of capital management effort examined below (Chapter 4, Section C), the essence of the property rights argument is encompassed in the concept of the "retention coefficient." It is specified that under capitalism, capital management effort is provided by capital owners, while under pragmatic market socialism it would be provided not by the general public which receives social dividend, as suggested above, but rather exclusively by the personnel of the Bureau of Public Ownership. Thus under socialism those who provide capital management effort receive only a small fraction (5 percent or less—the BPO retention coefficient) of the total property return paid to capital. The small retention coefficient under socialism may translate into low capital management effort, which may translate into low efficiency or "irrational calculation under socialism," to use the traditional Austrian phrase. The smaller retention coefficient of the capital managers under socialism than under capitalism may be interpreted as a diminishment of the property rights of the capital managers. An effort will be made both to formulate this argument, and to develop a socialist rebuttal to it, in analytical terms. The model utilized in this effort may be termed a neoclassical model rather than a property rights model because it uses several elements of standard neoclassical theory. But it would clearly be appropriate (and fashionable) to use the latter term. The point is, however, that this model may pose a chimerical problem if indeed, as is fully possible, the recipients of social dividend income under pragmatic market socialism (the general working population) would in fact exert the same capital management effort which is currently exerted by the recipients of property income under capitalism (the class of capital owners).

Property rights is merely one area of study in economics in which problems may be discerned for pragmatic market socialism—but if and when these problems are examined carefully, it is perceived that such problems are already fully operative under modern capitalism, and also that allegations as to the greater force of these problems under pragmatic market socialism are necessarily very speculative. Further examples of this lie in the related areas of information theory and principal-agent theory.[10]

One of the better-known economic journal articles of the twentieth century is Friedrich Hayek's 1945 paean ("The Use of Knowledge in Society") to the efficiency of the free market as a means of processing information. This article hardly constitutes a technical contribution to information theory: It is rather a statement of opinion such as might have been penned by one of the more enthusiastic French laissez-fairists around 1830. That the free market is very efficient, with respect to information, production, distribution, and many other variables, is not a point which any proponent of pragmatic market socialism would care to dispute. The question is: What are the practical implications of Hayek's contribution with respect to pragmatic market socialism? Any such implications are very hazy. The article suggests that Soviet central planning is inefficient, and considering Hayek's known aversion to socialism, a principal purpose of the article was no doubt simply to discredit socialism in the form of Soviet central planning. It scarcely needs much emphasis that the intention of pragmatic market socialism is not to emulate Soviet central planning. Thus, if it happens to be true that Soviet central planning is inefficient because the central planning authority is unable to effectively process the huge amount of information it gathers from the firms, that fact, while interesting, has no bearing whatever on the pragmatic market socialist proposal.

However, looking to the specific proposal of pragmatic market socialism, may we not discern problems stemming from "information"? For example, the Bureau of Public Ownership is supposed to evaluate the performance of corporation executives. But to do this effectively, would it not have to accumulate and process vast amounts of information regarding every aspect of corporate activity gathered from every tiny nook and cranny of the economy? To do the job *perfectly*, in principle it may well have to do this. But recall that its aspiration is only to do the job as well as the capital owners are currently doing it under capitalism. The capital owners under capitalism confront exactly the same information problems as would the BPO under socialism. Presuming the capital owners are not supermen, they are not able to resolve these problems completely, and they therefore do a more or less imperfect job of evaluating the performance of corporation executives.

If anything, pragmatic market socialism might have an advantage with respect to information. While a BPO agent assigned to a given corporation would be enjoined from issuing any instructions to its management, the agent would enjoy unrestricted access to the personnel and the documentation of the corporation. He or she could question employees and examine documents as much as desired. Moreover, as a person with experience in business management, the agent would be in a position to know which questions to ask and which documents to examine. Finally, the BPO agent would be devoting full time to corporate performance evaluation. Contrast this image with that of a typical stockholder in a large corporation under present-day capitalism: The stockholder would be barred from the corporate offices no less than any nonowner. The stockholder would learn about the operations of the corporation only that which the management deems it appropriate that he or she know, or that which legal requirements force them to disclose in annual reports. Most likely the stockholder is pursuing a demanding, full-time career in law, or medicine, or etc., and does not have much time or energy to devote to corporate performance evaluation in any event. It seems inescapable that the BPO agent would be in a far better situation with respect to the gathering and processing of information relevant to corporate performance evaluation than is the typical stockholder today.

The somewhat jargonistic term "asymmetric information" has become very popular in the currently flourishing literature on principal-agent relationships. The basic situation studied by this literature involves a principal who delegates authority to an agent. The agent's effort generates a return which is shared between the principal and the agent. The principal cannot fully monitor the agent's effort ("asymmetric information": the agent knows how much effort he is putting out, but the principal does not). The problem is to devise a method of sharing the return between the principal and the agent that is optimal in some sense. This basic problem applies under both capitalism and socialism. Under capitalism, the capital owners (the principals) delegate authority to the boards of directors (the agents); in turn, the boards of directors (the principals) delegate authority to the corporation executives (the agents). And so it goes, as higher corporation executives delegate authority to lower corporation executives, right down the line to the lowest employees. Under pragmatic market market socialism, the analogous chain goes from the general public (principals) to Bureau of Public Ownership personnel (agents), from BPO personnel (principals) to corporation executives (agents), and so on down the line. A closed-minded critic of pragmatic market socialism might propose that it could not possibly solve the terribly difficult principal-agent problem to even the crudest and most unsatisfactory degree of approximation. But such an objection would be vulnerable to the obvious response that if the problem cannot be solved very well under pragmatic market socialism, there is no good reason to believe that it is being solved very well under capitalism.

In the model of capital management effort developed in Chapter 4, the focus is on the first link in this chain under pragmatic market socialism. Property return produced by the capital management effort of BPO personnel is to be divided between the principals (the general public) and the agents (the BPO personnel). The agents' share is represented by the retention coefficient. The question is then whether the actual resolution of this problem under pragmatic market socialism would be at least as efficient as is the present resolution under capitalism. The model could thus be tagged a "principal-agent model" just as it could be tagged a "property rights model"—it is purely an arbitrary question of terminology.

A point made above is still relevant here: The incentives problem formulated by the model may be chimerical. In the model, there is no distinction between "capital owners" under capitalism and "members of boards of directors." However, if, as suggested above, under capitalism the capital owners delegate the responsibility of capital management effort to the members of boards of directors, then the proportion of total property return going to these members under capitalism would be analogous to the retention coefficient under pragmatic market socialism. Although precise statistics are not available, it seems fairly probable that those capital owners who are actually active on boards of directors under capitalism receive less than 5 percent of the total property return, which is the benchmark retention coefficient proposed for pragmatic market socialism. These considerations suggest that if under pragmatic market socialism roughly the same proportion of property return is retained by the Bureau of Public Ownership as is taken directly by members of corporate boards of directors under contemporary capitalism, then pragmatic market socialism will have solved the terribly difficult principal-agent problem just as well as does the contemporary capitalist economic system. It may therefore be surmised that the principal-agent problem would be no more insuperable under pragmatic market socialism than it is presently under capitalism.

It would be possible to continue in this vein indefinitely. But to do so would be both impractical and fruitless. Those whose minds are completely shut against pragmatic market socialism display marvelous fecundity and ingenuity in the production of objections to the proposal. No sooner does an advocate of the proposal begin to formulate a reasonable, sensible response to one particular objection than the closed-minded opponent announces that that particular matter is after all not really germane to the real issues involved, and proceeds to invent yet another extemporaneous objection. The advocate soon realizes that it is impossible to win this game. It can only be hoped that capitalist apologetics has not been so overwhelmingly successful in the non-Communist Western world as to forever preclude a novel form of socialism, the pragmatic market socialist form, to which only a very small part of the standard body of capitalist apologetics applies at all—and that part of it very imperfectly and unpersuasively.

NOTES

1. Francis Y. Edgeworth's well-known statement of the argument occurred in Part III of the three-part article "The Pure Theory of Taxation" published in the *Economic Journal* (1897). A celebrated postscript was added by Abba Lerner in Chapter 3 of *The Economics of Control* (1944). Skeptics of progressive taxation had particularly objected to the assumption in Edgeworth's argument that all individuals possess identical utility functions relating income to utility: These skeptics argued that it was quite plausible that some individuals would derive more utility from income than would others. In any event, since there was no objective way to measure utility, the Edgeworthian argument for progressive taxation rested upon the unscientific foundation of subjective judgment. In response to these points, Lerner argued that in the absence of knowledge of individual utility functions, equal distribution of income (given the other Edgeworthian assumptions and particularly the assumption of diminishing marginal utility of income) would maximize the *expected* sum of utilities.

2. Interestingly, John von Neumann and Oskar Morgenstern's seminal treatise, *The Theory of Games and Economic Behavior* (1947), was written during the period of von Neumann's involvement with the Manhattan Project. Among other things, the treatise deals with the significance of a concave utility function in income in terms of risk aversion, develops an axiomatic argument for the rationality of expected utility maximization as a basis for decision-making under uncertainty, and applies linear programming to the solution of zero-sum games. The work is considered to be the foundation of modern uncertainty analysis, as exemplified by the compendiums edited by Jacques Drèze (1974) and Peter Diamond and Michael Rothschild (1978).

3. The author has contributed an article (*Public Finance*, 1983) on the issue of consumption externalities (i.e., envy and altruism) in relation to optimal redistribution. Still other arguments for redistribution are contained in the compendium edited by Harold Hochman and George Peterson (1974). Most of the papers in that volume envision transfers from relatively advantaged groups to relatively disadvantaged groups, and frequently some sort of social welfare concept is employed. Among many public choice theorists, the notion of social welfare is disparaged, and it is argued that social decisions and policies eventuate from the interplay and competition among opposed private self-interests. Thus in his 1983 book on redistribution, the eminent public choice theorist Gordon Tullock argues that in actual fact in the contemporary United States the great majority of explicit and

implicit income transfers are the fruits of diligent self-seeking efforts by well-or-ganized special interest groups—such as farmers, retired persons, and auto workers—which are not, in general, particularly disadvantaged. A defense (of sorts) of the social welfare maximization concept is contained in the author's 1989 *Public Finance* article.

4. The phrase "equity-efficiency tradeoff" gained wide currency after Arthur Okun's 1975 exercise in popular economics: *Equality and Efficiency: The Big Tradeoff*. But the notion of an inherent opposition or conflict between equi-ty/equality and output/efficiency long predates Okun's book. For example, ten years earlier, the title of a book-length essay by James E. Meade—*Efficiency, Equality and the Ownership of Property* (1965)—came fairly close to the current nomenclature. In a 1984 paper in the *Journal of Political Economy*, Edgar Brown-ing and William Johnson estimate the current loss in output from redistribution in the United States to be quite substantial. The economic purposes of inequality in labor income, as perceived by standard neoclassical economics, are developed in Bronfenbrenner's 1971 survey volume, *Income Distribution Theory*. (See also Gian Singh Sahota's 1978 survey article for the *Journal of Economic Literature*.) A numerical assessment of the potential relevance of this argument to pragmatic market socialism is contained in a recently published article by the author in the *Eastern Economic Journal* (Yunker, 1991).

5. The argument described here was first developed in considerable detail in one of the author's most important papers on pragmatic market socialism, "The Microeconomic Efficiency Argument for Socialism Revisited" (*Journal of Economic Issues*, March 1979). This paper elicited a comment from Peter Murrell, published together with the author's reply (*JEI*, March 1981).

6. The hypothesis of weak accountability of high corporate executives under conditions of separation of ownership and control is occasionally recognized by the popular business press. For example, in its May 18, 1987 issue, *Business Week* ran a cover story entitled "Corporate Control: Shareholders vs. Managers." In a "Commentary" sidebar (pp. 108-109), the following comments on the contem-porary capitalist corporate economy were made: "The corporation, perhaps more than most institutions, is based on a series of myths. Managers serve owners. One share of stock gets one vote. Shareholders elect representatives to the board of directors. The free market disciplines winners and losers. All the myths have a purpose: to make us believe that the corporation is accountable and efficient. The truth of the matter is that the public corporation has been a benevolent autocracy for decades. Managers have run the show. Shareholder meetings have been elaborate ceremonies. Proxy votes have been foreordained rituals. People who have served as directors on boards have usually been friends of the boss... In 1932, Adolf A. Berle and Gardiner C. Means published *The Modern Corporation and Private Property*. In the corporation, they noted, shareholders surrender their wealth to outside management. The interests of those parties diverge. The problem gets worse as the number of shareholders increases and their influence grows even more diffuse. Management is often left to go its own way, accountable more in theory than in practice... Management rarely loses proxy battles, because the odds are

stacked in its favor. Executives can use company funds to reach voters with all the arguments they want to offer..."

7. Many pro-socialists in the past have taken note of various elements of capitalist apologetics, and have offered refutations of these elements. But by and large their discussions of capitalist apologetics have been brief and superficial. For example, in a lengthy paragraph in Volume I, Chapter VII, Section 2, of *Das Kapital*, Marx deals with some central components of capitalist apologetics. This occurs in the course of a counterfactual situation in which the capitalist does not receive property income (surplus value, in Marx's terminology) from his capital investment. The various protests made by the capitalist against this situation reflect various components of capitalist apologetics.

Marx states and replies to the capital management argument as follows: "Our friend [the capitalist], up to this time so purse-proud, suddenly assumes the modest demeanor of his own workman, and exclaims: 'Have I myself not worked? Have I not performed the labor of superintendence and of overseeing the spinner? And does not this labor, too, create value?' His overseer and his manager try to hide their smiles." Marx then states and replies to the saving argument as follows: "He [the capitalist] tries persuasion. 'Consider my abstinence; I might have played ducks and drakes with the fifteen shillings; but instead of that I consumed it productively, and made yarn with it.' Very well, and by way of reward he is now in possession of good yarn instead of a bad conscience; and as for playing the part of a miser, it would never do for him to relapse into such bad ways as that; we have seen before to what results such asceticism leads [i.e., business depressions]. Besides, where nothing is, the king has lost his rights: whatever may be the merits of his abstinence, there is nothing wherewith specially to remunerate it, because the value of the product is merely the sum of the values of the commodities that were thrown into the process of production. Let him therefore console himself with the reflection that virtue is its own reward." Although these responses do in fact contain valid points, they are far too sketchy and flippant to be effective.

Marx's scorn for capitalist apologetics is manifested in the conclusion of this paragraph: "Meanwhile, after a hearty laugh, he [the capitalist] reassumes his usual mien. Though he has chanted to us the whole creed of the economists, in reality, he says, he would not give a brass farthing for it. He leaves this and all such like subterfuges and juggling tricks to the professors of political economy, who are paid for it." Such rhetorical jibes at his intellectual opponents certainly lends a bit of amusement value to Marx's normally pedantic writing style. But both in Marx's time and in our own, the judgment that socialism represents a superior alternative to capitalism is by no means overwhelmingly dominant. In view of the strength of the opposition, Marx should perhaps have taken a more serious and reflective tone, and should not have dismissed opposed arguments so lightly. Capitalist apologetics is much too formidable to be vanquished with a few cleverly worded phrases.

8. As one of many possible examples of this, consider an article by Barry Nalebuff and Joseph Stiglitz entitled "Prizes and Incentives: Towards a General Theory of Compensation and Competition" (*Bell Journal of Economics*, 1983). The article develops a model of a single principal dealing with multiple agents,

with the agents competing against one another for prizes. Such an approach is suggestive of the sort of real-world competition between publicly owned business corporations envisioned under pragmatic market socialism. It is possible that with minor modifications, the model developed by Nalebuff and Stiglitz could be applied to the BPO problem.

9. The celebrated "Coase theorem," as explicated by Ronald Coase ("The Problem of Social Cost," 1960), is widely regarded as the taproot of the recent literature on property rights. The theorem states that over a wide variety of situations, the actual distribution of property rights has no impact on the efficiency outcome. It is arguable that the Coase theorem supports the pragmatic market socialist proposal, in that the reassignment of property rights to capital property return to labor income earners via the social dividend distribution mechanism, in place of their present assignment to the owners of financial wealth under the capitalistic distribution mechanism, would not result in any reduction in productive efficiency. Nevertheless, it is probably true that most of those who are enthusiastic about the notion of property rights would tend to be opposed to pragmatic market socialism, or to any other form of socialism. The use of the term "property rights" to describe the developing literature on the Coase theorem and related matters dates from the codification work of Eirik Furubotn and Svetozar Pejovich (1972, 1974). Included in the 1974 compendium was G. Warren Nutter's blast at the concept of market socialism: "Markets Without Property: A Grand Illusion," in which the doctrine of Ludwig von Mises that genuine markets are impossible under any form of socialism is reiterated with a degree of enthusiasm and dogmatism worthy of Mises himself. Another major survey article on property rights, covering work in the 1970s, was provided by Louis DeAlessi in 1980.

10. Some general surveys of the developing theory of incentive contracts between principals and agents include the following: Stanley Baiman and Joel Demski (1980), L. Peter Jennergren (1980), Stanley Baiman (1982), and Richard Zeckhauser (1985). Related and overlapping literatures are those on uncertainty (e.g., Steven Lippmann and John McCall, 1982), information (e.g., Jack Hirshleifer and John Riley, 1979), and the economics of organization (e.g., James Hess, 1983). "Asymmetric information" is the approved technical term for the fact that the agent will probably know more about the circumstances under which he or she works than the principal knows. "Moral hazard" is the approved technical term to describe the fact that the agent will probably utilize his or her superior information to obtain personal benefits which are not justified in a social welfare sense.

4

THE CAPITAL MANAGEMENT ISSUE

A. INTRODUCTION AND OVERVIEW

When the average person compares labor income in the form of wages and salaries with capital property income in the form of dividends, interest, and capital gains, an intuition automatically and naturally arises that the latter type of income is unearned. There is a much more obvious and direct connection between the efforts and contributions of a given person and that person's labor income than there is between those efforts and contributions and capital property income. To earn labor income, a person must work personally and directly: One cannot inherit labor from an ancestor as one can inherit capital property. And the labor must occupy a very substantial proportion of a person's waking hours. Even in as advanced and prosperous a nation as the United States, the typical job involves eight hours a day five days a week, with two to four weeks per year of vacation. The typical job, in other words, dominates a person's life, consuming by far the largest share of the person's time, energy, and attention.

The great majority of the adult population must absolutely find and retain employment in order to avoid personal catastrophe. Persons who are unwilling or unable to obtain employment very quickly find themselves in desperate conditions. Modern civilization is sufficiently compassionate that destitute individuals rarely perish directly from cold or hunger. But the conditions of life supportable by various forms of social welfare and private charity tend to be extremely spartan. Individuals living under these conditions are normally in poor health and subject to a high rate of mortality. Perhaps even worse is the implicit humiliation of being destitute, of having to admit that one cannot carry one's own weight, cannot make a worthy contribution to the larger society, cannot be an upright, independent member of society. It is fear of the physical and psychological toll of destitution which makes the vast majority of the population obsessed with employment, fiercely determined to get and to keep a job—however humble or exalted that job might be. To this vast majority, the loss of a job—particularly through the employer's dissatisfaction with the way that job is being done—is a nightmare desperately to be avoided. Once the fearsome event of being fired has taken place, one is looking directly into the face of destitution, if not into the face of death itself. And so begins a desperate search to find a new job to replace the one which has been lost. This search is carried on in full awareness that the only alternative to securing employment is the horror of destitution. Anyone who has experienced it can never forget the severe stress of a forced search for employment.

All this is the condition of the vast majority of human individuals. But of course, in modern capitalism, there exists a small minority of individuals who are exempt from this condition, who are immune to it. Who are these lucky individuals? How do they gain their immunity from a condition which is the lot of so many? They are the capitalists of society, and they gain their immunity from the need to find and retain employment through their ownership of capital wealth. The reality of this is so inherently off-putting and irritating to the rest of humanity that many individuals have a difficult time merely pronouncing such words as "capitalist" and "capital property income." Instead we hear of the "person of means" who possesses an "independent income." Such are the customary circumlocutions by which the irritating essence of capitalism is supposed to be rendered more bearable, more tolerable to the vast majority who *must* work for a living.

The ordinary, instinctive reaction of the typical individual who does *not* possess "means" and who does *not* receive an "independent income," upon being made aware that another individual *does* possess "means" and *does* receive an "independent income," is one of irritation and hostility. But this reaction normally is quickly suppressed, because the person has been thoroughly indoctrinated in capitalist apologetics. He or she has accepted that capitalism represents the best of all possible economic worlds, and that any feelings of irritation and hostility toward capitalists represent nothing more than childish envy. Thus such feelings must be bottled up and suppressed as quickly as possible. But it is the argument of this book that in fact those instinctive feelings of irritation and hostility have a solid basis in reality. They do not represent childish envy but, rather, *legitimate resentment*. They are just as legitimate as are feelings of irritation and hostility against a burglar who enters homes at night to steal articles of value. Capital property income received by capitalists in the modern capitalist economy is no more legitimately earned than were the political and economic privileges which long ago were taken and enjoyed by the hereditary aristocracy in the smug belief that they constituted "natural rights."

Not all capitalists are plutocrats. The definition utilized herein for "capitalist" is an individual whose capital property income *by itself* is capable of supporting at least a "comfortable" lifestyle. No doubt the large majority of individuals who fit this definition are not fabulously wealthy plutocrats. Many of us are personally acquainted with "minor" capitalists. They do not live extravagantly; rather, they live modest middle-class lives in modest middle-class homes. What sets them apart from the rest is that they do not work, do not have a job—even though they are far younger than the typical retired person. Or, if they *do* have a job, they seem quite unconcerned and lackadaisical about it, and/or they maintain a lifestyle substantially in excess of what can be reasonably afforded on their earnings. There is hardly any person in society so completely brainwashed by capitalist apologetics as not to entertain doubts, however nebulous and short-lived, that the privileges of these minor capitalists are absolutely necessary to the welfare of society.

At the other end of the spectrum are the "major" capitalists. These people move in a rarefied, elite world, and only a relatively small proportion of the noncapitalist majority has any personal acquaintance with them. These are the people who live in large mansions on substantial estates with high walls around them. They own additional residences, country homes and/or city condominiums, which the average person would deem palatial in their own right. They are found in the best restaurants, at the best clubs and hotels, behind the steering wheels of the best automobiles, aboard private yachts and private jets, in the boardroom—in general, wherever it is too expensive for the average person to venture.

"Major" capitalists have one salient characteristic in common with "minor" capitalists: To them, employment is optional. They *may* work (normally in top professional positions in corporate management, law, medicine, and so on), but they do not *need* to work. Quite a few of them disdain employment in favor of the classic pastimes of the idle rich: polo playing, horse breeding, gambling, yacht racing. Others go into politics—it does not concern them that the salaries of public officials are relatively modest. Although the average person normally has no personal acquaintance with plutocratic capitalists, he or she obtains a few glimpses of their lifestyles via the media. In providing these glimpses, the media concentrate far more on a handful of extraordinarily successful entertainers and entrepreneurs than they do on the large proportion of the very wealthy who attained their present status through substantial inheritances followed by financial speculation. But once again, the average person is normally not so completely brainwashed by capitalist apologetics as not to wonder occasionally if at least some of the rich and famous who are enjoying these fabulous lifestyles are doing so on the basis of unearned income.

Major capitalists, minor capitalists, and the entire intervening spectrum of capitalists have one distinguishing characteristic in common: The harsh, insistent, and perpetual need for labor, common to all those with little or no capital wealth to their name, does not apply, nor does there seem to be any apparent effort or contribution required of the capital wealth owner to realize capital income on the wealth. Let us consider a capitalist somewhere in the middle, neither a plutocrat indulging in an extravagant lifestyle nor a minor capitalist whose income just suffices for a modest lifestyle. Consider a person who owns, let us say, $10 million in financial capital. Three million may be invested in certificates of deposit in an array of banks, another $3 million in an array of corporate bonds, the remaining $4 million in an array of common stocks. That person may be, and probably is, seemingly completely uninvolved in the management of physical capital. That is, he or she may take little or no interest in the affairs of the corporations in which stock and bond investments are held. He or she may take little or no interest in the affairs of the banks with whom certificates of deposit are held. Yet interest is paid to the capitalist on the certificates of deposit and the bonds, and dividends are paid to the capitalist on the stock shares. Perhaps the capitalist will visit an investment counselor or a stockbroker for a few hours once a year, during which time he or she will sell some of the instruments in the investment portfolio and buy others, rearranging it slightly, and in the process realizing several hundred thousand dollars' worth of capital gains income to be added to the several hundred thousand dollars' worth of interest and dividend income already realized.

The owner of this large capital fortune seems to be enjoying a very substantial income, even a relatively huge income, without need of any significant expenditure of effort. Perhaps *by choice* the capitalist may read and study a great deal of literature about investments in general and about his or her own investments of the moment in particular—but there does not seem to be any *need* for such interest. Many capitalists appear to do quite well without taking any such interest. Many of them work at responsible professional employments in business management, law, medicine, and so on, employments that leave them little time or energy for their investments. Some of them dabble in the arts or go into politics. And some of them, of course, make a career merely out of spending money. "Risk-taking" is often invoked as a justification for capital property income, but there does not appear to be any particularly onerous risk involved, given that the capital fortune is sufficiently sizable and sufficiently dispersed. A few investments in a large portfolio may turn sour, but the law of averages virtually precludes their all turning sour. And if the fortune is converted into cash and hidden in a mattress, it is subject to the risk of being burned up in a fire or stolen.

Therefore neither effort nor risk seems to provide a legitimate justification for capital property income. When probate courts bestow large capital fortunes on the heirs of a deceased wealthy capitalist, these fortunes are never refused or given away on grounds that to manage their investment would be too difficult, or that the risks of these investments would so deprive the owner of peace of mind that life would become intolerable.

It may be alleged that "passive" capitalists of the sort described will inevitably lose their wealth to more "active" capitalists. But this allegation seems at odds with what is commonly observed. Once a given capital fortune has reached a critical mass, it seems that with a minor degree of caution in its investment, it is extremely stable. If anything, it is the "active" capitalists, with their often harebrained investment schemes, who seem more likely to lose out. The fact that the majority of capitalists seem to take a relatively conservative and passive approach to their investments suggests that this approach is favored by natural selection. The business media have little interest in the typical passive, conservative, drab capitalist. Thus the public receives information mainly on the tiny minority of flamboyant high-fliers among the capitalist class—individuals such as the much-publicized Donald Trump. The meteoric rises of these people often are soon succeeded by equally meteoric declines.

And so, on the basis of direct commonsensical impressions, capital property income does not seem to be earned. Apologists for capitalism thus confront a difficult task. They must argue that the direct testimony of common sense—to the effect that capital property income is unearned—is in fact illusory, and that by some indirect, roundabout, and more or less metaphysical means this income is earned in much the same way (or at least in somewhat the same way) that labor income is earned. But these arguments are constantly being challenged by common sense assisted by direct observation of the real world. It is the argument of this book that these common-sensical challenges are legitimate—that there is no substance nor validity to the indirect, roundabout, and more or less metaphysical means by which it is asserted that capital property income is earned.

There are two primary arguments that capital property income is an earned return to a significant economic contribution made by the capital owner: (1) that it is a return to the active role of the capital owner in the provision of capital management effort, and (2) that it is a return to the passive role of the capital owner in the provision of saving. Chapter 5 will consider the saving issue. The present chapter considers the capital management issue. The capital management argument is probably the more plausible in an economic theory sense, but it has the disadvantage of being more directly refuted by the common experience of mankind: In a modern economy such as that of the United States, there are tens of millions of persons who recognize from personal experience or observation that no significant and meaningful effort is expended by capital owners in managing the capital wealth from which they draw property income. The saving argument does not have this particular disadvantage because the "sacrifices of saving" are intuitively apparent to anyone who saves (i.e., the vast majority). On the other hand, when the saving justification is viewed in the cold light of contemporary economic theory, it fares even more poorly than does capital management.

Capitalist apologetics thrives best in a murky realm of semantic confusion and empty rhetoric. Thus any effort to reduce the question of whether capital property income is earned or unearned to the issues of capital management effort and/or saving will certainly be resisted. After all, where are such sanctified words as "entrepreneurship," "risk-taking," "innovation," and so on? Among members and admirers of the Austrian school of institutional economics, the term "capitalist" is rarely used, and the term "entrepreneur" is customarily substituted as a synonym. Thus through simple terminology the typical passive and parasitical capitalistic rentier is transformed into that most admirable and worthy member of society, the entrepreneur. This sort of shabby terminological subterfuge ought to be rejected as the crass dishonesty that it is. Only a tiny fraction of the contemporary capitalist class has any personal experience in the founding and operation of a business enterprise—and thus the great majority of it has absolutely no claim on the honorable status of entrepreneur. This issue will be examined further in Chapter 6 ("Investment, Growth, and Entrepreneurship"), along with such related issues as risk-taking. For now, suffice it to say that the term "capital management effort," as utilized herein, is intended to encompass *any and all* active effort expended in the management of both physical and financial capital. As the founding of a business enterprise involves active effort, entrepreneurship is included in capital management effort as a subcategory. Other forms of capital management effort include the supervision of existing business enterprises and the investment of existing financial capital in stocks, bonds, real estate, and so on.

With this broad understanding of "capital management effort" in mind, let us consider the argument that capital property income is earned by capital wealth owners through their capital management effort. The argument commences with the incontrovertible fact that the nonhuman factors of production are inert. Plant and machinery, per se, are nonliving, nonsentient, inanimate, inert objects. They will not, and in fact cannot, volitionally seek out their highest productivity employments. Human intelligence must guide them into these employments. Once established in some particular employment, a given factory or a given machine will not independently contribute to production in the same way a human worker will. The manner in which it contributes to production must be carefully planned and controlled by a human manager. Similarly, financial capital, as distinguished from physical capital, is inert. A pile of $1,000 bills earmarked for investment will not and cannot get up and go to the stock exchange in order to purchase shares of a promising stock. Once again, human intelligence must provide the necessary guidance. Without such human guidance, we could expect the allocation and management of both physical capital (plant and machinery) and financial capital to be very arbitrary and capricious. The actual contribution made by physical and financial capital to economic output and prosperity would be severely limited.

It is evident, therefore, that effective use of the nonhuman factors of production requires human effort. But human beings are notoriously lazy. Without incentives, they will not expend effort—or at least very much effort. The capitalist system has evolved a very straightforward, natural, and appealing solution to this dual problem in capital management and human incentives. Nonsentient capital is legally owned by human individuals who collect any and all payments for its use by business enterprises, government agencies, and private individuals. This in effect endows nonhuman capital with human attributes of intelligence, volition, and self-interest. Nonhuman capital therefore gravitates toward its highest return uses by virtue of the intelligence, volition, and self-interest of its human owners. Human owners expend effort in the management of capital because, and only because, they personally receive the return paid to capital.

Were socialism to disrupt this critical link between the self-interest of private individuals and the rational allocation and management of capital, then we could expect nothing more than totally arbitrary allocation and management of capital. Under socialism, the return paid to the nonhuman factors of production would not be received by those directly entrusted with their management. Instead, it would be dispersed over the entire population, even though the entire population obviously cannot collectively engage in capital management effort in any meaningful sense. Those entrusted under socialism with direct managerial control over capital, finding that no personal gain accrues to their capital management efforts, would have no incentive to engage in such efforts, and would therefore decline to do so. The consequence of arbitrary allocation and management of capital would be a disastrously low—or at least an unacceptably low—level of economic performance.

It is fully evident from the plan of pragmatic market socialism outlined in this book that this argument is taken very seriously. The plan in fact envisions positive pecuniary motivations to capital management effort analogous to those utilized by capitalism. Part of the capital property return generated by the market allocation of scarce capital would be retained as incentive income by agents of the Bureau of Public Ownership (BPO), the national government agency designed to perform under socialism whatever positive economic functions are performed under capitalism by private capital owners. Another part would be retained by the central office of the BPO to cover general administrative costs. It has been emphasized, however, that the percentage of capital property return retained for these purposes would be quite small, probably on the order of 5 percent or less. This small percentage is consistent with the socialist belief that capital property income under contemporary capitalism is *predominantly* unearned by its receivers (as opposed to *wholly* unearned).

To an apologist for capitalism interested in developing the capital management argument, however, capital property return under contemporary capitalism is *wholly* (or at least *predominantly*) earned by its receivers by virtue of their capital management efforts. As these efforts are in direct proportion to the pecuniary incentive to make them, if pragmatic market socialism drastically reduces the pecuniary incentive, it will drastically reduce the efforts made. If the property return received by the capital managers in the BPO under pragmatic market socialism is only a small fraction of that received by capital owners under capitalism, then the amount of effort expended on capital management under pragmatic market socialism will be a small fraction of what it is under capitalism, and the productivity of capital under pragmatic market socialism will be a small fraction of what it is under capitalism.

This argument is examined in the current chapter. The examination demonstrates that the argument is logically sound and coherent. Furthermore, it is intuitively plausible because it contains a kernel of truth. This kernel of truth is effectively conceded through the pragmatic market socialist proposal for an activist Bureau of Public Ownership which would retain a small fraction of the capital property return produced by the publicly owned business enterprise sector to cover its administrative and incentive expenses. This proposal implicitly recognizes that the small proportion of capital property return retained by the BPO represents an earned return to capital management effort. Or at least it recognizes a sufficient probability that this small proportion represents an earned return to justify its retention by the BPO. However, the pragmatic market socialist proposal also manifests the judgment that the preponderant majority of capital property return is in fact unearned. The following points very briefly summarize the evidence that supports this judgment.

The capital management defense of property income would no doubt be more compelling if economic production were conducted primarily on a small-scale basis using handicraft techniques. If each commodity were produced mainly by independent craftsmen using physical capital in the form of small, inexpensive, and uncomplicated tools, then it would be reasonable that the economically efficient use of these tools would require their personal ownership by the individuals using them. But in the modern industrial era, the capital management argument—if subjected to careful consideration in light of the self-evident characteristics of modern production—fails to ring true. Factory production has become the rule rather than the exception. Capital is applied in production not in the form of small, inexpensive, and uncomplicated tools but in the form of large, expensive, and complicated machines. A great many such machines are used even in a relatively small factory. Labor is applied in production not by independent craftsmen but by a great host of highly interdependent specialists ranging from unskilled laborers on the production line to professional managers in the executive suite.

Under modern industrial production, owners of capital do not take a direct, active, and personal role in the productive process. A craftsman engaged in handicraft production directly, actively, and personally uses his tools to manufacture products. But a modern capitalist does not directly, actively, and personally operate the machines he owns. Indeed, the capital ownership right has become generalized and financial in nature. It is no longer (if it ever was) the right to use a tool to produce a product. Rather, it is now clearly the right to claim capital property return—whether such return is generated by business enterprises engaged in the production of commodities, or by government agencies in need of revenue to finance public goods and services, or by private individuals in need of cash with which to purchase consumer durables such as homes and automobiles.

Quite obviously a great deal of effort is expended in the modern industrial economy in the interest of efficient use of existing physical capital (plant and machinery), as well as in the efficient allocation of financial capital among competing uses: physical investment by business firms, social uses by government agencies, consumption spending by private households. But practically none of this effort is contributed by the capital owners per se. (Many capitalists participate in the production process through various forms of labor employment—but there is a fundamental distinction between what they earn from that employment and what they receive on their capital wealth.) The productivity of capital is a function of the efforts of labor in all its myriad forms from unskilled labor to the most highly trained professionals. A particularly vital contribution is made to capital productivity through the labor of corporation executives: It is these individuals who provide "capital management effort" in its most readily apparent and convincing interpretation. But corporation executives are considered members of the labor force, and their salaries, bonuses, and perquisites, generous as they may be, are accounted as labor income and not capital property income.

It is the separation of ownership and control, more than any other single characteristic of the modern industrial capitalist economy, which points to the speciousness of the capital management justification of capital property income. But other significant indicators may be cited: Two of the more important include the dominant role of institutional investors in contemporary capital markets and the relative success of noncapitalist forms of production, as for example in nationalized industries and in the Communist nations. These points will be elaborated in the final Section D of the present chapter ("Circumstantial Evidence from the Real World").

Appealing to contemporary economic theory, we find that it does not provide any more evidence in favor of the capital management justification for capital property income than does informal examination of the contemporary real-world capitalist economy. In Section C below ("Theoretical Analysis of Capital Management"), it is demonstrated that the capital management justification is logically consistent with contemporary economic theory. But it is also demonstrated that the socialist rebuttal to this justification is equally consistent with contemporary economic theory. In general terms, we may cite one fundamental notion in contemporary economic theory which indirectly supports the capital management justification: the upward-sloping supply curve of labor. But at the same time, two equally fundamental notions may be cited which indirectly challenge this justification: the concept of the independent productivity of capital, and the concept of rental income. These concepts will be applied to the problem in the following Section B ("Surplus Value versus Unearned Income"), which proposes a revision and modernization of the classic Marxist theory of exploitation as the fundamental motivation for the pragmatic market socialist proposal.

B. SURPLUS VALUE VERSUS UNEARNED INCOME

Karl Marx based the proposition of surplus labor value exploitation on the labor theory of value, according to which all value is produced by labor. When Marx first studied economic theory, the labor theory of value was part of the body of orthodox, accepted economic principles. Certainly the classical economists (Adam Smith, David Ricardo, and so on) did not perceive the labor theory of value as a direct challenge to the ethical legitimacy of profit, interest, and other forms of capital property income under capitalism. Marx, on the other hand, did perceive this to be the case, and starting with the *Communist Manifesto* (1848) and continuing on through the several thick volumes of *Das Kapital,* he employed his interpretation of the labor theory of value as a moral bludgeon with which to chastise capitalism. According to Marx, since all value is produced by labor, it is ethically legitimate that all value be received by labor. However, all value is *not* received by labor under capitalism. Rather a substantial proportion of the total value produced, called "surplus value," is appropriated by the capitalist owners of nonhuman factors of production.

Surplus value is the differential between the total value produced by labor and the amount of subsistence value that must necessarily be paid to labor in order to enable the physical survival and continuance of the labor force. Thus a typical worker, laboring say ten hours per day, will produce an amount of value sufficient to sustain and reproduce himself after, for example, six hours. The remaining four hours' worth of value is appropriated by his employer, the capitalist. What enables the capitalist employer to carry out this appropriation? Why cannot the laborer demand the full ten hours' worth of value that his labor has created? The answer is that the capitalist, by virtue of legal ownership of the nonhuman factors of production, controls access by the laborer to these factors. Without access to the complex machinery of modern production, the laborer would be able to produce little or no value. Thus the capitalist is in an unassailable bargaining position with respect to the laborer.

The Marxist notion of property return as surplus labor value has its merits. The intuitive plausibility of the proposition is evident from the simple fact that for many decades it has been a virtually axiomatic assumption made by hundreds of millions of critics of Western capitalism living in the Communist nations. Nevertheless, it is probably not the best and the strongest interpretation possible of the hypothesis that property return is unearned by capital owners under contemporary capitalism. The non-Marxist interpretation of capital property return which motivates the pragmatic market socialist proposal rejects the labor theory of value. Rather, it postulates that in a true and legitimate sense, this capital property return is "earned" by the nonhuman factors of production. However, this income is *unearned by the human owners* of the nonhuman factors of production. Under contemporary capitalism, capital property owners claim for themselves a flow of property return created by the application of insensate and inanimate plant, machinery, and natural resources in the production process. The rational application of these nonhuman factors does indeed require a certain amount of human effort in capital management. But under contemporary capitalism, the great preponderance of this capital management effort is compensated by labor income in the form of the salaries and bonuses paid to corporation executives and other salaried employees directly involved in capital management.

The grounds on which the Marxist view is discarded as deficient—or at least as less satisfactory than the non-Marxist view—essentially comprise the critique of Marxist economics formulated in the late nineteenth and early twentieth centuries by such figures as Eugen von Böhm-Bawerk, Vilfredo Pareto, and John Bates Clark. It is well recognized by all but the most economically naive Marxists that the labor cost of production is totally irrelevant as far as the market price is concerned for at least two significant commodity categories: natural resources in a raw state, and commodities produced in the distant past (such as old master paintings). The usual Marxist response to this point is that the labor theory of value *does* apply to a far more significant type of commodity: one currently being produced in the economy. Neither raw natural resources nor old master paintings are currently being produced. Recognition that things not being currently produced nevertheless possess market value alerts us to the role of demand in the determination of market value. Some modern Marxists do not attempt to refute this role. They quite freely admit that once a commodity has been produced, its market value is determined entirely by the demand for it, and that this market value very frequently departs quite substantially from the commodity's cost of production in general, and its labor cost in particular. But the modern Marxist remains true to the Marxist tradition when asserting that whatever market value may be determined by demand for a currently produced commodity, the *source* of that value is labor and labor alone.

One might agree that labor does indeed breathe life into the entire apparatus of production, and even agree that it follows from this that labor is entitled to receive the entire productive return. But there is an important distinction between the fundamental philosophical identification of labor as the source of all value, and the practical need to design market mechanisms for the rational and efficient allocation of nonhuman factors of production. Such market mechanisms would treat the nonhuman factors of production as if they were making an independent contribution to production. These market mechanisms need not be contradictory to the philosophical identification of labor as the source of all value. The pragmatic market socialist system incorporates market processes that would ensure the efficient use of capital—while at the same time, the great preponderance of property return generated by these market processes would be returned to the working population via the social dividend. The proposed social dividend distribution of property return is obviously consistent with the principle that the *human source* of all value is labor.

The fact of the matter is that it was Marx himself who originally discarded the labor theory of value as a practical and relevant guide for the pricing of commodities. This was done (implicitly) in the course of his rebuttal of the "Great Contradiction" perceived in Marxist economics by Eugen von Böhm-Bawerk.[1] The Great Contradiction may be posed as follows: Marx asserts that labor is the source of all value, and that each laborer delivers to his employing capitalist a fixed amount of surplus value. Therefore capitalists should be eager to hire more laborers. However, even the most casual observation of conditions in the capitalistic real world (at least as of the late nineteenth century in the industrialized countries) suggests that capitalists are, in general, far more eager to replace laborers with machines than they are to hire more laborers. The machines obviously do the same work more cheaply, and raise the capitalists' profits. It would thus appear that capital makes an independent contribution to profit. Böhm-Bawerk formalized this insight by showing the logical inconsistency of three principles attributed to Marx: (1) the constancy of the rate of surplus value over all workers; (2) the constancy of the rate of profit over all firms; (3) variation in the organic composition of capital (the ratio of constant to variable capital) as between various firms.

In Volume III of *Das Kapital*, Marx proposed a refutation of Böhm-Bawerk's Great Contradiction in a table called the "Transformation Schema." This refutation, while technically correct, produces a serious flaw in the Marxist theory: It apparently removes the theory from the realm of theories which can be verified or refuted on the basis of empirical evidence. This is the case because, according to the Transformation Schema, the amount of observable profit in a particular firm is not equal to, nor even proportional to, the amount of surplus value in that firm. For Böhm-Bawerk, the profit rate for a firm would be the amount of surplus value in the firm divided by total expenditures in the firm, including expenditures on labor (variable capital) and expenditures on machinery and materials (constant capital). But in the exposition of the Transformation Schema, Marx defines the profit rate as the sum of surplus values *over all firms*, divided by the sum of total expenditures *over all firms*. It is postulated, therefore, that the capitalist class *as a whole* extorts surplus value from the laboring class *as a whole*. The application of a constant rate of surplus value to the entire labor force produces a pool of aggregate surplus value which is identical to aggregate profits. Aggregate profits are then divided among the capitalists in proportion to each capitalist's total expenditures, including expenditures on machinery.

The Transformation Schema demonstrates that basic Marxist economic theory does not necessarily incorporate a logical error. It was Marx's means of defending himself against the accusation that he was an illogical thinker. Be this as it may, non-Marxists are generally skeptical of Marx's Transformation Schema response to Böhm-Bawerk's Great Contradiction. Their comments on the debate are replete with references to the "mysticism" of Marxist economics, because its central hypothesis—the constancy of the rate of surplus value—is incapable of empirical verification. To Marxists, on the other hand, the non-Marxist invocation of the "empirical verification" issue reeks of obfuscation, obscurantism, and sophistry. To them, it is obvious from simple observation and common sense that the capitalist system is exploitative and that profits and other forms of property income represent surplus labor value—so that the Transformation Schema is merely a technical statement of a manifest reality. But even if the Marxist viewpoint on the issue were accepted, there would remain the practical questions of pricing and allocation of scarce capital.

The irrelevance of the labor theory of value, as far as the design of a practical, functioning economic system of production and distribution is concerned, is strongly suggested by the empirical fact that under the various national forms of communistic socialism, no significant effort has ever been made to price commodities at their average labor cost. A profit markup is almost universally applied to the costs of production in order to arrive at the price. Moreover, interest charges on capital borrowings are often included in the costs of production. Although these practices will not necessarily guarantee economic efficiency, they are certainly regarded as enhancing the likelihood of economic efficiency by Western economists. The significant point is that even those societies which regard Karl Marx as a demigod, and which endeavor to adhere as closely as possible to his various pronouncements, do not try to implement the labor theory of value as a practical means of pricing commodities.

As is well known, Marx was principally concerned with denouncing capitalism. He did not consider it worthwhile to provide a blueprint for the socialist system that would succeed upon the collapse of capitalism. It is certainly reasonable to speculate that had the question been posed to him, Marx would not have specified that prices under socialism must (or should) be equal to direct or indirect labor costs of production. As is also well known, Marx took a lively interest in conventional economics, and he endeavored to incorporate as much of it as possible into his critique of capitalism. Therefore it is fully possible that had he formulated this critique after the emergence of the neoclassical economic paradigm in the latter part of the nineteenth century, it would have closely resembled what follows here.

The non-Marxist interpretation of the unearned nature of capital property income under contemporary capitalism rests fundamentally on the self-evident physical distinction between nonhuman factors of production and the human owners of these factors. It is held that the contribution to production that is recognized in the form of capital property return is made by the nonhuman factors of production in an insensate, nonvolitional manner. Under capitalism, the property return paid out by business firms, government agencies, and households in a competitive bidding process for scarce capital resources, is collected by the individual human owners of these capital resources. A close analogy may be drawn to the system of slavery. Under slavery, the entire productive value created by the labor efforts of slaves becomes the personal property of the slaves' owners. Under capitalism, the entire productive value created by the productive contribution of capital becomes the personal property of the capital owners.

Of course it is the essence of capitalist apologetics to try to blur the obvious, self-evident, tangible, concrete distinction between a certain piece of capital such as a machine, and its human owner. The contribution of the machine, in capitalist apologetics, comes about through the alleged efforts and sacrifices of its owner. Chapter 5 will examine the allegation that the machine came about in the first place because of the saving sacrifices of its owner—this saving having provided the financial capital with which the machine was built. The present chapter examines the allegation that it is the capital management effort of the owner that endows an existing machine with productivity.

To begin with, the physical distinction between nonhuman capital instruments of production and their human owners suggests that there is a clear conceptual distinction between the productivity of nonhuman capital and the productivity of human capital managers (whether these managers be nonowners, as under socialism, or owners, as under capitalism). The capital managers have a claim, both from the point of view of justice and from the point of view of providing incentives to effort in the interest of economic efficiency and productivity, to that product which is attributable to their capital management efforts. But they do *not* have a claim, from either point of view, to that product which is attributable to the insensate and nonvolitional "efforts" of the nonhuman capital itself.

What grounds are there for supposing that the product attributable to human capital management effort is very small in relation to the product attributable to nonhuman capital "effort"? One may distinguish at least three separate notions of capital management effort. The first is the practical, day-to-day administration of business organizations, usually corporations, that own and utilize substantial aggregations of capital equipment. This is the direct management of capital. Anyone with any direct knowledge, or any sort of appreciation, from whatever source, of the complex problems and continual challenges encountered in the management of business enterprises, will not underestimate the effort that is applied by business executives to the direct management of capital. The physical and mental stresses of this sort of employment are no doubt severe. The direct management of capital indeed demands a great deal of effort. But it is also the case that under contemporary capitalism the direct management of capital is mostly handled by salaried executives whose principal remuneration, in the form of salaries, bonuses, stock options, perquisites, and so on, is accounted for as labor costs of the firm.

The two remaining notions of capital management effort are "motivational enforcement" and "financial allocation." The first refers to efforts expended in establishing an incentive system toward profit maximization for the corporation executives. The second refers to efforts expended in deciding among various competing investment opportunities. Neither of these, in contrast with direct management of capital, would seem to require, under modern conditions, a substantial outlay of effort. The basic rule for a contemporary financial capital owner is to put his or her financial wealth into capital instruments which promise a good, safe return. This rule simultaneously solves the problems of motivational enforcement and financial allocation. It gives the corporation managers an incentive to earn profits so that the owners will have good, safe returns paid to them and will thus be willing to leave their financial capital invested in the respective corporations. At the same time, it puts financial capital into those uses in which it is most productive.

In principle the problems of motivational enforcement and efficient allocation of capital are difficult, challenging problems. As a matter of fact, a truly compelling theoretical formulation and analytical solution of these problems is well beyond the capacity of contemporary economic and managerial science. However, under modern institutional conditions, the class of capital owners, as such, exerts little or no significant, effective effort toward the solution of these problems. From the point of view of the typical capital owner, the problem devolves to very elementary terms: "I currently own some bonds or stock shares in corporation X. Should I sell these instruments or retain them?" The answer to this question is usually dictated by some crude, arbitrary, ad hoc rule of the sort that may be found in any popular tome of investment advice, such as "Sell if the value of the instrument has dropped on average more than 10 percent per year since acquired (since its value is apparently headed toward oblivion), or if the value has risen on average more than 25 percent per year since acquired (since it will soon peak); otherwise retain." The relevant numbers may be plugged into the ad hoc rule and the sell-retain decision made in a matter of minutes. Similar rules govern decisions to buy stocks and bonds. It may require one afternoon a year to reshuffle a multi-million-dollar portfolio. It matters very little which particular set of ad hoc rules govern the buying and selling behavior of a particular capital owner: The performance of his or her portfolio is little influenced by the particular set selected.

Of course, the numbers which are substituted into these rules are the numerical outcome of a very considerable amount of effort expended in the direct management of capital by salaried corporation executives. These numbers are the critical elements in the imperfect solution that the market system obtains with respect to the problems of motivational enforcement and efficient allocation of financial capital. Once the numbers are generated, the work of any particular capital owner in reshuffling his or her portfolio in response to the figures is very easy and automatic. The capital owner's role in tackling these problems is thus very limited, and the contribution which he or she makes is very small and approaches insignificance. Thus the return that the capital owner has a moral right to expect in recompense for effort expended in capital management, is also very small and approaches insignificance.

These points imply that under pragmatic market socialism only a very small fraction of the property return would have to be retained by the capital managers of the Bureau of Public Ownership in order for capital to be managed as effectively as it is under contemporary capitalism, and for the economy to be as efficient as it is under contemporary capitalism. In the terminology of neoclassical economics, this translates into the assertion that capital property income in a modern market economy is either entirely, or almost entirely, rental income. Rental income is defined as an income stream for which the rate of remuneration has little or no effect on the quantity supplied of the commodity being remunerated.

The ideological implications of the rent concept are highly controversial. Some of the more conscientious defenders of the capitalistic status quo refuse to allow that the rent concept is anything more than a purely theoretical abstraction with absolutely no bearing on the real-world capitalistic economy. But a great many orthodox economists of more moderate views, while they are by no means drawn strongly toward socialism, nevertheless perceive that some real-world incomes are totally or predominantly rental in nature—that is, unearned. The astronomical incomes of a handful of popular music stars, for example, are customarily described as "quasi-rents." That is, these incomes mostly represent payments to fixed elements of personality, style, appearance, and so on. The supply of these fixed elements to society is not increased by paying these pop music stars more. As another example, payments made to a landowner for oil drilling rights are frequently described as rents, particularly when the landowner acquired the land in the distant past, before there was any hint of its possessing oil, and when the landowner is not personally engaged in exploration for oil.

The fact is that the concept of rent as unearned income entered mainstream economics long ago, and has consistently maintained a respectable status in the conceptual toolbox of the discipline because it seems, in some cases, to reflect reality quite accurately. The notion of "Ricardian differential rent," introduced in the early nineteenth century, is still standard material in economics textbooks.[2] David Ricardo (1772-1823) sided with the nascent industrial bourgeoisie in Britain in their long conflict against the remnants of the feudal landowning nobility. His theory of land rent as an unearned income may have helped to undercut the social power of the landowners. The declining power of this class in Britain was dramatically manifested by the repeal of the Corn Laws in 1846. Ricardo's role was to enunciate a theory in which the landowners were portrayed as parasitical drones devoid of any positive productive role in society. This portrayal undoubtedly inspired the industrialists and their allies, and demoralized (to some extent at least) the landowners and their allies. The Ricardian theory may be briefly summarized as follows.

Imagine a large number of perfectly competitive farms supplying some agricultural commodity, so that any one farm can sell all it is able to grow at the going market price. The farms come in two types: marginal and inframarginal. Marginal farms have high average cost per unit produced; inframarginal farms have low average cost. At the profit-maximizing equilibrium, the high-cost marginal farm makes no profit, while the low-cost inframarginal farm makes a profit. Ricardo makes two assertions about this situation. The first is that it is permanent. The reason for the difference in costs between the two types of farms has nothing to do with differences in the skills of the farmers or the methods with which the land is farmed. It is, rather, that the inframarginal farm has a better quality of soil than the marginal farm, or alternatively that the inframarginal farm is located closer to the urban food market and thus has lower transport costs.

The second assertion is that the profits received by the inframarginal farms will be taken by the landowners in the form of rental payments. Ricardo assumes a typical pattern of absentee landownership. The absentee landlords rent their land to tenant farmers. As the market expands and the price of food rises, the profits of inframarginal farms rise, and the absentee landlords raise the rents they charge to tenant farmers in order to appropriate these profits. But why cannot the tenant farmers demand to retain a portion of these profits? Because, says Ricardo, the profit is not the result of the special skills, abilities, and efforts of the tenant farmers. It is purely a function of exogenous variables: the productivity of the soil, or the proximity of the land to the urban market.

From Ricardo's exposition of the theory of differential rent, it is clear that he would have regarded as absurd any attribution of the rental income of the British landlords to their land management efforts. He obviously regarded the landlords' extraction of agricultural profits from their tenant farmers in the form of rental payments as a more or less automatic market process requiring little or no time, effort, or ability. The rental payments were definitely deemed unearned income in a strict sense. While not going so far as to recommend the social ownership of land, Ricardo clearly felt that certain methods of of reducing rental income on land (such as the repeal of the Corn Laws) would be socially beneficial.

Ricardian rent theory is the intellectual forerunner of the theory espoused here that capital property income is either wholly or very predominantly unearned. Ricardo held that the source of rent lies in the natural, inherent productivity of land. The present theory holds that the source of capital property return in general (including rent as one subcategory) lies in the natural, inherent productivity of capital in general (including land as a subcategory). Ricardo perceived a process by which profits accruing to inframarginal farms, which are not in any sense earned by the farmers working these farms, are appropriated in the form of rent by landlords, by virtue of their legal ownership of the land. The present theory perceives a process by which profits accruing to inframarginal corporate firms, which are not in any sense earned by the corporate executives administering these firms, are appropriated in the form of property income by capitalists, by virtue of their legal ownership of the capital. Ricardo perceived the British landowners to be recipients of an unearned rental income in no way economically attributable to their efforts in land management. The present theory perceives modern capital owners to be recipients of an unearned capital property income that is only very minutely attributable—if at all—to their efforts in capital management.

C. THEORETICAL ANALYSIS OF CAPITAL MANAGEMENT

It may be helpful to consider, at the outset of this theoretical examination of the capital management justification of capitalism, what could be a basic conflict of opinion dividing proponents and opponents of pragmatic market socialism. One of the foundation stones of contemporary neoclassical economic theory is the aggregate production function $Y = F(K,N,X)$, where Y is real national output, K is the stock of nonhuman capital (machines, factory buildings, etc.), N is the stock of nonhuman natural resources (agricultural land, mineral deposits, etc.), and X is the amount of effort provided by human workers. By "effort" is meant some type of active behavior or tangible activity that is physically and/or psychologically demanding and stressful, and which the individual would avoid in the absence of some form of material reward for undertaking it. Effort X may be broken down into two subcategories: "ordinary labor," denoted by L, and "capital management effort," denoted by E. Ordinary labor L is that commonly understood labor which is recompensed by "wage and salary income" or "compensation of employees" in the national income accounts. Capital management effort E represents that effort which is presently exerted by capital owners under capitalism, and which would be exerted by BPO personnel under pragmatic market socialism.

A technical interpretation of an extreme version of the capital management justification of capital property income is that the nonhuman factors K and N derive value only from the E effort expended by the owners: that if the E contribution of the owners were not to be provided, it would be as if these factors did not exist. This proposition may be incorporated into the neoclassical production function as follows: $Y = F(K(E),N(E),L) = F(L,E)$, where $K(0) = N(0) = 0$. Among neoclassical economists, it is axiomatic that a condition for economic efficiency is that factors of production be paid their marginal products. In the eyes of some defenders of the capitalist status quo, this proposition in turn implies that the human owners of the nonhuman factors K and N should receive the full marginal products of K and N, as these factors derive their productivity directly and entirely from the E contribution made by the owners.

In contrast, a proponent of pragmatic market socialism believes that the stock of K and N is an existent reality at any point in time which is independent of the E contribution of the owners under capitalism, or of the BPO personnel under pragmatic market socialism. The proponent asserts that the neoclassical production function should be written as $Y = F(K,N,L,E)$ and not as $Y = F(L,E)$. This is based on the commonsensical observation that machines, factory buildings, agricultural land, mineral deposits, etc., do not derive their fundamental physical existence directly from the E contribution of owners. (We are concerned here with the current active social contribution of owners represented by E. The alternative justification for capitalism, that property return rewards the past passive social contribution of owners in undertaking the saving from which K was derived, will be considered in Chapter 5.) The pragmatic market socialist viewpoint agrees completely with the neoclassical proposition that all factors of production should be paid their marginal products. The institutional structure of the pragmatic market socialist economy would guarantee that the nonhuman factors of production, K and N, are paid their marginal products, just as they are under capitalism. But the marginal productivity of K and N, the social contribution of the nonhuman factors, is not the same thing as the marginal productivity of E, the social contribution made by capital owners under capitalism and by BPO personnel under socialism.

A more moderate version of the capital management justification for capital property income would concede that the aggregate production function is properly written as $Y = F(K,N,L,E)$—but it would maintain that as between K, N and E, the relative importance of K and N is very small compared with that of E. The relative importance issue is readily appreciated in the case of the Cobb-Douglas production function. Using a, b, c, and d as the power coefficients of K, N, L, and E respectively, the function is represented as $Y = K^a N^b L^c E^d$. According to basic neoclassical distribution theory, the coefficients a, b, c, d represent the shares of the respective factors of production in national output. If the Cobb-Douglas production function is assumed to be linear homogeneous, then $a+b+c+d = 1$, and the various shares add up to the total product (the product exhaustion theorem). The proportion of national output going to ordinary labor L would be c, leaving the rest for capital K, natural resources N, and capital management effort E: $1-c = a+b+d$. The remainder of national output after payments to labor have been deducted represents property return: Therefore $a+b+d$ is the proportion of national output going to the owners of capital K and natural resources N, who are the providers of E (under capitalism).

A defender of the capitalistic status quo could claim that a and b are very small relative to d: that capital property income received by capital owners mostly represents a marginal productivity return to capital management effort E. A proponent of the pragmatic market socialist proposal would claim, to the contrary, that a and b are very large relative to d: that capital property income going to capital owners mostly represents a marginal productivity return to capital K and natural resources N. It would be agreed by both that the providers of L, ordinary labor, are economically and ethically entitled to the marginal product of L, and that the providers of E, capital management effort, are economically and ethically entitled to the marginal product of E. But the proponent of pragmatic market socialism insists not only that the providers of E definitely are *not* economically and ethically entitled to the full marginal products of K and N, but also that the great majority of capital property income received by capital owners under contemporary capitalism does in fact represent the marginal products of K

and *N*. This fundamental issue provides a useful background to the theoretical analysis of capital management effort undertaken in this section.

Of all the questions that might be raised concerning the potential performance of the pragmatic market socialist system, the following is quite possibly the single most important and fundamental question: Would the Bureau of Public Ownership under pragmatic market socialism be able to establish as intense a profit motivation among the corporation executives as currently exists under capitalism, given that it would be required to distribute to the general public as social dividend income the overwhelming preponderance (95 percent or more) of the property return produced by the corporations? Under capitalism, the totality of this income is paid to private owners in proportion to their personal ownership of material and financial capital assets. Under pragmatic market socialism, the two tiers of the BPO, comprising the corps of agents and the central office personnel, would together retain only 5 percent or less of this income to cover the incentive payments to the agents and the administrative expenses of the central office. Could the BPO, given this limitation, be as effective as the private owners in establishing the desired profit incentive in the publicly owned business enterprise sector? In other words, could society obtain the same efficiency that exists under capitalism, at a much lower "direct administrative cost"?

The present section will endeavor to establish that the question posed cannot be answered unambiguously on the basis of the standard presumptions of contemporary economic theory. There is no logical conflict between these presumptions and the proposition that property income is mostly unearned by capital management effort, or the proposition that it is mostly earned by such effort. Given the status of theory, the question is an empirical one rather than a theoretical one. This is not to say that the theoretical enunciation of the issue presented here is devoid of value. Presumably a precise analytical understanding of a question improves the reliability of a tentative answer to it, even though the tentative answer must necessarily be based to a large extent on intuitive judgment.

The theoretical enunciation developed here is a specialization of the "standard textbook model" of the labor-leisure decision by the individual.[3] The neoclassical model examined herein focuses on the capital management effort (*e*) provided by the representative capital manager as between contemporary capitalism and pragmatic market socialism. Two terms may be employed to describe capital management: "corporate supervision" (rather than corporate management—which is done by salaried executives) and "investment analysis." Corporate supervision refers to effort expended in the evaluation of corporate performance for the purpose of deciding upon retention and remuneration of corporate executives. Under capitalism, much of this effort is presumably expended by members of boards of directors. Under pragmatic market socialism, the direct analogue to the boards of directors would be the personnel of the Bureau of Public Ownership. Investment analysis refers to effort expended in the evaluation of potential corporate performance (as well as the potential performance of other prospective borrowers, such as government agencies and private households) for the purpose of deciding upon the allocation of a given amount of financial capital among competing investments. Under capitalism, investment analysis is performed by loan officers and portfolio managers of financial intermediaries, as well as by private investors. The former would continue to function under pragmatic market socialism as they do under capitalism. The latter would not exist under pragmatic market socialism, but investment analysis performed by employees of existing financial intermediaries might be augmented under pragmatic market socialism by a National Investment Banking System and a National Entrepreneurial Investment Board.

While reading the following discussion, it would probably be most natural to think of a "typical capital manager" under capitalism as a stock-owning capitalist, while the "typical capital manager" under socialism would be a BPO agent whose powers would be roughly analogous to those of the capitalist. This image confines the notion of capital management to "corporate supervision," and also does not precisely describe the BPO central office employees. In addition to complications concerning the relative nature of the typical capital manager as between capitalism and pragmatic market socialism, there is another important question which is not addressed by the following model: the relative number of capital managers as between capitalism and pragmatic market socialism. Of course, it must be recognized and appreciated that any effort to encompass a substantial number of the myriad institutional and interpretational complexities surrounding the question of capital management in a single model would lead to an impossibly complicated construction. There is an inevitable tradeoff between apparent realism and analytical manageability, and the model to be discussed incorporates a number of key aspects of the problem in a relatively accessible manner.

Readers with some background in mathematics and economic theory should read the following in conjunction with Section A of the Analytical Appendix at the end of the book. In an effort to avoid injecting too heavy a dose of analytics into the main text of the book, at various points the detailed mathematical manipulations and results will be consigned to the appropriate section of the Analytical Appendix. The main text will endeavor to convey the important implications of the mathematical analysis in a relatively informal manner. Also, in the case of the capital management model, some graphical illustrations based on the analysis will be presented in the main text.

The model consists of five endogenous variables and five equations. It is an optimizing model: The capital manager maximizes his utility subject to a budget constraint. The fundamental variable is capital management effort (e), determined by the first-order utility maximization condition. Once e is determined, the other four variables (h, r, y, and u—defined below) are determined by the other four equations of the model. The utility maximization problem is stated formally as follows:

maximize $u = u(y,h)$ subject to $y = \alpha(f + \beta r(e)k)$

where u = utility, y = income, h = leisure = $1-e$, r = rate of return on capital as a function of capital management effort. The four parameters included in the general function version of the model are as follows: f = exogenous income, k = capital responsibility (i.e., capital ownership in the case of capitalism), α = retention coefficient, β = effectiveness coefficient. Two general functions are included in the model: the production function $r(e)$ translates capital management effort e into a rate of return r on capital; the utility function $u(y,h)$ translates the two goods income y and leisure h into a level of utility. The usual neoclassical assumptions apply to these two functions. The $r(e)$ function displays positive, diminishing marginal product; while the $u(y,h)$ function displays positive, diminishing marginal utility in the two goods.

Figure 4.1 illustrates the utility maximization equilibrium of the representative capital manager in the e-y plane (for a case in which exogenous income $f = 0$). Owing to the properties of the $r(e)$ function, the budget constraint is represented by a concave upward-sloping curve. Owing to the properties of the $u(y,h)$ function, the utility isoquants for the utility function are convex upward-sloping curves. The utility-maximizing equilibrium occurs where the highest possible utility isoquant is just tangent to the production function constraint, that is, at the point where the the slope of the tangent line to the utility isoquant (u_y /u_h) is equal to the slope of the tangent line to the constraint function ($1/y'(e)$). In Figure 4.1, u* represents the highest level of utility which the capital manager can attain given the budget constraint $y = \alpha(f + \beta r(e)k)$.

The equilibrium point is determined by the four explicit parameters f, k, α, and β, plus whatever additional parameters are embodied in the $r(e)$ and $u(y,h)$ functions. Changes in these parameters will displace the equilibrium. The effect of any particular parameter on equilibrium capital management effort e is that parameter's "comparative statics effect" on e. Only one of

FIGURE 4.1
Utility–Maximizing Equilibrium

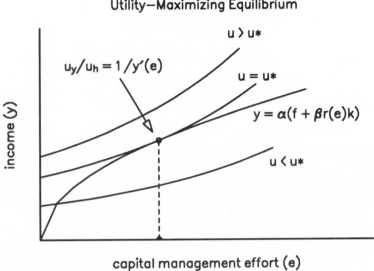

capital management effort (e)

the four comparative statics effects is unambiguous in sign: de/df is unambiguously negative, that is, an increase in exogenous income f will decrease the equilibrium effort level. Exogenous income f is a device used to clarify the distinction between substitution and income effects. All three of the parameters k, α, and β multiply the basic production function $r(e)$; thus their effects are basically symmetric. The three parameters determine the "wage" of capital management effort, or equivalently the "price" of leisure. An increase in any of the three parameters tends to decrease effort through the income effect: The more prosperous individual is induced to consume more of the superior good leisure. But at the same time an increase in any of the three tends to increase effort through the substitution effect: The individual confronts a higher "price" of leisure in terms of forgone consumption. Thus the total effect, being the sum of the income and substitution effects, cannot be theoretically predicted.

Figure 4.2 illustrates the indeterminacy for a variation in the retention coefficient α. With $\alpha = 1.0$, the utility-maximizing equilibrium is at point o. If α is then reduced to 0.2, the budget constraint function swivels downward. The new equilibrium will lie on the lower budget constraint. Three possible new equilibrium points are shown: a, b, and c (the corresponding utility isoquants for each possibility are omitted to simplify the appearance of the diagram). If the new equilibrium is at a, the reduction in

FIGURE 4.2
Reduction in Retention Coefficient

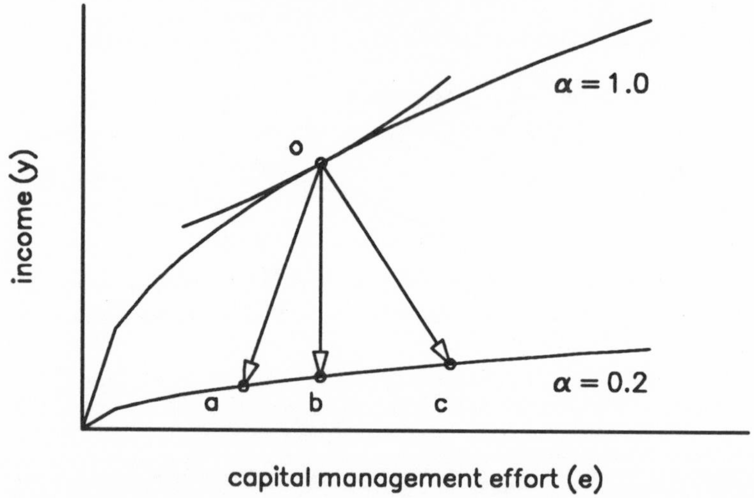

capital management effort (e)

the retention coefficient reduces the amount of capital management effort. If it is at b, there is no effect on capital management effort. And if the new equilibrium is at c, the reduction in the retention coefficient increases the amount of capital management effort.

It is a fairly conventional presumption in economics that for the typical worker the supply curve of labor is backward-bending (or "bow-shaped"). For a low wage and income the substitution effect of a wage increase will dominate, while for a high wage and income the income effect will dominate. It seems reasonable to suppose that the same situation would apply to the representative capital manager, where the "wage" may be interpreted as the factor $\alpha\beta k$, the factor which is multiplied into $r(e)$ to produce the endogenous component of income y. This possibility is illustrated in Figure 4.3, which shows the k-expansion path as a dashed curve (the k-expansion path represents the various utility-maximizing values of e for various values of k). If e were then graphed against k, the result would be a backward-bending supply curve of e. For k below 2.50, the substitution effect dominates, while for k above 2.50, the income effect dominates. For fixed values of two of the three parameters α, β, and k, we could draw this type of supply function for the other parameter.

We may now address the question of interest in terms of results obtained from this model. Clearly an effort is made by pragmatic market socialism

FIGURE 4.3
Backward—Bending Effort Supply

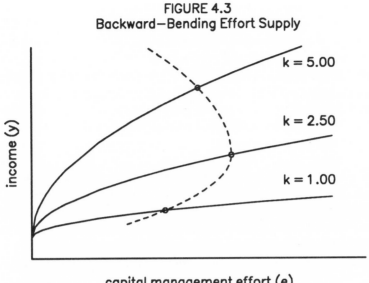

capital management effort (e)

to reproduce the incentive system of market capitalism. The BPO is allowed to retain a fraction of the property return produced by business enterprises, the BPO's objective is the instillation of a profit motivation in the business managers, and the BPO's agents are individually compensated in proportion to the profits earned by the individual business enterprises for which they are responsible. But opponents might object that the proposed retention coefficient (α) under pragmatic market socialism would be drastically inadequate. Under capitalism, the value of α is 1.00; under pragmatic socialism it would be 0.05 or less. Under capitalism, capitalists are assiduous in corporate supervision and/or investment analysis because they personally receive the full benefits in the form of capital property income. If socialism replaces the capitalist class with a public ownership agency, the BPO, whose employees and agents receive only a tiny fraction of what capitalists receive under capitalism, the efforts of these people in capital management would be a tiny fraction of the efforts of the capitalists, and consequently economic efficiency would be a tiny fraction of what it is under capitalism. The model demonstrates that this proposition is logically possible. The effect of an α decrease may be an e decrease, given merely that the representative capital manager under capitalism is operating on the upward-sloping part of the supply curve of e with respect to α, and that pragmatic market socialism brings about no offsetting changes in β or k.

The primary point in favor of this argument is that it is merely an extension of a very widely accepted proposition in modern economics: that of the upward-sloping supply curve of labor. As a matter of fact, the hypothesis of an upward-sloping supply curve of labor in the real world is *not* strongly supported by either theoretical or empirical evidence. In terms of theory, it is easy to specify plausible labor-leisure models in which the supply of labor would be either completely unresponsive to changes in the wage rate or a negative function of the wage rate. In terms of econometric research, a large body of statistical results on labor supply exists in which the estimated labor supply elasticity is either approximately zero or negative.[4] But a great many economists simply ignore this evidence because it seems intuitively plausible to them that by and large, people will work more if their rates of remuneration are higher. In light of the fairly strong consensus among economists that labor supply curves in the real world are upward-sloping, it would be inappropriate to lay much emphasis on the possibility that they are not.

No doubt a stronger and more widely acceptable argument against the capital management justification of capital property income is that in the modern industrial economy, capital management effort is provided under qualitatively different circumstances than labor; thus the assumption of a strongly upward-sloping labor supply curve does not necessarily imply a strongly upward-sloping supply curve of capital management effort and/or that capital management effort under pragmatic market socialism would necessarily be appreciably less than it is under capitalism. There are two principal hypothetical possibilities that a proponent of pragmatic market socialism might raise. The first is that the production function relating capital management effort e to rate of return r has a "plateau" configuration. The second is that pragmatic market socialism would possess considerable institutional flexibility, so that the k and β parameters could be influenced in such a manner that capital management effort is encouraged.

The plateau production function concept is a technical specification of the traditional socialist belief that property income is primarily of a rental nature. The idea is motivated by the perception that the interests of enterprise owners in modern industrial economies are sufficiently effective that no significant effort need be expended by the owners in order to establish a strong profit motivation among corporation executives. Capital management effort under contemporary capitalism, consisting as it does of mere performance evaluation of corporation executives in terms of the profitability of their corporations, is an inherently undemanding task. The real human effort is involved in the ordinary labor of corporation employees and corporation executives which produces the profits, and in the ordinary labor of accountants, statisticians, and economists which measures, reports, and analyzes the profits. Once all this work has been done, it is an easy matter to fire the executives of badly performing corporations—or, if that is too drastic, to lower their remuneration. Any of a large number of commonsensical rules tying executive remuneration and/or retention to indicators of present and future profitability will serve the purpose, and no appreciable effort is involved in specifying and applying such rules.

Technically, this would mean that the $r(e)$ function approaches an asymptotic upper limit very abruptly with a small or even negligible input of effort, so that it could be described as having a "plateau" configuration. In the extreme case, the rise to the top of the plateau would be instantaneous, so that the function would become horizontal at the asymptotic upper limit. The implication of such a production function would be that capital management effort under capitalism is already very small, so that the implementation of pragmatic market socialism probably would not affect matters much. In particular, even if the α reduction reduced e, this would not reduce rate of return r by very much.

A possible mathematical function incorporating the plateau production function proposition would be a power form in which the power coefficient is a small number approaching zero: $r = \bar{r}e^{\gamma}$ where $0 < \gamma < 1$. In this function $\bar{r}$ represents the asymptotic upper limit on rate of return, while γ represents the capital return elasticity (more precisely, the elasticity of rate of return r with respect to capital management effort e). The intercept of this function is at the origin, and the parameter γ governs how fast the function approaches its upper asymptotic limit of $\bar{r}$. The lower the γ value, the more rapid is the approach to the upper asymptotic limit, and the more the function takes on the plateau configuration. In Section A of the Analytical Appendix, this explicit form is combined with the Constant Elasticity of Substitution (CES) utility function to enable an explicit function analysis of the model. One of the key results of this analysis is illustrated in Figure 4.4: As γ becomes smaller and the $r(e)$ function begins to take on the plateau configuration, the equilibrium level of capital management effort necessarily becomes smaller.

The explicit function version of the model, incorporating the power rate of return function for $r(e)$ and the CES utility function for $u(y,h)$, may be used to obtain more precise results than is the case with the general function model. For example, we find that the elasticity of substitution between income and leisure in the utility function (σ) plays a particularly important role. Given $f = 0$, if $\sigma < 1$, then the retention coefficient α has a negative effect on capital management effort e; if $\sigma = 1$, then α has no effect on e; and if $\sigma > 1$, then α has a positive effect on e. To date there have only been

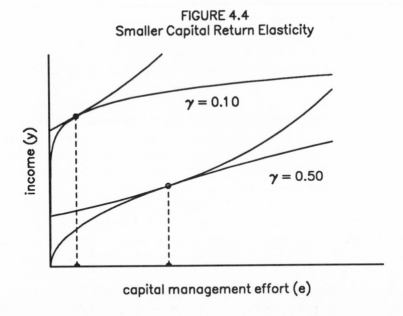

FIGURE 4.4
Smaller Capital Return Elasticity

a few attempts made at econometric estimation of σ, but those few indicate that σ is either close to 1 or somewhat less than 1.[5] This of course supports the socialist side of the argument, in that it suggests a slight effect of the retention coefficient α on capital management effort *e*. Another finding is that sufficient conditions for the case of backward-bending supply of *e* are that σ < 1 and f > 0.

The explicit function version of the model may also be used to obtain numerical solutions for various numerical specifications of the parameters. Such solutions demonstrate tangibly the crucial importance of the numerical value of the γ parameter: the capital return elasticity. If γ is a very low value, say 0.01, we see a numerical verification of the socialist critique of capital property income as unearned. Whether the retention coefficient α is high or low, the level of capital management effort *e* exerted by the capital manager is very low, but the rate of return on capital *r* is close to its upper asymptotic limit. It is also seen that under capitalism (where α is high), most of the capital manager's utility is producer's surplus: that is, very little of the total utility achieved is offset by the disutility of capital management effort (since capital management effort is very low, so too is its disutility). In sum, the plateau production function demonstrates clearly the logical consistency of the socialist argument that capital property income under contemporary capitalism is unearned. Of course, logical consistency does not necessarily imply empirical validity. But it is nevertheless an important step in the indictment of capitalism.

The second hypothetical possibility is that socialism could utilize its institutional flexibility to adjust the k and β parameters in such a way as to overcome any potential decreasing effect on effort e of the reduction in the retention coefficient α. Consider first the parameter k, the capital value managed by the representative capital manager. Figure 4.3 above illustrates that there may be some k value at which the supply of capital management effort bends back. Under pragmatic market socialism, an effort could be made to establish the capital responsibility of the typical BPO agent at this level. Presumably this level would be such that at a good rate of return, the agent would receive a high but not astronomical income.

Under capitalism, in contrast, much of the total stock of financial capital assets is contained in either quite small or quite large personally owned capital accumulations. Small-scale investors are physically unable to devote much time to capital management, because in order to earn a reasonable living, they need a normal labor occupation of some sort; nor do they have much incentive to devote much effort to capital management in any event, because even at a very high rate of return the absolute income on a small amount of k would be relatively insignificant. At the other end of the spectrum, very wealthy capitalists do not have much incentive to capital management effort because their very large k's mean that they receive large capital property incomes even if the rate of return is quite modest. In other words, small investors may be well back in the forward-falling segments of their supply curves of capital management effort (with respect to k), while wealthy capitalists may be well back in the backward-bending segments.

Turning to β, the effectiveness coefficient, it could be argued by a proponent of pragmatic market socialism that socialism could in all probability increase the β parameter by which a given $\alpha r(e)k$ is multiplied into income y. One possibility is that the typical BPO agent would tend to be more energetic and capable than the typical capitalist. The institutions of property ownership and transfer under contemporary capitalism concentrate a great deal of capital property in the hands of elderly individuals, well past their primes, in the hands of surviving spouses of the primary owners, these spouses frequently being devoid of experience and ability in capital management, and finally, through inheritance, in the hands of the primary owner's children, who also are frequently devoid of significant experience or ability in capital management. In contrast, under pragmatic market socialism, persons recruited into capital management would be qualified individuals in their prime working years; and having no ownership rights to their positions, they could be removed in the event they were not demonstrably successful at their task.

The second reason is probably far more important: The concentration of the legal rights of capital ownership in the BPO under pragmatic market socialism might overcome the pernicious effects on the incentives to effort of corporation executives of the separation of ownership and control phenomenon under capitalism. The institutional role of the BPO agent assigned to a particular corporation might be described as that of a "one-person board of directors." In the capitalistic real world of today, most corporation presidents are hardly intimidated by the boards of directors to which they are nominally subservient. Typically the board members are amateurish outsiders with little knowledge of the firm, they personally represent only a tiny fraction of the outstanding voting stock, and they are guided in their ostensible deliberations by a chairman who is either the present president or a past president of the corporation. In contrast, under the tentative provisions set forth above for the BPO, the ownership power over a typical large corporation, including the all-important power to dismiss the corporation's president—which under capitalism is ordinarily spread thinly over a vast throng of widely dispersed stockholders—would be mostly concentrated in the hands of a single BPO agent. The physical concentration of the legal powers of ownership into one individual might make the ownership power more active and formidable, and thereby subject the corporation executives to a tighter and more unified discipline than that to which they are accustomed under contemporary capitalism.

It should be clear from the above discussion that the conventional neoclassical economic theory of effort supply does not provide any compelling grounds for rejecting the proposition that pragmatic market socialism would achieve a level of economic efficiency at least equivalent to that of contemporary capitalism. The argument that a decline in the retention coefficient will reduce capital management effort via the reduction in the effective wage of capital management effort is merely a speculation— a speculation which may be countered by other speculations, of equal a priori plausibility, to the effect that the decline in the retention coefficient is not likely to have a serious adverse impact on economic efficiency. If the $r(e)$ production function relating capital management effort e to rate of return r has a plateau configuration, capital management effort under both capitalism and socialism will be quite low, but the rate of return will nevertheless be near its asymptotic maximum. Aside from this, it is also possible that even if there were a relatively strong positive relationship between the retention coefficient α and capital management effort e, the downward effect on e of reducing α might be counteracted if pragmatic market socialism could simultaneously adjust the k and β parameters of the representative capital manager so as to increase equilibrium capital management effort. When a priori theory fails to answer a question definitively—as it does in this case—reference must necessarily be made to empirical evidence.

D. CIRCUMSTANTIAL EVIDENCE FROM THE REAL WORLD

The previous section argued that the question of whether capital property income is justified by the capital management efforts of its recipients under capitalism cannot be answered unambiguously on the basis of standard neoclassical economic theory. Quite possibly more elaborate and sophisticated theoretical approaches to the question will be taken in the future. But it is very doubtful that such approaches will completely eliminate all ambiguity. They may be useful to the extent that they facilitate a better conceptualization of the problem and hence provide assistance to intuitive judgment. But they are unlikely to point directly to the problem's resolution.

The question is therefore an empirical one, and we must seek relevant empirical evidence. Of course, the only more or less conclusive piece of empirical evidence would be a controlled experiment in which one national economy would retain capitalism while another, identical in all other respects, would adopt pragmatic market socialism. If at the end of ten or twenty years, the pragmatic market socialist economy was operating as well as or better than the capitalist, we could safely conclude that capital property income is unearned under contemporary capitalism. The impossibility of such a controlled experiment is self-evident. In its absence, recourse must be had to evidence which has only a rather indirect and tangential bearing on the issue at hand. This empirical evidence is no more conclusive, in the sense of definitive formal proof, than is the theoretical evidence reviewed above. But it constitutes worthwhile circumstantial evidence on which to base a judgment. Four areas of empirical evidence will be surveyed, each of which sheds an appreciable amount of illumination on the question: (1) the separation of ownership and control; (2) institutional investing and capital markets; (3) the economic performance of public enterprises in non-Communist nations; (4) the economic performance of Communist economies.

Separation of Ownership and Control. Stock ownership rights in the typical contemporary corporation are widely dispersed over a large number of outside individuals, and even though these rights are distributed very unevenly, it still requires a fairly large number of the largest stockholders to constitute a controlling majority. The direct implication of this dispersion is that the executive team which manages the typical corporation on a daily basis normally possesses only a tiny fraction of the total legal ownership rights outstanding, and thus receives only a tiny fraction of the total property return generated by the business operations of the corporation. It is a matter for speculation whether this separation of ownership and management has been "forced" on financial capitalists by the more rapid rate of increase in the capital value of the typical business enterprise than in the capital value of the typical personal fortune, or whether it has more been facilitated by the financial capitalists' voluntary dispersion of their fortunes over a range of investments for risk-spreading purposes. One might well have to go back to the Middle Ages to find a time when owner-management was the norm in business enterprise, but it was not until the early twentieth century that the separation trend was systematically documented in the pioneering work of Berle and Means.

The statistical documentation of the separation phenomenon by Berle and Means and their successors has inspired considerable speculation and debate on its potential economic and social consequences.[6] Among economists, the central controversy revolves around whether the separation phenomenon has significantly weakened the profit motivation of the typical large corporation. The phrase "separation of ownership and control" carries the implication that the stockholders are no longer able to enforce their interests on the corporation executives (i.e., to control them). But of course the statistical evidence adduced by Berle and Means and others, strictly speaking, demonstrates only a physical separation between stockholders and executives. Such a separation could occur, and yet the stockholders could still so effectively enforce their interest in profitability on the executives that the physical separation would not significantly affect the locus of effective control. The phrase "separation of ownership and control" is therefore misleading, and a better one would probably be "separation of ownership and management."

The hypothesis that the separation of ownership and management has appreciably reduced the profit motivation of corporate enterprise might be based on the notion that the physical dispersion of stock ownership rights reduces the degree of cohesion among the stockholders in their efforts to control the executives. It is commonplace wisdom among military analysts that the effective power of a military unit is not simply proportional to its numbers, nor even to the degree of homogeneity in the interests of its members. A significant additional factor in determining a unit's effective power is its *cohesion*, the extent to which it is physically concentrated in one place, internally disciplined, tightly organized, and subject to unambiguous command by a single leader. The military concept of cohesion might certainly carry over into social relations, including those between stockholders and managers.

That many economists take seriously the possible attenuation in the profit motivation brought about by the separation of ownership and management is amply demonstrated by the development of a range of alternatives to profit maximization as theories of corporate enterprise: the sales maximization hypothesis of Baumol, the behavioral theory of Cyert and March, the managerial slack model of Williamson, and various managerial utility maximization models. A few efforts have been made to test various implications of these theories empirically. Some investigators have found indications that corporate sales are a stronger determinant of managerial remuneration than corporate profitability; others have found indications that owner-controlled firms are more profitable than manager-controlled firms.[7] As is usually the case, efforts to verify or falsify theoretical hypotheses with econometric evidence are here confronted with very formidable problems, including poorly measured variables, inadequate sample variation in independent variables, missing variables, misspecifications, and identification problems.

Just as the models of imperfect competition analyzed by Joan Robinson and Edward Chamberlin in the 1930s have failed to supplant the perfect competition model in orthodox theory, so too none of the alternatives to profit maximization inspired by Berle and Means have supplanted the profit maximization assumption.[8] The hypothesis that the separation of ownership and management has not appreciably reduced the profit motivation of corporate enterprise may be based on two distinct approaches. The first approach holds that the managers are in complete control, but that their interest is still in "true" profits, defined as sales revenue less production costs and lower-to-middle-level administrative costs. This differential represents a pool from which nominal profit and high-level administrative costs (i.e., high executive remuneration) is drawn. Thus the difference between manager-controlled and owner-controlled firms would not affect any significant aspect of firm operations, but rather merely the accounting issue of the distribution of "true" profits between nominal (or "reported") profits paid to stockholders and remuneration of high executives: Manager-controlled firms would show a higher ratio of the latter to the former, but otherwise would be indistinguishable from owner-controlled firms. The second approach perceives as the predominant source of profit discipline not the owners' direct enforcement of profitability criteria in the performance evaluation of corporation executives, but rather the competition among managers for the financial resources held by the owners. Such competition is variously manifested in competition between managers for high executive positions, in competition between firms for markets, and in competition between firms in the capital market for investment resources. In this second approach, control still resides fully in the owners, in the sense that they are able to enforce their interests absolutely on the corporation executives.

The principal relevance of the controversy sketched out above to the unearned property income question is that if those who suspect that the separation of ownership and management has significantly reduced the profit motivation of corporate enterprise are correct, then the implementation of pragmatic market socialism might well produce a stronger profit motivation in corporate enterprise than exists under contemporary capitalism, owing to its consolidation of presently dispersed stock ownership rights in the Bureau of Public Ownership. If this were the case, it would mean that higher productive efficiency is achievable at a considerably lower administrative cost (i.e., lower payments to BPO capital managers than to present-day capital owners). This of course strengthens the possibility that capital property income is mostly unearned.

But does the converse possibility, that the separation phenomenon has *not* significantly reduced the profit motivation of corporate enterprise, proportionately weaken the possibility that property income is mostly unearned? Such a proposition would seem dubious. Property income may be deemed unearned if pragmatic market socialism can attain as high a level of profit motivation and productive efficiency as does capitalism; there is no requirement that pragmatic market socialism outperform capitalism on these bases. At the same time, the arguments of those who maintain that the separation phenomenon has not adversely affected the profit motive suggest that given the institutional nature and structure of the economy, the profit motive is virtually self-enforcing, so that its enforcement requires no appreciable effort by the owners. These arguments imply, in short, that the observed property return is of a rental nature.

In terms of the analytical concepts of the previous section, if those who say separation reduces the profit motive are correct, it suggests that the effectiveness coefficient β would be higher under pragmatic market socialism; while if those who say that separation does not reduce the profit motive are correct, it suggests that the production function $r(e)$ relating capital management effort to rate of return on capital is of the plateau form. In other words, the separation of ownership and management, in and of itself and without regard for its consequences for the profit motive, provides prima facie evidence that property income is unearned. This has long been intuitively appreciated by proponents of socialism. Even Karl Marx referred to the separation phenomenon as exploding the argument that property income could be justified as the "wages of management and supervision."[9]

Institutional Investing and Capital Markets. The separation of ownership and management has progressed to such a point that many capitalists virtually ignore the voting rights contained in the common stock shares they own. This voting right is rarely regarded as an appreciable consideration in evaluating common stock instruments against alternative property income-producing instruments such as corporate and government bonds, Treasury bills, bank certificates of deposit, savings accounts, and so on. It is very widely recognized that the task of the modern capitalist is not directly administering the business enterprises and government agencies which issue property income-producing financial capital instruments—nor even of supervising the performance evaluation of the executives of these business enterprises and government agencies. The real effort of the modern capitalist—such effort being held by the apologists for capitalism to validate the assertion that property income is earned—lies in the solution of the difficult and demanding problem of how to allocate a given amount of financial capital over a wide range of competing investment opportunities. It is the diligence of capitalists in performing this function that guarantees the efficient allocation of scarce financial capital resources.

In reality in the modern capitalist economy, a very considerable proportion of this allocation work is performed not by private individuals acting on their own behalf, but by salaried employees acting on behalf of financial intermediaries such as banks, insurance companies, pension funds, and mutual funds.[10] Let us assume that the observed property return on a set of investments is a legitimate earned reward to the individual who decides on that set of investments, because if the property return is not paid, either entirely or mostly, to that individual, he or she will lose interest in the allocation process, it will be performed sloppily, and the resultant set of investments will produce little or no return. Presumably this situation would hold whether the individual doing the investment allocation work was a private citizen or an employee of a financial intermediary. It follows that financial intermediaries should pay a substantial proportion of the property return produced by their investments to the individuals who analyze investment opportunities and make investment decisions.

It would appear that real-world financial intermediaries in the contemporary capitalist economies do *not* reward their investment analysts particularly generously. It seems that in the view of those who manage financial intermediaries, investment analysis is a routine and not exceptionally demanding task. In his study of the investment process in insurance companies, James E. Walter writes (1962, p. 7): "A striking feature of securities investment departments is their insignificant expense, when expressed as a ratio to the dollar amount of investments outstanding. For the larger life companies, dollar investments per member of the securities staff typically are well in excess of $50 million and rise as high as $242 million." This information, in conjunction with other information, suggests that insurance companies pay to their investment analysts not more than 1 or 2 percent of the property return produced by the investments these analysts make.[11] Pension funds sometimes pay outside money management firms to handle their investments. In a 1982 article in *Institutional Investor*, it was reported that the modal money management fee as of the early 1980s was one quarter of 1 percent of the portfolio value.[12] This was at a time when high interest rates practically guaranteed a nominal return of 10 percent even on amateurishly managed money. Therefore the modal management fee, expressed as a percent of property return produced by the portfolio value (assuming a 10 percent return) was 2.5 percent.

Why is it that financial intermediaries such as insurance companies, pension funds, and others treat the investment function rather casually and do not reinvest a major proportion of investment earnings into investment analysis bolstered by special incentive schemes? One plausible reason is that they keep learning from experience that such reinvestments do not pay off. The futility of investing heavily in investment analysis is strongly implied by the much-debated efficient capital market hypothesis, according to which the capital asset markets "instantly" (or at least "very rapidly") incorporate any new information concerning the potential future return to a given asset into that asset's market price.[13] The hypothesis suggests that only two types of capital investors will continue to receive a significantly above-average rate of return over a long period: those who have continuing access to inside information and those blessed with superhuman investment skills. While some groups, such as editors of popular business-oriented periodicals and adherents of the Austrian school, firmly believe in the existence and critical social importance of the latter type of investor, many serious students of capital markets are dubious about his very existence, let alone his practical significance in capital markets and economic processes generally. The other side of the coin is that efficient capital markets would protect and preserve lazy and/or incompetent investors, who select their investments in an apparently rather frivolous and haphazard manner. Such investors, over the long term, could expect to receive the same average rate of return as those whose investment choices are made in a seemingly more rational and informed manner.

How much time is devoted to investment analysis by the typical private investor? Although there are some well-known cases of professional venture capitalists and the like, impressionistic evidence suggests that most capitalists, even excluding the small investors whose modest capital accumulations would not yield enough to live on even at a very good rate of return and who are therefore forced into ordinary labor occupations, do *not* devote a great deal of time to pondering and selecting investments. One tangible indication of the validity of this impressionistic deduction lies in statistical information published by the U.S. Internal Revenue Service. Although the income of those in the highest brackets is dominated by property income, the large majority of these individuals report wage and salary income, and even though this wage and salary income is a small proportion of their total income, it is quite large in an absolute sense. For example, in 1975, 78 percent of those in the top bracket (adjusted gross income over $1 million) reported wage and salary income amounting to an average of $156,685 per taxpayer, by far the highest labor income of any bracket. (It should be noted that of the 22 percent not receiving labor income, a large number were undoubtedly elderly and retired.) Even though this is a large labor income in an absolute sense and obviously results from full-time, responsible employment, it accounted for only 10.46 percent of the adjusted gross income of taxpayers in the top bracket, relative to 32.16 percent derived from dividends and 33.33 percent derived from capital gains.[14] These data suggest that capital investing is not a significantly time-consuming occupation even for the wealthiest capitalists: They need ordinary labor jobs in order to "keep busy." Another significant indication is provided by data from the 1971 Purdue University Survey of the Individual Investor. Only 15.4 percent of the respondents to the survey, all of whom were active in the stock market, spent more than 20 hours per month on investment analysis. The mean time devoted to investment analysis by the entire group of respondents was approximately 9 hours per month: that is, only slightly over one working day in a month.[15]

Two conclusions are suggested by this information. The first is that the work ethic is so strong in modern society that even among wealthy capitalists in no serious need of labor income, the great majority do in fact have ordinary labor jobs, jobs which preclude them from being personally describable as "social parasites." However, these jobs, although reflecting well personally on the capitalists who hold them, seriously undercut the plausibility of the argument that property income recompenses capital management effort in the form of investment analysis. The average labor income realized by wealthy capitalists is high enough to suggest serious, full-time, professional work in law, medicine, or business administration. It stretches credulity to the breaking point to speculate that these wealthy capitalists regularly come home after a long, tiring day at the office, and spend long, tiring evenings assessing their portfolios of investment assets. However, if it is perceived that property income is essentially unearned or rental in nature, it is fully understandable, given the prevalent social work ethic in conjunction with the psychological propensity in humans toward boredom and discontent in the absence of systematic activity, that even the wealthiest capitalists, who clearly have no financial need to work, would nevertheless work.

Therefore apparently most individual investors, no less than the institutional investors, have decided that the allocation of a substantial amount of time and energy to capital investment decisions is not worthwhile. This policy is of course fully consistent with the efficient capital market hypothesis. In turn, the efficient capital market hypothesis supports the concept of the plateau production function, discussed above, with respect to effort applied to financial capital investment. Just as the separation of ownership and management suggests that capital property income is not earned through the efforts of capitalists in supervising corporate enterprise, so too the evidence concerning institutional and private investment activity in the capital markets suggests that capital property income is not earned through the efforts of capitalists in investing financial capital.

Public Enterprise in Non-Communist Nations. Even in such a bastion of capitalistic free enterprise as the United States, there are a few pockets of public production of priced goods, mostly in the area of municipal utilities such as electricity, water supply, and refuse collection. In many if not most of the other advanced non-Communist nations, notwithstanding the recent trend toward privatization, a sizable fraction of economic production is still carried on by government-owned enterprises.[16] Public production of priced commodities in nations where private ownership of business enterprise remains the rule tends to be a controversial issue. The same theoretical reasons which justify private ownership as a general rule cast doubt on the efficacy of public production. Public enterprise must therefore be justified on the basis of "exceptional" conditions such as external effects or natural monopoly.

Many efforts have been made to evaluate the performance of public production relative to the private alternative.[17] Generally speaking, this research is unfavorable to public production. For example, a 1982 survey article by Borcherding, Pommerehne and Schneider summarized no fewer than fifty studies covering nineteen different activities in five advanced nations (the United States, Canada, Australia, West Germany, and Switzerland). The overwhelming preponderance of this evidence indicates the lower efficiency of public production relative to private. Of the fifty studies, only three indicated lower average cost in public production relative to private, while another five studies found no significant difference in average cost as between public and private production.

Those who believe that lower efficiency is an inherent and unavoidable characteristic of public ownership per se sometimes enunciate their arguments in terms of property rights.[18] In particular, the property rights in a public enterprise are dispersed over a huge throng of "citizen owners." Although as a body the citizen owners have an interest, both as taxpayers and as consumers, in the efficiency of public enterprise, the gains from higher efficiency are so much dispersed and diluted that no one citizen has an appreciable incentive to try to monitor and improve public sector efficiency. For their part, the managers of public enterprises have no significant incentive toward efficiency because their lack of property rights in these enterprises denies them any claims to the pecuniary benefits that would flow from higher efficiency. The proponents of this view heavily discount any pressures toward efficiency that might be generated by the seemingly vigorous competition among public enterprises and other government agencies over budgets, promotions, and other desiderata, and by the seemingly intense competition among political parties for government offices which is typical of modern democracy.

Only a relatively small minority of economists who have studied relative public-private efficiency have made the firm and explicit judgment that public enterprise efficiency tends to be lower simply and unavoidably because of the perverse structure of property rights inherent in public enterprise.[19] Some plausible alternative hypotheses have been suggested. For example, Caves and Christensen, in a study of Canadian railroads (1980), suggest that in some cases the critical element is that public enterprises are not subject to competitive forces. During the more recent era, in which the public and private railroads in Canada have competed in a relatively vigorous and unregulated fashion, public and private costs have been similar. Funkhouser and MacAvoy (1979), in a comparison of 100 Indonesian public and private corporations, tentatively attribute the higher costs of the public corporations to their greater susceptibility to pressures from local governments to hire an excessive amount of local labor and to buy materials from expensive local suppliers. Absence of direct competition, as in the Canadian public railroad case, is to be expected for many public enterprises, since one principal justification for public ownership in basically nonsocialist economies is natural monopoly. Complex and ambiguous motivations, as in the case of the Indonesian public corporations, are also to be expected in many public enterprises because another principal justification for public ownership is external effects.

Under the pragmatic market socialist proposal, the typical publicly owned business enterprise would operate under a relatively simple and straightforward profit maximization incentive, and would also be in direct competition with other publicly owned business enterprises producing the same or a similar product line. Departures from this standard norm of commercial motivation and competitive environment would have to be justified on the same grounds on which departures from the private owner-ship norm are currently justified under capitalism. Only if the observed efficiency shortcomings of public enterprises are the inherent result of public ownership, and not of other factors such as noncompetitive environ-ments and/or noncommercial motivations, would these shortcomings imply the inefficacy of the pragmatic market socialist proposal. It is thus highly significant that a great many authorities on public enterprise would agree that if the strong social consensus was that public enterprises should be profit maximizers, it would not be difficult for the executive arm of government to establish this motivation in the public enterprise managers. For example, Alec Nove has written (1973, p. 18): "Let us make an elementary observation. A public monopoly, if instructed to operate 'commercially,' will tend to behave in exactly the same way as a private monopoly."

Communist Economic Performance. In 1917, for the first time in history, the Bolshevik Revolution established socialism in a large national economy. Contrary to the expectations of many pre-1917 anti-socialists, socialism did not quickly prove itself an unviable economic proposition. Rather, the Russian national economy developed quite impressively under the com-munist version of socialism into what was for a long time—prior to the recent disruptions engendered by the perestroika program—the second strongest national economy in the world, after that of the United States. While Soviet ideologues extolled the rapid industrialization of the Russian national economy as proof of the superiority of socialism over capitalism, Western analysts remained highly skeptical of Soviet economic perfor-mance. They attributed the rapid growth of the Soviet economy to the inordinate investment rate forcibly imposed on the Russian population by the Communist oligarchy. While this brutal imposition resulted ultimately in a much larger economy in an absolute sense, the growth itself was highly inefficient, and the contemporary Soviet economy remains highly ineffi-cient. Statistical evidence of Soviet inefficiency has been adduced, for example, by Berliner (1964); Gisser and Jonas (1974); Bergson (1978); and Desai and Martin (1983).[20]

In addition to the scholarly studies just cited, an enormous amount of journalistic criticism of Soviet economic performance has been published in the popular media over the decades since the Bolshevik Revolution. Journalistic criticism of Soviet economic performance has recently inten-sified. The first fruits of Mikhail Gorbachev's perestroika campaign to restructure the Soviet economy more along the lines of market capitalism in the West are widely reported as virtual economic collapse. There is no doubt that the Soviet Union is undergoing a great deal of economic, political, and social turmoil at the present time. But reports of economic collapse are almost certainly exaggerated. First and foremost among the evidence cited to support the economic collapse scenario are widespread shortages and queuing. However, it is elementary economics that such shortages and queuing problems as the Soviet economy is experiencing may be very quickly and thoroughly abrogated by means of upward price adjustments. But the Soviet leadership is very reluctant to apply this particular cure, because Soviet consumers have become extremely accustomed to price stability. The point is that shortages and queuing do not, by themselves, necessarily imply an unacceptably low level of consumption and/or productive efficiency.

Understandably, in view of the protracted international conflict between the Communist East and the non-Communist West, which has generated, among other things, an all-out propaganda battle, very little sensible and intelligent analysis is found on either side concerning the relative economic and social performance of the other side. Certainly Communist ideologues have ridiculously underrated the performance of the capitalistic West—and anti-Communist ideologues have reacted in kind. Particularly in the Western popular media the economic performance of the Soviet Union has consistently been denigrated and underrated. But the fact remains that despite the severe drag on Soviet economic performance imposed by an extremely heavy military burden and by inadequate participation in the world economy, the material consumption of the typical Russian consumer is currently at a respectable level by world standards. Average Russian consumption is in fact significantly higher than it is in many capitalist nations, such as India or even Brazil.[21] The point here is not that the Soviet economy is just as prosperous and efficient as the advanced capitalist economies— clearly it is not. The point is, rather, that the actual shortfall in terms of prosperity and efficiency is not as large as it is often imagined to be in the West.

While few if any dissents to the inefficiency proposition are to be found among serious Western students of the Soviet economy, public ownership of productive enterprise, per se, is rarely cited by these students as an important source of inefficiency.[22] Far more attention has been paid to such potential sources of inefficiency as the following: (1) the constraints placed on enterprise flexibility by the existence of the central planning system; (2) the guidance of both current production and capital investment by political decisions rather than economic criteria; (3) perverse enterprise motivations involving such things as output levels and labor employment to a greater extent than more legitimate criteria such as profits and unit costs; (4) excessive wage egalitarianism and job security among the Soviet labor force; (5) the depressing effect on incentives to effort and general social morale of the dominant position of the oligarchically organized Communist Party in Soviet society. All of these deficiencies, as well as many others, are potentially avoidable within the context of public ownership.

Pragmatic market socialism would not involve the obvious departures of the Soviet economy from the principles of decentralized economic decision-making, consumer sovereignty, commercial motivations, and market alloca-tion. Certainly no such departures are intended. Neither is there any intention to emulate the political and social characteristics of the Com-munist nations, and such characteristics quite possibly also have an adverse effect on economic performance. Therefore it may be seriously questioned whether the economic liabilities of communistic socialism would apply to pragmatic market socialism.

But it is certainly arguable that the case for pragmatic market socialism is indirectly strengthened by the fact that the economic performance of the Soviet economy in particular and the Communist economies in general has been reasonably respectable, all things considered. If even the highly flawed communistic version of socialism has managed to achieve a reasonable level of economic performance, clearly a much higher level of economic perfor-mance may be expected of a socialist economic system which fully incor-porates the Western consensus concerning the efficiency of decentralized economic decision-making, market allocation, price flexibility, profit max-imization, and so on. The performance level achieved by the Communist economies therefore indirectly but significantly supports the expectation that pragmatic market socialism would achieve at least the efficiency level of contemporary capitalism, while surpassing the equity performance of contemporary capitalism through social dividend distribution of capital property return. And this expectation in turn reinforces the judgment that capital property income under contemporary capitalism is not in fact an earned return to the capital management effort of capital owners.

NOTES

1. The "Great Contradiction" in Marxist economic theory was explicated in Eugen von Böhm-Bawerk's *Karl Marx and the Close of His System*, which first appeared in book form and English translation in 1898 and which quickly gained the reputation of being a more or less definitive refutation of Marxist economic theory. The essence of the argument had been stated earlier, in the chapter on Marx in Böhm-Bawerk's treatise *Capital and Interest* (1884). In 1949, *Karl Marx and*

the Close of His System was republished by Augustus M. Kelley under the editorship of Paul M. Sweezy, the noted American Marxist. Sweezy included essays by Rudolf Hilferding and Lasislaus von Bortkiewicz, originally published in 1904 and 1907 respectively, which constituted replies from the Marxist camp to Böhm-Bawerk's critique of Marx. These essays retain considerable interest even today as seminal points of what eventually became a substantial technical literature, produced by both "believers" and "nonbelievers," on the Transformation Problem. The extent of this literature may be assessed from the 1971 *JEL* survey article by the prominent mainstream economist Paul Samuelson (a nonbeliever).

    2. Ricardian rent theory is a standard topic in textbooks on the history of economic thought. A few randomly selected examples are as follows: Robert Lekachman (1959, Chapter 7); Overton Taylor (1960, Chapter 8); John Fred Bell (1967, Chapter 10); Ingrid Rima (1978, Chapter 6); Mark Blaug (1985, Chapters 3 and 4). Normally these discussions include the fascinating real-world postscript to Ricardian rent theory: the single-tax movement in the United States based on Henry George's celebrated tract *Progress and Poverty* (1879). Ricardo and George are also typically covered in chapters on rent in principles of economics textbooks. Such textbooks are too numerous and too homogeneous to be worth citing.

    3. The model discussed here was initially developed in the author's first published paper on pragmatic market socialism: "Capital Management under Market Socialism" (*Review of Social Economy*, 1974). Some technical nuances were added in a 1976 paper appearing in the *ACES Bulletin*. Additional technical nuances were explored in a lengthy 1987 working paper: "Is Property Income Unearned? A Survey of Some Relevant Theoretical and Empirical Evidence." The model's most recent appearance in the published literature was in "A New Perspective on Market Socialism" (*Comparative Economic Studies*, 1988), a concise survey of some major economic questions pertaining to pragmatic market socialism.

    This model is essentially a slight modification of what might be termed the "standard textbook model" of the household labor supply decision. The standard household labor supply model is covered in most textbooks on intermediate and advanced microeconomic theory. Ten examples, arranged alphabetically by author, are as follows: (1) Edgar Browning and Jacqueline Browning (1986, Chapter 15, Section 2); (2) James Henderson and Richard Quandt (1980, Chapter 2, Section 5); (3) Jack Hirshleifer (1988, Chapter 12, Section A); (4) K. C. Kogiku (1971, Chapter 1, Section 5); (5) Heinz Kohler (1986, Chapter 10, Section on "Supply: The Case of Labor"); (6) P. R. G. Layard and A. A. Walters (1978, Chapter 11, Section 1); (7) Edwin Mansfield (1982, Chapter 13, Section 9); (8) Walter Nicholson (1985, Chapter 16); (9) Dominick Salvatore (1986, Chapter 14, Section 4); (10) Eric Solberg (1982, Chapter 5, Section I).

    4. For example, theory tells us that if a household has a Constant Elasticity of Substitution utility function in consumption and leisure, and no nonlabor income, then the value of the elasticity of substitution between consumption and leisure will determine the relationship between wage rate and labor supply. Labor supply will be unaffected by the wage rate if the elasticity of substitution is 1 (the Cobb-

Douglas special case). Also, the supply curve of labor with respect to the wage rate will be upward-sloping or downward-sloping as the elasticity of substitution is, respectively, greater than 1 or less than 1. As far as empirical work is concerned, Mark Killingsworth's large-scale survey of the theory and empirics of labor supply (1983) cites a large number of econometric estimates of labor supply elasticity. Counting endpoints of ranges, between his Tables 3.2, 3.3, and 4.3, which cover both "first generation" and "second generation" estimation methods, Killingsworth lists 73 labor supply elasticity estimates for men, spread out over 32 studies, and 100 estimates for women, spread out over 36 studies. The mean estimate for men is −0.134 with a standard error of 0.185; the mean estimate for women is 1.040 with a standard error of 2.464. Given these standard errors, the null hypothesis that the true labor supply elasticity for both men and women is zero cannot be rejected at any reasonably conservative level of statistical confidence.

5. See Yunker (*Public Finance*, 1989, p. 120) for discussion of current econometric work on the elasticity of substitution between consumption and leisure. Although results are mixed, on the whole this work is not at all inconsistent with a unitary value of this coefficient.

6. *The Modern Corporation and Private Property* (1932), by Adolf Berle and Gardiner Means, established the phrase "separation of ownership and control" (sometimes referred to herein as "separation of ownership and management") in the common currency of the economics profession in the early 1930s. Further empirical work by Gordon (1945) and Larner (1966, 1970) suggests that the trends originally studied by Berle and Means are continuing apace. Popularly written commentaries on the phenomenon include James Burnham's *The Managerial Revolution* (1941) and Adolf Berle's *Power without Property* (1959).

Probably owing to the disruption of the Great Depression and the advent of Keynesian macroeconomic theory, it required almost three decades before the economics profession acknowledged that the separation phenomenon might entail serious questions about the realism of the prevailing core economic theory of the profit-maximizing firm. William Baumol's revenue maximization model and Oliver Williamson's managerial slack model were developed, respectively, in *Business Behavior, Value and Growth* (1959, rev. ed. 1967) and *The Economics of Discretionary Behavior: Managerial Objectives in a Theory of the Firm* (1964). Robin Marris developed a growth maximization model, which might be regarded as a dynamic version of Baumol's static revenue maximization model, in *The Economic Theory of Managerial Capitalism* (1964). Another important source from the early 1970s is the compendium edited by Robin Marris and Adrian Wood (*The Corporate Economy*, 1971), to which a number of eminent economists contributed. J. R. Wildsmith's book-length survey of this and related theoretical work appeared in 1973. There have been various additional attempts, less widely known, to model the corporate firm based on the idea of managerial utility maximization: for example, M. A. Crew et al. (1971) and Azariadis et al. (1972).

In the 1980s, the *Journal of Economic Literature* published two important survey articles relevant to these matters: the first by Robin Marris and Dennis Mueller (1980) and the second by Oliver Williamson (1981). On the salient

question of whether the modern corporate economy is consistent with the traditional hypothesis of profit maximization by firms, the summary statements of the
authors of these *JEL* surveys are as follows. Marris and Mueller (1980, pp. 58-59):
"In the present paper we have tried to show that a large literature has now evolved
within the formal bounds of the discipline that is as much at odds with the invisible
hand theorem as was the previous 'heterodox,' institutionalist, or Marxist literature.
The new literature is rigorous, amenable to empirical testing and, we would argue,
more consistent with empirical evidence than the neoclassical model, where the
two differ in their predictions. It thus meets the criteria of positive economics.
Where it differs from the traditional theory most fundamentally is in its normative
implications. There either are none, or they are negative. Managerial pursuit of
self-interest need not lead to maximum present value of investment streams; too
much may be retained, too much reinvested..." Williamson (1981, p. 1559): "This
has a bearing on the problem of separation of ownership and control, noted by
Adolph Berle and Gardiner Means in 1932. Thus they inquired, 'have we any
justification for assuming that those in control of a modern corporation will also
choose to operate it in the interest of the stockholders' (1932, p. 121). The answer,
then as now, is almost certainly no..."

7. For empirical work on the effect of the separation of ownership and control
on the profit rates of firms, see David Kamerschen (1968); R. Joseph Monsen, John
Chiu, and David Cooley (1968); Brian Hindley (1970); H. K. Radice (1971);
Kenneth Boudreaux (1973); John Palmer (1973). Closely related work is that on
the determinants of managerial emolument. A 1962 study by Joseph McGuire, John
Chiu, and Alvar Elbring suggested that sales revenue has a stronger impact on
managerial salaries than profitability. This work was later challenged by Wilbur
Lewellen and Blaine Huntsman (1970) and Wilbur Lewellen (1971) on grounds
that it did not take account of stock options and other managerial benefits dependent
on profitability, and that when these factors are taken into account, it is apparent
that profitability has a strong impact on total managerial remuneration. In turn,
David Ciscel (1974) critiqued Lewellen and Huntsman's work on statistical
grounds.

8. Not long after the emergence of an explicit challenge to the core theory of
profit maximization by business firms, based on the separation of ownership and
control, a vigorous counterattack commenced. In 1976, Michael C. Jensen and
William H. Meckling published a lengthy article on the theory of the firm in the
Journal of Financial Economics, which more or less codified the "doctrine of
irrelevance," that is, the proposition that the separation of ownership and management has not significantly attenuated the profit orientation of the large modern
corporation. The "doctrine of irrelevance" gained a prominent champion in Eugene
Fama, famous for his earlier work on capital markets, when he published "Agency
Problems and the Theory of the Firm" in the *Journal of Political Economy* in 1980.
Shortly thereafter Fama and Jensen collaborated to produce yet another important
statement of the doctrine: "Separation of Ownership and Control" (*Journal of Law
and Economics*, 1983). In the 1980s, Jensen edited "Symposium on the Market for
Corporate Control" (*Journal of Financial Economics*, 1983,) and shortly afterward

"Symposium on Management Compensation and the Managerial Labor Market" (*Journal of Accounting and Economics*, 1985, co-edited with Jerold L. Zimmerman). In general, the papers in these symposia find statistically significant positive relationships between measures of stockholder welfare and measures of managerial remuneration and job security.

A considerable bulk of statistical work has thus been accumulated which indicates that to an appreciable extent corporation executives are accountable to stockholders and that the executives consequently pursue, to an appreciable extent, the objective of stockholder welfare. Nevertheless, it is also true that this work does not necessarily validate the "doctrine of irrelevance" as expounded by Jensen, Meckling, Fama, and others. "To an appreciable extent" is not the same as "to the maximum extent" or "to the optimum extent." All that the extensive statistical work that has been done in this area establishes is that the separation phenomenon has not destroyed the profit motive; but by its nature it cannot establish that the separation phenomenon has not weakened the profit motive. In their editor's introduction to the 1985 *Journal of Accounting and Economics* symposium, Jensen and Zimmerman make the following concession: "Unfortunately, the studies in this volume do not address the complex issues associated with the frequently made, but unsupported, assertion that executive compensation is 'too high.' Although it is possible to make equally plausible, but also unsupported, assertions that executive compensation is 'too low,' such arguments have received no attention in the media. More work is required, to address the difficult and important economic issues associated with whether executive pay is 'too low' or 'too high.'" But this very question, unaddressed by the research, is in fact the critical question. For if executive pay is in fact "too high," this constitutes evidence that corporation executives are inadequately accountable. The costs of inadequate accountability are not merely grossly overpaid executives but, more important, suboptimal incentives to managerial effort among these executives.

9. In view of the central relevance of the separation of ownership and management to the capital management justification of property income, it is interesting to note what Karl Marx had to say on the matter well over 100 years ago. The following quotes are from *Das Kapital*, Volume III, Part V, Chapter XXIII (1967 International Publishers edition):

"The wages of management both for the commercial and industrial manager are completely isolated from the profits of enterprise in the cooperative factories of laborers, as well as in capitalist stock companies. The separation of wages of management from profits of enterprise, purely accidental at other times, is here constant... Stock companies in general, developed with the credit system, have an increasing tendency to separate this work of management as a function from the ownership of capital, be it self-owned or borrowed. Just as the development of bourgeois society witnessed a separation of the functions of judges and administrators from land-ownership, whose attributes they were in feudal times. But since, on the one hand, the mere owner of capital, the money-capitalist, has to face the functioning capitalist, while money-capital itself assumes a social character with the advance of credit, being concentrated in banks and loaned out by them instead of its original owners, and since, on the other hand, the mere manager, who has no title whatever to the capital, whether through borrowing it or otherwise, performs all the real functions pertaining to the functioning capitalist as such, only the functionary remains and the capitalist disappears as superfluous from the production process..."

"Profit of enterprise and wages of supervision, or management, were confused originally due to the antagonistic form assumed in respect to interest by the surplus of profit. This was further promoted by the apologetic aim of representing profit not as a surplus-value derived from unpaid labor, but as the capitalist's wages of work performed by him. This was met on the part of socialists by a demand to reduce profit actually to what it pretended to be theoretically, namely, mere wages of supervision. And this demand was all the more obnoxious to theoretical embellishment, the more these wages of supervision, like any other wage, found their definite level and definite market-price, and the more they fell, like all wages for skilled labor, with the general development which reduces the cost of production of specially trained labor-power. With the development of co-operation on the part of the laborers, and of stock enterprises on the part of the bourgeoisie, even the last pretext for the confusion of profit of enterprise and wages of management was removed, and profit also appeared in practice as it undeniably appeared in theory, as mere surplus-value, a value for which no equivalent was paid, as realized unpaid labor."

10. Counting all the many textbooks in money and banking and in corporate finance, there is a very large literature on capital markets and institutional investors. This literature is so extensive, homogeneous, and widely known that references to it will be omitted. The professional journal and treatise literature is also very extensive. Unfortunately, there is very little in this large body of published writing on capital markets and institutional investors that is precisely relevant to our present purposes. The key question here is what proportion of the property income received on the investments of institutional investors goes to those individuals directly responsible for making investment decisions. This is not a matter on which information is readily available.

11. According to the *Life Insurance Fact Book, 1981* (Washington, D.C.: American Council of Life Insurance), p. 69, the net rate of investment income on mean invested assets was 4.11 percent in 1960 (a year from the era of Walter's study). This rate applied to $50 million produces $2.055 million in property income per year. Considering that Walter uses $10,000 as a benchmark to differentiate low salaries from high salaries (p. 210, Table IV-5), it would seem that the average salary of the security staff members could not have exceeded $25,000. Such a salary would be 1.2165 percent of $2.055 million.

12. "Pension Forum: Are High Management Fees Worth It?" *Institutional Investor* 16(7): 133-136, July 1982. From the article, it would appear that as a general rule pension funds do not retain outside investment management firms. The customary pattern seems to be that these firms are occasionally retained for a little while on the basis of their good performance in the recent past, but are discharged as soon as their good performance falters, as it inevitably does sooner or later. The

inability of these firms to sustain a high rate of return indicates that over those periods when they do happen to be earning a high return, they are simply the beneficiaries of good luck, and the high rate of return has nothing to do with superior investing prowess.

13. Eugene Fama's 1970 survey article on the theory and empirics of the efficient capital market hypothesis summarized the substantial work on the subject done during the 1960s, and initiated the even more impressive wave of work that continued throughout the 1970s and into the 1980s. Simon Keane provided a book-length survey of the evolving literature in 1983. A chapter-length survey was provided in the same year by Steven Sheffrin in his book on rational expectations (1983, Chapter 4). A great many studies have been published which allegedly support the efficient market hypothesis by showing that capital instrument prices react very quickly to new information, or that various seemingly clever rules for investing do not produce above-average returns over a long period of time. Among numerous academic specialists, the efficient capital market hypothesis, despite various anomalies that are generally deemed no more than curiosa, is considered sufficiently verified for all practical purposes of real-world decision-making. Thus one authority, Simon Keane, in summarizing the practical implications of the hypothesis for the private investor, is quite unequivocal on the following points (1980, pp. 19-22): (1) paying for "expert advice" on investments is a waste of money; (2) the risk-averse investor should diversify to at least some minimum extent (fifteen different assets is suggested as a guideline); (3) the investor should follow the buy-and-hold policy, in order to reduce brokerage expenses, unless a truly extraordinary situation emerges.

14. See James Yunker and Timothy Krehbiel (1988, pp. 90-91). These data are computed from U. S. Department of the Treasury, Internal Revenue Service, Publication Number 79 (5-78), *Statistics of Income 1975: Individual Income Tax Returns*.

15. The following data from the Purdue University Survey of the Individual Investor, reported in Yunker and Krehbiel (1988, Table 2), pertain not just to capital owners as a whole, but to a subset of stock market activists (the survey was addressed to customers of a nationwide stock brokerage house). Individuals active in the common stock market are likely to engage in more investment analysis activity than the norm. Nevertheless, even among these individuals, the allocation of time to investment analysis is not very generous.

Investment Analysis Time (in hours per month)	Percentage of Respondents
less than 3	32.9
3 to 5	21.5
5 to 10	18.2
0 to 20	12.0
20 to 30	6.4
greater than 30	9.0

The mean number of hours per month devoted to investment analysis within the entire sample is 9.184, with a standard deviation of 10.401. The proposition that it is "well known from casual empiricism" that on the whole capital owners devote little time to investment analysis, may be supported by the choices provided by the designers of the survey instrument used by the Purdue study. The designers did not ask if "20 working days per month, 25 working days per month," etc., were devoted to investment analysis, but rather if "less than 3 hours per month, 3-5 hours per month," etc., were devoted to investment analysis. Only in the mythology provided by such apologists for capitalism as Austrian school economists and the editors of popular business periodicals is it seriously proposed that real-world capital owners exert themselves seriously in the analysis of investment opportunities.

16. Although state-owned enterprises occur throughout the non-Communist world, the British nationalized industries have had a particularly strong impact on abstract thinking about state-owned enterprises. Illustrative references on the British nationalized industries, ordered chronologically, are as follows: Ben Lewis (1952); William Robson (1962); William Shepherd (1965); Graham Reid and Kevin Allen (1970); Richard Pryke (1971); Rolf Kelf-Cohen (1973); Richard Pryke (1981). Theoretical economic work on public enterprises is exemplified by William Baumol and David Bradford (1970), Abram Bergson (1972), Michael Crew and Paul Kleindorfer (1979), and Dieter Bös (1986). The connection between the economic theory of public enterprise and real-world public enterprise seems rather tenuous. In place of the properly specified problems in mathematical optimization studied in the theoretical literature, real-world public enterprises substitute vague references to social welfare. For example, Yair Aharoni states (1986, p. 134): "Most SOEs [state-owned enterprises] have officially declared objectives. These formal objectives laid out in statutes, memoranda of incorporation, official published government documents or declarations are usually very broad, vague, and not easily made operational and not necessarily a guide to actual action... Vagueness prevails in SOEs because it is deliberately designed both to leave room for future interpretation and because certain goals to be pursued are never officially stated." For an effort to make economic sense out of official directives, see Jack Wiseman (1963) on the British nationalized industries.

17. One of the earliest "serious" contributions (i.e., academic rather than journalistic) on the public sector relative performance question was William G. Shepherd's 1965 study of the British nationalized industries, originally a doctoral thesis at Yale University. Shepherd found that many of the popular criticisms of the British nationalized industries did not stand up to close scrutiny. Shepherd's positive verdict on the performance of the British nationalized industries was seconded in 1971 in the first of Richard Pryke's two books on the subject. But after the high-water mark of liberal sentiment was reached in the 1960s, the 1970s witnessed the resurgence of conservative sentiment. As a consequence, general opinion of "public enterprise efficiency" declined. An increasing number of studies appeared in which public enterprise came out on the short end in relative efficiency comparisons. By the time of the Thomas Borcherding et al. survey article (*Zeitschrift für Nationalökonomie*, 1982), findings in favor of public sector relative efficiency were very much in the minority. Some relatively recent general discussions of public-private relative performance are to be found in William Baumol

(1980); Pierre Marchand et al. (1984); and Yair Aharoni (1986).

18. One example of attribution of public sector inefficiency to inherent incentives problems owing to the attenuated property rights of public enterprise managers is provided by David G. Davies in his work on the relative performance of Australia's two airlines, one of which is publicly owned and the other privately owned. Davies published two articles in the *Journal of Law and Economics* (1971 and 1977), and later responded to a critique by P. J. Forsyth and R. D. Hocking in the *Economic Record* (1980). Davies's conclusions have also been contested by Douglas Caves and Laurits Christensen, in their examination of an analogous situation: public ownership of one railroad company and private ownership of the other in Canada (1980).

19. The reluctance of economists to conclude that public enterprise is authentically inefficient, despite the apparent evidence, is illustrated by Thomas Borcherding et al. (1982, p. 143 and p. 145): "The theme of this paper has been generally contrary to the view of efficient public supply through state owned firms. This puts an economist in a rather awkward position. Economists use as their organizing principle the notion that waste will be minimized, given the transactions costs of engaging in exchange. This means that inefficiency is a magnitude that rational economic actors will, mistakes and ignorance aside, attempt to reduce as far as it pays to do so. Why then would such a supply device be so often used if it is so inefficient? The answer must lie in a misinterpretation... Any real differences in efficiency must be explained, therefore, by differing 'frictions,' i.e., the differential transactions costs associated with different behavior under one institutional regime rather than another. Waste in a practical sense, therefore, cannot exist, unless there is a persistent and remediable error in the choice of societal institutions. The latter possibility, willful ignorance, cannot be readily accepted, however, without seriously compromising the economist's commitment to the rational choice paradigm. If our paradigm is to be retained, the answer to the hypothesis that inefficiency is present is to suggest the accuser look instead for other explanations. What one (especially the uninformed outsider) might term waste might, in fact, be the best means of accomplishing an otherwise unrealizable end."

20. Abram Bergson's 1978 study represents a major contribution to the professional literature on the numerical relative performance of the Soviet economy. The seminal contributions in this area were published in 1964 by Joseph Berliner and Bela Balassa. Berliner essayed a static total factor productivity comparison of the United States and the Soviet Union in 1960, while Balassa addressed the rate of growth of total factor productivities over comparable eras in the economic histories of the United States and the Soviet Union. Some additional work on past and/or potential Soviet economic performance includes Micha Gisser and Paul Jonas (1974); Padma Desai and Ricardo Martin (1983); Abram Bergson and Herbert Levine (1983); Padma Desai (1987); Gur Ofer (1987); John Cole and Trevor Buck (1987); and Edward Hewett (1988). Not all of this work deals directly with relative efficiency, which consists of two aspects: relative performance (one versus the other), and efficiency (ratio of output to inputs). For example, Desai and Martin present evidence indicating that the distribution of capital over the various sectors

of the Soviet economy is not such as to satisfy the Pareto conditions for productive efficiency. But quite possibly an analogous study for the U.S. economy would indicate that a similar situation exists.

21. In 1975, per capita GNP in the United States was $7,098 in current dollars. For the same year and the same monetary units, the Office of Economic Research of the Central Intelligence Agency estimated Soviet Union real per capita GNP to be $3,400 (Joint Economic Committee, U.S. Congress, *Soviet Economy in a New Perspective* [Washington, D.C.: U.S. Government Printing Office, 1976], Table 1, p. x). The ratio of Soviet to U.S. real per capita GNP is thus 0.479. A Physical Quality of Life comparison between the U.S. and the Soviet Union was given in a *Time* Magazine cover story, "Socialism" (March 13, 1978). The PQL index, based on life expectancy, infant mortality and literacy, ranges from 0 to 100. The U.S. was rated at 94 and the Soviet Union at 91. Interestingly, the per capita GNP comparison given in the same story diverges fairly substantially from that given above. According to *Time*, U.S. per capita GNP was $7,890 (presumably in 1977), while Soviet per capita GNP was only $2,760, which represents a ratio of 0.349 to the U.S. figure. This suggests the substantial range of error that exists, even with respect to this very fundamental and vitally important measure.

22. An example of this is provided by Abram Bergson in his 1964 book, *The Economics of Soviet Planning*. In the section "Sources of Inefficiency," running from page 329 to page 340, Bergson discusses seven primary sources of inefficiency: (1) the perverse effect of allowing the invalid labor theory of value to exercise some influence over economic decision-making; (2) the central planning system; (3) arbitrary and unresponsive price system; (4) inappropriate managerial success criteria; (5) the agriculture sector; (6) the pursuit of economic autarky; (7) the substitution of planners' for household preferences. Bergson is typical in placing the planning system near the top of the list. The classic works delineating the adverse effects of the Soviet planning mechanism on managerial flexibility and initiative are those of Joseph Berliner (*Factory and Manager in the U.S.S.R.*, 1957) and David Granick (*Management of the Industrial Firm in the U.S.S.R.*, 1954; *The Red Executive*, 1960). In a more recent contribution (*Job Rights in the Soviet Union: Their Consequences*, 1987), David Granick argues that an even greater problem for the Soviet economic system than planning and wage egalitarianism is excessive job security. One of the more serious lacunae in the economic theory of labor supply is that while almost everyone recognizes that in the real world the possibility of dismissal for inadequate performance of work is a very important incentive to effort, there is no important body of known theory that addresses this particular incentive.

5

THE SAVING ISSUE

A. INTRODUCTION AND OVERVIEW

As a justification for capital property income, the return to saving argument has certain advantages and disadvantages relative to the return to capital management argument. Perhaps its strongest advantage is that it is not in such direct conflict with intuition and common sense. For natural purposes of psychological self-esteem, capital owners want to believe that they are entitled, on both economic and moral grounds, to the capital property income which they receive. But the great majority of capital owners in the contemporary capitalist real world are no doubt quite well aware of the fact that they do not actually earn the capital property income which they receive via capital management effort of any meaningful sort. They do not personally administer or supervise the business enterprises and government agencies which pay them property return, nor do they typically expend much time and effort in selecting their investments.

On the other hand, by saving and investing some of their income rather than spending it all on current consumption, they are rendering a service to society by making available funds for investment or consumption loans to others. Providing this service is not devoid of apparent costs to the saver. There are always many attractive options for spending money which has been saved. Also there is always some degree of risk in saving: The assets representing the saving may decline in value, or the saver may die before having a chance to realize their value in consumption. Meanwhile, the immense value to society of savings resources with which to support capital investment can hardly be doubted by any sensible person: Plant and machinery obviously constitute the essential foundation on which our prosperity rests. Therefore it is very easy to persuade capital owners—whether they be rich, poor, or anything in between—that the capital property income which they receive represents a legitimate earned return to saving.

One significant disadvantage of the return to saving justification is that it obviously does not apply to natural resources. Human owners of natural resources receive property income no less than human owners of produced capital such as plant and machinery. Clearly the natural resources did not come about through the "saving sacrifices" of their human owners. The fact that the return to saving justification clearly does not apply to a major component of property income raises suspicions that it is generally invalid. Another disadvantage is that the subjective "sacrifices of saving" are much less onerous for wealthy capitalists who enjoy extravagant living standards than they are for noncapitalists of modest means—and yet a very large proportion of capital property return under modern capitalism goes to individuals at the high end of the wealth spectrum. Clearly the relationship between the intensity of saving sacrifices and the property income reward for these sacrifices is rather tenuous.

But no doubt the foremost disadvantage of the return to saving line is that it does not stand up very well to careful reflection, whether that reflection be in terms of informal observation and reasoning, or in terms of formal economic theory and econometric investigation. The fact is that the return to saving justification for capital property income depends on not one but two extremely problematic propositions: (1) the supply of private saving is positively related to the rate of property return (i.e., the rate of interest); (2) public intervention in total saving through the provision of public saving to supplement private saving would generate significant inefficiency.

The pragmatic market socialist proposal envisions the termination of real interest income on savings deposits and similar assets on the basis of the same judgment which justifies the termination of dividend and capital gains income on stock shares. The return to saving justification for interest income is regarded as a no less specious pretense than the return to capital management justification for dividend and capital gains income. Interest income and dividend/capital gains income are perceived as merely superficially distinct components of the same basic flow of property return. The pragmatic market socialist proposal encompasses a Bureau of Public Ownership (BPO) which would actively enforce a profit maximization incentive in the publicly owned business enterprise sector, thus providing a substitute for the capital management effort allegedly provided by private capital owners under capitalism. It cannot be predicted in advance whether the termination of property return on privately owned financial asset accumulations would appreciably decrease the flow of voluntary saving by private households, and thus require a substantial allocation to business capital investment out of general government revenues. But even if such an allocation becomes necessary, no special institutions need be established to accommodate this need. An auxiliary proposal described earlier would establish a National Investment Banking System (NIBS) and a National Entrepreneurial Investment Board (NEIB) financed directly from a national government appropriation. But this proposal is not part of the core pragmatic market socialist proposal. In the absence of an NIBS and NEIB, the national government treasury would simply deposit the business capital investment appropriation in existing business sector financial intermediaries under BPO ownership.

The argument that failure to pay property return on personally owned accumulations of financial assets would, through its effect on saving, have an appreciable adverse effect on social welfare, may be classified into a crude version and a sophisticated version. Both versions agree that the rate of property return (often termed, more restrictively, the "rate of interest") has a strong positive impact on private saving. Such an impact is consistent with the proposition that saving involves disutility and the rate of property return counterbalances this disutility. Thus (according to the argument) if socialism were to deny property income to private savers, private saving would decline quite drastically.

At this point the two versions diverge. According to the crude version, the decline in personal saving would lead directly to a severe shortage of investment funds for capital maintenance and expansion. The economy would quickly become capital-starved, and economic production would plunge. The sophisticated version stipulates that a rational society would probably not allow the capital starvation envisioned in the crude version to transpire, but would probably fill in the gap produced by the decrease in private saving with an equivalent increase in public saving.

But this would shift the determination of the total saving rate from the realm of private choice to the realm of public choice. Even if it were granted that public saving resources would be allocated to business enterprises in a competitive and commercial manner, it could still be held that the simple fact that the total saving rate was determined by the government would probably entail a nonoptimal total saving rate in an economic welfare sense. It could be held that an efficient aggregate saving rate is that rate generated by fulfillment of the microeconomic efficient saving condition: that the disutility of saving to each private household exactly equals the marginal productivity of capital investment to each business enterprise. If socialism abrogates interest payments on private savings accumulations, this equality would break down and the economy would be violating an important condition for microeconomic efficiency.

There are thus two basic questions to be considered. First, would the termination of property return payments to private savers result in a substantial decline in private saving? If the answer to the first question is presumed to be affirmative, then (and only then) it is necessary to address the second question: Would public determination of the total saving rate be appreciably less efficient than private determination? The first question is considered informally in the present section of this chapter; the following section presents a formal consideration of the economic theory of private household saving. Thus the first two sections demonstrate the dubiousness of an assumption that the supply curve of saving is upward-sloping with respect to the interest rate. The third section goes on to the second question. Presuming that there *is* in fact an upward-sloping supply curve of saving, and that consequently there is a significant reduction in private saving under pragmatic market socialism (because of the reduction of the real rate of interest to zero), how likely is it that the government intervention in saving which would become necessary would be significantly detrimental to economic performance? It will be argued in the third section that there are no convincing grounds for assuming that this intervention would generate serious economic performance problems.

In assessing the potential impact on saving of the abrogation under pragmatic market socialism of real interest payments on private savings accumulations, it is first of all important to be aware of how private household saving fits into the overall saving picture. There are actually three distinct sources of saving resources for use in capital investment: private household saving, business saving, and government saving. Although the emphasis herein will be on potential changes in private household saving and government saving, the fact is that a substantial part of capital invest-ment by business firms under modern capitalism is financed directly out of business saving (i.e., retained earnings). According to the basic principles of pragmatic market socialism, business executives would have exactly the same authority and motivations with respect to retained earnings as they do presently under capitalism. Under both economic systems, retained earn-ings reduce the current property return payout of the firm and hence endanger the current security of its executives, but at the same time they enhance the future property return payout of the firm and hence enhance the future security of its executives. In deciding on a level of retained earnings, executives endeavor to balance future security appropriately against present security. This decision process would be exactly the same under the two systems. Therefore the largest source of business capital investment expenditures—business saving rather than private household saving—would remain exactly the same under the two systems.

With respect to private household saving, it is impossible to predict whether it would be lower under pragmatic market socialism than it is under capitalism, or the reverse. It is elementary common sense to be prepared for the worst. The basic pragmatic market socialist proposal therefore envisions the formal establishment of national government responsibility for the level of overall saving through a regular annual appropriation out of tax revenue for business physical capital investment. This would be done purely as a precautionary measure: If private household saving does *not* decline substantially under pragmatic market socialism, then this national government appropriation to business physical capital investment need not be very large.

As to private household saving, there are two key aspects of the core pragmatic market socialist proposal which would tend to mitigate the impact of the transition. These are the two proposed exceptions to the general rule prohibiting the payment of interest (or other forms of property return) on private savings accumulations: (1) interest payments compounded into personal pension fund accumulations; (2) inflation-neutralizing interest payments by financial intermediaries. Currently under capitalism retirement income plans offered by pension funds and insurance companies typically involve compounded interest. Such plans would be available on exactly the same terms under pragmatic market socialism. Therefore that important component of private household saving which represents provision for retirement income (that is, pure life cycle saving) would be entirely unaffected by a transition from capitalism to pragmatic market socialism. In fact, the only component of private household saving that might be strongly affected would be the relatively minor "discretionary saving" component. Under the second exception, banks and other financial intermediaries holding time deposits or savings deposits of private households would be required by law to pay an interest rate on these deposits equal to the current national rate of inflation. The intention of pragmatic market socialism is to equate the net rate of interest on personally held financial assets to zero, but if no provision were made for inflation, the actual net rate would be negative. The idea is to eliminate the overall inflation rate as a consideration in the household's saving decision. Thus under pragmatic market socialism individuals would not refrain from saving on grounds that "without interest, inflation just eats up the savings."

The justification of property income as a return to saving, no less than its justification as a return to capital management, has a long history dating back to the early nineteenth century. Nassau Senior first elaborated the idea formally in the economic literature, using the famous term "abstinence" to specify that contribution made by savers which is rewarded by interest income. In one of the more vigorous and effective passages in *Das Kapital*, Karl Marx ridiculed Senior's abstinence theory as both illogical (because abstinence, per se, is unproductive) and absurd (since much, if not most, saving is done by wealthy capitalists who engage in extravagant personal consumption).[1] Late in the nineteenth century, the Austrian economist Eugen von Böhm-Bawerk, in response to Marx's critique of Senior, replaced the dubious "abstinence" terminology with the more neutral-sounding "time preference" terminology which is utilized today. However, aside from terminology, there is little practical difference between Senior and Böhm-Bawerk: Both argue that the payment of interest on savings accumulations is necessary to elicit such accumulations. The concept of time preference, invented by Böhm-Bawerk for use in capitalist apologetics, is today regularly applied in technical economics in the discounting of future consumption or utility in dynamic optimal saving studies. But it is used in these studies in a conventional and formalistic manner, and it is no doubt safe to say that the vast majority of economists who have contributed to this literature have never devoted any serious thought to the reasonableness of the time preference assumption.

The time preference proposition is that a certain consumption experience or level of consumption at the present time is invariably preferred to the same consumption experience or level of consumption at some future time. Clearly the proposition possesses a certain amount of intuitive plausibility. First, any saver, whether rich or poor, is constantly beset with temptations to spend his or her accumulation of savings. Second, in a capitalist economy in which private individuals may receive an interest return on accumulations of money, a sum of money now will invariably be preferred to the same sum of money later. However, the fact remains that these indisputable realities do not by themselves constitute a compelling case for the validity of time preference, as the concept is applied both in capitalist apologetics and in technical economics.

First, by adding to or retaining a certain accumulation of savings, a saver is in effect purchasing higher current utility from such goods as anticipated future consumption (particularly during the retirement years), personal financial security against adverse developments (loss of job, illness, etc.), and enhanced financial flexibility with which to take advantage of unexpected consumption opportunities which may arise in the future. In other words, there are several important motivations to save aside from augmented future consumption through the realization of interest income on savings. These motivations arguably provide an economically and morally sufficient reward for saving, so that an additional interest reward is not needed.

Second, the fact that money now is always preferred to money later does not necessarily imply that consumption now is always preferred to consumption later. Money is external to the individual, and unlimited amounts of it may be held in bank accounts without imposing any physical strain on the individual. Consumption, on the other hand, is often a directly physiological process (as in eating and drinking); and it always entails at least some degree of physiological involvement—even goods not intended for current use must be shopped for and stored. Economists like to speak of "unlimited wants," and it is certainly true that given sufficient time and financial opportunity, human individuals have shown themselves capable of prodigious feats of consumption. But such feats are not accomplished instantaneously; typically they are spread out over a long period of time. At a single moment in time, there appear to be definite limitations on what can be reasonably consumed, so that the "invariable" preference of current over future consumption is not to be lightly assumed.

Apart from the direct appeals to intuition mentioned above, not a great deal has been offered in its defense over the lengthy career of the time preference proposition. Proponents of time preference seem little disposed to attribute much importance to what is probably the most commonsensically acceptable basis for time preference: the possibility of death. Quite possibly this is the unconscious result of the important role of the time preference concept in providing an ideological justification for interest income. If the main reason for interest in the real world is time preference among elderly capitalists owing to the proximity of death, then it would be apparent that interest received by nonelderly capitalists is in the nature of a Ricardian rent: a producer's surplus, an unearned return. But if it is proposed that time preference applies equally at all ages, then interest return becomes a legitimate earned return at all ages.

As a rule, contemporary economists have little to say about time preference, either pro or con. An important exception to this rule is a 1981 article by Mancur Olson and Martin J. Bailey in which they claim that the case for positive time preference is "absolutely compelling." The essence of their argument is that in the absence of positive time preference, the optimal lifetime consumption of the representative individual, owing to the availability of interest on savings accumulations, would consist of extreme abstemiousness in the youthful years, rising gradually to prodigious consumption in the elderly years. Clearly this is not the typical pattern in the real world, ergo (conclude Olson and Bailey) the existence of positive time preference is proved. But in fact there are a number of plausible alternatives to positive time preference in explaining relatively stable lifetime consumption in the real world: relatively low intertemporal elasticity of substitution, relatively high psychological subsistence consumption, recalculation in each period of optimal consumption over the remaining lifespan, uncertainty concerning the future, discontinuities in the lifetime budget constraint, asymptotic upper limits on instantaneous utility, bequest motives, and so on.[2] Therefore the evidence offered by Olson and Bailey in support of positive time preference is in fact far short of "absolutely compelling," and their use of this particular phrase constitutes a gross overstatement.

When arguing at the level of casual empiricism, apologists for capitalism developing the return to saving justification for property income customarily make reference to the time preference of the individual which makes saving inherently sacrificial, and to the risk-taking which saving entails, particularly when the savings are put into investment assets. But the sacrifice of present consumption in the act of saving is balanced by a gain in future consumption. And the risk of depreciating financial assets is balanced by the greater security in confronting an uncertain future enjoyed by an individual who possesses financial assets. These considerations suggest that the gains and losses in saving might balance out fairly closely even in the absence of a property income return on savings accumulations—that is, that the abrogation of property income under pragmatic market socialism would have relatively little impact on the saving decisions of private households.

The issue of the presence or absence of a positive rate of time preference relates to the subjective evaluation of the ethical legitimacy of interest payments on savings accumulations. To the extent that savers are undergoing psychological stress owing to their fending off insistent time preference, we deem the interest reward to be ethically acceptable. But from a strictly logical point of view, time preference is not the essential question. A logically more important question is whether the abrogation of interest payments on private savings accumulations would reduce the rate of private saving. Contrary to widespread misapprehension a positive rate of time preference by no means guarantees an upward-sloping supply curve of private saving with respect to the interest rate. A still more logically important question is whether the aggregate saving rate determined under pragmatic market socialism, comprising public as well as private saving, would over the long term generate more or less social welfare than the saving rate currently holding under capitalism—keeping in mind that the social welfare level is determined by many other things beside the aggregate saving rate (such as the distribution of property return).

With respect to the first question above, casual empiricism at the household level suggests that the rate of property return is not an important determinant of private saving. The primary motivations for saving, as far as conscious awareness is concerned, include provision for old age, emergencies caused by illness or injury, children's education, and the acquisition of expensive consumer goods. Surveys indicate that even very wealthy respondents list these as the primary reasons for saving, and not the accumulation of a source of property income.[3] The minimal impact of the interest rate on saving decisions of households is intuitively apparent whether the households are only moderately prosperous or are very wealthy. In the case of small-scale savers, the tiny amount of property income received on their modest financial accumulations is too negligible to play a significant role in their calculations. As for wealthy capitalists, they already receive adequate property income—on the savings accumulations of their ancestors which they have inherited—so there is no need to save a great deal from their current income.

Therefore, we observe that people—whether rich or poor—do *not* consult current interest rates when making saving decisions. We observe that much saving is in the form of long-term contractual obligations which are often proportional to current income (e.g., insurance premiums, pension contributions). We observe that noncontractual, discretionary saving is normally governed by crude rules of thumb which are unrelated to the current rate of interest. The foremost economic authority of the twentieth century, John Maynard Keynes, looked at this kind of evidence and concluded that it is practically self-evident that income is the dominant determinant of saving, and that the effect of the interest rate is more or less negligible. Another input to Keynes's judgment on this question is the conventional economic theory of private household saving, which provides scant grounds for an assumption that the interest rate has a significant positive effect on private saving.

B. THEORETICAL ANALYSIS OF PRIVATE SAVING

Turning to the economic theory of private household saving, the first and foremost point to be made is that the presumption of an upward-sloping supply curve of saving with respect to the interest rate, a presumption made by Eugen von Böhm-Bawerk and other nineteenth-century classical economists and by their contemporary counterparts, blithely ignores the income effect of a change in the interest rate. One might well ask how such an elementary oversight is possible. Of course there is the role of ideological preconception: Capitalism is (supposedly) good, and a positive interest elasticity of saving (supposedly) helps to justify capitalism. But aside from the ideological factor, there may be a certain amount of honest confusion about elementary economic theory. Some economists may subconsciously imagine that since the demand curves of households for consumption goods are most probably downward-sloping, then the supply curves of households of primary factors (labor and saving) are most probably upward-sloping. Such an expectation would, however, be an unwarranted generalization.

The proposition that household demand curves are downward-sloping is supported both by introspection (a form of casual empiricism) and by the standard theoretical assumptions. Introspection tells consumers that if the prices of many, if not most, of the goods that they buy were substantially lower, they would buy more of them. Standard theory indicates that the two separate effects of a price change, the income effect and the substitution effect, will support one another for a superior consumption good—and most consumption goods seem to be superior. As for the few inferior goods, it would be necessary for one of them to be unrealistically important in the expenditures of the consumer for the income effect to outweigh the substitution effect sufficiently to produce an upward-sloping demand curve for that consumption commodity.

But the story is completely different with respect to primary factors of production. Given that leisure is a superior good, the income effect of a wage change *conflicts* with the substitution effect, and it can only be an unsubstantiated assumption that the substitution effect dominates the income effect to make the supply curve of labor upward-sloping. And given that future consumption (or possibly "expected future consumption" or "future security") is a superior good, the income effect of a change in the rate of property return *conflicts* with the substitution effect, and it can only be an unsubstantiated assumption that the substitution effect dominates the income effect to make the supply curve of saving upward-sloping. This theoretical ambiguity is reflected in introspective ambiguity. Not many individuals can respond truthfully and confidently in the affirmative that if their rate of labor remuneration rises, they will increase their labor time and/or intensity, or that if the rate of property return increases, they will increase their rate of saving.

Theoretical approaches to saving, as usual, yield insights rather than conclusions. The standard textbook neoclassical economic model of the private saving-consumption decision is a two-period model in which first-period saving yields an interest income which is added to available income in the second period.[4] The model proposes that in choosing a level of saving, the household is endeavoring to maximize a utility function dependent on consumption in both periods. The saving problem may be stated formally as follows:

maximize $u = u(c_1,c_2)$ with respect to c_1 and c_2

subject to the budget constraints:

$c_1 = y_1 + ra_o - s$ and $c_2 = y_2 + (1+r)(a_o+s)$

There are four parameters in the problem, as follows: (1) y_1 = period 1 income; (2) y_2 = period 2 income; (3) a_0 = initial assets; (4) r = interest rate. Similarly there are four variables in the problem as follows: (1) c_1 = period 1 consumption; (2) c_2 = period 2 consumption; (3) s = saving; (4) u = utility. Readers interested in the mathematical details of the analysis of this model are referred to Section B of the Analytical Appendix. At this point in the main text, the major implications of the analysis will be summarized in relatively informal terms.

The two constraints give, respectively, period 1 consumption c_1 and period 2 consumption c_2 in terms of saving s. If these constraints are substituted into the utility function, utility u is made a function of the single decision variable saving s. The first-order condition for the maximization of u with respect to s provides the basis for a comparative statics analysis of the effects of the four parameters (y_1, y_2, a_0, and r) on the equilibrium level of saving. Using the conventional economic assumptions concerning the utility function, we find that the effect of y_1 is unambiguously positive (an increase in period 1 income increases saving), while the effect of y_2 is unambiguously negative (an increase in period 2 income decreases saving). These results are obviously acceptable to commonsense intuition. Further analysis brings to light results that are perhaps less intuitively obvious. The effects of both initial assets a_0 and the interest rate r on saving are ambiguous in sign: It cannot be predicted on the basis of conventional theory whether increases in a_0 and r would increase or decrease saving. In both cases, there are two separate effects: One of these effects is analytically equivalent to an increase in y_1, and the other is analytically equivalent to an increase in y_2. The two effects are therefore in conflict with one another and the net effect is uncertain.

In the theoretical analysis of the capital management justification of property income presented above in Chapter 4, Section C, it was shown that a change in the retention coefficient α would have both an income effect and a substitution effect. The substitution effect would support the anti-socialist conclusion that the decrease in α under socialism would tend to decrease effort in capital management. The income effect, on the other hand, would support the pro-socialist conclusion that the decrease in α would tend to increase effort in capital management. An analogous situation applies to the two-period saving-consumption decision. A decrease in the rate of property return r received by the representative saver would have both a substitution effect and an income effect. The interest rate r may be interpreted as the price of future consumption (period 2 consumption) in terms of present consumption (period 1 consumption). A decrease in the interest rate lowers the price of future consumption in terms of present consumption and induces the individual to "buy" more present consumption (i.e., reduce saving). But the interest rate may also be interpreted in terms of the income which it produces in the future. Therefore a decrease in the rate of interest would reduce the amount of present consumption which the individual can "afford" (i.e., increase saving).

Both the jargon and the logic of this interpretation of an interest rate decline are rather convoluted and unnatural (which is of course typical of economic theory)—but the implications for our present purposes are straightforward enough. The substitution effect tends to support the anti-socialist proposition that the decrease in the interest rate would decrease personal saving. The income effect, on the other hand, tends to support the pro-socialist proposition that the decrease would tend to increase personal saving. Which effect—if either—dominates in reality is an empirical question and not a theoretical question.

An explicit function version of this model is obtained by using the widely applied Constant Elasticity of Substitution (CES) form for the utility function:

$$u = u(c_1, c_2) = \left[v c_1^{-\rho} + (1-v)c_2^{-\rho} \right]^{-1/\rho}$$

where the two new parameters added to the model are: (1) v = relative preference coefficient: period 1 versus period 2 consumption; (2) σ = elasticity of substitution between period 1 and period 2 consumption ($\sigma = 1/(1+\rho)$). This explicit mathematical specification of the utility function enables the derivation of an explicit supply function of saving. This function may be used to verify the comparative statics results obtained from the general function version of the model, and also to obtain additional results pertaining to this special case.

Among these additional results is the important role of the elasticity of substitution σ in determining the relationship between the interest rate and the private household saving level. In particular, the lower is this elasticity (i.e., the lower the degree of substitutability between consumption at different points in time), the greater the likelihood that the income effect dominates the substitution effect and that the relationship between the interest rate and the level of saving is negative. Although it must be conceded that the basic conceptual issue is somewhat nebulous, certainly it is not severely contradictory to intuition that the level of intertemporal consumption elasticity is rather low. Imagine, for example, an individual who possesses enough food to last comfortably for seven days—there would be no question of starvation, enforced weight loss, or anything of that sort. It seems reasonable that the individual would plan his or her consumption of the food so that it is consumed more or less evenly throughout the seven days. That is, the person probably would not binge for two or three days in the knowledge that severe hunger would ensue later on, nor would the person be likely to undergo severe hunger for two or three days in order to binge later on. This example may suggest to some that the intertemporal elasticity of substitution is generally low in the real world; to others it may suggest no such thing.[5]

No doubt the safest conclusion to be drawn from the two-period model of saving is that the impact of the interest rate on private household saving is a complicated question. It is sufficiently complicated even within the context of a very elementary economic model of saving. The two-period model of saving applied here is standard textbook material in economics. It is sometimes the case that textbook economics and applied professional economics diverge. Oddly enough, the divergence is not always in the expected direction of more complicated models being used in applied professional economics than in pedagogic economics.

For example, a great deal of contemporary work on saving examines "life cycle saving": saving which is undertaken over a working career of approximately thirty-five years to support consumption over a retirement period of approximately fifteen years. The fact that fifty periods are involved instead of the two periods of the textbook model naturally tends to inject a great deal more complexity into the mathematical analysis. One frequent response to this added complexity has been the adoption of a simplifying special case in which utility received in any period is assumed "separable" from utility received in any other period. Separable utility functions implicitly incorporate the assumption of infinite elasticity of intertemporal consumption. The two-period model using the CES utility function considered herein indicates that the effect of interest rate on saving will be positive so long as the elasticity of substitution is merely greater than 1—let alone being equal to infinity. Therefore it is not surprising that many of the current simulation studies on saving show a positive interest elasticity of saving. But no doubt many, if not most, of the economists working in this area would concede, if questioned on the matter, that the assumption of a separable utility function is based far more on the need for analytical tractability than it is on the inherent plausibility of infinite intertemporal elasticity of substitution.

To some analysts it has been obvious for quite a while that inequality in wealth ownership generally, and inequality in capital wealth ownership particularly, is too extreme to be importantly attributable to life cycle saving (accumulation of savings solely to provide retirement income). To these same analysts it has also been obvious that inheritance plays an extremely important role in the inequality of wealth ownership, and particularly of capital wealth ownership. Other analysts have until fairly recently tended to resist these implications, possibly since they were subconsciously regarded as subversive to the capitalistic status quo. But perhaps the capitalistic status quo now seems so completely impregnable as to render former qualms obsolete. Or perhaps it is simply a matter of the orderly advance of scientific knowledge. In any event, the minor role of life cycle saving and the major role of inheritance in generating capital wealth inequality is now far more openly acknowledged among the authorities than was formerly the case. At the present moment, therefore, the intertemporal utility functions used in the study of saving typically include a bequest motive. According to the theory, the typical household derives part of its utility from passing along financial assets to the next generation, and this is an important motivation to saving.

It is predictable that some economists will discern in bequest motives yet another objection to pragmatic market socialism. Given that a major motivation to saving is the provision of bequests to heirs, if pragmatic market socialism prohibits such bequests, this motivation to saving would be abrogated and saving would plummet. This particular objection is based on the faulty premise that pragmatic market socialism would either prohibit bequests or at least tax them at a virtually confiscatory level. There is nothing in the core pragmatic market socialist proposal against bequests and inheritances per se. The proposal aims at the elimination of property income on financial asset accumulations, but it is not necessarily opposed to the transfer of such accumulations between generations. If there were no property income on assets, then a $1 million inheritance would represent exactly $1 million worth of purchasing power—it would not represent a virtually perpetual source of capital property income stretching into the remote future. Assuming, therefore, that the pragmatic market socialist system allows for bequests and inheritances, the issue of saving, and in particular the issue of the potential effect on saving of reducing the real rate of interest to zero, would be the same as before. Whether the objective of saving is to provide for the individual's own future consumption or to provide for the enhanced consumption of that individual's heirs after his/her death, the reduction of the interest rate to zero would have both a substitution effect and an income effect. Which effect would dominate is still an open question, a question which no doubt can be answered convincingly only by means of experimentation.

Another important postscript to this theoretical discussion is that the potential impact on private saving of the implementation of pragmatic market socialism is not confined to the reduction of the interest rate on financial asset accumulations to zero. It should always be kept in mind that pragmatic market socialism intends a *redistribution* of capital property return rather than the abolishment of capital property return. What this means is that while the private household would be deprived of capital property income, it would receive as replacement social dividend income. For the great majority of households, the amount of social dividend income gained would significantly exceed the amount of capital property income lost. While elementary economic theory is ambiguous about the effect of the interest rate on private saving, there is no such ambiguity concerning current income: An increase in current income will definitely increase saving. Therefore, even if there were a tendency toward reduced saving on account of the abolition of interest on savings, for most households this reduction could be more than offset by the increase in saving from increased income. The upshot of this is that even if there is positive interest elasticity of saving in the real world, this does not necessarily indicate that private household saving would be lower under pragmatic market socialism than it is under capitalism.

C. PUBLIC AND PRIVATE SAVING

No doubt the single most dramatic development in Western economics during the twentieth century was the Keynesian revolution from approximately 1940 to 1960, a development in intellectual history precipitated by the Great Depression in the real world. The Keynesian revolution called into serious question the laissez-faire prescription of classical economics, at least insofar as it applied to macroeconomic equilibrium. Despite the "revolution" terminology, the ultimate impact of Keynes's thought was conservative and preservative: The whole point of the exercise was that severe business depression is avoidable without adopting the socialist recommendation of abolishing the capitalist economic system. During the height of the Keynesian revolution, certain conventional propositions of "classical" (i.e., pre-Keynesian) economics fell into disrepute. But as soon as it became reasonably evident that the Keynesian viewpoint was sufficiently well established to render any future repetitions of the Great Depression experience very unlikely, a reaction set in against various alleged "excesses" of the Keynesian revolution—a reaction which restored some of the former credibility and acceptance of these classical propositions. Among the rehabilitated classical propositions is that of the upward-sloping supply curve of saving with respect to the interest rate.

Despite the earnest Keynes debunking put forth by the conservative wing of the economics profession over the last half-century, the median economist still holds John Maynard Keynes in very high esteem. Therefore Keynes's personal judgment that the impact of income on saving virtually swamps the impact of the interest rate on saving remains highly influential to the present day. Another reason for the continued influence of this judgment is that it is consistent with the implications forthcoming from the basic microeconomic theory of private household saving: that the impact of current income on saving is definitely positive, while the impact of the interest rate on saving is inherently ambiguous owing to conflicting substitution and income effects. Of course, ambiguous comparative statics results from theoretical models utilizing no more than such axiomatic principles as diminishing marginal utility are the rule rather than the exception. These ambiguities are supposed to be resolved by statistical (econometric) investigations. Unfortunately, the data, specification, and identification problems normally confronting econometric investigations are sufficiently formidable that the results of such investigations possess little force unless they are strongly supported by casual empiricism and common sense. Therefore, in practice econometric investigations rarely resolve theoretical ambiguities to any substantial extent.

The aggregate consumption function is an essential component of Keynes's macroeconomic theory, and throughout the Keynesian revolution one of the most important purposes of econometric research was the estimation of aggregate consumption functions. As saving is income less consumption, any factor which tends to increase (decrease) consumption will at the same time tend to decrease (increase) saving. Thus the intensive work on consumption during that period implicitly constituted work on saving. This was also the period which witnessed the birth and rapid evolution of the large-scale macroeconomic model estimated by econometric techniques. Invariably consumption functions formed an important component of such models. Generally speaking, econometric work on consumption functions done from the 1940s through the 1960s, whether concerned solely with consumption or as part of a larger macroeconomic model-building project, omitted the interest rate from the list of variables included as determinants of consumption (and by implication saving), on the basis of the widespread consensus—based on Keynes—that the interest rate is an unimportant determinant of consumption and saving.[5]

The situation changed as the conservative counterrevolution made substantial inroads against the Keynesian revolution of 1940-1960. Now more often than not econometrically estimated consumption functions (and saving functions) contain an interest rate variable. And more often than not the statistical indication is that the interest rate has a statistically significant positive effect on saving.[7] Does this evidence establish that there is an upward-sloping supply curve of saving in the real world? Any knowledge-able econometrician will attest that although this evidence is consistent with the hypothesis of an upward-sloping supply curve of saving, it does not establish the hypothesis to any high degree of certitude. The estimation of static, microeconomic, cross-section relationships from dynamic, macro-economic, time series data is inherently problematic. This is particularly the case owing to the pro-cyclical movements of interest rates and saving rates. These movements create a difficult identification problem for econometric estimation. Contemporary econometric methodology consists mostly of various elaborations on ordinary least squares estimation, and it is well recognized by most practitioners that ordinary least squares merely iden-tifies statistical associations among variables—and that such associations may have little or no causative significance. Therefore the finding of positive statistical associations between interest rates and saving rates in macroeconomic data in and of itself provides only very modest support for the hypothesis that a decrease in the interest rate will *cause* a decrease in private household saving.

However, it is clearly necessary for intelligent advocates of socialism to admit that the prevailing uncertainty about the effect of the rate of property return on private saving does not add up to the proposition that the termina-tion of interest payments to private savers under pragmatic market socialism would not substantially reduce private saving. It is certainly within the realm of possibility that the interest elasticity of private saving is indeed positive and numerically appreciable. If this turned out to be the case, social saving out of tax revenue would have to be undertaken to replace the private saving lost because of the abolition of interest payments on private savings. While the government would endeavor (implicitly rather than explicitly) to match the marginal disutility to the representative taxpayer of paying taxes ear-marked for business capital investment to the marginal productivity of capital investment to the representative business enterprise, it would doubt-lessly be true that the marginal disutility of paying these taxes to each and every taxpayer would not be equal to the marginal productivity of capital investment to each and every business enterprise.

In assessing this problem, it is important to be clear about its limits. A conventional criticism of socialism is that it would politicize and/or bureaucratize all manner of economic decision-making, including that pertaining to investment. This conventional criticism is blunted by the institutional proposal of pragmatic market socialism. Pragmatic market socialism would reproduce the commercial motivations and market forces currently operative under capitalism, including those pertaining to investment. That is, government savings would be put into deposits with investment banks operating under the standard profit motivation of the business sector, or perhaps into national government investment agencies (the NIBS and the NEIB) whose motivation would be only slightly different from the standard motivation. These resources would therefore be lent out to the highest bidders among the business enterprises seeking investment capital. The question is therefore strictly confined to the potential consequences of public intervention in the determination of the *aggregate saving rate*—it does not involve inefficiencies in the way that saving rate is converted into capital investment. Under capitalism, so it could be argued by its supporters, the marginal disutility of saving is equated to the uniform interest rate by utility-maximizing individuals, while at the same time the marginal productivity of capital investment is equated to the uniform interest rate by profit-maximizing business enterprises. Thus the marginal disutility of saving is equated to the marginal productivity of investment over all individuals and firms. This is the same marginal-benefit-equals-marginal-cost condition which must hold for every commodity (saving resources being a commodity) in order to achieve Pareto optimality.[8]

The counterargument to this objection to pragmatic market socialism is that failure to meet this alleged microeconomic efficient saving condition would be unimportant in a practical sense. The counterargument relies on the dubiousness of the condition itself and the apparent absence of its fulfillment under capitalism—together with the consensus that regardless of this absence, capitalism is maintaining an adequate (or workable) level of efficiency. It would probably be naive to suppose that *either* contemporary capitalism or pragmatic market socialism could achieve the true conditions for the maximization of *either* physical output or social welfare. In all probability, the simple equations (such as $MC = p$) which are frequently represented in economics textbooks as being first-order maximization conditions for these things are meaningless for practical purposes. This is because of the probable abundant presence in the real world of three critical factors: (1) external effects in both production and consumption; (2) imperfect competition; (3) distortive taxation and regulation.

The proposition that utility maximization by individuals and profit maximization by firms will result in an optimal condition depends critically on an absence of all three of the above factors. Mathematical demonstrations of the invisible hand proposition have a reassuringly scientific air about them, and they are certainly useful as training exercises and as stepping-stones to what will be, it is hoped, a more satisfactory body of economic theory in the future. But to take such demonstrations seriously as guides to proper social policy—particularly when they clash strongly with a common-sensical appreciation of real-world affairs—would represent dubious rationality indeed. Also, it is perhaps significant that the microeconomic efficient saving condition has not yet been convincingly linked up with the optimal saving rates developed by the extensive optimal growth literature based on aggregate models of the economy. At this point, it is not at all clear that the optimal growth rates proposed by this literature would be achieved by an economy which leaves the aggregate saving rate entirely to private determination.[9]

There is a rather striking episode in the intellectual history of market socialism that clearly demonstrates the frequent indifference of economists to the efficiency principles which they themselves propound—when it comes to making practical policy judgments. The reference is to the manner in which the economics profession casually shrugged off the Langian market socialist proposal. As the only indubitable price-takers in the modern economy are small-scale independent farmers, it seems self-evident that some sort of oligopolistic or imperfect competition theory would apply more accurately to the large corporations which dominate contemporary economic life than would the perfect competition theory. Yet only under perfect competition would profit maximization lead to satisfaction of the Pareto-Hotelling $MC = p$ efficiency condition. It is therefore very plausible that this efficiency condition is *not* satisfied in the real world, and that the real-world economy suffers whatever economic efficiency losses are caused by this. Lange proposed that under market socialism firms be required to produce according to $MC = p$, thus removing these efficiency losses. The proposal is generally regarded by economists as impractical on the grounds that the "monitoring costs" to get the firms to set $MC = p$ would be excessive. But on what basis is it judged that the monitoring costs of enforcing $MC = p$ would be greater than the efficiency gains from having the rule fulfilled? Clearly not on grounds of the elegance of the theoretical considerations. After all, there is no worthwhile theory of monitoring costs (at least no widely recognized theory), while the Pareto-Hotelling $MC = p$ rule is backed up by a chapter full of handsome equations which have been diligently studied by generations of theoretical economists. But all this elaborate Pareto-Hotelling theoretical baggage was simply shrugged off, as common sense ruled the monitoring costs to be the more important factor. The weight of common sense was greater than that of a superficially imposing theoretical edifice.

This should also be the case with respect to the microeconomic efficient saving condition. First, there is no good reason to suppose that the condition is a worthwhile approximation of a true efficiency condition, as the external effects of the private saving decision—which may well be significant—are ignored. Second, the condition clearly does not hold at present in the real world because of the effect of taxation, and yet the real-world economies in such nations as the United States seem to be doing quite well. Finally, the condition simply ignores the equity consideration: It defies common sense to propose that society continue to put up with wealthy capitalists maintaining luxurious lifestyles by means of the disproportionate share of property return they receive on inherited capital fortunes, simply to support a dubious efficiency principle derived from a drastically simplified model of economic reality. The equity consideration will be considered further in Chapter 7 below on the "people's capitalism" defense of capitalism. Evidence will be presented to the effect that approximately 94 percent of the U.S. population would receive more social dividend income if property return were distributed as a social dividend supplement to earned labor income under pragmatic market socialism, than they currently receive under the present capitalist system in which property return is distributed to individuals in proportion to personally owned capital wealth (i.e., savings accumulations). Given the feeble and uncompelling nature of the microeconomic efficient saving condition, it does not constitute a serious counterweight against this significant equity advantage.[10]

The efficient saving condition is a concept rather equivalent to marginal cost pricing and lump sum taxation. Lump sum taxation obviously does not exist in the real world, and many economists would grant that given the apparent prevalence of imperfect competition, marginal cost pricing may not be very applicable to the real world either. And yet, the real-world economies of advanced nations such as the United States seem to perform quite impressively. While the theoretical cases for lump sum taxation and marginal cost pricing are clear enough, even theoretical economists entertain serious doubts as to the practical significance of their presence or absence in the real-world economy. Such commonsensical doubts have received a certain amount of empirical support—for example, in the form of findings by Arnold Harberger (1954) and others that the "costs of monopoly" are numerically minimal. Such doubts may well also legitimately apply to the importance of the microeconomic efficient saving condition.

It is definitely part of the core pragmatic market socialist proposal that aggregate saving and capital investment be not less than they are at present under capitalism. Thus, if private household saving were to decline as a result of the termination of interest payments on savings accumulations, the slack would most definitely be taken up by public saving out of tax revenue. Under contemporary capitalism, the practical upshot of the elaborate theoretical paraphernalia of "efficient microeconomic saving" is simply the allegation by conservative economists that saving is too low because taxation of property income discourages it. Certainly no economist who invokes the idea does so with the intention of arguing that saving is too high. Therefore the true argument against pragmatic market socialism embodied in the microeconomic efficient saving idea is simply that saving would be lower under pragmatic market socialism than it is under capitalism. But this argument conflicts with the basic nature of the pragmatic market socialist proposal, and therefore it can possess genuine merit only to someone who simply assumes that pragmatic market socialism, as described in this book, is inherently impossible.

It will be argued in Chapter 6 that, if anything, pragmatic market socialism would probably maintain a *higher* rate of capital investment than is currently maintained under capitalism. As for those who currently invoke the notion of microeconomic efficiency in saving as a means of trying to influence public policy in the direction of lower taxes on property income for the avowed purpose of increasing saving and investment, these individuals ought to recognize in pragmatic market socialism a potential instrument toward their avowed purpose.

NOTES

1. Karl Marx castigated Nassau Senior bitterly in *Das Kapital*, Volume I, Chapter XXIV, Section 3: "The hour of vulgar economy had struck. Exactly a year before Nassau W. Senior had discovered at Manchester, that the profit (including interest) of capital is the product of the last hour of the twelve [a reference to Senior's unpersuasive 'last hour' argument], he had announced to the world another discovery. 'I substitute,' he proudly says, 'for the word capital, considered as an instrument of production, the word abstinence.' An unparalleled sample this, of the discoveries of vulgar economy! It substitutes for an economic category, a sycophantic phrase—that's all there is to it... All the conditions for carrying on the labor-process are suddenly converted into so many acts of abstinence on the part of the capitalist. If the corn is not all eaten, but part of it also sown: abstinence of the capitalist. If the wine gets time to mature: abstinence of the capitalist. The capitalist robs his own self, whenever he 'lends' (!) the instruments of production to the laborer, that is, whenever by incorporating labor-power with them, he uses them to produce surplus-value out of labor-power, instead of eating them up, steam-engines, cotton, railways, manure, horses and all; or as the vulgar economist childishly puts it, instead of dissipating 'their value' in luxuries and other articles of consumption. How the capitalists as a class are to perform that feat, is a secret which vulgar economy has hitherto obstinately refused to divulge. Enough, that the world still jogs on, solely through the self-chastisement of this modern penitent of

Vishnu, the capitalist. Not only accumulation, but the simple 'conservation of a capital requires a constant effort to resist the temptation of consuming it.' The simple dictates of humanity therefore plainly enjoin the release of the capitalist from this martyrdom and temptation, in the same way that the Georgian slave-owner was lately delivered, by the abolition of slavery, from the painful dilemma, whether to squander the surplus-product, lashed out of his niggers, entirely in champagne, or whether to reconvert a part of it into more niggers and more land."

2. The first three of the mentioned alternatives to positive time preference as an explanation for relatively stable lifetime consumption are developed analytically by the author in a recent contribution (Yunker, *Journal of Post-Keynesian Economics*, 1992).

3. Examples include the following. In 1964, the annual *Survey of Consumer Finances* (done by the University of Michigan Survey Research Center) asked survey respondents: "In your case, what are the main purposes of saving?" For the highest income group ($10,000 or over in annual income), the most important responses were to provide for emergencies (39 percent), to provide for retirement (46 percent), and to provide for children's education (32 percent). The percentage of respondents referring to interest income was small enough to be lumped into the "other" category (15 percent). See George Katona et al. (1965, Table 7-1, p. 111). Also in 1964, the Survey Research Center carried out a special nationwide survey for the Brookings Institution of affluent households (income above $10,000 per annum), which asked essentially the same question on saving motivations. The percentage of respondents mentioning "To invest it; earn a return on it" is reported as 10 percent. See Robin Barlow et al. (1966, Appendix E, Section 1, p. 198).

4. This standard theory of household saving is covered in the majority of textbooks on intermediate and advanced microeconomic theory. Ten examples, arranged alphabetically by author, are as follows: (1) Edgar Browning and Jacqueline Browning (1986, Chapter 4, Section 5); (2) James Henderson and Richard Quandt (1980, Chapter 12, Section 2); (3) Jack Hirshleifer (1988, Chapter 14, Section A); (4) K. C. Kogiku (1971, Chapter 6, Section 2); (5) Heinz Kohler (1986, Chapter 15, section on "Households as Savers"); (6) P. R. G. Layard and A. A. Walters (1978, Chapter 12, Section 1); (7) Edwin Mansfield (1982, Chapter 18, Section 2); (8) Walter Nicholson (1985, Chapter 17); (9) Dominick Salvatore (1986, Chapter 16, Section 1); (10) Eric Solberg (1982, Chapter 11, Section II). Every one of these authors states that owing to opposed substitution and income effects of a change in the effective interest rate, the net effect of the effective interest rate on the supply of saving cannot be theoretically predicted, and several authors include a backward-bending supply curve of saving equivalent to the backward-bending supply curve of labor.

5. It is worth noting that there is a small literature on the direct estimation of the intertemporal elasticity of substitution between adjacent-period consumptions. In a 1983 *AER* article, Owen J. Evans cites six different estimates of this sort, four of which had been published and two of which were in working paper form at that time. All six indicate an intertemporal elasticity of substitution well under 1. Another significant indicator is that recent simulation work done by Laurence

Kotlikoff, probably the leading contemporary authority on the effect of taxation on saving, uses 0.25 for the baseline value of this coefficient (Kotlikoff, 1984, p. 1601).

6. The "classic" econometric models of the U.S. macroeconomy did not include the interest rate as a determinant of consumption and saving: the Klein-Goldberger model (Lawrence Klein and Arthur Goldberger, 1955), the Brookings model (James Duesenberry et al., 1965), and the Wharton Econometric Forecasting Unit model (Michael Evans and Lawrence Klein, 1967). Some of the more recent models do include the interest rate: for example, FairModel. Ray C. Fair's short-run forecasting model was initially published in 1971, and it has become particularly important over the last several years owing to the application of its current version (dating from 1976) as a microcomputer teaching aid for use in courses in macro-economic theory, econometrics, and so on. The model listing in a recent edition of the student workbook (Blackburn and Case, 1985, pp. 157-178) shows a short-term interest rate used as an explanatory variable for consumer expenditures on both services (equation 1) and nondurable goods (equation 2). In these equations, the coefficients of the interest rate variable are significantly negative, consistent with Boskin (1978). At this point, econometric models of the U.S. macroeconomy are somewhat passé as a research topic, which means that few of the newer models are published in the professional literature. Thus it would be difficult to say what proportion of the total number of econometric models currently in use do utilize an interest rate in the consumption/saving equations, and what proportion do not.

7. Possibly the first serious econometric evidence that there is an appreciable positive interest elasticity of saving (i.e., that the substitution effect outweighs the income effect) was provided by Colin Wright in an *American Economic Review* note published in 1967. Wright followed up in 1969 with a more comprehensive investigation, which reached the same conclusion. Warren Weber, in papers also published in the *American Economic Review* (1970, 1975), presented serious econometric evidence pointing to the opposite conclusion: that in fact the interest elasticity of saving is negative (i.e., that the income effect outweighs the substitu-tion effect). In 1978 Michael Boskin published an influential paper in the *Journal of Political Economy* that supported Wright's conclusion over that of Weber: that is, that the substitution effect dominates the income effect and the interest elasticity of saving is positive. Boskin's results were immediately challenged by Philip Howrey and Saul Hymans (1978), who argued not only that the Boskin results were not robust against minor specification changes, but also that if saving is measured by a method designed to isolate that part of household saving available for capital investment, no effect of the interest rate on saving is found. Nevertheless, Boskin's article might be considered a turning point, as evidenced by the fact that in a 1980 survey article by Paul Wachtel, Weber's results showing a negative interest elas-ticity of saving are described as a "curious exception." But in this same survey article, Wachtel reaches basically agnostic conclusions (1980, p. 163): "The con-clusion that emerges is that saving may or may not be sensitive to real interest rates and that it probably is positively related to nominal interest rates on saving. Since the effect of inflation on real returns is also ambiguous, no conclusion can be reached on that issue. Inflation does increase nominal interest rates, so that the

positive nominal interest elasticity of saving may be viewed as an indirect positive inflation effect."

8. It is somewhat ironic that this particular objection to socialism may be supported by the authority of none other than Oskar Lange, the founder of the market socialist idea in contemporary Western economics. On the other hand, Lange certainly did not believe that the "arbitrary saving rate" under socialism constitutes a decisive consideration (1938, p. 108): "Against these advantages of a socialist economy the economist might put the disadvantage resulting from the arbitrariness of the rate of capital accumulation, if accumulation is performed 'corporately.' A rate of accumulation which does not reflect the preferences of the consumers as to the time-shape of the flow of income may be regarded as a diminution of social welfare. But it seems that this deficiency may be overbalanced by the advantages enumerated. Besides, saving is also in the present economic order determined only partly by pure utility considerations, and the rate of saving is affected much more by the distribution of incomes, which is irrational from the economist's point of view." Perhaps in this last sentence "arbitrary" would be a safer choice of words than "irrational." But Lange's point is well taken that it is inconsistent to worry about one "arbitrariness" without worrying about another which is seemingly just as important.

9. Illustrative references from the seminal period of this literature include Edmund Phelps (1966) and Karl Shell (1967).

10. The possibility of social saving replacing private saving in a potential socialist economy in which private households would not receive an interest return on savings is fairly well recognized by the contemporary economics profession, although it would be excessive to say that the critical implications of this recognition, with respect to the legitimacy of property income under capitalism, have been well and truly assimilated. An example of the half-awareness of this possibility is provided by Mark Blaug (1985, p. 193), who concludes a lengthy paragraph on John Stuart Mills's version of Nassau Senior's abstinence theory with the following casual remark: "The bulk of rentier income, as Mill makes clear, consists of intramarginal surpluses, pure Ricardian 'rents,' which accrue to the saver through no effort of his own. And, of course, there is nothing in the theory that justifies the private ownership of property as such. If abstinence is required for capital accumulation, society as a whole can bear the burden just as well."

6

INVESTMENT, GROWTH, AND ENTREPRENEURSHIP

A. INSIGHTS OF THE AUSTRIAN SCHOOL

Careful examination of both the textbook and the journal literature will quickly establish that economics is the most highly mathematized of the social sciences. Nevertheless, realistic practitioners of economics will usually concede that despite the voluminous application of higher mathematics in economics, economic inquiry is still far more art than science—at least as "science" is understood in physics, chemistry, engineering, and similar disciplines. No doubt the most serious impediment to genuinely scientific inquiry in economics is the usual impracticality of applying controlled experimentation to investigate theoretical hypotheses. Despite the obvious limitations on the scientific aspirations of economics, the vast majority of contemporary Western economists are still firmly convinced that advanced mathematical methodology is essential to worthwhile investigation of complicated social questions. Mathematics is needed to develop precise, testable hypotheses, and even though empirical testing of such hypotheses in economics normally leaves much to be desired, it is widely agreed that imperfect testing is better than no testing at all. Aside from the role of mathematics in specifying theories in such a way that they become empirically testable, it is also an effective safeguard against the possibility of logical error. The analyst may specify a certain set of assumptions, and then may determine precisely, using mathematics, what set of conclusions may—or may not—be logically based on that particular set of assumptions. Given the dominant consensus in favor of higher mathematics in contemporary economics, it is understandable that almost all of those economists who have been awarded the Nobel Prize in economics have utilized mathematics extensively in their work. There is, however, one notable exception to this rule: Friedrich von Hayek.

Hayek is quite possibly the single most important and influential twen-tieth-century exemplar of the Austrian school, a school characterized, among other things, by its championship of institutional economics over analytical economics.[1] Institutional economics eschews advanced mathematical analysis of strategically simplified representations of reality (models) in favor of broad-based, informal, descriptive consideration of numerous historical, political, legal, sociological, and psychological factors bearing upon the topic of interest. Only the simplest logical rules are utilized to tie together the varied strands of the analysis, and judgmental conclusions are based on intuitive deductions from a mass of particularistic details. To the typical mainstream analytical economist, the predominantly nonmathematical methodology of institutional economics is ill-suited to the derivation of useful insights and sound conclusions regarding social and economic reality. It is generally believed that without strategic theoretical simplification, the human mind is quickly overwhelmed by an immense welter of unrelated facts, so that intuitive judgment becomes randomized and unreliable. The minority of institutional economists, for their part, are of the opinion that mathematics, particularly in the absence of a sound institutional understanding of society, tends to be sterile and even perverse.

No opinions will be offered here on the debate between analytical and institutional economists. Straightforward application of the "happy medium" principle would suggest that there exists some appropriate blend of institutional and mathematical knowledge. As to whether, as claimed by the institutionalists, the median economist errs in the direction of too much mathematical knowledge and too little institutional knowledge, this is an intriguing but no doubt unanswerable question. What is relevant to the present purpose is how a Nobel Prize in economics can be awarded to an individual, Friedrich von Hayek, who openly and completely disdains the mathematical methodology which so thoroughly permeates the discipline of economics. There are a number of possibilities. Even among analytical economists, there is continuing concern over possible excessive mathematization of the discipline, and Hayek's award may have been regarded as a means of redressing a possible imbalance. Respect for Hayek as a person may have played a role: Among other things, during the Nazi era Hayek emigrated from his homeland rather than become subservient to a noxious regime. There is the fact that since Hayek has always avoided mathematics, his voluminous writings seem accessible to nontechnical readers—they believe they are learning something from him. Last but not least, over the last several decades Hayek has become a darling of the increasingly influential conservative movement among the intelligentsia. His tireless and un-compromising advocacy of laissez-faire and minimalist government, in the alleged interest of freedom, liberty, and efficiency, has become increasingly fashionable over the second half of the twentieth century.

Among the most dogmatic judgments of Friedrich von Hayek and other like-minded Austrian luminaries, especially Ludwig von Mises, is that socialism, both in theory and in practice, is an unredeemable failure.[2] They hold socialism, in whatever way, shape, or form it may occur, to be the equivalent in human society of cancer in the human body. According to Austrian preachments, the idea of socialism is founded on gross mis-understandings of the nature of human society—misunderstandings so absolutely gross that they can only proceed from stupidity, ignorance, or psychopathology. It follows, therefore, that any and all efforts to implement this malignant idea in the real world must inevitably result in stagnation, possibly leading to catastrophe. Such a blanket condemnation of socialism as pronounced by Friedrich von Hayek and Ludwig von Mises is not, nor can it be, based on logical, orderly, impartial scientific inquiry as it is understood in mainstream economics.

It is ironic that so many mainstream economists, who generally decry completely nonmathematical and intuitive methods of inquiry as hotbeds of false deduction and faulty judgment, nevertheless deem the writings of Mises and Hayek to constitute a devastating intellectual critique of socialism.[3] This particular irony would seem to represent yet another victory of ideological preconception over sensible judgment. Perhaps if these mainstream economists were to familiarize themselves sufficiently with the work of Mises and Hayek, they would recognize it as the gaseous, opinionated, confused, and inconclusive speculation that it actually is. In reality, the critique of socialism provided by Mises and Hayek contains extremely little that would be relevant to a serious, objective analysis of socialism, since it consists merely of endless variations on commonplace, superficial attitudes and opinions—delivered with such haughty dogmatism as to be thoroughly off-putting to anyone not already in complete agreement with these attitudes and opinions.

These negative comments on Mises and Hayek should not be taken to imply that there is a great deal of direct opposition between Austrian economics, generally considered, and the pragmatic market socialist proposal being put forward in this book. The essence of Austrian economics is that the free and unregulated economic market is an extremely powerful mechanism for the efficient elicitation and use of productive resources, both in the short term and (especially) in the long term. Any proponent of pragmatic market socialism must necessarily subscribe strongly to exactly this proposition. Austrian critics of socialism understand "socialism" in generalized terms of social intervention in market outcomes: specifically as government planning of various sorts (ranging from Keynesian anticyclical policy to Soviet-style central planning), as comprehensive and extensive government regulation of business enterprise and private activity, and as a highly egalitarian policy of economic redistribution through progressive taxation and the welfare state. It has been amply emphasized herein that pragmatic market socialism has no necessary connection with any of these institutions and practices: It does not call for planning, it does not call for regulation, and it does not call for redistribution—beyond transforming capital property income into social dividend income.

On the other hand, pragmatic market socialism is not inherently *opposed* to these things; it is merely *neutral* toward them. Sensible social analysts, whether economists or otherwise, recognize in the rhapsodic glorifications of the free market penned by Mises, Hayek, and like-minded writers an attitude which verges perilously close to rank naiveté. One cannot sensibly react to each and every specific proposal for planning, regulation, or redistribution, of whatever it may consist, with the same unthinking negative verdict—based on nothing more than the crude and unqualified opinion that any and all social interventions in the workings of the market system will necessarily be disadvantageous. The limited usefulness of Austrian economics lies in its superficiality; in the fact that it consists of little more than the endless reiteration of exactly this crude and unqualified opinion.

The degree of illumination—or lack thereof—of social institutions, processes, and policies to be found in the work of Mises and Hayek need not be debated here. It is certainly within the realm of conceivability to imagine an individual who would simultaneously be an enthusiastic devotee of Austrian economics and at the same time favorably disposed toward the pragmatic market socialist proposal. This is the case because in the voluminous writings of Ludwig von Mises and Friedrich von Hayek, there is very, very little that has any direct bearing on the concept of market socialism in general, let alone pragmatic market socialism. To begin with, only a small fraction of the overall corpus of work produced by Mises and Hayek is devoted to criticism of socialism. And the vast majority of that criticism is directed against the revolutionary excesses and planning system of Soviet socialism, and against the social interventionist proposals of the social democratic Marxist political parties. But the direct application of the respective cases against communistic socialism and social democratic socialism against pragmatic market socialism is simply begging the question, and it ought not to be taken seriously by a fair-minded judge.

Excluding some brief passing comments scattered here and there throughout their work, the entire body of critical writing by Mises and Hayek on market socialism consists of a grand total of approximately forty printed pages. In 1940, Friedrich von Hayek published an article in *Economica* attacking the Langian plan of market socialism advanced a few years before in Oskar Lange's essay "On the Economic Theory of Socialism." As pragmatic market socialism is quite different from the Langian plan, we need not be concerned here with Hayek's critique of Lange. In the 1951 English edition of *Socialism: An Economic and Sociological Analysis*, Ludwig von Mises criticized a concept of socialism, which he designated the "artificial market," in a six-page passage on pages 137-142. From Mises's sketchy characterization of this concept, it appears to be essentially the same as pragmatic market socialism.[4] Therefore it is highly relevant to the present purpose to examine Mises's critique of the artificial market. Mises describes the proposal of "some of the younger socialists" for an artificial market in the following terms (*Socialism*, 1951, p. 138):[5]

> The advocates of the artificial market, however, are of the opinion that an artificial market can be created by instructing the controllers of the different industrial units to act as if they were entrepreneurs in a capitalistic state. They argue that even under Capitalism the managers of joint stock companies work not for themselves but for the companies, that is to say, for the shareholders. Under Socialism, therefore, it would be possible for them to act in exactly the same way as before, with the same circumspection and devotion to duty. The only difference is that under Socialism the product of the managers' labors would go to the community rather than to the shareholders. In such a way, in contrast to all socialists who have written on the subject hitherto, they think it would be possible to construct a decentralized, as opposed to a centralized, Socialism.

This proposal might well be satisfactory, according to Mises, were the duties of corporation executives confined strictly to matters of current production and marketing, as they are explicated in the standard economic theory textbook account of cost minimization with respect to factors of production and profit maximization with respect to the output level. The proposal collapses, however, as soon as it is recognized that the more important aspects of business enterprise involve planning for investment and growth in an unpredictable and dynamically changing world:

> Now it is a complete fallacy to suppose that the problem of economic calculation in a socialist community relates solely to matters which fall into the sphere of the daily business routine of managers of joint stock companies. It is clear that such a belief can only arise from exclusive concentration on the idea of a stationary economic system—a conception which is no doubt useful for the solution of many theoretical problems but which has no counterpart in fact and which, if exclusively regarded, can even be positively

misleading. It is clear that under stationary conditions the problem of economic calculation does not really arise. When we think of the stationary society, we think of an economy in which all factors of production are already used in such a way as, under the given conditions, to provide the maximum of the things which are demanded by consumers. That is to say, under stationary conditions there no longer exists a problem for economic calculation to solve. The essential function of economic calculation has *by hypothesis* already been performed. There is no need for an apparatus of calculation. To use a popular but not altogether satisfactory terminology we can say that the problem of economic calculation is of economic dynamics: it is not a problem of economic statics. (Mises, *Socialism*, p. 139)

Mises does concede, however, that the managers of joint stock companies ("corporation executives" in more contemporary terminology) under pragmatic market socialism would not simply ignore the matter of investment and growth. He is prepared to stipulate that in addition to managing current production and marketing, they would prepare proposals for investment projects. But these proposals would reflect only the limited information and overoptimistic expectations of the executives of individual corporations. Investment funds would be doled out to corporations by uninterested state employees merely on the basis of a crude numerical comparison of the dubious profitability estimates on various investment projects provided by corporation executives. Under capitalism, in contrast, investment projects proposed by corporation executives are presented to private capitalists (rather than to uninterested state employees) in the hope of obtaining capital. These capitalists, because of their personal financial stake in the outcome of these investment projects, evaluate them very closely and assiduously, with attention not merely to their anticipated profitability but also to their degree of risk, and in the light of all competing investment projects. As a result, the allocation of investment capital is performed in a highly rational and efficient manner:

> Faced with this difficulty, the socialist is likely to propose that the socialist state as owner of all capital and all means of production should simply direct capital to those undertakings which promise the highest return. The available capital, he will contend, should go to those undertakings which offer the highest rate of profit. But such a state of affairs would simply mean that those managers who were less cautious and more optimistic would receive capital to enlarge their undertakings while more cautious and more skeptical managers would go away empty-handed. Under Capitalism, the capitalist decides to whom he will entrust *his own* capital. The beliefs of the managers of joint stock companies regarding the future prospects of their undertakings and the hopes of project-makers regarding the profitability of their plans are not in any way decisive. The mechanism of the money market and the capital

market decides. This indeed is its main task: to serve the economic system as a whole, to judge the profitability of alternative openings and not blindly to follow what the managers of particular concerns, limited by the narrow horizon of their own undertakings, are tempted to propose. (Mises, *Socialism*, p. 140)

The principal problem with Mises's argument is that it ignores the important role played by institutional investors in modern capital markets. Rather, it envisions financial capital being provided to firms exclusively by private capitalists. In actual fact, nonfinancial firms, in the sale of stock and bond issues and suchlike transactions for obtaining investment capital, deal as much or more with institutional investors (investment banks, insurance companies, pension funds, etc.) as they do with individual investors. The loan officers and investment analysts of these institutional investors receive as personal income only a tiny fraction of the property return generated by the investments they make, and yet the performance of institutional investors in these markets is on the whole at least comparable with, and probably superior to, that of private investors.

Under pragmatic market socialism, private investors would be excluded from financial asset markets, but these markets would provide an arena for vigorous competition among independently managed and evaluated financial intermediaries of various types. The competition among these financial firms, and the efforts of their loan officers and investment analysts, would provide rational economic calculation on the supply side of the investment capital market—just as the efforts of the employees and executives of corporations in evaluating the specific investment opportunities of their own firms would provide rational economic calculation on the demand side of the investment capital market. Mises can perceive only private capitalists as sources of such calculation, and thus in his judgment rational economic calculation is "impossible" under socialism. He handles the obvious idea of socialized institutional investors simply by flatly denying their possibility:

Now if it is to remain socialistic, the socialist State cannot leave to other hands that disposition over capital which permits the enlargement of existing undertakings, the contraction of others and the bringing into being of undertakings that are completely new. And it is scarcely to be assumed that socialists of whatever persuasion would seriously propose that this function should be made over to some group of people who would "simply" have the business of doing what the capitalists and speculators do under capitalistic conditions, the only difference being that the product of their foresight should not belong to them but to the community. Proposals of this sort may well be made concerning the managers of joint stock companies. They can never be extended to capitalists and speculators, for no socialist would dispute that the

function which capitalists and speculators perform under Capitalism, namely
directing the use of capital goods into the direction in which they best serve
the demands of the consumer, is only performed because they are under the
incentive to preserve their property and to make profits which increase it or
at least allow them to live without diminishing their capital. (Mises,
Socialism, p. 141)

Mises's argument on the "artificial market" concept of socialism reflects
two major developments in economics during the 1930s. One development
was the statistical work of Berle and Means which compellingly documented the separation of ownership and control in large-scale corporate
enterprise. This work was the final nail in the coffin of the interpretation of
capital management effort as direct supervision and management of business enterprises, an interpretation that had been very important in
nineteenth-century capitalist apologetics. The second development was
Oskar Lange's "On the Economic Theory of Socialism." Lange's proposal
for marginal cost pricing under social ownership of capital was founded
squarely on conventional neoclassical economic theory, and the proposal
greatly weakened the formerly widespread judgment among mainstream
economists that socialism would necessarily be inefficient.

Mises's response to the separation of ownership and control was that it
applied only to current production by existing corporations, and not to the
disposition of new capital for investment and growth. His response to
Lange's proposal was that the attainment of static efficiency, in and of itself,
whether in the context of the Langian market socialist system or any other
market socialist system, would be of little consequence—since the inefficient utilization of new investment capital under socialism would entail a
lamentably low level of long-run performance. It was probably imprudent
for Mises to concede as much as he did. A more plausible argument might
have been that market socialism would be both statically *and* dynamically
inefficient—because capital owners would not receive the full capital return
to the existing physical capital stock in current use, nor would capital owners
receive the full capital return to new financial capital in future applications.
Once it is conceded that full receipt by capital owners of the capital return
is *not* necessary to the efficient use of existing physical capital in current
production, the best part of the capital management defense of capital
property income is lost. This is because the practical realities of investment
in the modern economy demonstrate that investment is simply part of the
"daily business routine" of both financial and nonfinancial corporations,
which are characterized equally, whether they be financial or nonfinancial
in nature, by the separation of ownership and control.

In light of these realities, Mises's invocation of the issue of "dynamic performance," as distinguished from "static performance," is revealed as a classic red herring. The next section of this chapter will consider practical aspects of investment, growth, and entrepreneurship under pragmatic market socialism. The present section will conclude with some brief comments of a more theoretical nature to the effect that the essential logical core of Mises's argument against the artificial market is merely a reworking of the capital management objection to pragmatic market socialism examined in Chapter 4.

The strict dichotomy proposed in Austrian economic thinking between "static" problems and decisions and "dynamic" problems and decisions is not particularly helpful, and if insisted upon, it can constitute a major obstacle to clear thinking. To begin with, the actual length of the time period in any given piece of "static" analysis is normally quite indeterminate, and in practice would depend on the particular application. The Austrians seem to have in mind that the period of time involved in "static" analysis is extremely brief, and of insufficient duration to alter any particular economic decision variable significantly. But in actual fact *any* kind of analysis, properly understood, must envision a period of time sufficient to alter the decision variables—otherwise there would be no point to analysis. Furthermore, *any* economic decision variable may be subjected to analysis if an appropriate time interval is taken. For example, the standard textbook problem of "minimizing the cost of production with respect to the factors of production," which no doubt is taken by the Austrians as a "static" problem having nothing to do with investment, might in fact, by imagining the time period to be of considerable length, involve substantially altering the level of capital input by means of constructing a huge new factory. Thus "static" analysis can be extended to the "dynamic" problem of investment merely by adjusting the time period appropriately.

This is not to say that a sensible technical distinction cannot be made between the conventional type of economic analysis that seems most naturally applied to current production and marketing, and possible alternative types of analysis that seem more naturally applied to investment. In mainstream economics, static analysis is differentiated from dynamic analysis on the basis of the former being restricted to one time period while the latter embraces several time periods. Another relevant distinction in mainstream economics is between certainty analysis, in which all the parameters are known constants, and uncertainty analysis, in which some parameters are random variables, whose values do not become known until after the economic decision-maker has set the decision variables. A very large amount of work has indeed been done by mainstream analytical economists on mathematical models of dynamic decision-making and

184 SOCIALISM REVISED AND MODERNIZED

decision-making under uncertainty.[6] Very little of this work has as yet become established in core economic theory as explicated in standard textbooks. One reason is the mathematical complexity of the work; another is that the results obtained are usually not radically opposed to those obtainable with the simpler mathematical methods of static certainty analysis. (This latter point is consistent with the point mentioned above that the time period utilized in static analysis is indeterminate and may in some applications be quite lengthy.)

It is interesting to note that the prominent Austrian economists have contributed nothing to the analytical literature on dynamic decision-making and decision-making under uncertainty: They apparently find it easier to snipe from the sidelines at the alleged deficiencies of static certainty analysis than to learn sufficient mathematics in the areas of dynamic optimization and mathematical statistics to make a useful contribution to the alternatives to static certainty analysis. Or perhaps they assume that unaided intuition can reliably answer questions and solve problems which sophisticated higher mathematics cannot fathom.

Obviously the Austrian luminaries Friedrich von Hayek and Ludwig von Mises believe that the allocation of investment capital, undertaken as it is in a multiperiod context and under conditions of uncertainty, can be performed efficiently only in a capitalist economy in which capital property is privately owned. They have not, of course, produced any analytical models of dynamic decision-making and/or decision-making under uncertainty to back up this opinion. Nor have any of their many admirers.[7] Clearly it would be impractical at this point to undertake a careful examination of the issue, backed up by analytical models. However, some informal comments might be worthwhile on two specific questions raised by applying the notions of dynamic decision-making and decision-making under uncertainty to the pragmatic market socialist proposal. One question is the extent to which pragmatic market socialism might deny the capital manager the *future* return on *current* decision-making, and thus reduce the incentive to apply serious effort to current decision-making. A second question is the extent to which pragmatic market socialism might deny the capital manager an adequate return on the *risk-taking* which is necessarily undertaken by the decision-maker under conditions of uncertainty.

In real-world business enterprise, the interrelated processes of investment, growth, and innovation are not determined, let alone dominated, by the solitary, entrepreneurial capital owners of Austrian mythology. They are, rather, the outcome of a complicated process, involving elements of cooperation and elements of competition, in which a great many individuals besides wealthy capitalists participate: engineers, accountants, marketers, executives, loan officers, investment analysts, and so on. Each of these many individuals has his or her personal time horizon determined by such factors as age, health, and the relative costs and benefits of retirement. Many of these individuals will no doubt be long gone before the final consequences of the investment decisions in which they currently participate have been fully worked out: Thus they will not be able to fully reap the benefits of efforts which they apply now. Therefore it seems plausible, for example, that elderly individuals involved in the investment process would have smaller incentives to effort than would younger individuals. This situation is obviously not restricted to pragmatic market socialism; it applies equally to contemporary capitalism.

Therefore the first and most important point is to recognize and appreciate that the conditions and incentives of the great majority of individuals who are directly involved in the investment process would be exactly the same under capitalism and under pragmatic market socialism. For example, the corporate CEOs under pragmatic market socialism would have basically the same expected tenure in office as they do under capitalism, and could also have incentives tied to the firm's security prices closely analogous to the stock option plans utilized under capitalism: These prices would be determined in a capital market operating exactly like that of capitalism, except for the absence of private investors. The primary distinction between capitalism and pragmatic market socialism would be the replacement of private capital owners, who possess the right to sell their capital property instruments in the capital market, by agents of the Bureau of Public Ownership (BPO), who receive a percentage of the property return produced by the corporations within their sphere of responsibility during their tenure in the position, but who may not sell the corresponding property rights in the capital market. The Austrian contention is that because the socialist counterpart of the capital owner (i.e., the BPO agent) could not sell the capital property rights implicit in the position, he/she would thereby be prevented from laying claim to the capital return generated in future periods by intelligent investment decisions in the current period. Thus his/her incentive to make intelligent investment decisions in the current period would be drastically reduced.

There are several points to be raised against this particular objection. To begin with, the standard term of office for the typical BPO agent (five to seven years) is not excessively brief, and it could be extended if that were deemed advisable. The proposal also envisions the BPO agent retaining a diminishing fraction of the return generated by a particular responsibility for several years after leaving the position. In view of the inevitable uncertainties regarding the more remote future, in real-world business decision-making the relevant time horizon is not more than a few years, and this interval of time would be adequately encompassed by the personal time horizons of the great majority of currently serving BPO agents. Another important consideration is the very minor and indirect role of capital owners/BPO agents in the investment process. The important work of investment analysis and the key investment decisions are made by corporate employees, particularly by corporate executives. In effect, the capital owners/BPO agents merely pass judgment on past investment decisions in terms of the profitability of the current production process; they do not participate meaningfully in the current investment decisions which will affect future corporate profitability. Finally, it is worth noting that aside from the nuance of differentiating the current period from future periods, the Austrian contention essentially comes down to the allegation of an inadequate return on capital management effort under socialism. It is nothing more than a somewhat messier restatement of the capital management apology for capital property income considered above in Chapter 4. The same points apply as applied above: the opposed income and substitution effects, the possibility of a plateau production function in capital management effort, and so on.

Turning to risk-taking as a justification for property income, it is instructive to note the close parallels between this idea and the abstinence idea produced by Nassau Senior in the early nineteenth century. Both abstinence and risk-taking were developed mainly as ex post facto rationalizations of capital property income against the socialist accusation that capital property income is economically and ethically unearned. They are both generalizable: Abstinence is usually applied to saving, but it can be generalized to capital management effort because the provision of such effort requires the capital owner to "abstain" from the good leisure; risk-taking is usually applied to the active process of capital management effort but it can be generalized to saving because just as the investor might lose his/her capital, so too the saver might lose his/her savings. Abstinence and risk-taking have roughly the same level of appeal to commonsense intuition: Just as all savers, large and small, are conscious of the sacrifices of abstaining from consumption, so too all investors, large and small, are conscious of the risks of investing.

As justifications for property income, the two ideas of abstinence and risk-taking are also subject to analogous objections. Just as the wealthy capitalist, with his/her extravagant consumption, receives far more property income than is sensibly attributed to the sacrifices of saving, so too he/she receives far more than is sensibly attributed to risk-taking. A very large capital fortune is effectively insulated against risk through the elementary expedient of diversification. The law of averages constitutes an extremely effective form of insurance, and the level of actual risk-taking involved in large-scale, highly diversified investing is nil. Furthermore, neither abstinence nor risk-taking is in itself a primary factor of production; they are merely ancillary conditions to the provision of a primary factor of production. As such, these conditions apply as much to the provision of labor as they do to saving and capital management effort. Just as the saver abstains from consumption, so too the laborer abstains from leisure. Just as the provision of capital management effort involves a risk that the effort will not prove financially fruitful, so too does the provision of labor. Therefore if the argument is made that capital property income is needed to compensate the abstinence from consumption of the saver and the risk-taking of the capital manager, the argument may equally be made that social dividend income is needed to compensate the abstinence from leisure of the laborer and the risk-taking of the laborer.

Quite a lot of careful work has in fact been done over the past few decades on decision-making under uncertainty—not by the nonmathematical Austrian economists but by mainstream analytical economists. It is widely agreed that the typical human participant in economic decision-making is risk averse, and thus the greater the degree of uncertainty in the decision-making environment (in terms of larger variances in the probability distributions of parameters), the lower the equilibrium levels of the decision variables. In particular, uncertainty and its consequent risk does in fact operate as a deterrent to the provision of primary factors of production such as capital management effort and saving. But it does not follow from this that there is a positive relationship between the rate of property return and the supply of either capital management effort or saving. It may indeed seem intuitively plausible to propose that since risk discourages capital management effort and saving, the role of capital property return under capitalism is to offset risk and encourage capital management effort and saving. But this is a case of opposition between intuition and analysis, and a good example of why it is that analytical economists believe that total reliance should not be placed purely on intuition unassisted by analysis.

The addition of uncertainty to the models of capital management effort and saving examined above (respectively in Chapters 4 and 5) does not appreciably alleviate the ambiguity of the effect of the retention coefficient on capital management effort and the effect of the abolition of interest payments on private household saving.[8] As to the specific effect of risk on capital management effort, a reasonable proposition in light of current understanding is that yet another reason why real-world capital owners do not devote much time to investment analysis (aside from the plateau-shaped capital return function) is that the tremendous degree of uncertainty regarding future price movements of individual securities operates as a severe deterrent to investment analysis. The practical consequences of this proposition for present purposes are similar to those of the plateau-shaped capital return function: The replacement of capitalism by pragmatic market socialism would have a minimal impact on the inevitably low level of capital management effort (in the form of investment analysis) and consequently a minimal impact on capital return and overall economic efficiency.

B. THE INVESTMENT MECHANISM

Critics of socialism, whether from the Austrian school or from other schools of thought, habitually maintain that socialism would be undynamic and unprogressive. The application of this customary allegation to pragmatic market socialism is certainly very dubious. The pragmatic market socialist proposal is based on a keen and thorough appreciation of the vital role of investment and innovation in economic growth and the general improvement of human welfare. But the proposal is also based upon a properly skeptical evaluation of the more or less preposterous interpretations of real-world capitalism put forward by exponents of Austrian economics and like-minded viewpoints.

When one looks realistically and objectively at the contemporary economic real world in the advanced, industrialized nations, what does one see? One sees large corporations as the dominant instrumentality in all economic processes ranging from "static" production and marketing through to "dynamic" investment, innovation, and growth. As much as capitalist apologetics apotheosizes the lone entrepreneur, in reality the role of such entrepreneurs in the real world is very modest. In practice the only way the lone entrepreneur can build up a viable and successful business enterprise (outside of the realm of handicraft production) is to develop a large, bureaucratically organized, echeloned and pyramidal structure, involving hundreds if not thousands of employees, as quickly as possible. The usual alternative is the rapid extinction of the enterprise, and the reduction of the entrepreneur to the status of employee. By its nature, truly entrepreneurial activity is extremely ephemeral. If it does not rapidly evolve into standard administrative activity, then it usually aborts.

This is not to say that no provision should be made under socialism for the lone entrepreneur. It is a central element of the pragmatic market socialist proposal that private entrepreneurs be able to exercise a personal ownership interest in the firms which they found so long as they remain personally active in their management, and that they be able to personally claim the full capitalized value of that ownership interest when they depart from management. In practice, this simply means that any successful private entrepreneur who becomes wealthy under capitalism would also become wealthy under pragmatic market socialism. Entrepreneurial activity might also be supported by a well-financed national government agency, the National Entrepreneurial Investment Board (NEIB). Some of the NEIB's funds would be loaned to outside entrepreneurs, and some would be utilized by staff members who would make careers in the establishment of new entrepreneurial firms. Independent private entrepreneurship and NEIB entrepreneurship would be supplemented—and probably considerably out-weighed—by the same type of entrepreneurship which is already dominant in the contemporary capitalist economy: the establishment of subsidiaries in new markets by existing large, multidivisional firms, these new firms entering into competition with firms already established in the respective markets.

Among both journalistic and academic apologists for capitalism, the image of the independent entrepreneur is a veritable religious icon. Their "theories" of entrepreneurship are perhaps more appropriately described as "idolatries" of entrepreneurship. Very frequently such apologists will actually use the term "entrepreneur" in place of the term "capitalist." However, as has been pointed out, use of the term "entrepreneur" as a synonym for "capitalist" is questionable, to say the least. First, the vast majority of wealthy capitalists obtained their personal fortunes through means other than entrepreneurship: Appreciation of inherited financial assets is doubtless the major factor in the development of most large capital fortunes. These asset accumulations are kept safely invested in securities issued by the large, established, nonentrepreneurial firms which in fact dominate the economy. Second, many of the individuals directly involved in the planning and initiation of entrepreneurial firms are salaried employees; as in the case of the entrepreneurial subsidiaries mentioned above. The invalid blending of an indubitably productive activity (such as entrepreneurship) with the passive and unproductive condition of financial capital ownership is a fundamental technique of capitalist apologetics.

Pure entrepreneurship, the establishment of brand new business enterprises, does indeed play an important role in the dynamic progress of the economy. But a realistic appraisal of the contemporary real-world economy indicates that this role is more of a catalytic nature rather than being numerically important in its own right. In other words, the estab-lishment of new firms with new products and/or production techniques tends to force established firms in the same industry to adopt these innovations more quickly than they otherwise would have. But the fact remains that as far as strict numerical importance is concerned, the great majority of innovative investment activity—that investment activity associated with the introduction of new products and/or production techniques rather than with the maintenance of existing products and production techniques—is carried on by large, existing, nonentrepreneurial firms. This activity is a constant, ongoing component of the competitive quest for markets and profits by these existing firms. As long as pragmatic market socialism maintains a strong profit motivation in the publicly owned corporate business enterprise sector, supplemented by an adequate level of competition among the publicly owned firms, the dynamic efficiency of investment and innovation will take care of itself, no less than the static efficiency of production and marketing.

The employees of a corporation, from production line workers on up to the top executive team, are like sailors on a ship embarked on an endless voyage. If the ship goes down—whether it goes down today, tomorrow, next year, or next decade—most of them will be highly inconvenienced. Thus they are not merely concerned that the ship stays afloat today and tomorrow, but that it remains afloat next year and next decade. It is not merely a matter of seeing to it that the engines are running and the propellers are turning; it is also a matter of maintaining the ship so that it does not develop leaks in the future, and of navigating the ship so that it does not run aground on shoals in the future. The point of the metaphor is that business enterprise is naturally, inherently, and simultaneously both static and dynamic in nature. Investment and innovation are no less a part of the daily business routine than are production and marketing. It may well be that mainstream economic theory has more to say about the static issues of production and marketing than it does about the dynamic issues of investment and innovation. If so, so much the worse for economic theory; this situation is not evidence against the practicality of the pragmatic market socialist proposal. The pragmatic market socialist proposal is based far more on a proper perception of the institutional nature of the real-world industrial economy than it is on mainstream economic theory.

Investment and innovation are motivated by the prospect of future profitability. And the primary focus of this concern lies in the corporate employees, from unskilled labor up to top managers—the people who actually perform the nitty-gritty work of innovating and investing (in the sense of converting money into machines). The ship metaphor presented in the preceding paragraph suggests that their major motivation is simply to avoid future bankruptcy. This is of course an oversimplification. A more accurate perception is that the welfare of the employees is directly proportional to the welfare of their corporations. The more profitable a corporation, the more generous it is with respect to wages, salaries, benefits, and perquisites, and the more relaxed it is with respect to employee retention and employee performance evaluation. Working for a profitable corporation means higher pay, better working conditions, and less stress. Of course there tends to be a feedback cyclical process. Higher pay, better working conditions, and less pressure on the employees eventually erode profits, so that some degree of retrenchment becomes necessary for a while. But over the long term, working for a consistently profitable corporation is better than working for a consistently unprofitable corporation. This simple fact is the primary goad to efficient innovation and investment in the real world, just as it is the primary goad to efficient production and marketing.

The separation of ownership and control, with its dire consequences for the economic and ethical legitimacy of the capitalist system, is relevant to both static and dynamic economic processes. The argument of Ludwig von Mises on the artificial market, examined in the preceding section of this chapter, is essentially that the separation of ownership and control casts serious doubt on the proposition that capital management earns property return only when capital management is understood as corporate super- vision, but that the proposition is fully valid and defensible when capital management is understood as investment analysis. This variant of the capital management argument can be taken seriously only by someone who is oblivious to—or who chooses to ignore—the dominant role in the modern economy of what might be termed "corporate investment analysis." Much investment in the modern economy is financed internally by nonfinancial corporations from retained earnings. The analysis of such investments is performed by salaried employees. Then there is the role of such recognized financial intermediary corporations as banks, insurance companies, and pension funds, whose investment analysis is mostly performed by salaried employees. Finally there are such agencies as mutual funds and investment counseling firms, which in effect are financial intermediaries, and once again whose investment analysis is mostly performed by salaried employees. Therefore, even with respect to financial capital, it would appear that many owning capitalists have delegated control to the various financial intermediaries in which they hold their wealth, just as the stockholders of nonfinancial corporations have delegated control of the physical capital which these corporations own to the corporation executives.

But of course *some* capitalists purchase investment assets such as cor- porate common stock and corporate and government bonds on their own personal account, without going through any form of financial intermediary. Apologists for capitalism allege that it is the laborious effort undertaken by such capitalists in choosing their investments which simultaneously guarantees efficient allocation of financial capital and morally justifies the capitalists' receipt of property income. But it would appear that the laborious effort undertaken by the thousands of salaried analysts for the financial intermediaries, and for the corporations which self-finance their investment, would be sufficient to bring the level of efficiency in financial capital allocation to very near its asymptotic upper limit, so that the private capitalists active in these markets are merely getting a free ride on the efforts of others. This view of reality is consistent with evidence mentioned earlier which suggests that most wealthy capitalists pursue demanding careers in various professions, and that they devote very little time to portfolio review and selection of assets. At the same time, there is no systematic evidence whatsoever that "activist" capitalists receive a higher rate of capital property return than do "passive" capitalists. If activist capitalists did indeed do appreciably better than passive capitalists, we would expect many more capitalists to be activist than seems to be the case.

Financial asset markets are often alleged to be stern discipliners of corporations. If a corporation is being managed badly, the value of its assets in these markets will be low, which will raise the cost of capital to the firm for purposes of capital maintenance and modernization. It will thus in the long term be forced out of business by other firms that are managed effectively, whose assets command a high price in financial asset markets. Thus the buying and selling of a firm's securities in the financial capital market is perceived to be an important contributor to the firm's profit motivation. Questions may clearly be raised about the effectiveness of this rather indirect mode of discipline, particularly in view of the extent to which established corporations take investment funds out of their own profits in the form of retained earnings. The "long term" in this case may be *very* long indeed.

However, whatever the degree of rigor in the discipline imposed on firms by the trading of their assets in financial markets, a similar discipline would exist under pragmatic market socialism because the proposal envisions the maintenance of such markets. While a publicly owned corporation could not issue and sell voting stock, it could issue and sell nonvoting financial instruments such as bonds. These sales could not be made to private individuals, but they could be made to other corporations, primarily financial intermediaries such as insurance companies which hold such assets as part of their standard mode of business operation. These financial intermediaries would then trade among themselves, and in so doing create a market price for the instruments issued by a particular corporation. This market price would affect the cost of new capital to the firm. The executives of this corporation would therefore have as much incentive to keep the prices of these assets high as they do under capitalism. High asset prices, in turn, are assisted both by intelligent static decision-making on current production and marketing, and by intelligent dynamic decision-making with respect to innovation and investment.

Under modern capitalism, the capital owners, as such, have little to do with the dynamic processes of innovation and investment—just as they have little to do with the static processes of production and marketing. Their role is simple and straightforward observation of the relative success of the various corporations in the economy, and the direction of financial capital toward the more profitable corporations. The real and meaningful effort in the economy is that put forth by the corporate employees in achieving whatever level of profitability which their respective companies are capable of achieving. Thus the capital owners, as capital owners per se, are merely parasitical rentiers who appropriate the fruits of other people's labor. This reality may be obfuscated—but it can never be abrogated—by means of the "dynamic" smoke screen pumped forth by the Austrian economists and their intellectual allies. In the real-world economy, whatever benefits may be derived from entrepreneurship, enterprise, innovation, discovery, rivalrous process—or whatever other catchword or catchphrase is utilized—are not derived to any appreciable extent from the efforts of the capital owners.

C. THE LEVEL OF INVESTMENT

According to Karl Marx's seminal socialist critique of capitalism, developed in the mid-nineteenth century, it is not the moral impropriety of surplus labor exploitation which will bring down the capitalist system but its propensity toward ever-worsening business depressions. But the evidence of approximately 150 years has, to a reasonable degree of certainty, falsified Marx's prediction. The Great Depression of the 1930s did indeed demonstrate that the nineteenth-century classical economists had been excessively complacent about business depressions, but even so, the unprecedentedly severe hardships imposed on the populations of the capitalist nations by this depression came nowhere near to igniting a socialist revolution. Moreover, the capitalist nations emerged from the Great Depression armed with Keynesian anticyclical policy, which according to standard macroeconomic theory offers reasonable assurances against a repetition of the acute economic ailment which afflicted the capitalist world economy throughout the 1930s. As a result, the macroeconomic stabilization argument for socialism has been rendered effectively null and void.

While the pragmatic market socialist viewpoint shares with the Marxist viewpoint the judgment that contemporary capitalism is inferior to an available socialist alternative, there are important points of difference between the two. For one thing, the pragmatic market socialist viewpoint makes no prediction that capitalism will eventually be abolished, because no drastic and intolerable efficiency shortcomings are perceived, either static or dynamic (such as catastrophic business depressions), in the contemporary market capitalist economy. Rather, the moral impropriety of highly unequal distribution of unearned property return (as opposed to surplus labor exploitation) is perceived to be the critical shortcoming of capitalism. This is a shortcoming which may or may not ultimately be recognized and acted upon by the population.

However, there are certain other shortcomings of contemporary capitalism which, while more speculative than the highly unequal distribution of property return, are nevertheless worthy of some consideration. One of these is suggested by the thinking of Karl Marx, John Maynard Keynes, and others on the phenomenon of business depressions ("recessions" in the customary modern diminutive terminology). It is widely agreed among contemporary mainstream economists that recessions occur because of a temporary decline in discretionary investment expenditures by business firms. It is only slightly less widely agreed that the reason for this temporary decline is a temporary flourishing of the opinion among corporation executives that investment spending has become, for the moment, unprofitable. This flourishing generates the painful irony of a self-fulfilling prophecy: Business executives *believe* that investing would be unprofitable, they cut back on investing, the economy sags, and as a result investing *does* become unprofitable. If the investment cutback reaches the proportions of a collapse, as it did in the early 1930s, and the economy is consequently plunged into an abyss of bankruptcy and unemployment, then Karl Marx's protestations that capitalism's propensity to business depression constitutes a serious social problem are not so easily shrugged off as misguided alarmism. But on the basis of almost fifty years since the end of World War II without a really severe business depression, the contemporary Western economics profession is confident that Keynesian monetary and fiscal policy holds the key to the prevention of excessively severe business depressions.

But the mere fact that a cycle problem exists under capitalism and has to be dealt with suggests the possibility of a serious conflict of interest between the capital-owning minority and the rest of the population. Business executives are cautious about capital investment, and are liable to the waves of pessimism which generate depressions, because of the strong concern for profitability enforced on them by the capital owners. It is customarily assumed that this conflict of interest is rendered harmless and irrelevant to the extent that successful implementation of Keynesian stabilization policy eliminates or greatly moderates business depressions. This customary assumption is quite possibly erroneous. Implementation of Keynesian stabilization policy implies a long-term retardation in the rate of growth of business physical capital. During the expansion phase of the cycle, the accumulation of savings is to be reduced through redistribution from rich to poor, and/or investment spending is to be contained through restrictive monetary policy. During the contraction phase, the decline in business capital investment is to be counteracted by an increase in discretionary public spending and/or an increase in private consumption, the latter to be inspired by a reduction in personal taxes.

Thus the rate of business capital accumulation is to be purposely retarded during the expansion period; while during the contraction period, the decline in the rate of business capital accumulation is to be accepted, and the potential adverse effect on overall economic activity is to be forestalled by replacing the flow of business capital investment with some other expenditure flow. The point of the exercise is to keep the rate of accumulation of business capital in the long term sufficiently low to maintain continuously a rate of profitability regarded as adequate by the capital owners. It may be, therefore, that in a society in which the capital owners did not constitute a distinct subset of the population with interests significantly different from those of the rest of the population, a higher long-term rate of business capital accumulation might be deemed socially desirable than the rate currently maintained under capitalism.[10]

But to the extent that the problem of suboptimal business capital accumulation exists under capitalism, the same problem would exist under the core pragmatic market socialist proposal. The Bureau of Public Ownership would enforce upon executives of both nonfinancial and financial corporations the same strong concern for profitability presently enforced upon them by the class of capital owners. To counteract the potential adverse effect on business physical capital investment of the concern for high profitability among executives of established business corporations, it would be necessary to undertake additional institutional alterations. The first alteration would be the establishment of a new category of national government expenditure: business physical capital investment. It has already been indicated that such an appropriation must be established in any event on precautionary grounds: to counteract a possible decline in private household saving owing to the elimination of interest payments on private savings accumulations. The annual appropriation for this purpose would go through the usual budgetary process. The second alteration would be the establishment of two new national government agencies, independent of the BPO, for the disposition of this budgetary appropriation into the business sector: (1) the National Investment Banking System (NIBS); (2) the National Entrepreneurial Investment Board (NEIB). These two agencies would supplement, not replace, the investment activity carried on by firms under BPO ownership. Such BPO-owned firms would include nonfinancial corporations which "lend" investment funds to themselves via retained earnings, and financial intermediary corporations such as banks, insurance companies, and pension funds, which lend investment funds to, and purchase securities from, other business corporations.

As indicated above (Chapter 2, Section D), the NIBS and the NEIB would be significantly different from the standard BPO-owned financial intermediary sector. Performance evaluation of the investment analysts and loan officers of the standard sector would be in terms of the profitability of *all* their past loans and investments, while performance evaluation of NIBS loan officers and investment analysts would be in terms of the profitability of their *recent* loans and investments, and the performance of NEIB executives and agents would be in terms of the profitability of *recently* established firms of the NEIB. Thus, in deciding upon the disposition of investment funds, NIBS and NEIB personnel would be uninhibited by concerns over the possible adverse effects of new investment activities on the profitability of older capital and established firms.

The upshot of this policy could be a higher rate of capital accumulation and economic growth under pragmatic market socialism than under capitalism.[11] Section C of the Analytical Appendix sets forth a model designed to illustrate this argument. The core of the model is a set of recursive equations econometrically estimated using quarterly U.S. data from 1950.1 through 1988.4. These estimations provide statistical support for the following hypotheses: (1) there is a positive effect, with a relatively long lag, of the rate of property return on the rate of business capital investment; and (2) there is a negative effect, with a relatively short lag, of the rate of investment on the rate of property return. Both of these hypotheses are intuitively appealing. It is obvious that high profitability both enables and encourages higher investment by business firms. And the negative impact of investment on profitability is simply a verification of the declining Marginal Efficiency of Investment (MEI) schedule, a Keynesian proposition which became ingrained in the macroeconomic theory textbooks as long ago as the 1950s. The core recursive model is then embedded in a larger model accounting for labor supply, capacity utilization, and national output.

Three variants of the model are developed. In the first variant, labeled the "pre-Keynesian capitalist," total potential output, as determined by the available capital and labor stock, is not completely achieved. Rather, actual output is related to potential output via a capacity utilization variable which is itself positively related to the investment rate. A higher investment rate means higher capacity utilization, and a closer approach of actual output to potential output. The second variant, the "post-Keynesian capitalist," presumes that the problem of underutilization of capacity has been completely abrogated. In this model the capacity utilization variable is always 1, regardless of the investment rate. (Of course, in the post-Keynesian real world, this level of anticyclical control has not yet been achieved. It is merely a conceptual device to imagine that the objectives of Keynesian recession control policy have been fully realized.) Finally, the "pragmatic market socialist" variant of the model assumes full capacity utilization, plus a higher level of responsiveness in the investment rate to past rates of property return. That is, the intercept coefficient of the statistically estimated relationship between rate of property return and rate of investment for the U.S. economy from 1950 to 1988 is raised to represent the potential effect of a national government appropriation to business physical capital investment distributed throughout the economy by an NIBS and an NEIB. Key results from simulations of the three variants of the model from 1952 to 1988 are presented in Table 6.1 and Figure 6.1.

The improvement between pre-Keynesian capitalism and post-Keynesian capitalism is seen in the fact that post-Keynesian capitalism succeeds in ironing out the recessionary downward wiggles in the national income growth line, and in achieving a slightly higher rate of growth in national income over the entire time period. But pre-Keynesian capitalism and post-Keynesian capitalism are exactly alike in their long-term average rates of capital accumulation and property return. In contrast, pragmatic market socialism succeeds in achieving a significantly higher growth rate in national income, by means of a significantly higher long-term average rate of capital investment. The cost of this higher growth is seen in the lower long-term rate of property return. Since under pragmatic market socialism, all property return would be returned to the general population as a supplement to earned labor income, the "cost" of a lower long-term average rate of property return would not be meaningful. But under capitalism, there exists a class of wealthy capitalists primarily dependent on property income, and to them this cost *would* be meaningful. Moreover, under capitalism the interest of this class in a high rate of property return is an influential force. Thus it may be suggested that the abolition of the special influence of the capitalist class in economic decision-making could allow for a higher rate of investment.

TABLE 6.1

Key Indicators from Three Variants of a Model of Aggregate Investment

Indicator (%)	Model I pre-Keynesian capitalist	Model II post-Keynesian capitalist	Model III pragmatic market socialist
average rate of business capital investment	9.11	9.11	11.85
average rate of property return	16.04	16.04	15.01
average annual growth rate of national income	5.98	6.07	6.30

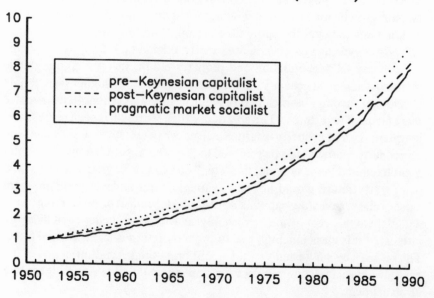

FIGURE 6.1
Potential Growth in National Income (1952 = 1)

It goes without saying that the three variants of this model are all extremely crude approximations of their respective real-world analogues. As one example out of many, the "pre-Keynesian capitalist" version of the model does not display a realistic amount of variability in the national income growth line. Also, the numerical parameter values used in the simulations are purposely adjusted to keep the solution results for the three variants within a narrow range of variation. This is done to avoid overstating the argument. What the model results do clearly demonstrate, however, is the conceptual distinction between the stabilization objective of Keynesian anticyclical policy and the issue of economic growth. They demonstrate that Keynesian anticyclical policy does not necessarily completely absolve capitalism from the traditional socialist accusation of inadequate dynamic performance. The same factors which lead to business depressions in the pre-Keynesian world are capable of retarding economic growth in the post-Keynesian world. Thus the complete elimination of business recessions does not necessarily mean that the capitalist economy is growing at the socially optimal rate.

Over the last two decades, numerous neoconservative economists have lobbied vociferously, both in the professional journals and in the popular media, for lower taxes on capital property income in the interest of increasing the rate of saving and investment. They have been largely successful, and wealthy capitalists owe these economists a large debt of gratitude. Through their efforts, these wealthy capitalists now enjoy significantly higher disposable incomes. Sales of fur coats, diamond necklaces, yachts, private airplanes, and large estates are thriving. But just how much of this added disposable income of the very wealthy is finding its way into increased saving and capital investment is a very problematic question.

One might well agree with neoconservative economists that a higher rate of saving and investment would be very desirable for purposes of raising productivity, enhancing innovation, improving economic performance and growth, and so on. Under pragmatic market socialism this desirable objective could be achieved by the simple and direct means of an increase in the national government appropriation to business physical capital investment. There would be no risk that the major impact of the policy would simply be to enhance the already extravagant living standards of the small minority of plutocratic capitalists.

NOTES

1. W. Duncan Reekie's survey of Austrian economics (1984), intended for the student and nonspecialist, is a concise and balanced effort to sort out the major

differences between the viewpoint and approach of Austrian economics relative to mainstream economics. It also contains brief biographical notes on some of the major figures in the tradition.

2. The Bolshevik Revolution of 1917 and the subsequent radical social and economic transformation of Russia lent a new urgency to academic debates concerning the potential economic workings and performance of socialism as defined by public ownership of the nonhuman factors of production. A far right-wing response to the news from Russia was formulated by Ludwig von Mises in "Economic Calculation in the Socialist Commonwealth," published in German in 1920 and shortly afterward in the first edition of *Socialism: An Economic and Sociological Analysis*, published in German in 1922. To Mises's way of thinking, the early news of economic hardship and famine in Russia was not so much the consequence of World War I and the Russian Civil War as it was evidence of inherent economic breakdown owing to the inability of a socialist economy to sustain "rational economic calculation." Both of these works were translated and published in English in the 1930s. "Economic Calculation" appeared in the compendium *Collectivist Economic Planning* (1935), edited by Friedrich Hayek. The first English edition of *Socialism* appeared in 1936; it was followed by a revised edition in 1951. The inability of socialism to sustain rational calculation (in the absence of outside guidance) is argued by Mises in Part I, Chapter II, of the 1951 edition of *Socialism*, and also in Chapter XXVI of *Human Action: A Treatise on Economics*, Mises's magnum opus (first edition, 1949; third revised edition, 1966). According to Mises, socialism could never amount to anything more or less than a giant bureaucracy, and his dim view of bureaucracy is well documented in his 1943 book on the subject. Mises's disdain for socialism as a concept was matched by his contempt for socialists as individuals. In *The Anti-Capitalist Mentality* (1956), Mises argues that throughout the history of the socialist idea, its adherents have been inspired by nothing more elevated than the envious resentment harbored by physically, intellectually, and psychologically inferior human beings against physically, intellectually, and psychologically superior human beings. The extremity of Mises's judgments, his intemperate rhetoric, and his supercilious attitude combined to make him somewhat of an embarrassment even to those who heartily subscribed to his negative view of socialism.

Friedrich von Hayek, although he may be considered a disciple of Mises, enjoys a more positive image. In his greatest popular success, *The Road to Serfdom* (1944), he attacks socialism more on political and psychological grounds than on economic grounds. Although Hayek questions the economic rationality of socialism in numerous obiter dicta throughout the large corpus of his published work in economics, political theory, and philosophy, much of his thinking on the economics of socialism may be ascertained from a mere three article-length pieces: his two editor's contributions to *Collectivist Economic Planning* ("The Nature and History of the Problem" and "The Present State of the Debate"), and his later critique of the Langian market socialist proposal in an article published in 1940 in *Economica* ("Socialist Calculation: The 'Competitive Solution'"). In his old age, with the help of an editor, Hayek produced one last blast against socialism: *The Fatal Conceit:*

The Errors of Socialism (1988). This extremely abstract and philosophical work contains little or nothing which is relevant to the evaluation of the pragmatic market socialist proposal. Evidence of this is the fact that Oskar Lange, the founder of the market socialist concept, is not mentioned anywhere in the book.

3. Illustrative of the mainstream attitude that Austrian economics constitutes a refutation of socialism is the recent analysis of Don Lavoie (1985) on the "socialist calculation debate" of the 1930s and 1940s. Lavoie argues that none of the pro-socialists of the period provided even marginally effective responses to the central accusation of Mises and Hayek that under socialism, rational calculation would be either literally "impossible" or at a minimum "highly ineffective." For example, the most famous pro-socialist of the period, Oskar Lange, provided a plan conceived on the basis of static neoclassical welfare theory. This plan, according to Lavoie, would almost certainly be grossly inadequate with respect to investment, growth, and entrepreneurship. In other words, whatever its theoretical merits in terms of conventional marginalist economic theory, its real-world implementation would almost certainly lead to economic stagnation and decay. Much the same appraisal has been advanced in contributions by Karen Vaughn (1980) and Peter Murrell (1983). Although these authors probably underestimate the potential dynamic performance of Langian market socialism, the main problem with their argument is that there are other plans of market socialism available (such as the pragmatic) which quite possibly constitute a more effective response to Austrian allegations of the inefficiency of socialism.

4. The analysis here follows the author's article in *Comparative Economic Studies*: "Ludwig von Mises on the 'Artificial Market'" (1989). Mises reiterated the argument discussed here in *Human Action* (1966, pp. 705-710).

5. Mises attributes the notion of the "artificial market" to "some of the younger socialists." Since the artificial market is none other than pragmatic market socialism, it would certainly be interesting to know more about the intellectual pedigree of the concept. Exactly who were these "younger socialists"? None of the important figures from the period during which Mises was preparing the revised English edition of *Socialism*, and whom he would have considered "younger socialists," seem to be likely candidates. The three most prominent contemporaries of Lange reputed to be sympathetic to socialism were Maurice Dobb, Henry Dickinson, and Abba Lerner. But in their published work, none of these economists advocated any plan of market socialism which is recognizable as pragmatic market socialism. Perhaps the idea of pragmatic market socialism was considered too simple and straightforward to form a basis for professional writing. Certainly these and other economists might have discussed the idea, and they might have thought of it as a sort of "backup" socialist proposal in the event that the more sophisticated proposals which they analyzed in their professional writing became overly entangled in theoretical or practical difficulties.

6. For general references on the economic literature concerning decision-making under uncertainty, see note 2, Chapter 3. Illustrative general references to dynamic optimization in economics include Edmund Phelps (1966), Karl Shell (1967), G. Hadley and M. C. Kemp (1971), and Morton Kamien and Nancy

Schwartz (1981).

7. It is fair to point out, however, that there has been at least one effort to vindicate the negative Austrian opinion of socialism: a 1984 article on market socialism by Peter Murrell, a mainstream economist who might be described as a "fellow traveler" of Austrianism. In the true Austrian spirit, Murrell endeavors to establish by purely logical means that an unnamed form of market socialism analogous to pragmatic market socialism must necessarily be inefficient. He departs from the tradition, however, in using mathematics rather than literary exposition as the medium of analysis. Murrell's proof of the inefficiency of market socialism is compromised by the fact that it starts from the assumption that all interest income is an earned return to saving and all profit income is an earned return to capital management effort. Under these assumptions, the inefficiency of market socialism follows directly without need of formal derivation: This is simply a matter of assuming that which is to be proved. Another fatal flaw in Murrell's argument is that it ignores distributional considerations. It is interesting to note that Murrell utilizes neither dynamic nor uncertainty methods to argue the inefficiency of socialism but, rather, the traditional static methods of classical calculus which most Austrians habitually denounce as uselessly restrictive and unrealistic.

8. The analysis on which this statement is based is too space-consuming and technical even to be included in the Analytical Appendix at the end of this book. The interested reader is referred to the author's article "Risk-Taking as a Justification for Property Income" (*Journal of Comparative Economics*, 1988).

9. Modern disciples of Austrianism would doubtless acknowledge as the high priest of the contemporary cult of entrepreneurship Professor Israel Kirzner of the University of Chicago, author of *Competition and Entrepreneurship* (1973), *Perception, Opportunity and Profit* (1979), and *Discovery and the Capitalist Process* (1985). Kirzner carries on in the tradition established at the University of Chicago by Frank Knight, author of *Risk, Uncertainty and Profit* (1921). There may or may not be any substance in the obscure but sonorous rhetoric of Knight and Kirzner as regards the role of the entrepreneur in the modern economy. But despite widespread opinion to the contrary, no one has yet demonstrated that the ideas of Knight and Kirzner constitute a serious argument against socialism in any form, let alone the pragmatic market socialist form.

10. The thesis stated here is derived from a number of diverse sources. Both Oskar Lange (1964, pp. 111-114) and Joseph Schumpeter (1962, pp. 96-98) consider a closely analogous question: the possible tendency for imperfectly competitive firms to delay the introduction of cost-reducing innovations in the interest of maintaining the value of existing capital. Lange, the socialist, regarded this tendency as a much more serious liability of the contemporary capitalist system than did Schumpeter, the nonsocialist. Lange and Schumpeter consider the problem as one of a certain unwillingness on the part of business enterprises to introduce technologically advanced equipment because of the adverse effect on the profitability of existing equipment, but it is a straightforward extrapolation of this idea to an unwillingness to introduce *any* new equipment because of the same adverse effect. Carl Landauer (1964, p. 194), in discussing the "disappointing

tempo of growth of industrial production in the United States" during the 1950s, says: "the creation of new productive capacity is slowed down whenever there is doubt as to the prospects of such capacity being used: Who would want to install new machines when there is a serious chance that much of the time they will stand idle for lack of orders?" None of the voluminous technical economic literature on the determinants of investment deals specifically with such possible tendencies.

11. This argument has been put forward in two of the author's prior articles. The 1978 *Rivista* article develops the argument via a simple theoretical model of the allocation of new saving resources. The model demonstrates that under reasonable assumptions about production and the effect of business physical capital on profitability, a socialist economy interested in the maximization of total income would allocate a larger proportion of new saving to business physical capital than a capitalist economy in which new saving is allocated in such a way as to maximize property income. The 1986 *JEI* article develops the argument via a small-scale macroeconomic recursive simulation model similar to the one specified and discussed herein.

7

PEOPLE'S CAPITALISM

A. INTRODUCTION AND OVERVIEW

The people's capitalism thesis in effect asserts the irrelevance of the traditional socialist complaint against capitalism that capital property income is unearned by its human recipients, the capital owners. This complaint is irrelevant, according to the people's capitalism argument, because the distribution of capital wealth (and hence of the capital property income which capital wealth produces)—when properly understood—is *not* in fact all that unequal. If this were true, then it would not matter that capital property income is *not* a return to capital management effort in the form either of corporate supervision or investment analysis, that it is *not* a return to the abstinence and other sacrifices of saving, that it is *not* a return to risk-taking, entrepreneurship, investment, innovation, discovery, and so on. It would not matter because everyone—or almost everyone—would already be receiving their fair share of capital property income (just as promised by socialism), and therefore no one—or almost no one—would be in a position to complain about possible injustice and inequity under capitalism.

The overall people's capitalism thesis may be subdivided into three major components: (1) the distribution of *current* capital wealth is not excessively unequal; (2) the distribution of *lifetime* capital wealth is not excessively unequal; (3) the distribution of *expected lifetime* capital wealth is not excessively unequal. The three components endeavor to convey the following respective messages to the subject: (1) "you *are already* a capitalist"; (2) "you *will become* a capitalist as you advance in years"; (3) "you *will probably become* a capitalist at some point in the future." Clearly there are some individuals in society to whom these messages properly apply—the question is to what percentage of the population. The argument of this chapter is that except to the tiny minority of existing capitalists and their direct heirs, these messages do not properly apply. In fact, these messages attempt to create in the subject the delusion that he or she has a significant personal stake in the preservation of the capitalist status quo, when in fact no such stake exists—at least if the socialist alternative to capitalism is the pragmatic market socialist economic system proposed herein.[1]

Capitalist apologetics flourishes best amid intellectual confusion: Thus one rarely finds in any given statement of capitalist apologetics emphasis upon one single aspect of the case for capitalism. Therefore, people's capitalism propositions are normally combined with various propositions to the effect that socialism would be inefficient, which is itself tantamount to the viewpoint that capital property income is somehow earned in an economically and ethically legitimate sense. But there remains a clear logical distinction between the argument that *all* individuals in society would tend to be be worse off under socialism because socialism would be generally inefficient, and the argument that *even* if socialism were as efficient as capitalism, a *large percentage* of individuals in society would nevertheless tend to be worse off because they personally would be ad-versely affected by a more egalitarian distribution of capital property return.

The various arguments that capital property income is earned, and that consequently socialism would be inefficient, have been considered in Chapters 4-6. At this point, attention will be focused on the logical essence of the people's capitalism argument itself. In order to permit this, it will be assumed, for purposes of the discussion of people's capitalism, that prag-matic market socialism would indeed achieve a level of short-run and long-run efficiency equivalent to that achieved by capitalism. The emphasis will be on what percentage of the population would be benefited and what percentage of the population would be harmed (assuming equal economic efficiency) by a shift from distribution of capital property return in propor-tion to financial assets under capitalism to distribution of capital property return as a social dividend supplement to labor income under pragmatic market socialism. These percentages, once determined or estimated, would then be adjusted according to expectations concerning relative efficiency. If it is believed likely that in practice pragmatic market socialism would be significantly less efficient than capitalism, then the percentage benefited by pragmatic market socialism would be adjusted downward. If it is believed likely that in practice pragmatic market socialism would be significantly more efficient than capitalism, the percentage benefited would be adjusted upward.

Of the three principal components of the people's capitalism argument, the first two (that current capital wealth is not excessively unequal, and that lifetime capital wealth is not excessively unequal) are more or less directly and definitively refuted by available statistical evidence. Nevertheless, these components remain extremely effective in practice because of the relatively small number of individuals who are fully aware and appreciative of this evidence. In other words, these components derive their effectiveness from the ignorance of most of the subject population to whom they are directed. The evidence on the third component (that expected lifetime capital wealth is not excessively unequal) is far less conclusive than on the first two. The argument to be made here is that inheritance and chance are by far the dominant determinants of lifetime capital wealthholding, and that the influence of such productive contributions as entrepreneurship is minimal. But the evidence supporting this proposition is admittedly not as fully compelling as one would like. The considerable practical effectiveness of this third component of the people's capitalism argument is not derived entirely, however, from the ambiguity of the available evidence: It also derives a large measure of its influence from its joint appeal to the subject's greed and pride.

The third component of the people's capitalism thesis minimizes the influence of inheritance and chance in the generation of large capital fortunes, and alleges that these fortunes are instead mostly the legitimate reward for the wealthholder's great personal industry, skill, and ability in providing essential enterprise and entrepreneurial services to society. The message, simply put, is that "The brightest, the boldest, and the best tend to get rich." The subject's instinctive pride naturally inclines him to the view that he personally is a member of the "brightest, boldest, and best." The subject's instinctive greed naturally inclines him to reveries concerning how pleasant it would be to be rich. Between the subject's instinctive pride and greed, the message takes on a high degree of potency and effectiveness. The message is no doubt most effective among capable, self-confident younger people just commencing their careers—people who have not yet been fully educated by experience in the salient distinctions between fantasy and real life.

The people's capitalism message is individualistically rather than socially oriented. Implicitly it tells the subject: "Don't worry about what socialism might do to society; rather, worry about what it might do to *you*. Perhaps it is true that socialism would benefit the losers and the little people. But you are not one of them; you are, rather, a winner, an individual of substance, one of the chosen. Capitalism may or may not be good for a lot of people, but capitalism is very definitely good for *you*." In its lowest and crudest form, this message may be directed even to individuals of very modest wealth and means. The message is successful to the extent that these people can be made to believe that personal ownership of a house, an automobile, a life insurance policy, a pension benefit, a savings account, or a few thousand dollars' worth of stock and bonds bestows upon them the status of "capitalist." A far more sensible definition of a "capitalist" is that which we have utilized throughout: one who personally possesses sufficient capital wealth that the capital property income on this wealth is sufficient by itself to support at least a comfortable lifestyle. By this definition, well under 1 percent of the population of an advanced capitalist nation such as the United States may be sensibly classified as capitalists. Clearly, the overwhelming majority of those who own houses, automobiles, life insurance policies, and so on, are not even distant cousins to capitalists.

At least some of the misunderstanding may be the fault of certain past extremists among the ranks of the socialists who have called for public ownership not merely of the capital means of production but of consumption goods as well. Perhaps even the well-known nineteenth-century slander against socialism that it calls for the "nationalization of women" is traceable to the ravings of some obscure, mentally unbalanced, self-described "socialist." The pragmatic market socialist proposal is typical of the mainstream socialist viewpoint that public ownership be confined strictly to capital goods used in large-scale, organized production. Personal owner- ship of anything and everything used directly by private individuals for their own personal purposes would be fully preserved: this would include residences, automobiles, and so on. It would also include insurance and pension benefits of all kinds; these would in no way be compromised or diminished by the inauguration of pragmatic market socialism. As for small accumulations of capital wealth in the form of stocks, bonds, and such instruments, these would be fully compensated in cash. The accumulations would thereby be fully preserved—although they would no longer produce any capital property income. For the great majority of households, however, even those with reasonably substantial capital wealth accumulations, the amount of social dividend income received under pragmatic market socialism would considerably exceed the capital property income which they had received under capitalism.

The people's capitalism thesis is essentially that capital wealth ownership is in reality quite widely dispersed throughout the population. Crude variants of the thesis attempt to support the proposition by blurring the distinction between capital wealth and noncapital wealth. This blurring is useful because certain important types of noncapital wealth have indeed become widely dispersed throughout the population, particularly houses and automobiles. Capital wealth consists of financial assets which directly produce monetary capital property income: stocks and bonds are the ar- chetypal examples. Noncapital wealth consists of other types of assets, mostly physical in nature, which do not produce this type of income. Among this latter type of wealth are houses used as personal residences and personal automobiles. Many economists insist that houses and automobiles bestow on their owners implicit income equal to the rental charges they would have to pay to use comparable houses and automobiles for their personal purposes. But such implicit income—in contrast with the explicit capital income produced by stocks and bonds—cannot be spent at the local grocery store or jewelry store. It cannot be used to support life: If a person owned only a mansion and a gold-plated limousine and chose not to work, that person would starve to death. However much "implicit income" may be produced by noncapital forms of wealth, this remains an extremely significant qualitative distinction between capital wealth and noncapital wealth.

Another component of generally defined wealth which has become much more widely dispersed as the twentieth century has progressed are pension benefits. Inasmuch as most pension plans involve compounded interest, the confusion of pension benefits with capital wealth is perhaps somewhat more excusable than the confusion of houses and automobiles with capital wealth. But there is still a very vital distinction: The power of true capital wealth to produce capital property income is not terminated by the death of the owner. The celebrated management guru Peter Drucker, in his book *The Unseen Revolution* (1976), has advanced a novel variant of the people's capitalism thesis based on the increasing importance of insurance companies and pension funds in the advanced capitalist economies, particularly that of the United States. The historic objectives of socialism, proclaims Drucker, have already been effectively achieved in the United States and similar nations. This is because a large proportion of the business enterprise system has come to be owned by pension funds and insurance companies. At the same time, the pension and insurance benefits owed by these financial intermediaries to the population are relatively widely dispersed and equally distributed among private households. Thus, without benefit of bloodshed or turmoil, the economy has been effectively socialized—or, alternatively, people's capitalism has prevailed. Thus Drucker provides a new version, this time from the right, of the familiar proposition that public ownership of capital has become "irrelevant."[2]

We have had occasion to comment extensively on the significant and even dominant role of financial intermediaries in contemporary capital markets. This large role constitutes compelling evidence against the proposition that capital property income is legitimately earned as a return to capital management effort in the form of investment analysis. But this large role does not imply that the distribution of capital wealth has been equalized. Just as the Gross National Product measure excludes transactions among business firms to avoid double counting, so too the wealth measure excludes financial assets owned by business firms. Properly defined, "wealth" refers to property directly owned by private households: This is how wealth has always been defined in economic thinking and in government documentation. This documentation demonstrates clearly that as far as *privately owned wealth* is concerned, it remains today just as it has been for as long as it has been seriously measured: very unequally distributed. "Pension fund socialism" à la Peter Drucker is simply another obfuscation of this bedrock reality about contemporary capitalism.

Table 7.1 presents the best data currently available, pertaining to the United States during the twentieth century, on a very popular measure of wealth inequality: the percentage of wealth owned by the wealthiest 1 percent of the population. Inspection of this data indicates a slight tendency toward equalization between 1920 and 1950—a tendency which has been terminated in the latter half of the twentieth century.[3] As to what was responsible for the apparent equalization between 1920 and 1950, explanations run to the vicissitudes of depression and war, along with a very considerable increase in the progressiveness of personal taxation. Another factor no doubt was the widespread diffusion of home and automobile ownership during the first half of the twentieth century. The fact that the

TABLE 7.1

Estimated Share of the Wealthiest One Percent of the U.S.
Population in Total Wealth, 1922-1982

Year	Share	Year	Share
1922	31.5	1958	23.8
1929	36.3	1962	22.0
1933	28.3	1965	23.4
1939	30.6	1969	20.1
1945	23.3	1972	20.7
1949	20.8	1976	20.8
1953	24.3	1982	19.7

Source: 1922-1972: U.S. Department of Commerce, Bureau of the Census, *Statistical Abstract of the United States, 1984*, Table 794 (p. 481). 1976, 1982: Martin Schwartz, "Preliminary Estimates of Personal Wealth, 1982: Composition of Assets," U.S. Department of the Treasury, Internal Revenue Service, *SOI (Statistics of Income) Bulletin*, 4(3), Winter 1984-85, p. 1.

wealthiest 1 percent of the population owns 20 percent of the total wealth in society indicates an extremely high level of inequality in wealth ownership. But it must be strongly emphasized that the inequality of *capital* wealth ownership is still more extreme than the inequality of *total* wealth ownership. As far as capital income-producing financial assets are concerned, it is quite likely that as much as 40 or 50 percent of the total amount of privately owned wealth of this type is held by the wealthiest 1 percent of the population.[4]

What, it may be asked, is the *practical* significance of the drastic inequality presently prevailing with respect to capital wealth, as evidenced by the large percentage of capital wealth owned by the wealthiest 1 percent of the population? Is this merely a numerical abstraction of purely academic interest—such as the large number of tons of water in an ocean, or the large number of stars in a galaxy? So long as the distribution of capital property return is regarded as a foreordained natural phenomenon with which it would be folly to interfere, then the large percentage of capital wealth owned by the wealthiest capitalists does indeed merit nothing beyond raised eyebrows and shrugged shoulders. But once the pragmatic market socialist alternative to capitalism is perceived to constitute a serious, viable alternative to the capitalist status quo, then the inequality of capital wealth becomes a very consequential matter. The direct practical implication of the extreme inequality of capital wealth ownership under contemporary capitalism is that the large majority of the population would receive more social dividend income under pragmatic market socialism than they currently receive capital property income under capitalism. In fact, using official national government data for the United States, it is possible to estimate the percentage of the population which would be financially benefited by pragmatic market socialism: approximately 94 percent. Section B of the present chapter explains how this estimate is obtained.

The estimate is based on current capital wealth ownership, as opposed to lifetime capital wealth ownership or expected lifetime capital wealth ownership. Section C adduces additional evidence that the percentage benefited by pragmatic market socialism would not be greatly reduced if the basis of comparison is lifetime capital wealthholding as opposed to current capital wealthholding. Section D proceeds to a consideration of the distribution of *expected* lifetime capital wealthholding, as opposed to "deterministic" lifetime capital wealthholding. The argument is that expected lifetime capital wealth is not significantly more equally distributed than are lifetime capital wealthholding and current capital wealthholding—and, furthermore, that the major factors in the generation and perpetuation of this high level of inequality are inheritance and chance, as opposed to personal ability, effort, and achievement. Thus, whether we take it to refer to current capital wealthholding, lifetime capital wealthholding, or expected lifetime capital wealthholding, the people's capitalism thesis constitutes an invalid justification for the preservation of the capitalistic status quo.

B. WHO WOULD BENEFIT FROM THE SOCIAL DIVIDEND?

In 1963, the U.S. Federal Reserve Board carried out a major survey on the wealth and income of the U. S. population. Results from the survey were presented in a report entitled *Survey of Financial Characteristics of Consumers*, authored by Dorothy S. Projector and Gertrude S. Weiss and published in 1966. To date, this survey and its report are unique in the annals of statistical documentation of the economic characteristics of the U.S. population. The survey has never been replicated, and one can only wonder if this is mainly because it was so expensive to carry out, or perhaps mainly because it brought to light cold facts about wealthholding in the United States which many individuals of influence would prefer to forget.[5] The fact that these data are at this point approximately twenty-five years old is of very little consequence. As is documented in the data shown in Table 7.1, there is no apparent long-term trend in wealth inequality in the latter half of the twentieth century. Furthermore, one might well conjecture that after more than ten years of hard work in Washington aimed at reducing the tax burden on the wealthy, the U.S. distribution of wealth is now somewhat more, rather than less, unequal than it was in the early 1960s.

Survey of Financial Characteristics of Consumers is unique in the fact that explicit data are presented not only on the distribution of *total* wealth but also on the distribution of *capital* wealth.[6] Considerable emphasis has been placed herein on the critical distinction between these two concepts of wealth. This distinction is especially vital to the present purpose because the objective of pragmatic market socialism is not to equalize total wealth but to equalize the distribution of the capital property return paid under capitalism to owners of capital wealth. *Survey of Financial Characteristics of Consumers* provides the distribution of capital wealth not only for the total population, but also for various age ranges. As will be discussed in Section C below, these latter data constitute a direct refutation of the hypothesis that inequality in capital wealth ownership is mainly a function of life cycle saving.

Table 7.2, derived from the *Survey*, presents information on the distribution of capital wealth and labor income, information which enables an estimate of the potential effect of social dividend distribution of capital property return. This information indicates the extremely high level of inequality in capital wealth ownership relative to inequality in labor income distribution. Probably the most popular single measure of inequality is the Gini coefficient, which has a range from 0, indicating complete equality, to 1, indicating complete inequality. The Gini coefficient for capital wealth, computed from the data in Table 7.2, is .9299, while the Gini coefficient for labor income is a relatively modest .3644. Pragmatic market socialism intends to distribute the flow of capital property income produced by business firms and other entities in a competitive bidding process for scarce financial capital, in proportion to labor income, instead of in proportion to capital wealth. Since labor income is far more equally distributed than capital wealth, this implies a substantial equalization of the distribution of capital property return. The question is exactly what percentage of the population would benefit from the social dividend distribution principle. The question is answered as follows:

Under capitalism, the property return income (*PRI*) of household i tends to be proportional to capital wealth (*CW*) by the factor *r*, representing the rate of return on *CW*. (In practice, of course, there is a strong random factor which affects the *r* of any particular household in any particular period of time; but this discussion is in terms of the statistically expected value of PRI.) Under pragmatic market socialism, the social dividend income (*SDI*) of household *i* would be proportional to its labor income (*LI*). Presuming that the average return factor *r* under capitalism would hold under pragmatic market socialism (this reflects the equal efficiency assumption), and that the Bureau of Public Ownership (BPO) would distribute as social dividend income the proportion $1-\alpha$ of the property return it receives (α is the BPO retention coefficient), the following result is obtained:[7]

$$SDI_i > PRI_i \quad \text{as}$$

$$(1-\alpha)\frac{LI_i}{MLI} > \frac{CW_i}{MCW}$$

where *MLI* is mean labor income and *MCW* is mean capital wealth. This may be put into words as follows: If the adjusted ratio of the labor income of a household to mean labor income in the population $(1-\alpha)(LI_i/MLI)$ is greater than the ratio of the capital wealth of that household to mean capital wealth in the population (CW_i/MCW), then that household would receive more social dividend income under pragmatic market socialism than it receives property return income under capitalism.

Table 7.2 gives the ratio CW_i/MCW for each wealth bracket in column (5), and the ratio LI_i/MLI for each income bracket in column (10). Figure

7.1 locates points representing cumulative percentages of the population and, respectively, the capital wealth ratio (CW_i/MCW), and the adjusted labor income ratio $(1-\alpha)(LI_i/MLI)$. By linear interpolation, the point may be estimated at which there is an intersection between the capital wealth ratio function and the labor income ratio function. The method is indicated in the notes under the figure. The intersection point occurs at a percentage of 94.21 and a ratio of 1.6657 for a BPO retention coefficient of $\alpha = .05$. It is estimated that 94.21 percent of the population has an adjusted ratio of labor income to mean labor income higher than the ratio of capital wealth to mean capital wealth. This is the percentage of the population which would receive a larger amount of social dividend income under pragmatic market socialism than they currently receive property income under capitalism. This, then, is the practical consequence of the inequity under capitalism of highly unequal property return distribution: 94.21 percent of the population is poorer under capitalism than they would be under pragmatic market socialism. Of course, the computed figure of 94.21 is only an estimate, and as such it is unlikely to be exactly correct. But it is not necessary to undertake

TABLE 7.2

Comparison of Capital Wealth Distribution with Labor Income
Distribution in the U. S. Population, 1962

A. Capital Wealth

Wealth Range ($) (1)	Number of Units (Mil) (2)	Mean Invest- ment Assets ($) (3)	Cumulative Percent of Units (4)	Ratio for Capital Wealth (5)
0-499	11.8	$0	20.38	0
500-1,999	14.3	5	45.42	.0007
2,000-4,999	7.4	902	75.82	.1286
5,000-9,999	4.9	2,704	84.28	.3855
10,000-24,999	5.2	8,290	93.26	1.1821
25,000-49,999	2.1	21,298	96.89	3.0369
50,000-99,999	1.0	51,944	98.62	7.4068
100,000-499,999	.7	196,273	99.83	27.9870
500,000-	.1	1,264,653	100.00	180.3298
all brackets	57.9	$7,013		

Table 7.2 continued:

B. Labor Income*

Income Range ($) (6)	Number of Units (Mil) (7)	Mean Labor Income ($) (8)	Cumulative Percent of Units (9)	Ratio for Labor Income (10)
0-2,999	16.3	$1,202	28.15	.2321
3,000-4,999	11.4	3,379	47.84	.6526
5,000-7,499	12.2	5,610	69.91	1.0834
7,500-9,999	9.0	7,788	84.85	1.5040
10,000-14,999	6.2	9,191	95.16	1.7750
15,000-24,999	2.0	11,729	98.61	2.2651
25,000-49,999	.5	15,167	99.48	2.9291
50,000-99,999	.2	21,484	99.82	4.1490
100,000-	—	42,375	100.00	8.1836
all brackets	57.9	$5,178		

Source: Dorothy S. Projector and Gertrude S. Weiss, *Survey of Financial Characteristics of Consumers,* Washington D.C.: Board of Governors of the Federal Reserve System, August 1966: Table A10 (pp. 114-121): Composition of Portfolio of Liquid and Investment Assets, Dec. 31, 1962, Part b: Mean Amount in Dollars of Equity (pp. 118-121); Table A33 (pp. 148-149): Characteristics of Consumer Units, Dec. 31, 1962; Table A36 (p. 151): Consumer Units in Survey Population, Dec. 31, 1962.

Notes: "Wealth Range" is Size of Portfolio of Liquid and Investment Assets. "Ratio for Capital Wealth" is Mean Investment Assets of the Wealth bracket divided by Mean Investment Assets for all Wealth brackets ($7,013). "Ratio for Labor Income" is Mean Labor Income of the Income bracket divided by Mean Labor Income for all Income brackets ($5,178).

*Table A33 of *Survey of Financial Characteristics of Consumers* gives Mean Income for each Income Range, where this is a total income measure including income from all sources. These Mean Total Income figures were converted to Mean Labor Income by using the ratios of Wage and Salary Income (WSI) to Adjusted Gross Income (AGI) reported for each Income Range, obtained from Table 2 (pp. 30 ff.) in *Statistics of Income 1963: Individual Income Tax Returns* (Washington, D.C.: Department of the Treasury, Internal Revenue Service). The proportions of AGI represented by WSI for the nine Income Ranges, from highest to lowest, are as follows: 0.1737, 0.3510, 0.4392, 0.6605, 0.8561, 0.9024, 0.9021, 0.8511, 0.7626. For all Income Ranges, the proportion of WSI to AGI is 0.8119.

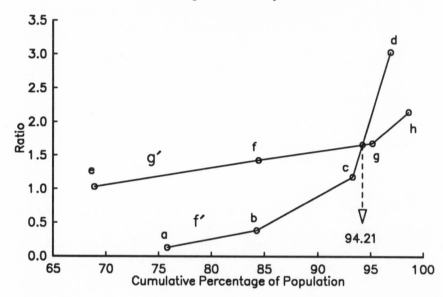

FIGURE 7.1
Percentage Benefited by Socialism

Notes:

Capital Wealth: f′ function			Labor Income: g′ function			
Point	Cumulative Percentage	Ratio	Point	Cumulative Percentage	Ratio	Adjusted Ratio
a	75.82	.1286	e	68.91	1.0834	1.0292
b	84.28	.3855	f	84.45	1.5040	1.4288
c	93.26	1.1821	g	95.16	1.7750	1.6863
d	96.89	3.0369	h	98.61	2.2651	2.1518

Equation of straight line segment between c and d:
Ratio = −46.51383 + (.5114063 x Percentage)
Equation of straight line segment between f and g:
Ratio = −0.60134 + (.0240384 x Percentage)

Intersection of straight line segments:
Percentage = 94.21   Ratio = 1.6657

complicated statistical analysis to know that a very high level of confidence attaches to the proposition that, assuming equal economic efficiency as between capitalism and pragmatic market socialism, at least 90 percent of the population would benefit from social dividend distribution of capital property return.

An obvious objection is that in order to achieve efficiency comparable with that of capitalism, the Bureau of Public Ownership would necessarily have to retain much more than 5 percent of property return to cover incentive payments to its agents. Such an objection constitutes a resort to the capital management argument dealt with in Chapter 4. It is interesting to note that unless the BPO retention coefficient were to become quite high, the percentage of the population benefited by social dividend distribution of property return would not be significantly diminished. Recalculation of the intersection point indicated in Figure 7.1 for higher retention coefficients shows the following:

BPO Retention Coeff.	Percentage Benefited
5 percent ($\alpha = 0.05$)	94.21
10 percent ($\alpha = 0.10$)	94.03
15 percent ($\alpha = 0.15$)	93.85
20 percent ($\alpha = 0.20$)	93.67
25 percent ($\alpha = 0.25$)	93.49

These results are striking testimony to the high degree of inequality in capital wealth distribution in advanced capitalist nations. So unequal is this distribution that even if the total pie of distributed property return were substantially reduced, the great majority of the population would still receive more social dividend pie under pragmatic market socialism than they currently receive capital property income pie under capitalism. Of course the core pragmatic market socialist proposal envisions quite a small BPO retention coefficient. But it is interesting to know that the distributional benefit of pragmatic market socialism does not depend critically on a very low retention coefficient.

C. THE MINOR ROLE OF LIFE CYCLE SAVING

An extremely important feature of the modern economy is the institution of retirement. Whether for reasons of efficiency or of humanity, individuals are not expected to work until they drop. Roughly speaking, the expected age of retirement is around sixty and the expected life span is around seventy-five. Therefore individuals must make provision for approximately fifteen years of retirement consumption unsupported by current labor income. Saving which is done for purposes of providing retirement income is called "life cycle saving." The argument may be advanced that capital wealth inequality (or total wealth inequality, for that matter) mostly reflects life cycle saving. There is obviously a kernel of truth in the argument: Clearly individuals late in their working careers are going to have a great deal more in the way of assets intended to provide retirement income than do individuals recently embarked on their working careers, or individuals well into their retirement years. At one time this argument may have been a great deal more plausible than it is today, but at the present time enough hard evidence has been accumulated to demonstrate compellingly that life cycle saving is responsible for only a very small fraction of existing inequality in both total wealth and capital wealth.[8]

As has already been pointed out, pension benefits are qualitatively different from capital wealth: Pension benefits are terminated upon the death of the beneficiary, while capital wealth in the form of stocks and bonds can, and often does, go on producing capital property income through several generations of inheritors. Pension benefits are normally a very important component of the total wealth of low-to-medium-income households; and the value of pension benefits follows the classic skewed inverted-V pattern associated with life cycle saving: a slow rise to a peak, followed by a relatively rapid decline. Low-to-medium-income households make provision for retirement almost exclusively through pension plans: They accumulate little or nothing in the way of true capital wealth throughout their working careers. For wealthy capitalistic households, on the other hand, the value of pension benefits is very minor relative to the value of stocks, bonds, and other forms of capital wealth. Moreover, there is no indication of a decline in the value of the capital wealth of wealthy capitalistic households with increasing age of the head of the household. Rather, the value of capital wealth typically increases continuously until the death of the owner.[9] Obviously these households can live very comfortably (not to mention luxuriously) solely on the income produced by their capital wealth, without having to sell any of it in capital markets. The wealth thus tends to appreciate in value at the standard market rate, so that upon the death of the parent capitalist, a new generation of children capitalists emerges through the mechanism of inheritance. The upshot of all this is that life cycle saving has little or nothing to do with the distribution of genuine capital wealth.

A considerable amount of evidence has been accumulated which indicates the minor role of life cycle saving in capital wealth inequality, but one of the most definitive pieces of evidence comes from the *Survey of Financial Characteristics of Consumers* utilized in the preceding section of this chapter to obtain an estimate of the percentage of U.S. households which would be financially benefited by social dividend distribution of property return. The report gives the distribution of capital wealth not only for the entire population, but also for four age brackets: age of head of household under 35, 35-54, 55-64, and 65 and over. Using this information, it is possible to estimate the percentage of the population within each of these age brackets which would benefit from social dividend distribution of property return. Also, it is a simple matter to reestimate the percentage benefited for different values of the BPO retention coefficient.

Table 7.3 shows the Gini coefficient of capital wealth distribution for the four age brackets and the overall population, as well as the percentage benefited for a range of BPO retention coefficients from a low of .05 to a high of .25. The retention coefficient has remarkably little impact on the percentage benefited, either for the overall population or for any of the age brackets. As for age, the slightly higher Gini coefficient for the overall population than for any age bracket indicates some positive impact of life cycle saving on capital wealth inequality, but this impact is apparently very slight. If life cycle saving were an important contributor to overall capital wealth inequality, capital wealth inequality within each particular age bracket would be substantially less than overall inequality. But, as can be

TABLE 7.3

Implications of Capital Wealth Distribution in the
U.S. Population, by Age and Overall

		Age Bracket			Overall
	-35	35-54	55-64	65-	
A. Gini Coefficient					
	.8732	.8819	.8636	.8956	.9299
BPO Retention Coefficient	B. Percentage of the Population Benefited by Social Dividend Distribution of Property Return				
.05	99.80	95.93	85.52	88.36	94.21
.10	99.72	95.84	85.01	87.53	94.03
.15	99.65	95.74	84.51	87.36	93.85
.20	99.58	95.65	84.01	87.20	93.67
.25	99.52	95.56	82.23	87.04	93.49

seen from the Gini coefficients in Table 7.3, capital wealth inequality within each particular age bracket is almost as high as overall inequality. As a result, even considering the wealthiest age bracket of the population (55-64), the age bracket which encompasses the usual age of retirement, the percentage of this age group which would be benefited by social dividend distribution is 85.52 percent for a BPO retention coefficient of .05, and it declines only to 82.23 for the substantially higher BPO retention coefficient of .25. In sum, neither a higher BPO retention coefficient (within reasonable limits) nor the life cycle saving factor materially affects the qualitative proposition that the overwhelming majority of the U.S. population would benefit financially from the abolition of capitalism and the inauguration of pragmatic market socialism—unless, of course, the latter were to suffer extraordinary efficiency ailments.

D. DETERMINANTS OF CAPITAL WEALTH MOBILITY

Even if an apologist for capitalism were forced to confront the above evidence and were to acknowledge its significance, there would still be one last line of defense on which to fall back. This line consists of the speculation that there is a great deal of age-independent capital wealth mobility in the population (poor today, rich tomorrow—and vice versa). The data from the *Survey of Financial Characteristics of Consumers* examined above simply indicate that at any point in time there is a great deal of inequality in the distribution of capital wealth, both within the overall population and within any particular age bracket. Thus at any point in time, a few people have a great deal of capital wealth, while most people have little or no capital wealth. What these data do *not* show, however, is that the few people who have a great deal of capital wealth at one point in time also tend to have a great deal of capital wealth at another point in time. Conceivably that small minority of the population which has a great deal of capital wealth at one point in time tends to have much less capital wealth at other points in time, both prior to and after the first point in time. In other words, the fact that the distribution of current capital wealth is highly unequal and the fact that life cycle saving has little to do with capital wealth inequality, do not necessarily rule out the possibility that a high degree of age-independent capital wealth mobility—mobility unrelated to life cycle saving—generates a relatively egalitarian distribution of expected lifetime capital wealth (using "expected" in the statistical sense of expected value or mean).

Needless to emphasize, the proposition of a great deal of capital wealth mobility conflicts sharply with the impression that most people gain through casual empiricism: that the poor tend to stay poor and the rich tend to stay rich. The proposition of age-independent capital wealth mobility is "empirically supported" mostly by Andrew Carnegie-style rags-to-riches anecdotes. But it is very dubious that these anecdotes describe a significant social phenomenon. What makes these anecdotes interesting, after all, is their extraordinary quality, the fact that they are so far removed from the common experience of mankind. But it is perhaps worth mentioning once again that the pragmatic market socialist proposal firmly and explicitly excludes entrepreneurial enterprise from public ownership. What this means is that if a fortune is indeed achieved through genuine, honest, Andrew Carnegie-style entrepreneurial enterprise under capitalism, that same fortune would be achieved by exactly the same means under pragmatic market socialism. Another relevant point is that a few large fortunes are achieved under capitalism without benefit of entrepreneurship but, rather, through an individual's achieving "superstar" status in sports, popular music, or the cinema. However enormous the incomes received by these individuals, they are technically labor incomes, and thus would be unaffected by a transition from capitalism to pragmatic market socialism. The type of fortune that *would* be jeopardized by pragmatic market socialism is the typical capital fortune generated by appreciation on an inherited base. Of course capitalist apologetics does its best to ignore this typical capital fortune, because it is so obviously *not* the result of any worthwhile, productive contribution by the owner.

As far as capital wealth mobility among wealthy capitalists is concerned, there are few, if any, systematic data. The popular business media pay a great deal of attention to the comparatively rare cases of meteoric rises and falls. But most of these cases involve multimillionaires rising to billionaire status and billionaires falling to multimillionaire status. Clearly multimillionaires and billionaires alike belong to the general category of wealthy capitalists. Serious social scientific panel studies of households over time indicate great constancy in wealth and income.[10] Such studies do not deal specifically with capital wealth or with particularly wealthy households, but they do support the general conclusion from casual empiricism that the rich tend to stay rich (or at least relatively rich) and the poor tend to stay poor (or at least relatively poor). In the absence of serious evidence to the contrary, there is no good reason to suppose that the great stability of economic status which is observed in low-to-middle-income groups does not also hold among very wealthy capitalists. The fact that most of the room at the top of the financial ladder is already occupied by people who have been there for a long time directly implies the unlikelihood of people farther down the ladder moving to the top.

Given a certain amount of age-independent capital wealth mobility, whether it be numerically large or numerically small, there remains the even more significant question of the *determinants* of this mobility. The same Andrew Carnegie-style stories which support the proposition of a large degree of capital wealth mobility also imply that this mobility is based upon the socially productive contributions, in the form of innovation, entrepreneurship, and such, of wealthy capitalists. Against these stories, however, may be arrayed a fair amount of serious evidence suggesting the crucial role in capital wealth mobility of two factors having nothing whatever to do with the alleged productive contributions of wealthy capitalists: (1) inheritance; and (2) chance.[11]

Systematic evidence on the role of inheritance in capital wealthholding is, for obvious reasons, hard to come by. Inheritors are normally very reticent, and detailed inquiries will normally elicit the "none of your business" response. There have, however, been some efforts to obtain information through voluntary surveys. The questionnaire utilized in the 1963 Federal Reserve Board survey, for example, contained an item pertaining to inheritance. Table A32 of the *Survey* demonstrates the increasing importance of inheritance with increasing wealth and income. Some 59 percent of the respondents in the highest wealth category admitted to having received "some" inheritance, although only 34 percent were willing to admit that their inherited assets constituted a "substantial" proportion of their current assets. The highest wealth bracket in the report was defined as total wealth of $500,000 or above—not a particularly large amount, especially when real estate is included. There is little doubt that if the highest bracket were defined in terms of capital wealth (as opposed to total wealth) of a really substantial amount, say $5 million or more, far more than 59 percent of the group would have received "some" inheritance. In considering evidence obtained from voluntary surveys such as this, one must always take account of the possibility of dishonest responses. Few wealthy inheritors are proud of their inheritances, and there is a strong temptation among them to "forget" these inheritances when responding to surveys or other queries.

There is also a strong temptation among wealthy inheritors to minimize the relative importance of inherited assets in relation to their total current assets. In particular, wealthy capitalists as a rule do *not* deem the appreciated value of an inheritance to be part of the inheritance. Thus if a capitalist inherits an amount of stock worth $5 million, and twenty years later, through simple appreciation, that same amount of stock is worth $20 million, the capitalist is quite likely to respond, in apparently good conscience, to a survey on inheritance that his/her inherited assets are a small proportion of current assets.

This tendency is clearly demonstrated by a result from a survey of the affluent conducted by James Barlow and associates in the 1960s. Chart 7.1 (p. 88) of the Barlow et al. report (1966) shows a plot of the percentages of respondents selecting each one of three possible choices for "main source of present assets," against the logarithm of income. The three choices are: (1) savings out of income; (2) gifts and inheritances; (3) appreciation of assets. "Savings out of income" declines steadily from a high of about 70 percent to a low of about 10 percent. This demonstrates that large accumulations of financial assets are not slowly and patiently accumulated out of labor income for life cycle saving purposes. "Gifts and inheritances" remains stable at about 7 percent over the entire range of income. But we know, from the Federal Reserve Board survey and several other sources, that the receipt of inheritances does in fact increase with income. However, the respondents to the Barlow et al. survey were not being asked "Did you ever receive an inheritance?" but "What is the main source of your present assets?" The third possible choice, "appreciation of assets," was selected as the main source of present assets by a steadily increasing proportion of respondents, from a low of about 15 percent at the lowest income level to a high of about 74 percent at the highest income level. This evidence clearly demonstrates that those individuals who currently possess large capital fortunes which were appreciated from inherited bases choose not to deem the "main source" of these fortunes to be inheritance. This aversion to reality is understandable under the circumstances, but it certainly ought to be taken into account in evaluating claims made by any particular wealthy capitalist that "*My* wealth was *not* inherited." Such claims are often naively accepted at face value, which explains why so many individuals who ought to know better hold the opinion that inheritance plays a minor role in large-scale capital wealthholding.[12]

Another source of systematic information on inheritance is the very laborious and difficult "probate record technique" first applied in Great Britain in the 1920s by Josiah Wedgwood. More recent work using this method has been done by Colin D. Harbury and associates in Great Britain, and by Paul L. Menchik in the United States.[13] In the "backward-searching" variant, applied by Harbury, a sample is obtained of financial estates of people dying at a certain time, and an effort is made to trace as many of their parents as possible, so that the sizes of the parents' financial estates may be ascertained and compared with those of their children. In the "forward-searching" variant, applied by Menchik, a sample is obtained of financial estates of a group of people dying at a certain time, and an effort is made to trace as many of their children as possible, so that the sizes of the children's financial estates may be ascertained and compared with those of their parents. Obviously this type of research is subject to a great deal of sampling error and bias, but one can well appreciate the amount of time and effort that goes into the accumulation of samples of this sort. And despite the shortcomings of the samples, they provide systematic evidence on the role of inheritance which cannot otherwise be obtained. Unlike surveys, the probate court technique is not subject to dishonesty or "forgetfulness" among the respondents.

Table 7.4 provides some illustrative evidence derived from the publications of Harbury and Menchik. In this table, results from Menchik's 1979 *Economica* article have been slightly rearranged to make them more comparable with the format chosen by Harbury and McMahon in their 1973 *Economic Journal* article. This format is designed to provide a meaningful answer to the question "Given that a son dies leaving a certain amount of wealth, how wealthy was his father likely to have been?" Starting with the first row, that pertaining to the wealthiest sons, the figures may be interpreted as follows: Some 26 men died in 1956-1957 leaving fortunes in excess of £500,000: of these 26, 23 percent had fathers who died leaving £500,000 or over, 42 percent had fathers who died leaving £100,000 or over, 69 percent had fathers who died leaving £25,000 or over, and 77 percent had fathers who died leaving £5,000 or over. It is important to note that even the "poorest" of the fathers, those leaving estates in the neighborhood of £5,000, were wealthy men by the standards of the times. Most of the fathers in Harbury's 1956-1957 sample died in the 1910s and 1920s. Taking the average of 1915-1916 and 1925-1926, 1.625 percent of those dying in England left estates of over £5,000, 0.64 percent left estates of over £25,000, 0.01 percent of over £500,000. It may be observed from the table, therefore, that 71 percent of all those men dying in Great Britain in 1956-1957 leaving estates of £100,000 or more had fathers who died leaving wealth that put them in the upper 1.625 percent of the population.

About one tenth of 1 percent (0.1 percent) of all those who died in England in 1956-1957 left estates of £100,000 or more. Thus possession of a fortune of this magnitude put its owner into the highest elite of wealthholding. According to the "inheritance counts for little or nothing" hypothesis put forward by exponents of people's capitalism, in this high elite will mostly be found "self-made men," who arose from humble origins and accumulated their wealth by dint of their own internal assets of intelligence, industry, and determination. This hypothesis is flatly contradicted by Harbury's empirical information. The Harbury sample indicates that fully 71 percent of those ending up in the richest 1 percent of the population had fathers who ended up in the richest 1.625 percent. Put another way, of every

TABLE 7.4

Probate Evidence on the Role of Inheritance in Wealthholding

A. Inheritance in Great Britain: C. D. Harbury

Son's Wealth current £	Cumulative Percentages Father's Wealth: current £				Sample Size
	>500,000	>100,000	>25,000	>5,000	
over 500,000	23	42	69	77	26
300,000-500,000	10	42	59	66	41
200,000-300,000	4	29	63	71	72
100,000-200,000	3	26	56	71	391
Fathers of all sons leaving £100,000 and over	5	28	57	71	530

B. Inheritance in Connecticut: P. L. Menchik

Parents' Wealth 1967 $	Cumulative Percentages Child's Wealth: 1967 $			Sample Size
	>1,000,000	>200,000	>50,000	
over 1,000,000	52	80	91	44
200,000-1,000,000	13	56	79	61
50,000-200,000	1	24	67	89
40,000-50,000	0	0	20	5
Children of all parents leaving $40,000 and over	16	45	75	199

Source Part A: Condensed from Table I in C. D. Harbury and P. C. McMahon, "Inheritance and the Characteristics of Top Wealth Leavers in Britain," *Economic Journal* 83(331): 810-833, September 1973. *Source Part B:* Derived from Table 3 in Paul L. Menchik, "Inter-Generational Transmission of Inequality: An Empirical Study," *Economica* 46(184): 349-362, November 1979.

Notes: In Part A, Wealth is defined as estate size at death. In Part B, Wealth is defined as "Peak Midparent Wealth," an adjusted weighted average of the estates of both parents. The Part A results were obtained by tracing the fathers of a sample of men dying in 1956-57 in Great Britain leaving estates of £100,000 or more in current £. The Part B results were obtained by tracing the children of a sample of parents dying in the 1930's and 1940's in Connecticut leaving estates of $40,000 or more in 1967 dollars.

ten very wealthy people, seven came from very wealthy parentage. Apparently most of the available room at the top is already occupied by those who started at the top.

Of course, Britain is reputed to be a relatively stratified society. What about a "frontier republic" such as the United States, in which socioeconomic mobility is reputed to be very prevalent? The results pertaining to the United States, shown in Part B of Table 7.4, are basically consistent with those in Part A, although the forward-searching variant of the probate record technique utilized by Menchik approaches the intergenerational transmission of wealth from the opposite angle. The backward-searching variant asks the question "How wealthy were the parents of wealthy children likely to have been?" The answer seems to be "Quite wealthy." The forward-searching variant asks the question "How wealthy are the children of wealthy parents likely to be?" Once again, the answer seems to be "Quite wealthy."

As indicated, the format of Part B of Table 7.4 is comparable with that of Part A. Starting with the first row, that pertaining to the wealthiest parents, the figures may be interpreted as follows: There were 44 located children of parents who died in Connecticut in the 1930s and 1940s leaving $1 million or over: of these 44 children, 52 percent died leaving wealth of over $1 million, 80 percent died leaving wealth of over $200,000, and 91 percent died leaving wealth of over $50,000. (All these figures are in terms of constant 1967 dollars.) While it is possible to quibble over whether 50,000 1967 dollars qualifies as a "large estate," clearly 200,000 1967 dollars does so. It appears, therefore, that 80 percent of the children of wealthy parents are also wealthy. Whereas Part A of Table 7.4 demolishes the myth of highly prevalent upward mobility ("rags to riches"), Part B demolishes the myth of highly prevalent downward mobility ("riches to rags"). Taking the two indications together suggests very considerable stability over time and between generations in the pattern of capital wealthholding by private individuals.

The information in Table 7.4 is certainly enlightening, and it clearly supports the qualitative proposition that inheritance is an "important" source of capital wealth inequality. But the question remains of exactly *how* important. As both Harbury and Menchik are economists, and by dint of hard work in the dusty archives of the probate courts had developed samples of parent wealth and child wealth, it would quite naturally occur to them to perform regressions of child wealth on parent wealth. The R-squared from a simple regression provides a summary statistic indicating the degree of association between two variables. It ranges from 0, indicating no association, to 1, indicating a perfect association. If causation may be inferred, the

R-squared indicates the causative importance of the independent variable in determining the dependent variable. Harbury and Menchik report a great many R-squareds from a variety of samples, some estimated using the original variable values and some estimated using log transforms of the values. Most of the estimates fall into the range from about 0.20 to about 0.60, suggesting that anywhere from 20 percent to 60 percent of child wealth is directly determined by parental wealth. An interesting result obtained by Harbury is that the R-squareds from regressions of child wealth on parent wealth are increasing over time: The more recent samples show higher R-squareds than the earlier samples.[14] This suggests that the influence of inheritance on wealthholding is increasing.

Although regressions of child wealth on parent wealth are informative, even more direct information would be obtained from a regression of a person's wealth at the time of death on inheritances received earlier by that same person. In a 1980 contribution, Paul Menchik utilized his data set to make estimates of inheritances received. Terminal wealth (i.e., wealth at the time of death) was regressed on estimated inheritance. Four such regressions were performed, one for each of four computational methods. For one of these methods, the R-squared was 0.36, but for the other three the R-squareds were all about 0.59. These results confirm the closer association to be expected between current wealth and inherited wealth than between current wealth and parental wealth. Menchik found an R-squared of 0.25 or less between current wealth (of the child at death) and parental wealth, but for the same sample found a higher R-squared of at least 0.39 and quite possibly as high as 0.59 between current wealth (of the child at death) and inherited wealth.

It is not at all extravagant to say, on the basis of this evidence, that possibly as much as 60 percent of capital wealth at a person's death is statistically directly attributable to inheritances received. But what of the remaining 40 percent? May this be attributed to the personal merit and social contributions of the capital owners? Does it represent "self-made wealth," to use the customary term? It *may* be attributed to the personal merit and social contributions of the capital owners, but it may also—with perhaps greater realism—be attributed to random variation in rates of capital wealth appreciation which have nothing whatever to do with the personal merit and social contributions of the capital owners. The extreme variability in rates of growth of investment asset values is universally recognized by all those familiar with capital markets. This variability suggests that even large and highly diversified individual portfolios of investment assets could experience substantial variability in growth rates between any two points in time.

To explore the implications of random growth on an unequal inherited asset base, consider a modest computer simulation experiment based on the elementary stochastic growth equation:

$$CW_{t+1} = (1 + g) CW_t$$

where CW is capital wealth, g is a normally distributed random variable representing the rate of appreciation, and t and $t+1$ represent two successive periods in time. The initial CW distribution (representing the distribution of inheritances) over 20 individuals is arbitrarily specified to be highly unequal (Gini coefficient = .7611). The overall level of inequality is generated by inequality among the first 10 individuals (ranging from individual 1 with initial CW of 50.0 to individual 10 with initial CW of 1.0), while individuals 11 through 20 are all given the same inherited initial CW of 0.5. The mean and standard deviation of g are set respectively at GM = 0.08 and GSD = 0.12.

Table 7.5 shows results from a single simulation of the model at ten-year intervals (t = 1, 10, 20, 30, and 40). For each of these periods capital wealth is rank ordered. The parenthesized figure in each column represents the initial (period 1) rank of the individual's capital wealth. The right-hand column gives rank-ordered average lifetime capital wealth. At the bottom of the table are two summary statistics: the Gini coefficient measures capital wealth inequality for a particular time period, and the R-squared is from a simple regression of current capital wealth on initial capital wealth (this is the analogue of the above-mentioned R-squareds of Menchik's regressions of wealth of child at death on inherited wealth). The Gini coefficient and R-squared for average lifetime capital wealth are at the lower right.

Two individuals are singled out in Table 7.5: individual 6, with initial CW of 2.5 (rank order = 6) and final CW of 1.9 (rank order = 16); and individual 16, with initial CW of 0.5 (rank order = 16) and final CW of 27.7 (rank order = 9). Boxes connected by arrows trace the movements of these two individuals through the capital wealth distribution. Individual 6 is a case of "riches to rags," an unlucky investor whose average annual rate of appreciation from period 1 through period 40 is a negative 0.68 percent. Individual 16 is a case of "rags to riches," a lucky investor whose average annual rate of appreciation from period 1 through period 40 is a positive 10.5 percent.

Examination of Table 7.5 brings to light some important points. To begin with, the results of the simulation for individuals 6 and 16 demonstrate that random chance provides a perfectly good explanation for the anecdotal evidence cited by exponents of people's capitalism to support the hypothesis of a great deal of upward and downward capital wealth mobility. Dramatic cases of rise and fall are to be expected from the workings of chance. But

TABLE 7.5

A Simulation of Random Capital Wealth Appreciation

Rank	Capital Wealth (CW) of Individual I at Period t = ...					Average Lifetime
	... 1	... 10	... 20	... 30	... 40	
	CW(I)	CW(I)	CW(I)	CW(I)	CW(I)	CW(I)
1	50.0(1)	110.7(1)	159.6(1)	138.1(1)	144.6(3)	123.5(1)
2	25.0(2)	16.7(2)	33.7(2)	46.8(8)	141.2(1)	41.8(3)
3	10.0(3)	11.0(3)	22.9(4)	43.3(12)	117.0(4)	35.3(8)
4	5.0(4)	7.8(4)	18.7(8)	42.9(3)	99.8(8)	32.0(4)
5	5.0(5)	7.0(8)	18.6(5)	41.7(4)	40.9(2)	29.4(2)
6	2.5(6)	6.9(5)	16.8(3)	38.7(5)	39.3(5)	19.2(5)
7	2.5(7)	4.3(7)	9.2(7)	29.6(2)	27.7(16)	11.0(12)
8	1.0(8)	3.7(18)	8.9(12)	20.6(16)	21.6(7)	9.9(16)
9	1.0(9)	3.3(6)	3.7(16)	12.2(9)	14.3(11)	8.1(7)
10	1.0(10)	2.4(13)	3.2(9)	9.9(7)	6.7(17)	5.4(9)
11	.5(11)	1.6(12)	3.0(18)	7.4(11)	6.6(9)	5.1(11)
12	.5(12)	1.4(16)	2.7(13)	3.2(17)	5.5(18)	3.3(13)
13	.5(13)	1.1(10)	2.1(6)	2.0(10)	4.1(12)	2.5(6)
14	.5(14)	.9(9)	1.4(11)	1.9(13)	3.8(13)	2.5(18)
15	.5(15)	.7(14)	.9(19)	1.5(14)	2.8(19)	2.0(17)
16	.5(16)	.5(19)	.8(17)	1.2(15)	1.9(6)	1.3(19)
17	.5(17)	.5(11)	.8(14)	1.1(18)	1.7(15)	1.2(14)
18	.5(18)	.4(17)	.8(15)	1.1(6)	1.0(14)	1.1(10)
19	.5(19)	.4(20)	.4(20)	.8(19)	.9(10)	.9(15)
20	.5(20)	.4(15)	.3(10)	.1(20)	.4(20)	.4(20)
Gini	.7611	.7676	.7430	.6390	.6732	.6722
R-Sq	1.00	.8853	.9033	.7116	.3735	.9239

Note: GM = 0.08; GSD = 0.28.

at the same time, the table demonstrates that chance is not an inherently equalizing force, and that it is naive for poor and middle-income people to expect that the workings of chance are likely to raise them to a very high level of wealth. The reason is that chance is as likely to decrease relative wealth as it is to increase it. Thus as a rule (despite the atypical cases of individuals 6 and 16 in Table 7.5), individuals tend to remain pretty close to their initial position within the wealth distribution as time proceeds. To see this principle at work in Table 7.5, consider the fact that the wealthiest individual in the initial period is still the wealthiest individual in terms of lifetime wealth. Consider also the fact that out of the richer individuals 1 through 10 in the initial period, only one (individual 6) ends up in in the poorest ten (i.e., rank 11 through 20) in terms of lifetime capital wealth. Meanwhile, only two individuals in the 11 through 20 rank in the initial period (individuals 12 and 16) make it into the top ten in terms of lifetime capital wealth.

Another indication of the neutral overall effect of chance on wealth inequality is the fact that the Gini coefficient of wealth inequality, computed in each period from 10 through 40, and also for average lifetime capital wealth, is very close to the initial period Gini coefficient. In this particular experiment, the Gini coefficient for lifetime capital wealth (.6722) is only slightly less than the Gini coefficient for initial capital wealth (.7611). Although chance is often casually thought of as the "great equalizer," in fact it tends inherently to generate a certain amount of *inequality*. This propensity is known as Gibrat's Law, and it is illustrated in Table 7.5 by the fact that the initial capital wealth of individuals 11 through 20 is equal, while the final (period 40) capital wealth of these same individuals is quite unequal, and their average lifetime capital wealth is quite unequal.

Table 7.5 shows a single simulation of a random capital wealth appreciation model. Further insight into random capital wealth appreciation is gained by a "Monte Carlo" experiment in which several simulations are done and the mean summary statistics are computed over the set of simulations. Table 7.6 contains results from such an experiment. Each row of the table shows average Gini coefficient and R-squared over ten simulations. These summary statistics are shown at five-period intervals from period 5 through period 35, and also in lifetime terms (average from period 1 through period 35). Part A of Table 7.6 pertains to cases in which the initial capital wealth distribution is equal (each individual has initial $CW = 1$); Part B pertains to cases in which the initial capital wealth distribution is unequal (the initial CWs are those shown in Table 7.5). Each part of the table contains results for four different values of the standard deviation of the growth rate g (GSD $= 0.04, 0.12, 0.20, 0.28$). The higher the standard deviation of g, the greater the variability of the rate of capital wealth appreciation.

The results in Part A of Table 7.6 illustrate Gibrat's Law: the generation of inequality through the workings of chance. Since all individuals start with the same capital wealth, the Gini coefficient computed at period 1 would be 0. It is observed that the Gini coefficients increase over time from the base of 0 in a concave fashion: The initial increase in inequality is fairly rapid, but the increasing effect of time on inequality levels off as time proceeds.

TABLE 7.6

Average Gini Coefficient and R-Squared over Ten Random
Capital Wealth Appreciation Simulations

	\...5	\...10	\...15	Period T = ...\...20	\...25	\...30	\...35	Life-time
A. Equal Initial Distribution								
GSD = 0.04								
Gini	.0398	.0588	.0725	.0816	.0920	.1050	.1121	.0835
R-Sq	—	—	—	—	—	—	—	—
GSD = 0.12								
Gini	.1253	.1844	.2173	.2471	.2682	.2924	.3192	.2396
R-Sq	—	—	—	—	—	—	—	—
GSD = 0.20								
Gini	.2016	.2860	.3590	.4183	.4573	.5020	.5339	.4183
R-Sq	—	—	—	—	—	—	—	—
GSD = 0.28								
Gini	.2915	.4051	.4950	.5649	.6214	.6590	.7016	.5625
R-Sq	—	—	—	—	—	—	—	—
B. Unequal Initial Distribution								
GSD = 0.04								
Gini	.7635	.7663	.7663	.7691	.7732	.7738	7744	.7716
R-Sq	.9980	.9953	.9913	.9913	.9889	.9846	.9841	.9909
GSD = 0.12								
Gini	.7536	.7480	.7533	.7579	.7607	.7667	.7779	.7625
R-Sq	.9753	.9550	.9546	.9296	.9129	.9076	.8975	.9325
GSD = 0.20								
Gini	.7819	.7744	.7800	.7869	.7990	.8067	.8075	.7901
R-Sq	.9456	.9125	.8612	.8182	.8571	.8828	.7467	.8597
GSD = 0.28								
Gini	.7707	.7666	.7582	.7852	.7985	.8115	.8086	.7838
R-Sq	.8697	.8284	.7362	.5617	.5606	.5145	.5779	.6349

The lifetime Gini is somewhat below the upper limit of the final (period 35) Gini. It is furthermore observed that the greater the variability of rate of capital wealth appreciation g (i.e., the higher the GSD), the higher the final (period 35) level of inequality. The R-squared is omitted in Part A of Table

7.6 because the independent variable (initial capital wealth) is constant: All individuals have an initial CW of 1. If observations on the independent variable all have the same value, regression is impossible and no R-squared can be computed.

From the Gini coefficient results in Part B of Table 7.6, we may infer that if the initial level of inequality is greater than the upper level of inequality from Gibrat's Law, then chance has little effect on the level of inequality over time: The level of inequality at any point in time and the level of lifetime inequality tend to be the same as the initial level of inequality. Since the independent variable of initial capital wealth varies in the experiments reported in Part B, regressions of current and lifetime capital wealth on initial capital wealth may be performed, and the R-squareds from these regressions computed. These R-squareds refer to the degree of association between current capital wealth and initial capital wealth, and lifetime capital wealth and initial capital wealth. Note the following important points: (1) the degree of measured association between current and lifetime capital wealth and initial capital wealth decreases as the variability of capital wealth appreciation (measured by GSD) increases; (2) the degree of measured association between current capital wealth and initial capital wealth declines as the interval between the initial period and the current period lengthens; (3) even for a very high level of variability of capital wealth appreciation, there is a high degree of association between both final (period 35) capital wealth and initial capital wealth, and lifetime capital wealth and initial capital wealth. The last point directly contests the hypothesis put forward by exponents of people's capitalism that initial capital wealth (i.e., inheritance) has very little effect on current or lifetime capital wealth.

It is obvious, however, that by specifying the GSD to be an extremely high value, it would be possible to reduce the R-squared between final period capital wealth and initial capital wealth to a very low value. The same would be true of the R-squared between lifetime capital wealth and initial capital wealth. But such an extremely high GSD value would most probably be highly unrealistic: a drastic overestimate of the analogous real-world value. But even stipulating, purely for the sake of argument, that such an extreme degree of capital wealth appreciation variability existed in the real world would not vindicate the vital *moral component* of the conventional people's capitalism argument. The logical essence of the people's capitalism defense of capitalism is simply that there is a great deal of capital wealth mobility in the population. If true, this would mean that currently nonwealthy people would have a fair and reasonable chance of becoming wealthy capitalists at some point in the future. But the moral component of the people's capitalism defense goes beyond this to the assertion that the high degree of capital wealth mobility which exists in society is mostly determined by the personal abilities and merits of various individuals in society. That is, people who become wealthy capitalists are not merely the beneficiaries of blind luck; rather, they are extraordinarily capable individuals who utilize their extraordinary capabilities to benefit society through entrepreneurship, innovation, enterprise, discovery, and so on. The moral component of people's capitalism blends by degrees into the capital management argument dealt with in Chapter 4. Obviously that entire discussion cannot be recapitulated here. Instead, the present chapter on people's capitalism will conclude with some informal comments on the relative plausibility of the merit hypothesis versus the chance hypothesis in explaining the inequality of capital wealth ownership in the contemporary capitalist economy.

Various evidence exists, from casual empiricism to the formal investigations of Harbury and Menchik, that inheritance plays at least an "appreciable" role in the perpetuation of capital wealth inequality over time.[15] Whether that "appreciable" role is more accurately described as "major" or perhaps as "minor" will at this point be left to the judgment of the reader. But what about the amount of capital wealth inequality—large or small, as the case may be—which is *not* directly attributable to the institution of inheritance? How much of this "residual" capital wealth inequality is to be attributed to differentials in the personal merit of individuals, and how much is to be attributed to differentials in the random luck of individuals? The normal position of an apologist for capitalism is that chance is a very minor contributor relative to merit. The position underlying the pragmatic market socialist proposal is the diametric opposite: that as far as large capital fortunes are concerned, merit plays an inconsequential role and chance plays the dominant role in the determination of that residual element of capital wealth inequality, large or small, which is not directly attributable to inheritance.[16]

To begin with, as may be ascertained from Tables 7.5 and 7.6, a very simple model of random capital wealth appreciation provides a straightforward and plausible explanation for observed patterns of wealth inequality and wealth mobility in the real world. By the principle of Ockham's Razor, simple hypotheses are preferred to complex hypotheses—so long as the simple hypotheses do as well in explaining reality as do the complex hypotheses. What makes the merit hypothesis "complex" relative to the chance hypothesis is that there is no practical and reasonable measure available to represent the "merit" concept invoked by the people's capitalism thesis. Recognized measures of human merit, from physical strength to higher intelligence, are more or less normally distributed with relatively modest standard deviations. The distribution of capital wealth is completely alien to the distributions of these known measures of merit: Instead of being symmetric, it is drastically skewed to the right, and instead of having a relatively modest standard deviation, it has an extremely high standard deviation. This fact suggests strongly that merit has little to do with the distribution of capital wealth. The apologist for capitalism responds to this difficulty by positing that the relevant merit in this context is "entrepreneurial courage and vision"—or some such completely speculative, quasi-mystical, unmeasurable, and probably nonexistent hypothetical construct. Such constructs are not reasonable and rational inductions from the common experience of mankind—they are blatantly apologetic inventions designed to justify an institutional status quo which offends common sense and common morality.

In capitalist apologetics, the entrepreneur is a superhuman figure more relevant to the realm of myth and legend than to the capitalistic real world of today. The popular business media occasionally endeavor to lend substance to the myth by describing the current exploits of the "new rich" of self-made entrepreneurs. For obvious reasons the popular business media have no interest in the typical drab, inheriting, passive type of capitalist—the type of capitalist in whose hands the majority of capital wealth is no doubt concentrated. Aside from the extreme scarcity in the real world of the "self-made" individuals eulogized by the popular business media, and aside from the typical exaggeration of their financial success by the media (gross worth is invariably cited rather than net worth), the simple fact remains that the only evidence which the media can adduce to support the "superman" interpretation is that these people are typically very industrious and unusually self-confident. But industry and self-confidence, in and of themselves, do not necessarily yield extraordinary benefits to human society.

When we reflect on the true heroes of human civilization, on those who have, clearly and unquestionably, made extraordinary contributions to political, scientific, and cultural progress, our minds evoke statesmen such as Washington and Churchill, scientists such as Newton and Einstein, philosophers such as Locke and Dewey, writers such as Dickens and Tolstoy, inventors such as Edison and the Wright brothers, artists such as Rembrandt and van Gogh, and composers such as Beethoven and Tschaikowsky. Did these individuals achieve great wealth through their clear and undeniable contributions to human civilization and human culture? Hardly. While it is true that the majority of these sorts of individuals achieve very comfortable living standards throughout their lives, few if any of them become truly wealthy, to the point where they accumulate vast capital fortunes with which to nurture generations of inheriting descendants.

There has in fact been little or no overlap between the most significant figures in human history and the richest figures in human history. The famous individuals mentioned above are hardly to be confused with the founders of the Rothschild and Rockefeller financial dynasties. This is not to deny that Mayer Rothschild and John D. Rockefeller may have made useful contributions to human society. But it seems clearly absurd to propose that Mayer Rothschild, for example, made a larger contribution to human civilization than did George Washington because Mayer Rothschild founded a financial dynasty and George Washington did not. Yet this absurdity is exactly what is implied by the people's capitalism argument that large-scale capital wealth mostly signifies and rewards the economic and social productivity of the wealthy capitalist.

In sum, people's capitalism fails to justify the capitalist economic system. The large majority of the population would benefit from social dividend distribution of capital property return under pragmatic market socialism. This fact is a direct consequence of the extreme inequality of capital wealth ownership under contemporary capitalism. This extreme inequality is not to be explained by life cycle saving for purposes of providing retirement income; such saving accounts for a very small proportion of the total inequality in capital wealth ownership. Furthermore, this extreme inequality does not reflect, to any appreciable extent, the relative merit and the relative social contributions of the various members of society. Rather, it reflects, almost entirely, the workings of inheritance and chance, two phenomena which have absolutely nothing to do with merit and social contributions. The high degree of effectiveness of the people's capitalism line in the real world proceeds not from its logical and empirical plausibility but from its insidious appeal to three of the more negative, albeit deeply rooted, human characteristics: ignorance, greed, and pride. It is to be hoped that ignorance, greed, and pride will not forever remain capitalism's salvation.

NOTES

1. The term "people's capitalism" was apparently invented in the 1950s by the Advertising Council. The thrust of the Ad Council's argument was that the growth of common stock ownership and profit-sharing plans had created a great horde of "ordinary citizens" with a direct financial stake in the capitalistic status quo. A derisory professional appraisal of the argument by Victor Perlo was published in the *American Economic Review* (1958). Perlo's general conclusion was stated as follows: "'People's capitalism,' that the rank and file of the population are becoming owners of the means of production, is without foundation in fact. The widespread diffusion of this theory signifies only the effectiveness of organized

propaganda." A "skeptical evaluation" of people's capitalism by the present author was published in the *ACES Bulletin* in 1982.

2. The thrust of Peter Drucker's argument is suggested by the following quotes from *The Unseen Revolution* (1976). Page 1: "If 'socialism' is defined as 'ownership of the means of production by the worker'—and this is both the orthodox and the only rigorous definition—then the United States is the first truly 'Socialist' country." Pages 2-3: "In terms of Socialist theory, the employees of America are the only true 'owners' of the means of production. Through their pension funds they are the only true 'capitalists' around, owning, controlling, and directing the country's 'capital fund.' The 'means of production,' that is, the American economy—again with agriculture the only important exception—is being run for the benefit of the country's employees. Profits increasingly become retirement pensions, that is 'deferred compensation' of the employees. There is no 'surplus value'; business revenue goes into the 'wage fund'." Page 4: "In other words, without consciously trying, the United States has 'socialized' the economy but not 'nationalized' it. America still sees herself, and is seen elsewhere, as 'capitalist'; but if terms like 'socialism' and 'capitalism' have any meaning at all, the American system has actually become the 'decentralized market socialism' which all the Marxist church fathers, saints, and apostles before Lenin had been preaching and promising, from Engels to Bebel and Kautsky, from Viktor Adler to Rosa Luxemburg, Jaures, and Eugene Debs."

3. This particular indication was well established in the consciousness of the American economics profession by Robert Lampman's book, published in 1962, which examined U.S. wealth distribution from 1922 to 1956. A 1974 study by James D. Smith and Stephen D. Franklin, covering the years 1922-1969, reinforced Lampman's conclusions.

4. For example, from James Smith and Stephen Franklin (1974, Table 1), it may be ascertained that in 1969 the richest 1 percent of the population owned 50.8 percent of corporate stock, compared with only 23.8 percent of total assets.

5. Just prior to the Federal Reserve Board survey, some fairly influential books had been published alleging that the highly unequal distribution of wealth in the United States severely vitiated the nation's idealistic image of itself as the home of equality and democracy: in particular C. Wright Mills's *The Power Elite* (1956) and Gabriel Kolko's *Wealth and Power in America* (1962). The survey may have been a good-faith effort to ascertain whether there is any substance in the accusations of writers such as Mills and Kolko. Perhaps some of the policy-makers and bureaucrats responsible for the survey hoped that it would serve as a refutation of the critique of these writers. Certainly it is possible to interpret some of the data obtained in a manner favorable to contemporary capitalism in the United States. For example, in *Rich Man, Poor Man* (1971, pp. 157-158), Herman Miller asserts that the findings of the survey support the proposition that inheritance is a relatively minor determinant of capital wealth inequality. This particular point is certainly questionable. The very same evidence was cited somewhat later by Lester Thurow (*Generating Inequality*, 1975, pp. 129-131) in support of the opposite conclusion: that inheritance is a very important determinant of capital wealth inequality. The

survey results were also cited abundantly by Ferdinand Lundberg in *The Rich and the Super-Rich* (1968), a work in the direct line of Mills and Kolko.

6. The best-known U.S. government data source on personal wealth distribution is the intermittent Internal Revenue Service series *Supplemental Statistics of Income: Personal Wealth Estimated from Estate Tax Returns*. This source deals entirely with total wealth rather than capital wealth. The distribution of various types of capital property income, such as dividends and capital gains, may be inferred from the annual Internal Revenue Service series *Statistics of Income: Individual Income Tax Returns*.

7. The inequality may be developed as follows. We start with

$SDI_i > PRI_i$

Let CW be total capital wealth and LI be total labor income. The total amount of capital property return distributed as social dividend income under pragmatic market socialism would be $(1-\alpha)$ times r times CW. Each household receives the proportion of this amount equal to the proportion of its labor income to total labor income. Under capitalism, in contrast, total distributed capital property return is r times CW, and each household receives the proportion of this amount equal to the proportion of its capital wealth to total capital wealth:

$$\frac{LI_i}{LI}(1-\alpha)\, r\, CW > \frac{CW_i}{CW}\, r\, CW$$

Cancel the r times CW term on both sides, and divide both denominators by the number of households, so that LI and CW are replaced, respectively, by MLI and MCW (mean labor income and mean capital wealth). Then transfer the $(1-\alpha)$ factor around to the front of the left-hand-side term, and the final result is obtained:

$$(1-\alpha)\frac{LI_i}{MLI} > \frac{CW_i}{MCW}$$

8. The argument put forward herein on the relative unimportance of life cycle saving with respect to overall capital wealth inequality is based on U.S. data. For analogous arguments based on U.K. data, see the articles by the British economists Anthony Atkinson and Nicholas Oulton (*Oxford Economic Papers*, respectively 1971 and 1976). Atkinson, a leading authority on wealth and income distribution, is the author of two books on wealth inequality in Britain: *Unequal Shares: Wealth in Britain* (1972), and (with A. J. Harrison) *The Distribution of Personal Wealth in Britain* (1978); he is also the editor of the authoritative compendium: *Wealth, Income and Inequality* (second edition, 1980).

9. See James Yunker (Winter 1982, Table 6) for substantiation of this statement. These data are taken from U.S. Department of the Treasury, Internal Revenue Service, Publication 482 (3-76), *Supplemental Statistics of Income 1972: Personal Wealth Estimated from Estate Tax Returns*, Table 27 (p. 31) and Table 40 (p. 47).

10. See, for example, the studies in Part III ("Income Distributions with Long and Short Accounting Periods") in the 1975 compendium edited by James D. Smith

(*The Personal Distribution of Income and Wealth*).

11. Significantly, this list omits crime, duplicity, guile, dishonesty, or whatever other term might be used to describe the role of immorality and wrong-doing in the accumulation of large-scale capital wealth. But of course there is a school of thought that attributes quite a large role to these factors. There is certainly plenty of anecdotal evidence to support it, from the well-known "robber barons" of the nineteenth century to the various operators and wheeler-dealers of the twentieth century: insider traders, junk bond scam artists, venal savings and loan executives, and so on. A typical contemporary pattern seems to involve the accumulation of a huge fortune, followed by arrest and conviction for white collar crime, for which the actual prison term served amounts to a few years. Upon emerging from prison, the culprit retires to a lifetime of luxury financed with ill-gotten gains salted away in Swiss bank accounts. To avoid accusations of sensationalistic exaggeration, no consideration will be given herein to this sort of thing.

12. One particularly glaring example of rank credulity is provided by Herman Miller, author of *Rich Man, Poor Man* (1971, esp. pp.157-158). Miller is very impressed by the fact that, according to Table A32 in the Federal Reserve Board *Survey of Financial Characteristics of Consumers*, fully 39 percent of those in the highest wealth bracket claimed to have received no inheritance at all. Aside from the fact that the highest wealth bracket is not all that high ($500,000 and above), and aside from the fact that 39 percent is not all that high, why did Miller not take into account the tendency for some recipients of inheritances to conveniently forget them for purposes of responding to surveys? Miller sums up his interpretation of the evidence with the following cheery little homily: "If you have given up hope of ever becoming a millionaire and you blame it on the system, you may just be looking for an alibi. Millionaires are being made every day, now more than ever before. They come from all walks of life and all ethnic and religious backgrounds. Most of them did it on their own, without inherited wealth. The key to their success according to the managing editor of the Wall Street *Journal*, who should know, is hard work, courage and individuality. A little luck helps too, but most experts don't seem to attach much importance to it." This is archetypal people's capitalism. Despite the incredible naiveté of this sort of thing, it seems nevertheless to be incredibly effective with a great many people.

13. Josiah Wedgwood's *The Economics of Inheritance* appeared in 1929. Harbury's work is contained in a series of three articles and a book: *Economic Journal* (1962, 1973); *Review of Income and Wealth* (1977); and George Allen and Unwin (1979). Menchik's work is contained in two articles: *Economica* (1979) and a contribution to a compendium volume edited by James D. Smith and published by the University of Chicago Press (1980).

14. See Harbury and Hitchens (1979, Table 7.3).

15. Additional empirical evidence on the importance of inheritance in the accumulation of capital wealth, not based on the probate court technique, is provided by John A. Brittain (1978). The methodology of this study is rather subtle, but the results are consistent with the probate court technique in strongly suggesting the primary significance of inheritance in large-scale capital wealthholding. In

another contribution (1977), Brittain analyzes the role of inheritance in the determination of economic status generally, as opposed to capital wealth specifically. A further source of raw statistical information on inheritance in the United States is the Internal Revenue Service publication *Statistics of Income: Fiduciary, Gift and Estate Taxes*. As is true of many raw data sources, the true significance of the information in this publication is not necessarily obvious. However, it does establish one basic point: that in an absolute sense a great deal of capital wealth is transmitted between generations through the probate courts.

16. That chance plays a greater role than ability in the accumulation of capital wealth is attested to by a great mass of anecdotal evidence. One such anecdote reveals the modesty of John Maynard Keynes regarding his much-vaunted success as an investor (*Journal of Political Economy* 96(3): back cover, June 1988). In a letter to the London *Times* published March 28, 1972, A. L. Goodhart, an acquaintance of Keynes, wrote as follows:

"Sir, In the spring of 1941, Maynard Keynes, Sir Wilfrid Greene and I were in Estoril on the outskirts of Lisbon, waiting for a seaplane to fly us to New York. One evening we went to the local casino where Keynes and Greene, who were following a carefully planned system, seemed to be inexorably unsuccessful while I, a novice, recouped our depleted finances.

"When we left, Keynes explained that a player's success depended more on intuition than on intelligence. He gave as an illustration his own reputation as an astute business man because he had made staggering profits both for King's College (Cambridge) and for himself by investing in the shares of a Chicago traction company.

"For no particular reason he had sold these holdings two weeks before the stock market collapsed in the autumn panic of 1929. If he had not done so the college would have been in serious financial difficulties and he would have been wiped out. It was not reason but chance that made him choose the crucial date. The fact that he was an economist, he said, was irrelevant."

For further systematic support of the thesis that chance is more important than merit in the accumulation of large-scale capital wealth, see Anthony B. Atkinson, *Unequal Shares* (1972), Chapter 3; and Lester Thurow, *Generating Inequality* (1975), Chapter 6.

8

CAPITALISM AND DEMOCRACY

A. CAPITALISM: BULWARK OF DEMOCRACY?

For a brief period during the 1930s, the economic efficiency argument against socialism seemed dangerously close to unraveling entirely. The entire capitalist world was wracked by severe business depression and mass unemployment. At last, the Marxist jeremiads, so long complacently dismissed by the mainstream Western intelligentsia as harebrained alarmism, seemed on the verge of realization. Meanwhile, the socialistic U.S.S.R. was surging ahead with its monumental collectivization and industrialization campaigns. As much as the mainstream Western intelligentsia deprecated the Soviet effort as bumbling and misguided, there was something very impressive, even awe-inspiring, in the vision of an entire nation-state trying to lift itself up by the bootstraps in order to thrust itself forward into the vanguard of economic and social development. And it was also obvious that should the retrograde tendencies in the capitalist world of the early 1930s and the progressive tendencies in the Soviet Union of the same period continue for very long, the Soviet Union would soon surpass the leading capitalist nations of the West both in aggregate production and in individual living standards. Under the extraordinary circumstances of the times, the traditional, more or less professorial admonitions as to the various alleged economic liabilities of socialism were beginning to sound hollow and unconvincing.

It was therefore welcome news to conservatives everywhere when in the latter 1930s unmistakable evidence began emerging, in the form of massive Communist Party purges, that the Soviet Union was in reality a far cry from the nascent workers' paradise that its leaders and supporters purported it to be. Until the famous purge trials of the 1930s, it might have been possible for a relatively impartial outside observer to interpret internal conflict and dissension within the Soviet Union, from the great Civil War of 1918-1921 to the kulak resistance to collectivization of the early 1930s, as the struggle of an enlightened, progressive, and worthy Communist Party organization against various selfish, recalcitrant, and unworthy reactionaries. But the possibilities for a sympathetic view of the Communist Party's role in the Soviet Union diminished drastically when the Stalin dictatorship began suppressing every vestige of internal opposition by means of humiliating and then executing highly placed officials, individuals who only a short time before had made important contributions to the success of the Bolshevik Revolution. The Communist Party purges of the latter 1930s clearly manifested the enormous stress being placed on the Russian people by the radical transformations undertaken by the leadership. They lent substantial credence to the view that whatever economic progress was being made by the Soviet Union was being achieved through the acute sacrifices and suffering of its people—sacrifices and suffering which would never have been permitted if the people had exercised any genuine democratic control over their fate. It was this period which witnessed a worldwide disillusionment with Soviet communism, along with the rapid development of a novel political argument against socialism as a supplement to the traditional economic arguments.

Friedrich von Hayek's tract *The Road to Serfdom* (1944) is generally deemed the seminal formulation of the political argument against socialism. But in actual fact Hayek's treatment of the issue is unfocused, freewheeling, and drastically overstated. Hayek argues that *any* sort of paternalistic state intervention in the economy—for example, in the form of progressive taxation, business regulation, welfare programs, and so on, through its inculcation of an overly dependent "slave mentality" in the population— will by imperceptible degrees tend toward the worst atrocities of the Hitler regime in Nazi Germany and the Stalin regime in the Soviet Union. However, only the most extravagantly libertarian mentalities find much merit in Hayek's contention that the watered-down social democracy of Roosevelt's New Deal in the United States, and similar policies in other capitalist nations in the 1930s, are inevitably the first steps on the easy downward path toward absolute dictatorship and unbridled totalitarianism.

Another reason for dispensing with consideration of Hayek's "broad version" of the political argument against socialism is its extremely limited applicability to the logical core of the pragmatic market socialist proposal. This logical core involves only public ownership of large-scale, established business enterprises: It is completely neutral on such questions as the proper extent of welfare programs, business regulation, progressive taxation, and so on. It is fully conceivable, for example, that a pragmatic market socialist United States of the future would display *less* in the way of welfare programs, business regulation, progressive taxation, and so on, than does the capitalistic United States of the present. Therefore it cannot be assumed that pragmatic market socialism would be any more conducive to Hayek's purported "slave mentality" than any existing, real-world capitalist system. In order to fully and unambiguously evade Hayek's argument as presented in *The Road to Serfdom*, it would be necessary to implement the laissez-faire ideal of the early nineteenth century: the state as nothing more and nothing less than a policeman. Only a tiny minority of radical fringe libertarians are seriously attracted by this possibility.

The "narrow version" of the political argument against socialism with which we will be concerned here dispenses with the conceptually nebulous and psychologically dubious "slave mentality" notion and instead merely holds that the combination of economic and political power under socialism would tend to suppress genuine democracy. The outward forms and trappings of democracy might remain (contested elections at regular intervals, ostensible freedom of speech and press, etc.), but these forms and trappings would have no authentic substance. More specifically, under socialism the incumbent political party in the national government would utilize its control over the economy to stifle political opposition and dissent. There are two primary mechanisms through which this would be accomplished. The first would be the dismissal from their employment with state-owned business firms of any and all individuals known to be members of or sympathizers with opposition political parties. Thus deprived of a means of livelihood, these individuals would be reduced to destitution, and their ensuing struggle for physical survival would prevent them from taking any meaningful part in the political process. The second mechanism involves the state-owned means of communication: The personalities, ideas, and policy proposals of any and all opposition leaders would be so prejudicially distorted and misrepresented by the state-owned media as to deprive them of any fair chance to influence public opinion and win elections.

Both the broad and the narrow versions of the political argument against socialism are often alluded to in capitalist apologetics, but fully worked-out statements of the argument are scarce, particularly for the narrow version. One such statement of the narrow version of the argument is to be found on pages 15 through 21 of Milton Friedman's book *Capitalism and Freedom* (1962). Although Friedman's work is far more moderate and balanced than that of Hayek, it still manifests the intellectual confusion and propagandistic distortion typical of capitalist apologetics. Such confusion and distortion are demonstrated by the title itself: From the bulk of its contents the book should be titled *Laissez-Faire and Freedom* rather than *Capitalism and Freedom*. The book consists almost entirely of arguments against various forms of state-initiated or state-condoned interventions in the free market, such as minimum wages and occupational licensure. The fact that most of the interventions which Friedman decries are already well established under contemporary capitalism in the United States and elsewhere, indicates that the "freedom" which he is concerned to augment is in no way necessarily connected with "capitalism," properly understood as private ownership of the nonhuman factors of production.

Exactly the same conclusion is derived from the observation that such things as minimum wages and occupational licensure could be eliminated under pragmatic market socialism, and the economy would be none the less "socialist" because of it. "Freedom" is of course a glorious and magnificent concept, and every rational person desires as large a measure of it as is reasonably practical. At the same time it is well understood by all sensible people that both the laws of nature and the laws of society inevitably place severe limits on individual human freedom. Whatever may be the higher purpose of the laws of nature is not for us to fathom, but the laws of society are based on the simple premise that too much freedom for some people can mean too little freedom for other people. Friedman's juxtaposition of the terms "capitalism" and "freedom" in the title of his book is clearly meant to convey the invalid impression that capitalism per se is conducive to freedom, and is thereby necessarily a very positive institution in human society.

However, in fairness to Friedman, it should be emphasized that out of the 202 pages of *Capitalism and Freedom*, there are indeed 7 pages (pp. 15-21) in Chapter 1 ("The Relation Between Economic Freedom and Political Freedom") which argue for a causative relationship between capitalism (in the sense of private ownership of business enterprise) and freedom (in the sense of participation in genuinely democratic political processes). Friedman chooses to develop the argument by contrasting the great ease with which pro-socialists under capitalism may campaign for the inauguration of socialism, with the great difficulties which would confront potential future pro-capitalists under socialism in campaigning for the restoration of capitalism. Friedman concedes that private capitalists under capitalism have both incentives and means with which to discourage pro-socialists, but he argues that the capitalists are not sufficiently self-aware and well-organized to pursue their interest effectively.

Thus, if one privately owned firm dismisses a known pro-socialist in order to hobble his or her political activity, another privately owned firm will hire that same pro-socialist because the owner's concern to acquire a productive employee will override qualms about the effect of possible future socialization on the owner's wealth. And if one privately owned publishing house rejects a manuscript advocating socialism for fear that it might foster future socialization, another privately owned publishing house will rush to publish it in order to gain the short-term profits to be earned from a persuasive and well-written advocacy of socialism. Moreover, alleges Friedman, under capitalism there are always a few eccentric capitalists who are very much in favor of socialism, even though its implementation would mean their own financial ruination. These capitalists actively seek out pro-socialists in order to provide them with generous living allowances and to subsidize the publication of their works.

Continuing with Friedman's argument, the situation would be entirely different under socialism. While the economic power held by capitalists under capitalism is relatively dispersed, political power is necessarily much more concentrated. If economic power is then subsumed under this concentrated political power, as under socialism, the incumbent political leaders in the national government would have a devastating weapon with which to negate the opposition. Friedman describes this power being used against the advocates of a restoration of capitalism, but clearly the power could be used against any opponents of the incumbent leaders, whatever the actual value judgments and policy preferences of these opponents. Orders would be given to all public enterprises to dismiss political opponents of the incumbent leadership, and there would be nowhere for these people to turn to reacquire employment. Poverty would force them into silence and inactivity. Orders would also be given to all publicly owned communications media to suppress all positive commentary on the personalities, ideas, and policy proposals of opposition figures. The only information made available to the public on these figures would be negative. Periodically the public might be permitted to troop to the polls to cast their votes, but the only candidates who would have any chance of success in these elections would be those selected and groomed by the incumbent political leaders. Economic power would be used first to establish and then to perpetuate the domination of society by a small, privileged oligarchy.

There are obviously some kernels of truth in this argument, and it behooves any sensible advocate of socialism to take it very seriously. All of the industrially advanced capitalist nations of today enjoy highly democratic political systems: Regular, strongly contested elections are supported by virtually unlimited freedom of speech and press. Although Friedman exaggerates the ease with which pro-socialists may argue their case under contemporary capitalism, pro-socialists obviously possess a reasonable amount of latitude (this book is evidence of that). Moreover, all of the Communist nations of the world, at least until very recently, have provided very sobering examples of the presence of socialism combined with the near-total absence of democracy. Certainly every aspect which Friedman describes of the potential suppression of opposition by the incumbent leadership under socialism—and then some—held completely true during the Stalinist period in the Soviet Union and the Maoist period in China. In fact, Joseph Stalin and Mao Tse-tung hardly contented themselves with depriving opposition figures of remunerative employment and either ignoring or harassing them in the media: These measures were supplemented by imprisonment and execution. Such drastic measures were ostensibly taken in the interest of the people and the state, but in reality they served mainly to consolidate the personal power of megalomaniac tyrants.

On what basis may it be argued that the anti-democratic outrages perpetrated in the past by the Communist nations would almost certainly not come about in the pragmatic market socialist society proposed in this book? On what basis may it be argued that political democracy would remain as viable and vibrant under pragmatic market socialism as it is currently in the advanced capitalist nations of the world? As to the absence of genuine democracy under communistic socialism, this is far more plausibly attributed to historical forces and conditions than it is to the nature of socialism itself. As to the preservation of genuine democracy under pragmatic market socialism, there are certain aspects of the core proposal which are specifically designed to impede and forestall the successful utilization of the government's public ownership authority in the consolidation, amplification, or perpetuation of the political power of the incumbent leadership.

But it is not argued that these formal institutional provisions would be sufficient in themselves to maintain authentic democracy. The real key to the preservation of democracy is the democratic tradition. If the citizen body has been thoroughly and intensively indoctrinated in the inherent moral superiority of the democratic political system, then the formal guarantees of democracy incorporated in the pragmatic market socialist proposal would be effective in practice. The pragmatic market socialist proposal has been initially and primarily designed with the advanced capitalist nations in mind. The proposal is completely compatible with both the tangible institutions of democracy and the psychological attitudes toward democracy which are common to these nations. Democracy would be guaranteed to the same extent under pragmatic market socialism that it is currently guaranteed under capitalism through mutually supporting institutions and attitudes favorable to democracy.[1]

The concluding comments of this section pertain to the absence of genuine democracy under Communism; the following section of the chapter will directly address the preservation of democracy under pragmatic market socialism. With respect to the absence of democracy under Communism, consideration will be limited to the U.S.S.R., both because it remains the single most important Communist nation (in terms of power and history) and because in key historical and political aspects, it is reasonably representative of the other Communist nations. Specifically, the Soviet Union is typical of the Communist nations in that prior to the revolution which inaugurated socialism, there existed no strong democratic tradition. Of course the fact that pre-revolutionary Russia possessed no appreciable democratic tradition does not imply that Russia was atypical. While the abstract idea of democracy is now extremely potent throughout the world, the kind of working institutions and actual popular mental attitudes which presently characterize nations such as the United States and those of Western Europe are still fairly uncommon. It is certainly to be hoped that these institutions and attitudes will one day be more or less universal, but this remains to be seen. In any event, Russia in 1917 was typical of most nations in possessing no strong democratic tradition.[2]

From the beginning, the Communist Party of the Soviet Union proclaimed itself a staunch champion of democracy. The various constitutions of the U.S.S.R. firmly guaranteed freedom of speech and political activity, and there were always regular elections for nominally important government offices. The aspiration toward democracy expressed by the Communist Party of the U.S.S.R. certainly counted at least slightly in its favor—at least the Communist Party never ridiculed and denounced democracy, as did the various fascist parties which played such a large role in the history of the first half of the twentieth century. But in the judgment of almost all qualified outside observers, the Communist Party of the U.S.S.R., despite its professed adherence to democracy, in reality continued the oligarchic political system that characterized pre-revolutionary Russia. Speech and political activity were free only to the extent that they supported the incumbent leadership, and elections were merely empty formalities since the incumbent leadership designated all the candidates.

Of course, it is also recognized by most outside observers that given the Communist Party's historical development and its radical program, it could hardly have been expected to rapidly establish genuine democracy in the Soviet Union. The Party's historical genesis was as a conspiratorial secret society, and when it came to power in Russia, its radical program of uncompensated expropriation at home and espousal of socialist revolution abroad immediately confronted it with hordes of determined enemies. The Soviet state barely survived a brutal civil war, and when that crisis was over, there loomed the possibility of invasion by a hostile capitalist outside world. Nor were the fears of invasion purely a paranoid delusion: Russia had been invaded a number of times in the past, and its socialization now lent an extra ideological incentive to potential invaders to supplement the traditional economic and imperialistic incentives.

Sure enough, in 1941, only a little over twenty years after the Bolshevik Revolution, Hitler's armies swept into Russia. In an effort to prepare for that eventuality, the Communist Party leadership under Joseph Stalin had pushed forward a crash program of agricultural collectivization and forced-pace industrialization, a policy which imposed severe hardships on every segment of the population from the rural kulaks to the urban proletariat. The policy did, however, achieve a sufficient level of internal resources, in conjunction with military aid from the Allies, to overcome the Nazi onslaught. However, the Soviet Union's efforts after World War II to provide itself with a buffer zone of satellite states in Eastern Europe rapidly brought on a cold war in which the traditional concern over foreign invasion was now augmented by the dreadful possibility of nuclear devastation. In sum, throughout its existence, the Communist Party of the Soviet Union has considered itself in a state of siege, surrounded by multitudinous deadly enemies both at home and abroad. Democracy as it is known in the United States and similar nations flourishes best under prosperous, stable, non-threatening conditions—conditions which have manifestly never prevailed throughout the history of the Soviet Union.

To apply the political argument against socialism, narrowly defined, against pragmatic market socialism, it is necessary to envision a slow and gradual strangulation of democracy by indirect means of economic intimidation (the dismissal of political opponents from their employment) and media harassment (uniformly negative commentary on political opponents in the printed and electronic media). This vision is completely divorced from the political history of the U.S.S.R. and the other Communist nations. The Communist Party of the U.S.S.R. did not slowly and gradually strangle democracy in Russia—democracy did not exist in Russia when the Party came to power. In maintaining its power, the Party relied far more on direct physical intimidation (concentration camps, executions, etc.) than it did on indirect economic intimidation and media harassment. In short, the fact that Communist nations have been undemocratic is an unfortunate historical circumstance which, however, has very little bearing on the course of democracy in potential pragmatic market socialist nations of the future.

B. PROSPECTS FOR DEMOCRATIC SOCIALISM

The absence of democracy in the Communist nations is more plausibly attributed to the nondemocratic historical traditions of these nations, and to the vigorous internal and external opposition to which the incumbent regimes have always been subject, than it is to the institution of socialism in and of itself. Nevertheless, the fact remains that pragmatic market socialism does envision a substantial aggregation of potential economic power into the hands of the national government. The dismal record of the Communist nations with respect to political democracy is a very sobering consideration. What assurances do we have that genuine democracy would not become extinct under pragmatic market socialism? It must be conceded at the outset that these assurances cannot be complete. Judging from history, genuine democracy is a fragile institution in the best of times, and it remains in some degree of peril whatever the prevailing economic system. After all, a capitalist economic system did not preserve Germany from the horrors of Nazi totalitarianism in the 1930s. The argument to be made, however, is that the degree of risk would not be substantially greater under pragmatic market socialism than it is currently under capitalism.

It goes without saying, to begin with, that the legislation establishing the pragmatic market socialist economy would explicitly prohibit any attempt to utilize the economic authority of the national government to benefit the incumbent government leaders in any way, either financially or politically. Government leaders would be specifically enjoined from directly claiming any part of property return produced by the publicly owned business enterprises as their personal income, and they would be equally enjoined from issuing any instructions to the managers of publicly owned firms designed to benefit their personal political power, such as the dismissal of political opponents from their employment or negative commentary on these opponents in the media. It would be completely clear from the founding legislation that any efforts of the incumbent government officials along these lines constitute a grave offense, punishable by impeachment, removal from office, and imprisonment. Of course formal provisions of this sort do not guarantee democracy, but at least they are a beginning. If a particular anti-democratic activity is declared immoral in principle and illegal in law, then it is more likely to be deterred in practice.

There are certain aspects of the basic economic institutions of pragmatic market socialism which would have important consequences in terms of practical deconcentration of political power. First, private ownership of small-scale business enterprises and entrepreneurial business enterprises would be maintained. Quite probably nonprofit enterprises would also be entirely independent of the Bureau of Public Ownership (BPO). These kinds of enterprises would provide employment opportunities for members of the political opposition, even in the unlikely event that firms operating under the BPO could be made to dismiss these members. Second and more important, the actual power of the BPO over the publicly owned business firms would be carefully delimited. Recall that the BPO would be firmly enjoined from issuing any instructions whatsoever to the publicly owned firms pertaining to any of the microeconomic decision variables of business enterprise: production, marketing, investment, and so on. Among these microeconomic decision variables are the hiring, retention, and dismissal of employees. Thus the BPO would be prohibited from ordering the firing of a particular employee *for any reason*, let alone for political activity against incumbent officials. The only grounds on which the BPO could legally dismiss the chief executive officer of a publicly owned business enterprise would be on objectively verifiable grounds of low profitability. Thus, if a particular corporation was earning an adequate rate of profit, the BPO could not touch it, and such a corporation would therefore provide a secure haven for political dissidents in search of employment.

One can certainly imagine the president of the United States, for example, wanting to engineer the dismissal of a vociferous political opponent who happens to be employed, say, by General Motors Corporation (GMC). But consider the chain of transmission that would be involved in implementing this desire. The president would have to communicate his order to fire the political opponent to the director of the BPO. But presuming the aggregate profit rate in the economy is adequate, the president would have no publicly acceptable grounds on which to dismiss the director if the director refused to pass along the order. The director of the BPO would have to communicate the order to the particular BPO agent within whose sphere of responsibility GMC fell. But presuming the agent spends a certain amount of time studying his or her corporations and is not serving time in prison, the director would have nothing with which to intimidate the agent who refuses to pass along the order, because the only grounds for dismissal of a BPO agent would be gross dereliction of duty or proven criminal activity. The BPO agent would have to communicate the order to the GMC CEO. But presuming GMC is making an adequate rate of profit, the agent would have no publicly acceptable grounds on which to recommend the dismissal of the GMC CEO if the latter refused to pass along the order. There are thus at least three key and reasonably well insulated individuals between the president and his intended victim: the BPO director, the BPO agent, and the CEO. None of these individuals would be likely to have a great deal to gain (directly and personally) from carrying out the order, but they would have everything to lose if they were discovered to be parties to a blatantly illegal conspiracy. And no doubt many other individuals would necessarily be involved. The outcome would almost certainly be a blown whistle: Someone in the chain of transmission would decide that it would be less risky, all things considered, to try to expose the conspiracy than to be a party to it.

Of course the reference to whistle blowing presumes that there would exist independent media through which the whistle could be blown loudly. Independent media of communication are essential to the success of a democratic political system in a mass society. On this basis it is proposed that all or a large part of the media of communication (i.e., book and magazine publishing houses, radio and television stations and networks, press services, and so on) be independent of the Bureau of Public Ownership. This is purely a precautionary measure, because in all likelihood these firms would be adequately independent even if they *did* fall under the formal authority of the BPO. However, because of their critical role in the transmission and dissemination of information, these firms would *not* fall under the purview of the BPO. Most of them would instead be operated as cooperative business enterprises (i.e., "self-managed," "labor-managed," etc.): The employees would periodically elect the top manager in an open and democratic manner. From the technical economic point of view, the objective of cooperative firms is the maximization of the welfare of their current employees. Employee welfare maximization has been rejected herein as a general rule for the operation of publicly owned business enterprise on grounds that profit maximization is likely to be more efficient and dynamic. But an exception would be made in the case of media enterprises on political grounds. Another form that might be appropriate in some cases (e.g., local newspapers and local radio and television stations) would be nonprofit enterprise under the direction of a board elected by and responsible to the population of the area in which the firm operates.

Cooperative or locally-owned media enterprises would be insulated from potential direct orders from BPO agents to engage in propaganda against the political opposition. However, they might still be subject to pressure through advertising revenues. Many, if not most, media enterprises engaged in the transmission and dissemination of politically relevant information, particularly newspaper and magazine publishers and radio and television stations and networks, derive a substantial proportion of their revenues from advertising. One might imagine a high government official offended by negative commentary in a certain magazine, for example, trying to engineer the withholding of advertising in that magazine by publicly owned firms. This official, of course, would confront exactly the same obstacles as he or she would in endeavoring to secure the dismissal of an employee of a publicly owned firm on political grounds. But as a supplement to the whistleblowing obstacle, there might also be established a program of mandatory financial subsidies to media enterprises to offset the threat from politically motivated withholding of advertising. For print media, the subsidies would be in proportion to sales to the public. By tying the subsidies to earned revenues, the efficiency costs of subsidies are mitigated, and by tying them to nonadvertising revenues, the potential indirect influence of the BPO on editorial policy would be mitigated. The problem is more difficult for electronic media (radio and television) because their revenues are derived entirely from advertising. Here the subsidies might be in proportion to population served. Obviously the negative effect of such subsidies on efficiency is more severe. But it would probably be justified to incur substantial economic efficiency losses in order to maintain fully independent media and thereby better ensure that the economic authority of the national government under pragmatic market socialism is not abused in the interest of the incumbent officials.

Of course, the success or failure of formal mechanisms for the preservation of democracy is heavily dependent on the prevailing attitude toward democracy in the citizen body. If the attitude toward democracy is positive, even reverential, the mechanisms will be effective in practice. It is submitted here that a conspiratorial effort by the party in power under pragmatic market socialism to destroy the political opposition through misuse of the public ownership authority, and to consolidate perpetually an oligarchic sociopolitical regime, is even more unlikely in practice than would be a conspiratorial effort by the military in the United States under the present capitalist economic system to suppress democracy and set up a totalitarian regime. Military dictatorship has been a fact of life in many different nations at many different points in history, and it is no less a fact of life at the present time than it has been in past times. Moreover, there is no tangible, physical defense against military dictatorship in any nation, including the United States, which has established a large, permanent military machine. If the soldiers and officers of the U.S. armed forces ever achieved a consensus in favor of military dictatorship, the civilian officials could be rounded up and executed overnight, and within a day or two the military could establish a reign of terror based on brute force from which there would be absolutely no escape. Relative to the automatic weapons and armored vehicles currently available to the U.S. military, the tools which would be available to the civilian leaders under pragmatic market socialism to suppress democracy (economic intimidation and media harassment) are veritably laughable.

But despite the absence of meaningful "formal mechanisms" against military dictatorship, to date the United States has not been subjected to military dictatorship. Any officers endeavoring to organize a military coup in the United States at the present time would be quickly exposed and no doubt duly consigned to psychiatric institutions for observation and treatment. The vast majority of the soldiers and officers of the U.S. military machine are completely loyal to the concept of electoral democracy, and they would regard any effort to overturn it through the use of military force as a heinous crime deserving of swift and terrible retribution. In the face of this nearly universal attitude, it would be practically impossible for the high leadership of the U.S. military establishment to successfully organize a coup.

For exactly the same reasons, it would be practically impossible for the high leadership in the national government under pragmatic market socialism to successfully engineer the destruction of genuine democracy through misuse of the government's economic authority over the publicly owned business enterprises. The first faltering steps along such a path would almost certainly bring down any national government officials sufficiently foolish and misguided as to undertake them. The fate of Richard M. Nixon in 1974—humiliated, threatened with impeachment, forced to resign— stands as a clear lesson to any future president of the United States under pragmatic market socialism who might toy with the notion of utilizing the Bureau of Public Ownership to suppress his opponents. In actual fact, Nixon's offenses, from the Watergate cover-up to the unsuccessful efforts to get the Internal Revenue Service to conduct tax audits of his enemies, were far less direct and serious offenses against the democratic institutions of the U.S. republic than would be misuse of the BPO to further the interests of the incumbent leadership. Thus the guilty public officials would fall even more quickly and dramatically than did Nixon.[3]

The political argument against socialism put forward by Friedman and others is based on the fallacious proposition of a complete commonality of interest among government personnel, and/or complete concentration of power within the government apparatus. In actual fact, the government consists of thousands and even millions of separate individuals, each one of whom has his or her own particular interests and ideals. Aside from a few historically extraordinary cases such as Adolf Hitler, the head of the government never achieves the kind of transcendent personal power and influence necessary to completely dominate the political and/or military apparatuses and thereby bend them to a singular will. But just such complete domination would be necessary for the suppression of democracy through public ownership under socialism, or through use of military force under any sort of economic system. In the normal state of affairs, the potential payoff to a conspiracy to suppress democracy to any particular member of the military or the government would be far too small and uncertain to constitute a meaningful incentive to action.

The political argument against socialism also relies on an unrealistic degree of selfishness and egotism among the government employees. Just as the military represents a relatively representative cross section drawn from the general population in modern society, so does the government. Just as the typical soldier or officer is more loyal to the nation as a whole than to any particular branch of the service, so the typical government employee is more loyal to the nation as a whole than to any particular government agency. And just as people in general possess moral standards and ideals, so do members of the military and members of the government. The vast majority of these members are therefore morally repelled by the thought of utilizing their special power and authority to suppress the hallowed institution of democracy. The vast majority of them would prefer to risk death than to be part of a conspiracy to destroy this vital component of the accustomed way of life. Of course, we cannot know whether the reverential attitude toward democracy will persist indefinitely into the future. But so long as it does persist, it constitutes an insuperable obstacle to those who would destroy democracy. And there is absolutely nothing in the pragmatic market socialist proposal that is in any way contrary to or prejudicial to the high moral status presently enjoyed by the democratic concept in the advanced industrial nations.

In fact, it is fully arguable that pragmatic market socialism would in fact *improve*—slightly but significantly—the quality of democratic social decision-making in nations such as the United States. The reason is that pragmatic market socialism would eliminate the excessive political influence of the class of wealthy capitalists in the democratic process. While it is clearly necessary to reject the traditional Marxist proposition that the capitalist class "dominates" the state, and thereby the entire society, there remains a kernel of truth in this proposition: It is probably fair to say that the capitalist class "unduly influences" the state, and thereby the entire society.

To begin with, it can hardly be disputed that any given individual's effective sociopolitical power is strongly related to that same individual's economic resources. People who are economically advantaged tend to have more time and energy to devote to political issues. They are liable to be better educated and more widely read, and thus more capable of persuasively defending an opinion and effectively communicating it to others. Thus they more readily become opinion leaders, both in small social contexts and in larger contexts. They are also more likely to graduate from informal opinion leading to formal opinion leading via direct participation in the political process, running for and serving in important government offices. Such advantages grow in proportion to wealth and income. Therefore, very wealthy capitalists whose property income absolves them from the need to work for a living are often to be found in both elective and appointive government positions. They do whatever they can to keep the salaries of these offices low, ostensibly to reduce the burden on the taxpayers but in reality to reduce the competition they confront from those of more modest means. Even if they do not opt for direct participation in the political process, wealthy capitalists are able to exercise considerable influence over direct participants, both by logical persuasion and, more important, by the financial support of campaigns for office. In modern mass societies, any particular aspirant to high government office is completely unknown to the vast majority of his or her intended constituents. It requires very large sums of money to buy the political advertising and other forms of publicity necessary to overcome this natural anonymity. Wealthy capitalists possess the necessary funds, and they will gladly support candidates whose viewpoints coincide with their own.[4]

It is also necessary to take into account the communication mechanism by which the politically active minority in a mass democracy stays in touch with the politically passive majority which does little more than its periodic voting duty at the polls. The judgments and attitudes of the politically active minority are transmitted to the politically passive majority principally through the media of mass communication (popular newspapers and magazines, network television, etc.). Under contemporary capitalism these media are mostly tightly centralized, privately owned corporations controlled by a small minority of wealthy capitalists and high executives, a subset of the larger group of wealthy capitalists and high executives who control the larger economy. This situation certainly has some appreciable effect in biasing the flow of information and commentary to the politically passive majority in a manner favorable to the attitudes, judgments and opinions of wealthy capitalists and high executives. It is not being alleged either that the mass media are totally subservient to the wealthy elite, or that public opinion is totally manipulated by the mass media, as if it were a marionette on strings. Clearly there are certain limits on the extent to which the "masses" can be made to think in exactly the same way that the wealthy elite thinks. At the same time, however, it seems inescapable that the wealthy elite has far more influence on how the masses think than vice versa.

It has been much emphasized herein that the purposes of pragmatic market socialism, in and of itself, are not excessively egalitarian. Pragmatic market socialism represents no threat whatsoever to the very comfortable living standards achieved by the upper middle class of prosperous professionals: physicians, lawyers, executives, and so on. Moreover, it represents no threat whatsoever to substantial wealth accruing to genuine personal effort: successful entrepreneurship, superstar status in sports or entertainment, and so on. Therefore, even if it were fully accepted that the distribution of effective political power closely corresponds to the distribution of economic resources, it could not be argued that an extremely pure form of democracy would be achieved under pragmatic market socialism, because pragmatic market socialism would not involve that great a degree of equalization of economic resources.

At the same time, however, pragmatic market socialism does indeed represent a threat—and no apologies are made for this—to large capital fortunes which represent nothing more exalted than higher-than-average random appreciation on an inherited capital wealth base. The various obfuscations of people's capitalism may possibly conceal, but they can never alter or mitigate, the fact that the vast majority of very large capital fortunes under contemporary capitalism are of exactly this nature. Therefore the inauguration of pragmatic market socialism would indeed bring about the termination of the extravagant financial privileges of a tiny minority of plutocratic capitalists. Consequently, it would bring about the termination of the excessive influence of these people in the ongoing democratic process.

It would be rash to speculate on how this would affect government policy. It does not necessarily imply, for example, that welfare spending would mushroom, because arguably there is sufficient resistance to this among the vast majority of middle- and upper-income individuals whose economic and political status would not be importantly affected by a transition to pragmatic market socialism. But whatever the future course of social policy under pragmatic market socialism, at least it would be a course more in consonance with the true interests of the majority of the population. The potential purification of the democratic process—at least to some appreciable extent—has to be taken into account in considering the political ramifications of a potential transition to pragmatic market socialism.

Capitalist apologetics insists on the threat which socialism would pose for democracy because of its combination of economic and political power. It has been argued here that the added threat to democracy from public ownership of large-scale, established business enterprise is not very significant. Nevertheless, it has to be conceded that there is at least some added threat, however tiny and negligible it may be. But against this liability of socialism should be set an offsetting advantage: the removal from the democratic political process of a class of excessively wealthy, excessively powerful, excessively conservative capitalistic rentiers. In the final analysis, the reader may agree that, all things considered, pragmatic market socialism would be better for political democracy than the contemporary capitalistic status quo.

NOTES

1. Another statement of the argument advanced here is contained in the author's 1986 article in *Polity*: "Would Democracy Survive Under Market Socialism?" The answer to the question posed in the title is "probably yes."

2. The force of history in shaping the authoritarian Soviet system has been amply acknowledged by Western historians and political scientists. For example, in *The Soviet Paradigm* (1970, pp. vii-viii), Roy Laird writes as follows: "Yet, at the beginning of the 1970's this student of Soviet affairs is impressed by how fundamentally similar the present system is compared to what it was under Stalin and how deeply its authoritarian roots are buried in long centuries of Tsarist absolutism. Indeed, most political change in Russia from early Tsarist times until now can be seen as a slow, relatively linear evolution toward a special type of political model... primarily dependent upon a highly disciplined and bureaucratic apparatus."

3. The Watergate affair and the consequent resignation of Richard M. Nixon was one of the most fascinating and significant episodes in the post-World War II history of the United States. In its immediate aftermath, a small library of books on the subject was published, many of them contributed by principals in the drama. Overviews include Theodore H. White (1975) and Clark Mollenhoff (1976). Of the many memoirs by principals, those of John Dean (1976) are probably the most significant. It is probably safe to say that in retrospect, a consensus has emerged that on the whole the Watergate affair provided evidence that the American political system is basically in good health. Particularly significant to the present concern were Nixon's futile efforts to enlist the IRS bureaucracy in the cause of his personal power. According to Nixon (*Memoirs*, 1978, pp. 676-677): "The Democrats, while in office, had made little effort to camouflage their pressure on the key government agencies. It seemed that even when they were out of power their supporters—particularly among the bureaucrats in the IRS—continued to do the job for them... I repeatedly urged Haldeman and Ehrlichman—though without apparent success—to have IRS checks made on McGovern's key staff and contributors."

4. This, for example, is clearly the judgment of George Thayer (*Who Shakes the Money Tree?*, 1973, pp. 282-283): "It is another truth that the ties between the Fat Cats and officeholders work in favor of the status quo... No other tie so impedes the orderly process of change in America than that which binds big contributors and office-holders together."

9

CAPITALISM AND HISTORY

A. POSSIBILITIES FOR IDEOLOGICAL HARMONIZATION

Up to this point, we have been concerned herein with what might be termed the "internal" case for pragmatic market socialism: the certain achievement of a substantially fairer and more equal distribution of unearned capital property return, the possible achievement of a somewhat higher level of static efficiency and dynamic performance, and the possible achievement of a purer and more unadulterated form of political democracy. These benefits of pragmatic market socialism are completely independent of the international situation: They would be the same for the United States, for example, even if the United States happened to be the only nation on the face of the globe. At this point, however, we must briefly append to the "internal" case so far developed a simple but highly important "external" consideration. The implementation of pragmatic market socialism in the militarily powerful nations of the West, particularly in the United States, might significantly improve international relations and thereby significantly reduce the possibility that the human race will one day suffer the catastrophe of nuclear war.[1]

It must be conceded that the "external" case for pragmatic market socialism is both highly speculative and extremely controversial. The dramatic and far-reaching events currently transpiring within the Communist world have rendered it even more so. In the eyes of many analysts, the cold war is definitely over, once and for all. It is certainly to be hoped that they are correct—but it may be a bit premature to *assume* that they are correct. Consideration of this aspect of the case for pragmatic market socialism will be confined to this one relatively brief chapter. However, the issue is so inherently important that it definitely merits some attention.

The argument is simply that the preservation of capitalism in the contemporary world not only is internally disadvantageous for the populations of the capitalist nations, but also contributes to an ideological conflict between communism and its alternatives which in turn fosters an acute psychological and military confrontation, and thereby the possibility of unlimited war. Pragmatic market socialism represents a reasonable compromise between communism and noncommunism: it implements the principles of market allocation and political democracy from the noncommunist side of the controversy, and it also implements the socialist principle of public ownership of nonhuman factors of production used in large-scale production from the communist side of the controversy. In other words, pragmatic market socialism combines the valid insights and principles from both sides of an ideological controversy which has fueled an international confrontation situation of the gravest peril. It is therefore a "painless" way of resolving this controversy, or at least of reducing the controversy to a more manageable level. In order to properly appreciate the significance of this aspect of pragmatic market socialism, it is necessary to be fully conscious of the gravity of the contemporary international situation, and of the important contribution which ideological conflict has made to this situation.

Of all the extraordinary technological achievements of the twentieth century, perhaps the single most important has been the development of nuclear weapons. These unimaginably destructive weapons do not merely exist: They have been manufactured in abundance; they are widely disseminated in aircraft, silos, and submarines around the world; and they are poised for virtually instantaneous use. The majority of these weapons are controlled by the military forces of the United States and the Soviet Union, two superpowers which have been locked in an extremely hostile confrontation ever since the end of World War II, a period of almost half a century. Should these weapons ever be unleashed against the population centers, the ensuing death and destruction would be so overwhelming that the present level of civilization might never be regained, and indeed the very existence of the human race might well be jeopardized. This truly nightmarish situation is a simple fact of life with which humanity has been living for several long decades.[2]

We are all hopeful, of course, that the extravagant costs of nuclear warfare have so reduced the probability of unlimited war that a nuclear World War III will never be fought. Numerous observers of the world situation are greatly impressed by the apparent stability of the present balance of terror, and they urge extreme caution in any movement toward strategic disarmament. But at the same time, it is also clear that the international nuclear confrontation which has characterized the second half of the twentieth century cannot be allowed to persist indefinitely. History unambiguously demonstrates mankind's strong proclivity toward warfare, whatever the cost. Moreover, even if it is agreed that the *current probability* of nuclear war in any particular year is very small, the laws of probability guarantee that over a sufficient number of years the *cumulative probability* of nuclear war will become very large. Sooner or later, if the present situation is allowed to persist indefinitely, such a war will indeed occur. Therefore, the present situation simply *must* be terminated peacefully.

By general consensus, the most dramatic chapters in human history, albeit the most painful, have been written by conquerors. It would appear that political leaders—and the populations which they represent—are at all times strongly attracted by the notion of imperialistic expansion, and that the only effective constraint on the imperialistic aspirations of any particular organized social group is the brute military force exercised by other organized social groups. Many important, currently peaceable nations have histories involving episodes of imperialistic expansion, of greater or lesser violence. By means of purchases backed by force, the United States appropriated the lands of the native Indian tribes in the nineteenth century. More recently, the German nation under the leadership of Adolf Hitler made a very creditable effort at world conquest from 1939 to 1945. In the aftermath of World War II, the Soviet Union used its occupying forces in Eastern Europe to topple the incumbent governments and install Communist governments subservient to the Soviet Union. These actions, in conjunction with the traditional Soviet Communist aspiration toward worldwide socialist revolution, were naturally interpreted in the West as evidence of Stalin's inclination to emulate Hitler: to achieve a universal Communist empire under the hegemony of the Soviet Union.

In the latter 1940s the policy of containment was undertaken lest the populations of the Western nations be reduced to a condition of bemused, benighted, antlike slavery such as depicted in George Orwell's famous novel *1984*. The hope in undertaking this policy was that eventually the Soviet Union would voluntarily and peaceably abandon its expansionist inclinations. Once this happened, there would be a much higher degree of international harmony, and hence a much smaller need for conventional and nuclear armament. What has made this desired outcome especially difficult to achieve, in the case of the Soviet Union and the other Communist nations, has been the complicating and exacerbating factor of Communist ideology. According to the traditional Soviet Communist viewpoint, worldwide socialization is not merely in the selfish national interest of the Russian people; rather, it is in the interest of all humanity.

Properly socialized human beings harbor an insistent need for self-justification. Therefore, they are constantly on the alert for correspondences between their own self-interest and the interests of others. A certain course of action may be appealing to a person on grounds of self-interest, but its degree of attractiveness is greatly enhanced if the person perceives reasons (which may or may not be valid) why that course of action would also be of benefit to others. Thus in the nineteenth-century United States, the appropriation of land from the Indian tribes was justified on the basis, probably legitimate, that the European immigrants could make better use of the land, and that even the Indians would benefit from adopting the imported European civilization. When Adolf Hitler sent his armies into Russia in 1941, he fancied himself a messiah to the Russian people, because he was freeing them from the oppressive shackles of Bolshevism. And equally so, when Stalin installed Communist governments in the Eastern European nations in the latter 1940s, he considered this to be a favor to the populations of these nations, since they were thereby being freed from the oppressive shackles of capitalism. This basic human need for self-justification accounts for the important role of ideology, generally defined, in human conflict.

An ideology may be defined as a subjective belief system concerning proper individual behavior and/or social organization which is simultaneously both highly controversial and almost completely unverifiable by logical, scientific means. Well-defined, fully self-conscious secular ideologies are associated with the modern historical era, but in fact ideologies, generally defined, are as old as human civilization. When the ancient Greek armies under Alexander and the Roman armies under Caesar marched forth to conquer, they considered themselves representatives of civilizations far superior to those which they intended to subjugate. This feeling in itself constituted an important inspiration and incentive to conquest ("We conquer these people for their own good").

Certainly the most important form of ideological inspiration to conflict throughout premodern human history was not social but religious. Most of the important religions have in common the idea of a Supreme Being to whom total fealty is required, along with a system of rules and rituals for the governance of human conduct. Human beings tend to discern enormous significance in what might be considered by objective observers to be minor differences in the Supreme Being's specific designation (Yahweh, God, Allah, etc.) and/or in the fine details of the rules and rituals. The fact that other humans do not subscribe to exactly the same religious belief system has throughout history filled believers with righteous wrath. Among the more dramatic examples of religiously inspired conflict are the Islamic wars of expansion, the Crusades, and the various conflicts between Protestants and Catholics in Western Europe during the early modern period which culminated in the devastating Thirty Years' War (1618-1648).

This is not to assert that military conflict has not often occurred between societies with very minor differences in religion, institutions, and customs.

And it is also not to assert that mundane motives of direct material aggrandizement cannot be perceived in any given historical conflict in which opposing belief systems have been involved. However, this is most definitely to argue that the *probability* of military conflict is larger, and the *intensity* of military conflict, if initiated, is stronger, when ideological differences are present than when they are absent. It is to argue that conflict is both more probable and more dangerous when societies display substantial differences in religion, institutions, and customs—and that this is especially true when societies are fully and consciously aware of the differences. And it is consequently to argue that the history of the twentieth century would have been much different, and that the risk of total nuclear war in the latter half of this century would have been much smaller, if it had not been for the ideological conflict between communism and noncommunism.

The success of the Bolshevik Revolution in Russia in 1917 afflicted both the leaders and the people of that nation with what can only be described as an ideological infection. Had the Bolshevik Revolution been unsuccessful, and capitalism been maintained in Russia, it is virtually impossible to conceive that world history throughout the remainder of the twentieth century would not have been dramatically different. More specifically, it is almost impossible to conceive that mankind would have experienced the severe post-World War II cold war, with its persistent militarization and perilous brinkmanship on the edge of nuclear disaster.

So long as the human race is unable to advance politically beyond the sovereign nation-state system, the best hope for the maintenance of peace remains the balance of power. Over the past 200 years of Western civilization, there have been two major breakdowns in the balance of power which precipitated lengthy periods of savage warfare. The "French wars" associated with the French Revolution and the Napoleonic era persisted from 1792 to the Congress of Vienna in 1815. The ideological overtones of this conflict involved rising bourgeois liberalism versus declining aristocratic traditionalism. The "German wars" associated with the Kaiser and Hitler persisted from 1914 to the Potsdam Conference of 1945. The ideological overtones of this conflict involved democratic pluralism versus oligarchic centralism. There are striking parallels between these two periods of rampant, uncontrolled warfare. But one of the most important *differences* between the two periods is that the Congress of Vienna established a highly stable and harmonious, relatively unmilitarized condition in Western civilization for several decades, whereas the Potsdam Conference did not.

The stability following the Congress of Vienna eventually broke down when modern Germany emerged in the latter half of the nineteenth century. Such breakdowns are more or less inevitable under the sovereign nation-state system. But the point here is that had it not been for the Bolshevik Revolution which socialized Russia in 1917, in all probability a lengthy period of stability and harmony would have followed the Potsdam Conference in 1945, just as one had followed the Congress of Vienna in 1815. This outcome would have been even more likely because, in addition to curbing German power, World War II led to the development of nuclear weapons of such transcendent destructiveness as to threaten the very existence of advanced human civilization. But instead of entering a lengthy period of stability and harmony, human civilization proceeded directly from World War II into a tense cold war situation characterized by massive militarization and a perpetual threat of nuclear disaster.

The conventional cynical interpretation of Soviet behavior since 1917 is that the Communist leadership has hypocritically employed Communist ideology to legitimize a standard nationalistic, imperialistic drive toward world domination. This interpretation leaves much to be desired. While the consensus judgment in the non-Communist world that the Communist leadership has been dangerously deluded and misguided may well be valid, we should at least grant these leaders the virtue of sincerity. They (almost certainly) were not conscious hypocrites: Their belief in the superiority of socialism over capitalism (almost certainly) was perfectly sincere. It is this strong and sincere belief which explains why the Communist leadership of the Soviet Union did *not* pursue a rational definition of Russian national interest after the Bolshevik Revolution of 1917.

The brutal program of uncompensated socialization implemented by the Bolsheviks under Vladimir Lenin instantly marked Russia off as a pariah among nations. Had they not been driven by strong ideological ideals and convictions, the Communist leaders would have reestablished capitalism in Russia as soon as it became evident, in the early 1920s, that the rest of the world was not, in the foreseeable future, going to follow Russia down the path of socialist revolution. Had they had any serious interest in world conquest for its own sake, the most promising path would obviously have been to build up Russia's industrial and military strength through full participation in the world economy. This was indeed the path taken by Germany and Japan in the same period.

But clearly the Communist leaders of the Soviet Union were never inspired by a vision of a world empire militarily dominated by Russia. Their fervent hope was merely that Russia would serve as a moral exemplar to the rest of humanity, and that socialization of the rest of the world would end Russia's perilous position as an outcast from the family of nations. Rather than give up the ideal of socialism, the Communist leaders of the Soviet Union have put themselves and their nation at severe risk throughout the twentieth century. In the last half of the twentieth century, they have continuously risked nuclear devastation for the sake of keeping alive the holy fire of socialism in the world. It does not make sense to interpret Soviet behavior throughout the twentieth century simply as "pursuing Russia's national interest." But it does make sense to interpret it as the outcome of ideological convictions so deep and so strong that they have overcome rational self-interest, national interest, and common sense.

The ideological conflict between communism and noncommunism comprises three major elements: (1) socialism versus capitalism; (2) planning versus the market; (3) oligarchy versus democracy. There are other important differences, principally in attitudes toward religion and toward international activism, but the above three elements are the most fundamental in a purely logical sense. Of these three elements, the vital crux has always been, and remains, the issue of socialism versus capitalism. Communism in the Soviet Union and elsewhere has been guided by the pronouncements of Karl Marx, who perceived in the capitalist economic system the sole root of all evil. According to Marx's theory of economic materialism, the entire legal, political, social, and philosophical superstructure is determined entirely by the economic foundation, consisting of the technology of production and the institutions of ownership. Thus everything that is bad about capitalism is due fundamentally to private ownership of capital, and everything that is good about socialism is due fundamentally to public ownership of capital. Even the most cursory study of the guiding works of communism, from Marx through Lenin and proceeding on down, will substantiate the proposition that the fundamental ideological quarrel which the Communist world has had with the non-Communist world concerns the capitalist economic system, and the capitalist economic system alone.

Anti-Communist literature almost invariably emphasizes the conflict between democracy (normally described by the sacred term "freedom") and oligarchy (characterized as "totalitarianism," "dictatorship," "slavery," etc.). But as was pointed out in Chapter 8, the Communist nations inherited the absence of democracy from pre-revolutionary times, and the failure of Communist governments to introduce democracy is attributable to the severe stress placed on these governments by extreme internal and external opposition and hostility. Communist ideology is not inherently opposed to Western democratic institutions. In fact, the Communist nations early on adopted the outward forms, if not the substance, of Western democracy. Communist criticism of Western "bourgeois" democracy has never been that this form of democracy is an inherently ineffective form of political governance but, rather, that owing to the surreptitious domination of society by the all-powerful capitalist class, the forms and trappings of democracy in the West possess no genuine substance.[3] (Note that this is a mirror image of the argument used by anti-Communists to assault Communist democracy.)

Similarly, the opposition between planning and the market as the basic mechanism of economic production and distribution is not the central crux of the matter. The Soviet Union adopted the current system of central planning well over ten years after the Bolshevik Revolution had socialized the Russian economy.[4] The central planning system was not based directly on the clear pronouncements of Karl Marx; rather, it was regarded as a necessary expedient for rapid development of a modern industrial economy. A modern industrial economy was desired both because it would permit a higher standard of living among the population and, perhaps even more important, because it would produce an abundance of up-to-date military equipment with which to protect the socialist economic system of the U.S.S.R. against potential invasions by hostile capitalist nations. As mentioned earlier, the forced-pace industrialization campaign under central planning in the 1930s may well have preserved the Soviet Union from conquest by the Nazi military machine in World War II.

To summarize, neither central planning nor the oligarchic one-party political system is necessarily prescribed by the ideological essence of communism. But socialism *is* most certainly prescribed by this essence. Therefore it would be much easier for the Communist world to implement political democracy along conventional Western lines, and to implement some type of market socialist economy, than it would be to implement capitalism per se. Movements are presently converging in the Communist world toward all three main components of Western non-Communist society: political democracy, free market allocation, and capitalism itself. Perhaps these movements will continue toward what many in the West consider their logical conclusions—and perhaps they will not. This important question will be considered in the next section of the chapter.

The present section will conclude with the statement that whatever the future may hold, the preservation of the capitalist economic system in the non-Communist West has for many decades contributed heavily to an ideological conflict which in turn has fueled a prolonged and bitter international confrontation which could easily have precipitated—and which may yet precipitate—a nuclear war. The typical advocate of pragmatic market socialism no doubt shares the consensus in the non-Communist world that the greater share of moral responsibility for the present situation lies with the Communist governments, particularly that of the Soviet Union. This is to say that while the advocate perceives pragmatic market socialism to possess significant advantages over contemporary capitalism, these advantages are certainly not worthy of the risk of nuclear war. Moreover, the contemporary Communist form of socialism, owing to its dysfunctional elements of central planning and oligarchic political governance, is on the whole inferior to contemporary capitalism. Thus, dire risks have been imposed on human civilization by the recalcitrant, paranoid, and hostile behavior of the Communist nations in the cause of an inferior form of socialism.

All this notwithstanding, it is nevertheless regrettable that the non-Communist Western nations do not move forward of their own volition to implement pragmatic market socialism. Such a transition would do much to defuse the ideological confrontation between the two systems, without imposing any penalties on the citizens of the capitalist nations. Such a transition would benefit the populations of the capitalist nations even if the international conflict situation did not exist. But given that this conflict situation *does* in fact exist, a transition to pragmatic market socialism would quite possibly dramatically improve the odds for genuine, permanent détente between the Communist and non-Communist worlds. The potential value of such détente is beyond calculation.

B. REFORM MOVEMENTS IN THE COMMUNIST NATIONS

It is extremely difficult for an enthusiastic supporter of the capitalist system to perceive and acknowledge the important role of ideological conflict in the potentially deadly international confrontation situation that has persisted throughout the second half of the twentieth century. The superiority of the capitalist economic system over the socialist economic system seems so completely clear and self-evident to such a supporter that the only available means to explain the professed dedication of the Communist leadership to socialism are stupidity, ignorance, or hypocrisy. Since stupidity and ignorance seem unlikely, that leaves only hypocrisy: The Communist leaders are employing the false issue of socialism to justify the pursuit of their own crass self-interest. But the fact remains (based on fundamental human psychology) that hypocrisy is almost as unlikely as stupidity or ignorance.

To a proponent of pragmatic market socialism, there remains yet another explanation for the mystery: The Communist leaders have stuck by socialism, through thick and thin over many hazardous decades, because it so happens that they are *right* about socialism. They are right to the extent that the logical essence of socialism, the public ownership of nonhuman factors of production utilized in large-scale ("socialized") production, is inherently superior to the logical essence of capitalism, private ownership of such factors. Therefore, even though their own realization of socialism is seriously flawed by central planning and the one-party state, they continue to sense the fundamental value of socialism in and of itself, and they continue to support socialism even at the risk of catastrophe.

Be this as it may, at the moment that this is being written, the Communist world is in the midst of what appear to be epochal transitions. The Eastern European nations are described as "having abandoned communism," the Soviet Union is "in the process of abandoning communism," and the People's Republic of China and the other Communist nations "will soon abandon communism." This pat perception of the matter is almost certainly, for the moment at least, both oversimplified and premature. The following comments are focused on the Soviet Union, because the Soviet Union has been, and remains, the ideological and military heart of world communism. If Eastern Europe does indeed rescind and renounce every last vestige of the social system introduced by the Communist governments installed by the Red Army in the aftermath of World War II, this may just as easily be attributed to the awesome force of nationalism as to any rational evaluation of the relative advantages and disadvantages of the social system. As for China and the other Communist nations, for the moment they do not possess sufficient military power to make what they do or do not do with their internal social systems of central interest to observers of the international situation.

As for the Soviet Union, the enthusiastic supporter of capitalism tends toward the optimistic view that the present turmoil within the Soviet Union is evidence of total ideological capitulation. Within a relatively short time, according to this view, the Soviet Union (or the various individual republics if the Union itself is dissolved) will be characterized by private ownership of capital, a free market economy, and a fully and genuinely democratic political system. Most of those who take this view seem also to expect that once full ideological capitulation has taken place in the Soviet Union, the likelihood of major strategic and conventional disarmament will be much enhanced, and the prospects for a peaceful resolution of the present nuclear confrontation will be greatly improved. Of course, if it were actually true, as these people would have argued in the past, that the socialization of the capitalist West would not improve prospects for peace (because ideology is just a hypocritical tool of the Communist leadership), then it follows that the capitalization of the Communist East will not improve prospects for peace. But now that it is the Communist East making adjustments in its ideology, the enthusiastic supporters of the capitalist status quo are finding it easier to perceive and acknowledge the true importance of ideology. It is of course almost certainly true that the capitalization of the East in the future would improve the prospects for peace, just as it is almost certainly true that the socialization of the West in the past would have improved the prospects for peace.

Does the reform movement in the Soviet Union, under the leadership of Mikhail Gorbachev, Boris Yeltsin, and others, signify a complete abandonment of communism, so that within a few years the Soviet Union will be just like a big, Russian-speaking United States? Will it be characterized by a democratic market capitalist social system exactly analogous to the social system currently prevalent in the United States and the other leading nations of Western capitalism? Although such an outcome would have seemed miraculous only a few years ago, at this point in time it must be acknowledged as a definite possibility. Any sensible advocate of pragmatic market socialism would welcome this outcome cheerfully, because its effect in reducing the threat of nuclear war is obviously of tremendously greater importance than would be the fact that the external case for pragmatic market socialism would thereby be rendered null and void.

But it would certainly be regrettable for the Soviet Union if in its eagerness to abandon oligarchic planned socialism, it skipped entirely over the possibility of democratic market socialism and went directly to democratic market capitalism. If socialism itself were abandoned, this would be the equivalent of throwing out the baby with the bathwater. It would certainly be in the interest of the Soviet Union, as well as of the other Communist nations, at least to experiment for a while with some sort of democratic market socialism, either the pragmatic variety or some other, before abandoning the principle of socialism altogether. It would also be of great interest to many individuals in the capitalist nations to see how market socialism performed in the Communist nations. These latter nations might provide a proving ground in which the potential performance of market socialism could at last be empirically tested. Although any sensible proponent of pragmatic market socialism would be happy to see the Soviet Union become capitalistic because of the favorable effect on international relations, that proponent would of course be even happier to see the Soviet Union adopt some form of market socialism, preferably a reasonable facsimile of the pragmatic variety. The adoption of democracy and the market would have a sufficiently favorable impact on the ideological conflict and hence on international relations, and this would at the same time give pragmatic market socialism a fair opportunity to prove itself.

The enthusiastic supporter of the capitalist status quo earnestly desires the Soviet Union to become fully capitalist, while the proponent of pragmatic market socialism earnestly desires the Soviet Union to experiment with market socialism, preferably of the pragmatic variety. But what actually *will* happen in the Soviet Union? At the present moment, the future of the Soviet Union is still very uncertain. One possibility, of course, is a sort of Thermidorean reaction which would depose Gorbachev, Yeltsin, and the other progressive leaders in the interest of moderation and stability. There must be millions of individuals in the Soviet Union, particularly in the Communist Party and the military, who want nothing so much as the end of the current turmoil and confusion. Thus far the only tangible consequences of the much-touted economic and political reforms seem to have been even greater scarcity and hardship than existed before. If very few people are directly benefiting from reform, then the reform movement's constituency will gradually evaporate. For the moment, at least, the Soviet Union appears ripe for the classic "man on horseback."

In the event that important institutional changes actually do emerge from the present situation, it is quite possible that they would be more of a political nature than of an economic nature, at least in the short term. At this point in time, the political purposes of the reform movement seem better defined than the economic purposes. A tremendous consensus has apparently developed in favor of eliminating direct Communist Party control over the state apparatus and establishing a genuinely democratic political system. This is not at all surprising since, from the beginning even the high Communist Party leadership, let alone the rank-and-file membership, has been ideologically uncomfortable with the oligarchic political system in the Soviet Union. The Party has always proclaimed itself a friend of democracy and has tried to maintain the appearance of democracy. It has been reasonably well aware of the fact that it was definitely on the losing side of the argument, in debates with anti-Communists, on the issue of democracy. Apparently the time is at last at hand when the Communist Party has accepted the fact that genuine democracy should become a reality in the Soviet Union.

Presuming that democracy does become a reality in the Soviet Union, the question remains of what effect the existence of democracy will have on the economic system. And when we come to the economic system, we must recognize that the centrally planned socialist economy established under Joseph Stalin in the late 1920s and early 1930s is extremely deep-rooted in the Soviet Union. There have been a number of economic reform efforts since the death of Stalin in 1953. Without exception, these efforts were supposed to alleviate the bureaucratic overload on the economy, to decentralize economic decision-making authority, and to place greater reliance on commercial motivations in the management of business enterprises. The most famous of these efforts were the Kosygin reforms of the mid-1960s, inspired by the free market exhortations of Evsey Liberman and others. The universal consensus among Western economists who have studied these reform efforts is that they have had extremely little impact on the practical functioning of the economy. When Gorbachev first arrived on the scene in 1985, calling for radical restructuring of the economy, the attitude of most Western authorities on the Soviet economy was merely "Ho hum, here we go again."[5]

By the 1990s, it has become clear that in historical perspective, Mikhail Gorbachev will go down as the most important Soviet leader since Joseph Stalin, or possibly even Vladimir Lenin. But it remains uncertain as to what the practical consequences of the Gorbachev period will be for the Soviet Union. Economic perestroika has apparently produced nothing more than a giant muddle, while glasnost has produced an apparently decisive challenge to the historical authority of the Communist Party along with separatist movements in a large number of the peripheral republics. Once the political situation has clarified itself, the economic situation will no doubt follow suit. But it would be very speculative at the present time to predict in what direction the economy will go.

After all is said and done, and the dust has settled, the economy may not be all that different from what it has been for several decades. Many of the same people who lustily demand economic reform as a nebulous ideal seem unable to accept the practical ramifications of reform. An obvious example is the price system. Soviet consumers are thoroughly accustomed to low and stable administered prices on a variety of necessities: basic foodstuffs, housing, and medical care. If free market allocation is to become a reality, the administered pricing system must be abandoned. Most of these prices must be allowed to rise to levels that Soviet consumers generally deem astronomical and intolerable. Up to the present point in time, all serious efforts at price reform have been abandoned in the face of anguished howls from the consuming public. The Soviet consumer apparently subscribes strongly to the following attitude: "If the government can't give us these commodities at a low price, then we'll get a government which can." Such an attitude is hardly conducive to meaningful economic reform. The establishment of genuine democracy in the Soviet Union would make it much easier for the public to change governments, which could operate as an even greater constraint on a transition to a genuine market economy.

The market is one thing, but private ownership of large-scale business enterprise is quite another. For generations, the Soviet population has been intensively indoctrinated, through the educational system and the media of communication, in the paramount virtues of socialism. The public ownership principle is most sacrosanct of all with reference to large-scale industrial enterprises, enterprises in which the production process is most clearly and obviously "socialized" in a technological sense. The genuine privatization of large-scale industrial enterprises would require a complete repudiation of the very soul of communist ideology. It is true that the various "500-day plans" currently afoot in the Soviet Union call for the privatization of such enterprises. But to date these plans remain aspirations; they have not been implemented in practice. Moreover, it is quite possible that the "privatization" called for by these plans means something far short of the meaning of the term in the West. If the potential future private owners are not given meaningful control over the managers of these enterprises (the ability to dismiss them, etc.), and if the owners are not given a substantial share of the profits earned by these enterprises, then "private ownership" would not possess the significance it possesses under Western capitalism.

Considering the central moral status of socialism in Soviet history and communist ideology, and considering the fact that a very high degree of reliance on market allocation may in fact be achieved without abandoning the core socialist principle of public ownership of large-scale, established business enterprises (such has been the argument of this book), it would seem rather more likely that the Soviet Union will eventually end up with some form of market socialism than that it will end up with pure and unadulterated capitalism such as is standard in the non-Communist nations. This is certainly to be hoped for, since it would provide an opportunity for market socialism to prove itself economically in a more or less definitive, empirical manner.

It is certainly arguable that since the Soviet Union and the other Communist nations may be moving in the direction of experimentation with market socialism, the Western non-Communist nations should hold off any experiments of their own with market socialism, of the pragmatic or any other form, so as to benefit from the experiences and errors of others. Against this argument is that the prospect of major transitions in the Communist world, transitions which are weakening an ideological conflict situation which has contributed heavily to the peril of human civilization, may inspire like transitions in the non-Communist world.

The Soviet Union and the other Communist nations are struggling desperately toward a higher form of social organization. At every step the progressive elements in these nations are being opposed and obstructed by reactionary forces who perceive these transitions as a form of crass capitulation to the ideological enemy—as something against which their basic pride and self-esteem rebel. Under the circumstances, it would provide a tremendous lift to the progressive elements in the East if the Western capitalist nations made a compensating accommodation in the form of pragmatic market socialism. Pragmatic market socialism embodies the core socialist principle, and its implementation in the West would deliver the extremely significant consolatory message that the West does not deem the entire Communist experience to have been a completely misguided and malevolent episode in human history.

This is simply to say that ideological convergence is a more promising scenario of future development than the ideological capitulation scenario currently envisioned by many in the Western capitalist world. Expectations that the Communist world will throw aside every aspect of Communist ideology, even the most central and sacred, may well be disappointed. On the other hand, if both East and West arrive, by mutual consent and free volition, at the common ground of democratic market socialism, then both sides will have made ideological concessions and accommodations. History demonstrates that peaceful conflict resolution almost always requires some degree of concession by both parties. Where human psychology and sensibilities are involved, such tangible expressions of mutual respect and esteem are almost always vitally necessary.

Therefore it is argued here that despite the turmoil and uncertainty presently prevailing throughout the Communist world, this is still a good time for the West to adopt pragmatic market socialism. In fact, this may be more than a good time—it may be the best time. We do not know whether the opportunities which presently exist for the amelioration of international tension and hostility will persist very much longer. The progressive elements in the Communist nations could all too easily be quickly overthrown and eliminated. They are more likely to suffer this fate if the West continues to stand by doing nothing, smugly and patiently awaiting total ideological capitulation by the East. Therefore pragmatic market socialism still offers the possibility of strengthening and accelerating the positive tendencies toward peace which have lately emerged. Pragmatic market socialism may still be an important instrumentality toward the final and definitive termination of a nightmarish condition in which human civilization labors under the daily peril of nuclear devastation.[6]

NOTES

1. The author's 1982 article in *Co-Existence* ("Ideological Harmonization as a Means of Promoting Authentic Detente: A False Hope?") contains a somewhat more detailed statement of the argument developed here. An updating of the argument is scheduled to appear in the same journal in 1992.

2. The situation is sufficiently familiar that elaborate scholarly apparatus is not required. The following official statement is typical. In the words of the Office of

Technology Assessment, U.S. Congress (1979, p. 94): "This case discusses a massive attack that one normally associates with all-out nuclear war. The attack uses thousands of war-heads to attack urban-industrial targets, strategic targets, and other military targets. The number of deaths and the damage and destruction inflicted on the U.S. society and economy by the sheer magnitude of such an attack would place in question whether the United States would ever recover its position as an organized, industrial, and powerful country."

3. A typical quasi-official statement of the traditional Soviet Communist viewpoint on Western democracy is as follows. M. A. Krutogolov (1980, p. 46): "Being one of the institutions of bourgeois democracy, the multi-party system does not alter the social content of capitalism. Though [the various political parties] alternate with each other as the ruling party, they do nothing to alter the exploitative nature of the capitalist system, but rather on the contrary, do everything they can to ensure that no working class party ever comes to power."

4. The standard interpretation of the origin of Soviet central planning is succinctly stated by Morris Bornstein and Daniel Fusfeld (1974, p. 17): "Comprehensive central planning and administrative control were adopted in the U.S.S.R. in the late 1920's to mobilize resources for rapid industrialization." Major sources for this interpretation include Alexander Erlich (1960); Nicholas Spulber (1964); and E. H. Carr and R. W. Davies (1969).

5. The rhetoric of reform and decentralization commenced almost as soon as Stalin died in 1953; and the so-called Kosygin reforms of 1966, based on the ideas of Evsey Liberman (1971) and others, were regarded as especially significant, eliciting book-length studies in the 1970s: George Feiwel (1972) and J. Wilczynski (1972). However, the consensus among Western authorities on the economy of the Soviet Union is that despite the abundant rhetoric, the actual pace of substantive change has always been very slow. This consensus viewpoint is clearly expressed in the title of a 1979 paper by Gertrude Schroeder: "The Soviet Economy on a Treadmill of 'Reforms'." The current economic news from the U.S.S.R. is dominated by the Gorbachev initiatives of perestroika (restructuring) and glasnost (openness). The initially dubious reaction to these programs among Western authorities was exemplified by the symposium edited by Susan Linz in *Comparative Economic Studies* (Winter 1987). Other commentaries on the current Soviet reform effort include Edward Hewett (1988), Padma Desai (1989), and Jan Adam (1989). By the early 1990s, most specialists on the Soviet economy are agreed that drastic alterations of the traditional economic system will probably soon occur—but few such specialists are willing to predict what these changes will be, when they will occur, and precisely how they will be implemented.

6. The larger potential of pragmatic market socialism in human history has been assessed by the author in a lengthy article entitled "Practical Considerations in Designing a Supernational Federation," published in *World Futures* in 1985. An important component of the scenario developed in "Practical Considerations" is an economic development effort tentatively designated the World Economic Equalization Program, discussed in two articles by the author published in the *Journal of Developing Areas* (1976) and *World Development* (1988). The ideas

developed in these three papers are highly visionary, to say the least, and as such they are also highly speculative and controversial. In the interest of conservatism, they are not discussed in this book. However, the author anticipates a full development of them in a future book.

10

PROSPECTS FOR CHANGE?

A. A PROPOSAL FOR ACTION

Let us briefly summarize the case for pragmatic market socialism put forward in this book. The central, primary, and most certain benefit of pragmatic market socialism may be described as both economic and moral in nature: It would significantly equalize the distribution of unearned capital property return, and thereby eliminate from society an unseemly parasitical element of wealthy capitalistic rentiers. There would be no significant efficiency losses to offset this equity benefit, in either the short term or the long term. This is because the various arguments that capital property income is earned income, either as a return to capital management effort in various forms (corporate supervision, entrepreneurship, etc.) or as a return to the abstinence and/or risk-taking sacrifices of saving, are merely ex post facto rationalizations of an institutional status quo, and as such they are devoid of validity and legitimacy. Equally invalid is the people's capitalism justification for capitalism: Careful examination of the available evidence suggests both that the overwhelming majority of the population would benefit from social dividend distribution of capital property return, and that the capital fortunes of wealthy capitalists are attributable far more to inheritance and chance than to any productive contributions made by these capitalists (either in the form of entrepreneurship or of anything else).

As far as short-term and long-term economic efficiency and dynamism are concerned, it is fully possible that pragmatic market socialism would be appreciably superior to capitalism: Distribution of property return in proportion to labor income might encourage labor, the sterner discipline over high corporation executives exercised by the Bureau of Public Ownership (BPO) might improve managerial performance, and there might be a higher rate of business physical capital investment and economic growth. On the political side, there is very little likelihood that the economic authority of the national government under pragmatic market socialism could be utilized to suppress political opposition and genuine democracy, while at the same time the elimination of the excessive power of the wealthy capitalist class in social decision-making would improve the quality of democracy. In the international area, pragmatic market socialism offers a means of reducing the ideological distance between communism and noncommunism, a means which imposes absolutely no sacrifice on the populations of the Western capitalist nations. Such a reduction would significantly increase the probability of avoiding nuclear war and (through significant disarmament) of shifting a large proportion of the economic resources presently being used for military armament into more productive employments.

Much effort has been devoted herein to avoiding overstatement of the case for pragmatic market socialism. Traditional advocacies of socialism have implied that capitalism is a kind of social cancer which is ruining and destroying human life and civilization. The present advocacy of socialism, on the other hand, concedes that modern capitalist societies are fully viable: The argument is, rather, that capitalism, at least at the present moment in history, is merely a kind of mildly debilitating ailment, such as a rash, a cold, or a wart. Nevertheless, this ailment is curable; it is not necessary for society to put up with it. Of course, should the cure (pragmatic market socialism) prove worse than the ailment (contemporary capitalism), as is clearly within the realm of possibility, then pragmatic market socialism, after a reasonable period of experimentation, should, and no doubt would, be abandoned and the capitalist economic system restored. What the moderately stated case for pragmatic market socialism loses in terms of drama and rhetorical force, it (one hopes) more than gains back in terms of basic credibility and plausibility.

Let us imagine a reader who has been more or less persuaded by the case for pragmatic market socialism set forth in the previous nine chapters. Such a reader may still have one very important objection left: that no matter how attractive pragmatic market socialism may appear in theory, it has no chance whatsoever in reality. According to this objection, every element of the population in the advanced capitalist nations, from unskilled laborers through the professionals and intelligentsia and on up to the political leadership, is so completely and totally opposed to socialism (in the sense of public ownership of capital) that they will never perceive the merit of the pragmatic market socialist proposal. Their negative opinion of socialism is too firmly fixed for them to engage in rational, objective consideration of pragmatic market socialism. Most will simply ignore the proposal, and of the small minority who deign to notice it, the vast majority will reject it thoughtlessly and unceremoniously on a variety of superficial, off-the-cuff, extemporaneous objections. Thus, regardless of the true pros and cons of the matter, the proposal has no more chance than the proverbial snowball in hell.

This tenth and final chapter will endeavor to answer this objection to the extent possible. In line with the realistic attitude maintained throughout the work, it has to be granted that this is a very serious objection. As a matter of fact, once the validity of the case for pragmatic market socialism has been recognized, the only possible explanation for why this, or some similar plan of market socialism, has not yet emerged into the realm of public discussion and debate is the immense prejudice in the population against the very notion of socialism, whatever the form or variety. The basic argument to be made here, therefore, is the only argument which *can* be made: that it would be an abrogation of our finer qualities of humanity to refrain from action on grounds that ignorance and prejudice are too deep-seated in our fellow humans ever to be successfully challenged. The negativism, cynicism, and pessimism of such a conclusion would simply be morally wrong.

The argument, of course, must and does deny that pragmatic market socialism has *no chance whatever*: Rather, it is based on the premise that owing to the solidity of the case for pragmatic market socialism, the proposal does in fact possess some perceptible chance of success despite the tremendous prejudice against socialism in the advanced capitalist nations at the present time. In order to properly assess this chance, it is necessary to look at least briefly at a possible scenario for the practical realization of pragmatic market socialism. Obviously it is much too early to be very precise and specific, but something needs to be said about the matter. The present section of Chapter 10 will propose some rough guidelines for a campaign toward the implementation of pragmatic market socialism. On the basis of these guidelines, the next section will assess the possibility of success. The argument will be made that there is an adequate possibility of success to merit action.

The objective of the campaign would be to enlighten a sufficiently large majority of the citizens of the advanced capitalist nations to enable a peaceful, orderly, democratic implementation of pragmatic market socialism. Some consolation may be derived from the thought that unanimity is not not required. It is fairly predictable that most of the capitalist class will allow their personal self-interest to override their social conscience, and it is also predictable that a considerable number of people who would in fact be personally benefited by pragmatic market socialism will continue to oppose it out of ignorance and prejudice, even after the majority of their fellow citizens have been sufficiently enlightened to change their minds and support it.

The campaign toward pragmatic market socialism would basically be a campaign of enlightenment against the force of entrenched ignorance and prejudice. It must be a peaceful, unhurried, good-natured campaign based on genuinely friendly persuasion. The rhetoric employed must be balanced, temperate, and well-considered. As far as public manifestations are concerned, the traditional "demonstration" must be studiously avoided. Instead, reliance should be placed on a superior type of public assembly to be known as a "gathering." Whereas the traditional demonstration is a noisy, obstructive, aggressive affair, the gathering would be quiet, peaceful, and friendly. The idea would be to attract the natural curiosity of passers-by—not to get their attention by frightening, annoying, or overawing them. In order to organize and focus the enlightenment campaign, there has to be a special interest group whose central purpose is the achievement of pragmatic market socialism. A tentative name for the group might be the Pragmatic Progress Society.

It is essential that the objective of the campaign be very specific, clearly stated, and fully understood by all. One reason for this is that socialism is so prejudicially misunderstood at the present time that most people will tend to interpret vagueness in a negative way: They will incorrectly imagine that pragmatic market socialism will involve changes to which they personally are opposed (e.g., a giant welfare state). Another reason is that a transition to pragmatic market socialism would inevitably involve a certain amount of confusion in the short term which will adversely affect productivity, living standards, and public support for the transition. The amount of confusion can be kept to a minimum if the specific nature of pragmatic market socialism is completely understood in advance. It would probably be advisable for the Pragmatic Progress Society to prepare draft legislation at a very early stage. A possible title for the draft legislation to establish pragmatic market socialism would be "An Act for Economic Justice." The act would outline exceptions to socialization, specify a procedure and timetable for socialization, establish the Bureau of Public Ownership, specify the extent and limitations of the BPO's authority, provide for social dividend distribution of capital property return earned by large-scale, established corporations, and deal with a variety of subsidiary issues such as foreign ownership, inflation-compensating interest payments by financial intermediaries, and so on and so forth. The purpose is to have available, from the outset, a piece of legislation which fully answers questions about what is intended by pragmatic market socialism, and which will enable relatively smooth and rapid implementation of pragmatic market socialism once sufficient political support for the transition has been achieved.

In arguing the case for pragmatic market socialism, great emphasis has to be placed on the relatively conservative nature of the proposal, and on its complete independence from a large number of negative ideas about socialism. It must be tirelessly reiterated that pragmatic market socialism does not involve Soviet-style central planning, or any other type of national or even indicative planning; that it does not imply a giant, paternalistic welfare state; that it does not intend radical redistribution and egalitarianism; that it has no communalistic aspirations; that it would not signify the triumph of bureaucratic homogenization over a healthy level of individualistic materialism. To anyone who has carefully studied the pragmatic market socialist proposal, it is obvious that the proposal is compatible with pursuit of material self-interest, competition, and individual achievement and recognition. It is obvious that the proposal fully incorporates strong material and psychological incentives to effort. So successful has capitalist apologetics been in the past, however, that it will be very difficult at first for a great many people to perceive these fundamental truths about pragmatic market socialism. But with time and effort, the truth may finally emerge and be recognized.

Among the most obvious means by which the moderation and sensibility of the pragmatic market socialist proposal may be demonstrated is the fact that the proposal is being put forward merely as a recommended experiment, not as a definite social reality for all time. Any sensible advocate of pragmatic market socialism must understand that the evidence in favor of pragmatic market socialism is not conclusive in a scientific sense. What has been argued herein is merely that the case for pragmatic market socialism is sufficiently strong to merit at least an experimental venture with the system. The argument concedes that pragmatic market socialism might not work as well in practice as is hoped, and the proposal incorporates a clear and definite provision that if, after a reasonable trial period, the performance of the pragmatic market socialist economy is clearly inferior to the performance of the capitalist economy, then capitalism would be reestablished: Publicly owned corporations would be privatized, the Bureau of Public Ownership would be abolished, and the economy would be restored to its prior condition. It must be insistently stressed to the public that opposition to pragmatic market socialism is opposition even to a mere *experiment* with pragmatic market socialism. Such opposition can only be based on what must be described, given the available evidence on the matter, as an irrationally strong certainty that pragmatic market socialism would be inferior to capitalism. The question must be asked over and over: "If the opponents of pragmatic market socialism are so positive that capitalism is superior to pragmatic market socialism, then why are they so afraid of an experiment with pragmatic market socialism?"

The experimental viewpoint inherent in the proposal will be especially important to the economics profession, whose input will be particularly influential throughout the enlightenment campaign. Like many other professions (law, medicine, management, accounting, science), the economics profession receives its fair share of criticism and negative publicity. Economists are renowned for their inability to agree on much of anything, and for their generally unsatisfactory record of forecasting. Nevertheless, when the time comes, economists are consulted by non-specialists just as earnestly on important questions which are relevant to their area of specialization as are other professionals. Thus, if and when pragmatic market socialism emerges into the general arena of public discussion, given that it is first and foremost an economic idea, other professionals and the general public will be very interested in the opinion of economists on the idea.

It is probably too much to expect that many professional economists would profess themselves personally in favor of conducting an experiment with pragmatic market socialism. Economics is a highly academic profession, in the sense that the vast majority of professional economists are employed in the higher education system. As a rule, professors have rather passive mentalities and attitudes. This is perhaps especially true of professors of economics because of the traditional bias in the profession, dating back to the invisible hand proposition of Adam Smith in *The Wealth of Nations* (1776), in favor of limited state intervention in the market economy. Owing to this passive mentality, it can be predicted that very little serious study of pragmatic market socialism will take place until the system either has been implemented or is on the verge of implementation. This is because most economists believe that their major purpose is to study the economy as it is, or as it will most likely become in the near future—not to study hypothetical economies that may or may not come to pass in the relatively remote future.

But while it is unlikely that many economists will come out in favor of implementing pragmatic market socialism, it may be realistic to hope that most of them, when consulted on the probable performance of pragmatic market socialism, will state that there is no clear-cut evidence from economic theory or empirics that pragmatic market socialism would be inferior to capitalism. Economists are more likely to take this neutral position if they fully appreciate the experimental nature of the proposal because, as a group, they are strongly influenced by the experimental ideals of physical science. The core of scientific inquiry is the experimental testing of theoretical hypotheses. All theoretical hypotheses fit the existing facts to some degree. The idea of experimentation is to accumulate additional facts with which to ascertain the relative plausibility of competing theoretical hypotheses which fit the existing facts to approximately the same degree. Economists are rarely able to rise to the ideal level of scientific inquiry set in the natural sciences because of the usual impossibility of controlled laboratory experiments. But they constantly aspire to this level, and they are completely dedicated to the experimental principle as a means of resolving theoretical controversies.

At the present point in time, the two competing theoretical hypotheses concerning pragmatic market socialism ("Pragmatic market socialism would be superior to capitalism" and "Pragmatic market socialism would be inferior to capitalism") are about equally consistent with the available empirical evidence. It has been argued herein that the weight of the existing evidence is somewhat in favor of pragmatic market socialism, but this is clearly a subjective judgment, and great care has been exercised to avoid overstating it. But if pragmatic market socialism were to be implemented in the real world, its performance thereafter would constitute far stronger evidence than anything we have available now. A much stronger judgment could be made on the relative performance issue.

It is true, of course, that even if pragmatic market socialism were to falter, its more enthusiastic proponents could attribute this to other factors (e.g., an oil price rise owing to another Mideast crisis) having nothing to do with its institutional nature. By the same token, even if pragmatic market socialism were to do very well, its more enthusiastic opponents could attribute this to other factors (e.g., resolution of another Mideast crisis) having nothing to do with it. But those with more moderate judgments will do their best to discount the various other factors which will occur around the time of implementation, and will then find the actual performance of pragmatic market socialism to be of great assistance in judging whether the system actually offers an inherent, institutional, systemic improvement over capitalism. Owing to their professional dedication to the ideal of scientific inquiry, economists are more likely than many other professionals to recognize in an experimental implementation of pragmatic market socialism the only fair, objective, impartial, and truly scientific means of evaluating its relative performance. Therefore economists are less likely to express reservations about pragmatic market socialism if the implementation campaign places strong and consistent emphasis upon the point that capitalism would be restored if pragmatic market socialism were to falter seriously.

While very few economists, particularly in the early going, are likely to go on record officially as supporting an experimental implementation of pragmatic market socialism, many of them might arrive at this judgment personally and thereafter endeavor to disseminate it by private, informal means. The important thing is not how many economists publicly support pragmatic market socialism but how many privately support it. The same is true of other groups. There are several distinct components of society to whom the message must be communicated. Economists are merely one small part of the intelligentsia. Distinct from the intelligentsia (i.e., educators, researchers, writers, journalists, and allied groups) are the practicing professionals in law, medicine, management, and so on. The general public is an even broader group encompassing all of the above, plus the very large proportion of individuals in blue collar employment and in low-to-middle-level white collar employment. A small but very significant group is the political leadership, including not only individuals currently serving in government offices but also those who are active and influential in political parties and interest groups.

Within each group of the population, from the smallest and most specific to the largest and most general, at any point in time there will be two critical numbers: (1) the percentage of the group which is aware of the pragmatic market socialist proposal; and (2) the percentage of the group which is in favor of the pragmatic market socialist proposal. For the proposal to be successful, it is necessary that these two percentages, within the general public as a whole and also within most subgroups, rise steadily toward a high level, well over 50 percent. The pattern of rise would follow the well-known logistic curve of disseminatory phenomena (rise at an increasing rate up to a point of inflection, followed by rise at a decreasing rate up to an asymptotic upper limit). If these figures are estimated over a certain interval of time, it will become possible to make an estimate of the upper asymptotic limit toward which the growth curve is headed. If this limit is well over 50 percent, then success is merely a matter of time. On the other hand, if this limit is *not* well over 50 percent, then failure must eventually be acknowledged.

B. WHAT ARE THE CHANCES?

What are the chances that in due course the percentage aware of pragmatic market socialism and the percentage in favor of it will rise to sufficiently high levels to permit its inauguration? Obviously it must be conceded that the chances appear at first sight to be minimal. The citizen bodies in the advanced capitalist nations are at the present moment firmly opposed to socialism in the public ownership sense. Most individuals in these nations condemn the notion of socialism in any form, and among that minority which professes support for socialism, most have in mind the social democratic concept of socialism—a concept which long ago abandoned the public ownership principle on interdependent grounds of expediency and irrelevancy. The negative judgment on socialism in the advanced capitalist nations is extremely strong and deeply rooted. Even among the intelligentsia, that group of the population which above all is supposed to be mentally open and receptive to new ideas and proposals (at least for purposes of study), there is extremely strong prejudice against socialism: The belief is dominant that the issue of socialism versus capitalism was settled a long time ago against socialism, and it would be merely a waste of time and energy to reopen the question now.

Allowing for the present dominant consensus against socialism, we must still ask the question "Has this dominant consensus against socialism been reached on the basis of a full understanding and consideration of the pragmatic market socialist proposal?" To ask the question is to answer it: The answer is clearly "No." It must be conceded even by an enthusiastic supporter of the capitalist status quo that the pragmatic market socialist alternative is almost completely unknown at the present time in the capitalist nations, among both the intelligentsia and the general public. Pragmatic market socialism is a truly novel approach to socialism, and is very distinct from many traditional concepts of socialism. It has been specifically designed to avoid the perceived problems and defects of these traditional concepts. At the same time it is fully consistent with the primary dictionary definition of socialism as public ownership of the capital means of production, a definition which dates back to the monumental codification of socialism by Karl Marx in the nineteenth century. Pragmatic market socialism represents a carefully worked out attempt to gain the equity benefits promised by the conceptual core of socialism while avoiding the economic and political liabilities of past socialist ventures. The proposal is based on a clear understanding and a respectful appreciation of the prevailing theories and attitudes of Western economics. It may well represent the most careful, complete, serious, and sensible advocacy of socialism to be produced in the twentieth century.

The skeptical question will certainly be asked: "If pragmatic market socialism is indeed as sensible and attractive as it is alleged to be, why has it not entered into public consciousness and debate long before the present time? After all, the basic institutional realities of contemporary capitalism to which pragmatic market socialism is opposed have been in effect for a very long time." This is a very good and effective question. But to begin to answer it, some reference must be made to the unpredictability of intellectual history. It is not always obvious why ideas which are later found to be important by humanity develop at one point in time and not at another. Why did not someone prior to Copernicus arrive at the conclusion that the earth revolves around the sun and not vice versa? Why did not someone prior to the American founding fathers develop a workable political system of constitutional, representative democracy? Should pragmatic market socialism come to pass in the real world, we may be sure that future analysts will discern all kinds of reasons why the time for pragmatic market socialism was ripe, and that its emergence was more or less inevitable. It is much easier to interpret the past than to prognosticate the future.

As to why there should exist such tremendous prejudice against socialism in the capitalist nations, given that forms of socialism are available, such as the pragmatic market socialist form, which would be superior to capitalism, there are at least two important contributory factors which are immediately evident. One is the excessive influence of the capitalist class in the formation of public opinion and social decision-making. The privately owned media of communication contribute to the distorted view of socialism which is prevalent in society, as does the disproportionate role of wealthy capitalists in the political process. This is not to allege that the media engage in a planned conspiracy to smear socialism, or that the political process is totally dominated by the campaign contributions and direct participation of wealthy capitalists. The reality is far less blatant than this: The public cannot be totally brainwashed by the media, nor can it be led about by the political leadership like a flock of mindless sheep. Nevertheless, it remains true that private ownership of the media and direct and indirect political activity by capitalists explain at least a part of the public's distaste for socialism.

The second important contributory factor to the public's distaste for socialism has been the international confrontation between communism and noncommunism, a confrontation which blossomed into a potentially deadly cold war after World War II. Socialism has been associated with a powerful and dangerous national enemy, an enemy bent upon forcing socialism on the capitalist nations of the world without regard for the preferences of their populations. This has engendered a potent emotional reaction against socialism, particularly in the United States and the other advanced capitalist nations. The typical United States citizen is fully prepared to fight to the death to prevent malevolent Communist leaders, in the Soviet Union and elsewhere, from "forcing socialism down our throats." The acute international confrontation situation, with its terrible overtones of potential nuclear annihilation, has greatly hampered any sort of rational, objective consideration of socialism itself. Socialism has become deeply implicated in an overall communist social system which the populations of the Western capitalist nations generally regard as utterly repugnant: as characterized by severe economic deprivation, total political repression, and an intolerable degree of subjugation of the individual to the state. As much as it is logically argued that socialism remains a small pearl of luminous value in an otherwise disastrous social system, the emotionally charged opposition to communism makes it very difficult for people in the West to perceive this pearl of value.

Of these two contributory factors to the public's distaste for socialism, apparently nothing can be done about the first: Until pragmatic market socialism is actually implemented, the excessive influence of the capitalist class in shaping public opinion and determining public policy will continue. But at this point in time, there are serious grounds for hope with respect to the second factor. Historic transitions are now occurring within the Communist nations which promise to considerably alleviate the international confrontation situation. It is very difficult to predict the exact amount of ideological convergence which will emerge from the present chaos and confusion in the Communist nations, but it seems inescapable that some appreciable measure of convergence will occur. Indeed, some convergence has already taken place, and there are signs of even more in the near future. The military and psychological threat represented by the Communist world seems to be ebbing, and with this there emerges the possibility of less emotional hostility toward socialism in the West.

No doubt to some it will seem highly paradoxical to propose that the amelioration of communist ideology, and an ideological approach of the Communist nations toward the non-Communist nations, will improve the prospects for socialism in the West. After all, the present transitions in the Communist world are widely heralded not only as the "death of communism" but also as the "death of socialism." But there is no true paradox once it is recognized that the economic principle of socialism is completely distinct from the political principle of one-party oligarchy, and the economic institutions and procedures of central planning. Historically, communism in the Soviet Union and elsewhere in the Communist world has been characterized by three conceptually quite distinct components: (1) socialism; (2) central planning; (3) the one-party state. As discussed in Chapter 9, a logical and mutually beneficial scenario of convergence would consist of a movement by the Communist East away from central planning and the one-party state, combined with a movement by the non-Communist West toward socialism. In this manner the Communist East and the non-Communist West could arrive, by free volition and mutual consent, at a pattern of democratic market socialism. A democratic political system combined with a market socialist economic system would combine the best elements of the ideologies of both sides. This would represent true ideological convergence rather than simple ideological capitulation in which one side admits total error in its previous viewpoints and attitudes. From the psychological point of view, true ideological convergence seems a more likely outcome than simple, unilateral ideological capitulation.

But even if the actual outcome is indeed full ideological capitulation by the Communist world, this could be a favorable outcome as far as the long-term prospects for pragmatic market socialism are concerned. Socialism would no longer be smeared through its association with a dreaded national enemy. The capitalization of the Communist world would also tangibly demonstrate the possibility of experimentation with socialism: It would show that it is possible to "return from socialism" if socialism proves to be unsatisfactory. Therefore, the issue of socialism could be examined in a calmer, clearer light, a light more conducive to rational judgment. This would substantially enhance the prospects for an actual implementation of pragmatic market socialism.

The twentieth century has witnessed huge and overwhelming catastrophes for the human race. The death and destruction of World Wars I and II, the barbarity of Hitler's Nazi regime and the repressiveness of Stalin-era Soviet communism, the post-World War II threat of absolute nuclear destruction—all of these have contributed to an onslaught of pessimism, cynicism, and spiritual ennui. But at the same time, as we near the end of the twentieth century, there are many positive signs. The human race has indeed avoided nuclear destruction. Although there are many short-term setbacks (recessions, inflation, natural disasters, etc.) and many severe long-term problems (excessive population growth, environmental degradation, fossil fuel exhaustion, etc.), in general impressive economic progress is being made at the present time. Throughout the world average living standards seem to be slowly but steadily on the rise. If relaxation of the international crisis enables redirection of a large proportion of the economic resources currently devoted to military production, future progress may be further accelerated. The wonders of science and technology continue rapidly apace, and there is scarcely any human being so remote and isolated as not to be positively affected by these advances.

In short, humanity may be on the verge of a spiritual rebirth. The idea of progress and the attitude of optimism may reemerge among mankind, and the twenty-first century may witness an epochal consolidation of the status of the human race, a consolidation through which its long-term prospects will be tremendously enhanced. Pragmatic market socialism is merely one small part of this incipient regeneration. But its symbolic importance may be far beyond its immediate material contribution.

Without doubt the easiest course at the present moment in history would be to dismiss pragmatic market socialism as merely a delusion—a utopian fantasy. Such a conclusion would be tantamount to a self-fulfilling prophecy. Obviously, if almost everyone believes that pragmatic market socialism is impossible, then it will become impossible in fact. Such an outcome would constitute an abrogation and betrayal of the finer qualities of our humanity. If the reader believes that pragmatic market socialism would probably benefit humanity, there exists a strong moral imperative to action.

ANALYTICAL APPENDIX

A. A MODEL OF CAPITAL MANAGEMENT EFFORT

The general function version of a model of capital management effort supplied by the representative capital manager consists of four parameters and five variables, as follows:

Parameters	Variables
(1) f exogenous income	(1) e capital management effort
(2) k capital responsibility	(2) h leisure
(3) α retention coefficient	(3) r return on capital
(4) β effectiveness coefficient	(4) y income
	(5) u utility

The variables e and h are interpreted as proportions of total time available $(0 < e, h < 1)$. The five variables of the model are determined by the following five equations:

Equations	Description/Properties	
$h = 1 - e$	definition of leisure	(A.1)
$r = r(e)$	capital return production function	(A.2)
	$r'(e) = dr/de > 0, \; r''(e) = d^2r/de^2 < 0$	
$y = \alpha(f + \beta r(e)k)$	definition of income	(A.3)
$u = u(y,h)$	utility function	(A.4)

$$u_y = \frac{\partial u}{\partial y} > 0, \quad u_{yy} = \frac{\partial^2 u}{\partial y^2} < 0$$

$$u_h = \frac{\partial u}{\partial h} > 0, \quad u_{hh} = \frac{\partial^2 u}{\partial h^2} < 0$$

$$u_{yh} = \frac{\partial^2 u}{\partial y \partial h} > 0$$

$du/de = 0$	first-order utility max condition	(A.5)

The first-order utility maximization condition (A.5) may be developed in a number of ways, of which the following are useful:

$$\frac{du}{de} = u_y \frac{dy}{de} + u_h \frac{dh}{de} = u_y y'(e) - u_h = u_y \alpha \beta r'(e) k - u_h = 0 \qquad (A.5a)$$

$$\frac{u_y}{u_h} = \frac{1}{y'(e)} = \frac{1}{\alpha \beta r'(e) k} \qquad (A.5b)$$

Equation (A.5b) equates the Marginal Rate of Substitution between leisure and income (u_y/u_h) to the Marginal Rate of Transformation between leisure and income ($1/y'(e)$). This is known as the "tangency condition" because of its graphical interpretation (see Figure 4.1).

Comparative statics analysis is based on implicit differentiation of the first-order utility maximization condition. Letting x stand for any one of the set of four parameters (f, k, α, β), de/dx is derived by differentiating (A.5) with respect to e and x and solving for de/dx:

$$\frac{\partial^2 u}{\partial e^2} de + \frac{\partial^2 u}{\partial e \partial x} dx = 0 \qquad (A.6)$$

$$\frac{de}{dx} = -\frac{\dfrac{\partial^2 u}{\partial e \partial x}}{\dfrac{\partial^2 u}{\partial e^2}} \qquad (A.6a)$$

Owing to the negative sign in front of the RHS expression in (A.6a) and the fact that $\partial^2 u/\partial e^2 < 0$ by the second-order maximization condition, the sign of de/dx is the same as the sign of $\partial^2 u/\partial e \partial x$. The signs of the four comparative statics derivatives are evaluated using the following schema:

x	$\dfrac{\partial^2 u}{\partial e \partial x}$	Sign
f	$\alpha(u_{yy}\alpha\beta r'(e)k - u_{hy})$	−
k	$\alpha\beta r(e)(u_{yy}\alpha\beta r'(e)k - u_{hy}) + u_y\alpha\beta r'(e)$	?
α	$(f + \beta r(e)k)(u_{yy}\alpha\beta r'(e)k - u_{hy}) + u_y\beta r'(e)k$	?
β	$\alpha r(e)k(u_{yy}\alpha\beta r'(e)k - u_{hy}) + u_y\alpha\beta r'(e)$	?
	$\qquad\quad(-)\qquad\qquad\qquad(+)$	

The expression governing the sign of de/df consists of only one term and this term is negative because $u_{yy} < 0$ and $u_{hy} > 0$. The negative sign of u_{yy} is from the diminishing marginal utility of income principle, which is regarded as virtually axiomatic in modern economics. Some economic theoreticians prefer to avoid an assumption regarding the sign of u_{hy}, but to do so precludes even the most fundamental and intuitively appealing results. If a sign *is* assumed for u_{hy}, it is invariably positive.

A rise in exogenous income f therefore unambiguously reduces capital management effort in the model. Thus the sign of de/dx for $x = f$ is minus. Notice now that the term governing the sign of de/df reappears in the first term of the other three expressions in the above schema. Thus the first term in these expressions represents the income effect of the respective parameter. This term is always negative. The second term is the substitution effect, and it is always positive. Since there is a conflict in sign as between the two terms in each expression, the overall sign of each expression is indeterminate—thus the question mark in the sign column. Figure 4.2 illustrates the indeterminacy for the parameter α.

An explicit function version of the model is obtained by using a power (or constant elasticity) form for the capital return function and a Constant Elasticity of Substitution (CES) form for the utility function:

$$r = r(e) = \overline{r}e^{\gamma} \tag{A.7}$$

$$u = u(y,h) = [\theta y^{-\psi} + (1-\theta)h^{-\psi}]^{-1/\psi} \tag{A.8}$$

The new parameters added to the model by these explicit forms are:

$\overline{r}$ maximum rate of return on capital
γ elasticity of capital management effort
θ relative preference: income vs. leisure
σ elasticity of substitution between income and leisure ($\sigma = 1/(1+\psi)$)

The maximum rate of return on capital $\overline{r}$ would be achieved when capital management effort equals its upper limit of 1. Using the axiomatic assumption in contemporary economics of diminishing returns to a factor of production, the elasticity of capital management effort γ is a positive number less than 1. The income relative preference parameter θ is also positive and less than 1: This numerical specification incorporates diminishing marginal utility of income and leisure. The elasticity of substitution between income and leisure σ is embodied in ψ through the relations $\sigma = 1/(1+\psi)$ and $\psi = (1/\sigma)-1$; σ may take on any value between 0 (no substitutability between income and leisure) through infinity (complete substitutability between income and leisure). This parameter measures the degree to which income and leisure are substitutable for one another in the individual's utility function.

If (A.7) and (A.8) are substituted into the first-order utility maximization condition (A.5), the following basic result is obtained:

$$\Phi = \Omega e^{\sigma(\gamma-1)} - \Omega e^{\sigma(\gamma-1)+1} - \Gamma e^{\gamma} - \alpha f = 0 \tag{A.9}$$

where $\Omega = (\theta'\gamma\alpha\beta\bar{r}k)^{\sigma}$, $\Gamma = \alpha\beta\bar{r}k$, and $\theta' = \theta/(1-\theta)$. The capital management effort supply function is implicit in this relationship, but this form is not explicitly solvable for e in the general case. However, certain insights concerning the capital management effort supply function may be obtained by analytical means, as described in the following. In addition, if the parameters of the model are numerically specified, equation (A.9) may be solved for e numerically. A computer program was written to ascertain the effects of numerical variation in the parameters (f, k, α, β, $\bar{r}$, γ, θ, σ) on the effort level e, and also on the other variables of the model (h, r, y, u). The analytical insights reported below were verified by a considerable amount of numerical experimentation using this computer program. The program also produced the illustrative numerical results reported at the end of this section.

One analytical approach is to simplify equation (A.9) by means of specific numerical assumptions regarding key parameters. For example, if the assumption of diminishing returns to effort e in the capital return production function is replaced by constant returns to effort (i.e., $\gamma = 1$), then (A.9) may be solved explicitly for the e-supply function:

$$e = \frac{\Omega - \alpha f}{\Omega + \Gamma} = \frac{(\theta'\alpha\beta\bar{r}k)^{\sigma} - \alpha f}{(\theta'\alpha\beta\bar{r}k)^{\sigma} - \alpha\beta\bar{r}k} \tag{A.10}$$

This effort supply function is equivalent to a standard labor supply function in a CES utility function model, where the exact equivalent of the constant wage rate w in the standard labor supply model is the factor $\alpha\beta\bar{r}k$. In this case comparative statics derivatives may be obtained by direct differentiation of (A.10). It may be ascertained, for example, that the numerical value of σ governs the sign of $de/d\alpha$. If $\sigma < 1$, then $de/d\alpha < 0$; if $\sigma = 1$, then $de/d\alpha = 0$; and if $\sigma > 1$, then $de/d\alpha > 0$.

Another interesting special case is when the elasticity of substitution $\sigma = 1$, and the general CES utility function reduces to the specific Cobb-Douglas utility function. In this case (A.9) remains impervious to explicit solution unless in addition exogenous income $f = 0$. If both $\sigma = 1$ and $f = 0$, another explicit solution may be obtained which is closely analogous to the explicit solution obtained when $\gamma = 1$ and $f = 0$ (compare (A.11) and (A.10)):

$$e = \frac{\Omega}{\Omega + \Gamma} = \frac{\theta'\gamma}{1 + \theta'\gamma} \qquad (A.11)$$

One of the most significant features of this e-supply function is that e is completely unaffected by four model parameters: α, β, $\bar{r}$, and k. That is, $de/d\alpha = de/d\beta = de/d\bar{r} = de/dk = 0$.

Returning to the general case in which γ is a positive number less than 1, comparative statics derivatives may be evaluated, as in the general function case, by means of implicit differentiation. Three such derivatives will be considered: $de/d\alpha$, de/dk, and $de/d\gamma$.

Dividing (A.9) by α and rearranging, the first-order maximization condition may be written:

$$\Phi' = \alpha^{\sigma-1}\Omega'\left[e^{\sigma(\gamma-1)} - e^{\sigma(\gamma-1)+1}\right] - (\Gamma'e^{\gamma} + f) = 0 \qquad (A.12)$$

where $\Omega' = (\theta'\gamma\beta\bar{r}k)^{\sigma}$ and $\Gamma' = \beta\bar{r}k$. By the implicit differentiation rule:

$$\frac{de}{d\alpha} = -\frac{\dfrac{\partial\Phi'}{\partial\alpha}}{\dfrac{\partial\Phi'}{\partial e}} \qquad (A.13)$$

Since $\partial\Phi'/\partial e < 0$ by the second-order condition for a maximum, the sign of $de/d\alpha$ is the same as the sign of $\partial\Phi'/\partial\alpha$. By differentiation of (A.12) with respect to α:

$$\frac{\partial\Phi'}{\partial\alpha} = (\sigma-1)\alpha^{\sigma-2}\Omega'\left[e^{\sigma(\gamma-1)} - e^{\sigma(\gamma-1)+1}\right] \qquad (A.14)$$

Dividing the bracketed expression in (A.14) by $e^{\sigma(\gamma-1)}$ yields $1 - e = h$, which is positive. Therefore the sign of $de/d\alpha$ is governed by the value of σ, the elasticity of substitution. If $\sigma < 1$, then $de/d\alpha < 0$; if $\sigma = 1$, then $de/d\alpha = 0$; and if $\sigma > 1$, then $de/d\alpha > 0$. This generalizes the result mentioned above for the special case of $\gamma = 1$. These possibilities are illustrated in Figure 4.2.

By an exactly analogous demonstration, it may be shown that the sign of de/dk is the same as the sign of the following:

$$\frac{\partial\Phi''}{\partial k} = (\sigma-1)k^{\sigma-2}\Omega''\left[e^{\sigma(\gamma-1)} - e^{\sigma(\gamma-1)+1}\right] + \frac{\alpha f}{k^2} \qquad (A.15)$$

where $\Omega'' = (\theta'\gamma\alpha\beta\bar{r})^{\sigma}$. If exogenous income $f = 0$, then the value of σ determines the sign of de/dk just as it determines the sign of $de/d\alpha$. In the case where $f > 0$, the right-hand term in (A.15) is greater than 0, so if $\sigma = 1$ or $\sigma > 1$, then $de/dk > 0$. But if $\sigma < 1$, there emerges the "backward-bending" supply curve of capital management effort with respect to k. If $\sigma < 1$, the left-hand term is negative. If k is small, the positive right-hand term $\alpha f/k^2$ is large, so that the positive right-hand term dominates and $de/dk > 0$. But as k increases, the positive right-hand term $\alpha f/k^2$ decreases until finally the negative left-hand term dominates and de/dk becomes < 0. The case of a backward-bending e-supply curve is illustrated in Figure 4.3.

Finally, consider $de/d\gamma$. The intuition of Figure 4.4 suggests that $de/d\gamma > 0$, so that as γ becomes small and approaches 0, the level of capital management effort e also becomes small and approaches 0. This intuition is confirmed in the special case of a Cobb-Douglas utility function ($\sigma = 1$) and no exogenous income ($f = 0$). From result (A.11), the limit of e as γ approaches 0 is also 0. To evaluate $de/d\gamma$ in the general case, take the partial derivative of (A.9) with respect to γ and obtain the following:

$$\frac{\partial \Phi}{\partial \gamma} = \sigma \gamma^\sigma \Omega_o \left((1/\gamma) + ln(e) \right) \left[e^{\sigma(\gamma-1)} - e^{\sigma(\gamma-1)+1} \right] - \gamma \Gamma e^{\gamma-1} ln(e) \qquad (A.16)$$

Taking into account the negative sign in front of the second term in (A.16), this second term represents a positive effect since $ln(e)$ is negative (e is less than 1, and the log of a number less than 1 is less than 0). As noted above, the bracketed expression in the first term is positive. Therefore a sufficient condition for $d\Phi/d\gamma$ (and hence $de/d\gamma$) to be positive is that the parenthesized term $(1/\gamma) + ln(e)$ is positive. That this term is in fact positive for sufficiently small γ may be established heuristically as follows:

As γ approaches 0, $1/\gamma$ becomes a large positive number. Possibly this large positive number could be offset and the parenthesized term could be negative if $ln(e)$ were a negative number large in absolute value. If, as γ becomes very small, e also becomes very small, then $ln(e)$ could in fact become a negative number large in absolute value. But if this is indeed happening, then $de/d\gamma > 0$ for this range of small γ values, which is precisely what is to be proved.

Of course the above argument is not mathematically rigorous. However, a large amount of numerical experimentation with the computer program mentioned earlier turned up no combination of parameter values for which e did not become very small as γ became very small. It may therefore be hypothesized with a reasonable degree of certitude that within the context of this model, $de/d\gamma$ is unambiguously positive for low γ.

Numerical solutions of the model obtained using the computer program also help to crystallize the capital management issue in a more tangible manner than is possible on the basis of general analytical results. The "pro-capitalist view" is that γ is fairly large, while the "pro-socialist view" is that γ is fairly small: These views may be respectively implemented in a γ value of 0.50 and a γ value of 0.01. Under capitalism the retention coefficient is high ($\alpha = 1.00$) while under pragmatic market socialism the retention coefficient would be low ($\alpha = 0.05$). In the following table the five variables e, h, r, y, and u are already defined, while UB, DU and PS have not yet been defined. UB stands for "bliss utility," defined as the utility the capital manager would achieve if he had the same income but did not have to exert any capital management effort; this is computed by evaluating the utility function with the actual y but setting $e = 0$. DU stands for "disutility" of capital management effort, obtained by deducting actual utility from bliss utility: This measures the reduction in utility from having to provide capital management effort to earn income. Finally, PS stands for "producer's surplus," defined as actual utility less disutility, as a proportion of actual utility. This is the proportion of actual utility which is not offset by the disutility of capital management effort, that is, the "surplus" of actual utility over "earned" utility, expressed in proportional terms.

Now consider the following table of four numerical solutions of the model for the various combinations of the capital return elasticity γ and the retention coefficient α mentioned above (using for the other parameters: $\theta = 0.25$; $\sigma = 1.2$; $f = 0$; $\bar{r} = 1$; $k = 1$; $\beta = 1$):

	pro-capitalist view $\gamma = 0.50$		pro-socialist view $\gamma = 0.01$	
var	capitalism $\alpha = 1.00$	socialism $\alpha = 0.05$	capitalism $\alpha = 1.00$	socialism $\alpha = 0.05$
e	0.12515	0.07626	0.00329	0.00200
h	0.87485	0.92374	0.99671	0.99800
r	0.35376	0.27614	0.94444	0.93974
y	0.35376	0.01381	0.94444	0.04699
u	0.70640	0.41196	0.98342	0.53118
UB	0.78396	0.44100	0.98586	0.53207
DU	0.07756	0.02904	0.00244	0.00089
PS	0.89021	0.92950	0.99752	0.99833

All the above solutions are based on $\sigma = 1.2$; since $\sigma > 1$, this means that $de/d\alpha$ is positive. Thus the potential reduction in α between capitalism and pragmatic market socialism would reduce capital management effort. Despite this particular numerical specification which incorporates an important proposition from capitalist apologetics (the upward-sloping supply curve of capital management effort), the table demonstrates that if the capital return elasticity is low, the potential reduction in α does not have a significant impact on economic efficiency. If γ is very low, then e is very low, whatever the value of α. However, even with low e, the rate of return on capital is close to its asymptotic upper limit (in this case, the numerical upper limit is $\bar{r} = 1$). Under capitalism, with the retention coefficient $\alpha = 1.00$, the rate of return on capital r is 0.94444; while under pragmatic market socialism, with $\alpha = 0.05$, r is 0.93974.

In the low γ case, since e is low, disutility is also very low and most utility is producer's surplus. This suggests that under capitalism the capital owner does little to earn his or her income; and also that under pragmatic market socialism the BPO agent would do little to earn his or her income. The difference between capitalism and pragmatic market socialism is that under the former, the capital owner receives high income and high utility (respectively 0.94444 and 0.98342), while under the latter the BPO agent receives very much lower income and somewhat lower utility (respectively 0.04699 and 0.53118). The reason why there is a smaller impact on utility than on income is the principle of diminishing marginal utility of income, incorporated into the model by specifying $\theta < 1$.

Contemporary capitalism perpetuates a highly unequal distribution of producers' surplus (that is, utility received but not "paid for" in terms of disutility of effort), which is itself based on a highly unequal distribution of capital wealth. The model solutions shown above suggest that the capitalist system pays wealthy capital owners a great deal for doing very little, while the pragmatic market socialist system would pay BPO agents a much more modest amount for doing very little. Pragmatic market socialism would not totally eliminate inequity, but it would reduce the amount of inequity.

B. A MODEL OF PRIVATE HOUSEHOLD SAVING

The general function version of a two-period model of private household saving consists of four parameters and four variables, as follows:

Parameters		Variables	
(1) y_1	period 1 income	(1) c_1	period 1 consumption
(2) y_2	period 2 income	(2) c_2	period 2 consumption
(3) a_o	initial assets	(3) s	saving
(4) r	interest rate	(4) u	utility

The four variables of the model are determined by the following four equations:

Equations	Description/Properties	
$c_1 = y_1 + ra_o - s$	period 1 budget constraint	(B.1)
$c_2 = y_2 + (1+r)(a_o + s)$	period 2 budget constraint	(B.2)
$u = u(c_1, c_2)$	utility function	(B.3)

$$u_1 = \frac{\partial u}{\partial c_1} > 0, \ \ u_{11} = \frac{\partial^2 u}{\partial c_1^2} < 0$$

$$u_2 = \frac{\partial u}{\partial c_2} > 0, \ \ u_{22} = \frac{\partial^2 u}{\partial c_2^2} < 0$$

$$u_{12} = \frac{\partial^2 u}{\partial c_1 \partial c_2} > 0$$

$du/ds = 0$	first-order utility max condition	(B.4)

The first-order utility maximization condition (B.4) may be developed as follows:

$$\frac{du}{ds} = u_1 \frac{dc_1}{ds} + u_2 \frac{dc_2}{ds} = -u_1 + u_2(1+r) = 0 \tag{B.4a}$$

$$\frac{u_1}{u_2} = 1+r \tag{B.4b}$$

Comparative statics analysis is based on implicit differentiation of the first-order utility maximization condition. Letting x stand for any one of the set of four parameters (y_1, y_2, a_o, r), ds/dx is derived by differentiating (B.4) with respect to e and x and solving for de/dx:

$$\frac{\partial^2 u}{\partial s^2} ds + \frac{\partial^2 u}{\partial s \partial x} dx = 0 \tag{B.5}$$

$$\frac{ds}{dx} = -\frac{\dfrac{\partial^2 u}{\partial s \partial x}}{\dfrac{\partial^2 u}{\partial s^2}} \tag{B.5a}$$

Owing to the negative sign in front of the RHS expression in (B.5a) and the fact that $\partial^2 u/\partial s^2 < 0$ by the second-order maximization condition, the sign of ds/dx is the same as the sign of $\partial^2 u/\partial s \partial x$. The signs of the four comparative statics derivatives may then be evaluated using the following schema:

x	$\dfrac{\partial^2 u}{\partial s \partial x}$	Sign
y_1	$-u_{11} + u_{21}(1+r)$	+
	$\quad(-)\quad\quad(+)$	
y_2	$-u_{12} + u_{22}(1+r)$	–
	$\quad(+)\quad\quad(-)$	
a_0	$[-u_{11} + u_{21}(1+r)]r + [-u_{12} + u_{22}(1+r)](1+r)$	?
	$\quad\quad(+)\quad\quad\quad\quad\quad\quad(-)$	
r	$[-u_{11} + u_{21}(1+r)]a_0 + [-u_{12} + u_{22}(1+r)]a_0 + u_2$	?
	$\quad\quad(+)\quad\quad\quad\quad\quad\quad(-)$	

Given the standard assumptions concerning the utility function ($u_{11} < 0$, $u_{22} < 0$, $u_{12} > 0$), the comparative statics effects of y_1 and y_2 are unambiguous: an increase in period 1 income y_1 increases saving s, and an increase in period 2 income y_2 decreases saving s. However, the comparative statics effects of a_0 and r are more complicated and their net effects are ambiguous. Note that the $\partial^2 u/\partial s \partial x$ expression for both $x = a_0$ and $x = r$ contains in brackets the expressions for y_1 and y_2. The signs below these brackets refer to the sign of the entire bracketed expression. As the terms in the brackets are of opposed sign, no conclusion can be reached concerning the sign of the overall expression.

An explicit function version of the model is obtained by using a Constant Elasticity of Substitution (CES) form for the utility function:

$$u = u(c_1, c_2) = \left[v c_1^{-\rho} + (1-v) c_2^{-\rho} \right]^{-1/\rho} \tag{B.6}$$

The new parameters added to the model by this explicit form are:

v relative preference: period 1 vs. period 2 consumption
σ elasticity of substitution between period 1 and period 2 consumption
   ($\sigma = 1/(1+\rho)$)

The period 1 versus period 2 consumption relative preference parameter v is positive and less than 1; this numerical specification incorporates diminishing marginal utility of consumption in both periods. If $v > 1-v$, period 1 consumption has a stronger effect on utility than period 2 consumption; this assumption would therefore incorporate the concept of positive time preference. The elasticity of substitution between period 1 consumption and period 2 consumption σ is embodied in ρ through the relations $\sigma = 1/(1+\rho)$ and $\rho = (1/\sigma)-1$; σ may take on any value between 0 (no substitutability between period 1 and period 2 consumption) through infinity (complete substitutability between period 1 and period 2 consumption). This parameter measures the degree to which period 1 and period 2 consumption are substitutable for one another in the individual's utility function.

If (B.6) is substituted into the first-order utility maximization condition (B.4), we may solve explicitly for the utility-maximizing level of saving s:

$$s = \frac{(1+r)^{\sigma}(v')^{-\sigma}(y_1+ra_o) - (y_2+(1+r)a_o)}{(1+r)^{\sigma}(v')^{-\sigma} + (1+r)} \tag{B.7}$$

where $v' = v/(1-v)$. This explicit supply function of saving verifies the comparative statics results obtained from the general function analysis. The parameter y_1 appears only once in the numerator with a positive sign: therefore $ds/dy_1 > 0$. The parameter y_2 appears only once in the numerator with a negative sign: therefore $ds/dy_2 < 0$. The parameter a_o appears twice in the numerator, once with a positive sign and once with a negative sign: thus the sign of ds/da_o is ambiguous. The same is true of r, which appears not only twice in the numerator with opposed signs but also in the denominator. Note that the saving level generated by this function could be either positive or negative. It is safe to say about the function that saving s is a complicated function of the parameters.

Under pragmatic market socialism the interest rate on financial asset accumulations would be zero ($r = 0$), and therefore in this model the private household's saving would be the following:

$$s = \frac{(v')^{-\sigma}y_1 - (y_2+a_o)}{(v')^{-\sigma} + 1} \tag{B.8}$$

This function demonstrates the probable fallacy of the simplistic proposition from capitalist apologetics: "There would be no saving if there were no interest." As a matter of fact, no general conclusion may be reached concerning whether socialist saving as determined by (B.8) would be greater than or less than capitalist saving as determined by (B.7). This result suggests that the saving question, no less than the capital management question, is basically an empirical issue rather than a theoretical issue.

Using the quotient rule of differentiation on (B.7), we may obtain an explicit equation for the comparative statics effect (ds/dr) of interest rate r on saving level s. The denominator of this expression is squared according to the quotient rule, so that the sign of ds/dr is the sign of the numerator expression. After algebraic manipulation of the initial results from differentiation, the numerator expression is shown to be equal to the following:

$$(\sigma-1)\left[(1+r)^{\sigma}(v')^{-\sigma}(y_1 + (1+r)a_o\right]$$

$$+ a_o\left[(1+r)^{2\sigma}(v')^{-2\sigma} + (1+r)^{\sigma+1}(v')^{-\sigma}\right]$$

$$+ y_2\left[(1+r)^{\sigma-1}(v')^{-\sigma}\sigma + 1\right]$$

There are three terms in this expression, each one of which contains a positive bracketed expression. The first bracketed expression is multiplied by $(\sigma - 1)$, which is positive, zero, or negative depending on the value of σ, the elasticity of substitution. The second and third bracketed expressions are multiplied respectively by a_o and y_2, which are both positive. Conclusions which may be based on the above expression as a whole are as follows: (1) the sign of ds/dr is ambiguous; (2) a necessary condition for $ds/dr < 0$ is that $\sigma < 1$, and given $\sigma < 1$, the lower is σ the more likely it is that $ds/dr < 0$; (3) the higher are a_o and y_2, the more likely it is that $ds/dr > 0$; (4) as the time preference parameter v' appears in all the bracketed expressions, its impact on ds/dr is ambiguous—thus, for example, if there is positive time preference $(v' > 1)$, this does not guarantee that $ds/dr > 0$.

C. A MODEL OF AGGREGATE INVESTMENT

The data utilized to estimate the following model are taken from *Business Conditions Digest*, a monthly publication of the Bureau of Economic Analysis of the U.S. Department of Commerce. Quarterly data from 1950.1 to 1988.4 are used on the following series (as reported in early 1989):

PROFA	286. Corporate Profits Before Tax, Adjusted
NI	288. Net Interest
NATINC	220. National Income in Current Dollars
INVNPE	100. Expenditures in 1982 Dollars for New Plant and Equipment
GNP	50. Gross National Product in 1982 Dollars

From the raw figures are computed the rate of property return p_t and the rate of investment i_t (in percentage terms), defined as follows:

$$p_t = ((PROFA + NI)/NATINC) \times 100$$

$$i_t = (INVNPE/GNP) \times 100$$

where the subscript t stands for the time period ($t = 1$ for 1950.1, ..., $t = 156$ for 1988.4). Now define a four-period moving average on p_t, lagged five periods, and a four-period moving average on i_t, lagged one period, respectively as follows:

$$\bar{p}_{t-5} = (1/4)\left(p_{t-5} + p_{t-6} + p_{t-7} + p_{t-8}\right)$$

$$\bar{\imath}_{t-1} = (1/4)\left(i_{t-1} + i_{t-2} + i_{t-3} + i_{t-4}\right)$$

An ordinary least squares regression of i_t on t and $\bar{p}_{t-5}$ produces the following estimated equation (t-statistics in parentheses):

$$\hat{\imath}_t = 3.6699 + 0.01277\, t + 0.27108\, \bar{p}_{t-5} \qquad\qquad R^2 = .729$$
$$\quad\ (5.926)\quad (8.288)\qquad (6.132)$$

The regression coefficients are highly significant by the customary t-test, and the R^2 is reasonably high, given that the variables are in ratio terms. The positive coefficient on t indicates an upward trend in i_t. The positive coefficient on $\bar{p}_{t-5}$ indicates that, controlling for the time trend, the lagged moving average rate of property return has a positive association with the current rate of investment.

An ordinary least squares regression of p_t on t and $\bar{\imath}_{t-1}$ produces the following estimated equation (t-statistics in parentheses):

$$\hat{p}_t = 16.4987 + 0.03624\, t - 0.38303\, \bar{\imath}_{t-1} \qquad\qquad R^2 = .610$$
$$\quad\ (15.211)\quad (10.753)\quad (-2.661)$$

Once again the regression coefficients are highly significant by the customary t-test, and the R^2 is reasonably high. The positive coefficient on t indicates an upward trend in p_t. The negative coefficient on $\bar{\imath}_{t-1}$ indicates that, controlling for the time trend, the lagged moving average rate of investment has a negative association with the current rate of property return.

These statistical results are respectively consistent with the following hypotheses: (1) a higher rate of property return tends to encourage a higher rate of investment, with a relatively long lag; (2) a higher rate of investment tends to have an adverse (negative) effect on the rate of property return, with a relatively short lag. Thus there is a recursive interrelationship between rate of property return and rate of investment.

This recursive interrelationship is shared by all three variants of a simple macroeconomic simulation model. The three variants are designated the "pre-Keynesian capitalist" (Model I), the "post-Keynesian capitalist" (Model II), and the "pragmatic market socialist" (Model III). The pre-Keynesian capitalist model allows for underutilization of the stock of factors of production. In this model, the coefficient of capacity utilization (c) varies positively with the amount by which the investment rate deviates from its time trend (in terms of a four-period, unlagged moving average), and the coefficient is usually something less than 1. In turn, the coefficient of capacity utilization determines how much actual output will be produced. The post-Keynesian and pragmatic market socialist models are alike in specifying that underutilization of capacity is not a problem: both specify that $c = 1$ regardless of the investment rate. Where the post-Keynesian and pragmatic market socialist models diverge is in the relationship between lagged rate of property return and current investment rate. The pragmatic market socialist model assumes that any given lagged rate of property return will produce a higher investment rate.

The three variants of the model are simulated over an interval from 1952.1 to 1988.4. This simulation interval matches the estimation interval for the two regression equations (some observations are lost from the front of the sample because of the use of lagged variables). An aggregate Cobb-Douglas production function is used to specify potential output. Labor is specified to grow at a constant rate, while capital increases by the amount of investment less a deduction for depreciation. Disturbance terms are utilized in the two estimated equations: These are normally distributed random variables with means of 0 and standard deviations equal to the standard errors of the estimated regression equations (respectively 0.5448 and 1.0123). Hypothetical values are used for the parameters of the nonestimated equations. For purposes of the simulations, the p and i variables are converted into proportional terms (from percentage terms). Notation for the additional variables is as follows: K = capital stock, L = labor stock, Y^p = potential output, Y = actual output, ε_{ti} = disturbance term in equation i, and i^d = deviation from time trend investment rate (only used in Model I). Initial values of K and L are set equal to 1: thus initial Y is 1.

The model equations are as follows:

pre-Keynesian capitalist model (Model I):

$$\bar{p}_{t-5} = (1/4)\,(p_{t-5} + p_{t-6} + p_{t-7} + p_{t-8}) \tag{C.I.1}$$

$$\bar{i}_{t-1} = (1/4)\,(i_{t-1} + i_{t-2} + i_{t-3} + i_{t-4}) \tag{C.I.2}$$

$$p_t = 16.4987 + 0.03624\,t - 0.38303\,\bar{i}_{t-1} + \varepsilon_{t1} \tag{C.I.3}$$

$$i_t = 3.6699 + 0.01277\,t + 0.27108\,\bar{p}_{t-5} + \varepsilon_{t2} \tag{C.I.4}$$

$$K_t = 0.95\,K_{t-1} + 0.01\,i_{t-1}Y_{t-1} \tag{C.I.5}$$

$$L_t = 1.01 L_{t-1} \tag{C.I.6}$$

$$Y_t^p = K_t^{.25} L_t^{.75} \tag{C.I.7}$$

$$i_t^d = i_t - (3.6699 + 0.1277\ t) \tag{C.I.8}$$

$$\bar{i}_t^d = (\tfrac{1}{4})(i_t^d + i_{t-1}^d + i_{t-3}^d + i_{t-3}^d) \tag{C.I.9}$$

$$c_t = 0.60 + ((\tfrac{1}{100})\ \bar{i}_t^d - 0.03)^{.25} \tag{C.I.10}$$

$$Y_t = c_t Y_t^p \tag{C.I.11}$$

post-Keynesian capitalist model (Model II):

$$\bar{p}_{t-5} = (\tfrac{1}{4})\ (p_{t-5} + p_{t-6} + p_{t-7} + p_{t-8}) \tag{C.II.1}$$

$$\bar{i}_{t-1} = (\tfrac{1}{4})\ (i_{t-1} + i_{t-2} + i_{t-3} + i_{t-4}) \tag{C.II.2}$$

$$p_t = 16.4987 + 0.03624\ t - 0.38303\ \bar{i}_{t-1} + \varepsilon_{t1} \tag{C.II.3}$$

$$i_t = 3.6699 + 0.01277\ t + 0.27108\ \bar{p}_{t-5} + \varepsilon_{t2} \tag{C.II.4}$$

$$K_t = 0.95\ K_{t-1} + 0.01\ i_{t-1} Y_{t-1} \tag{C.II.5}$$

$$L_t = 1.01 L_{t-1} \tag{C.II.6}$$

$$Y_t^p = K_t^{.25} L_t^{.75} \tag{C.II.7}$$

$$c_t = 1.0 \tag{C.II.8}$$

$$Y_t = c_t Y_t^p \tag{C.II.9}$$

pragmatic market socialist model (Model III):

$$\bar{p}_{t-5} = (\tfrac{1}{4})\ (p_{t-5} + p_{t-6} + p_{t-7} + p_{t-8}) \tag{C.III.1}$$

$$\bar{i}_{t-1} = (\tfrac{1}{4})\ (i_{t-1} + i_{t-2} + i_{t-3} + i_{t-4}) \tag{C.III.2}$$

$$p_t = 16.4987 + 0.03624\ t - 0.38303\ \bar{i}_{t-1} + \varepsilon_{t1} \tag{C.III.3}$$

$$i_t = 6.6699 + 0.01277\ t + 0.27108\ \bar{p}_{t-5} + \varepsilon_{t2} \tag{C.III.4}$$

$$K_t = 0.95\ K_{t-1} + 0.01\ i_{t-1} Y_{t-1} \tag{C.III.5}$$

$$L_t = 1.01 L_{t-1} \tag{C.III.6}$$

$$Y_t^p = K_t^{.25} L_t^{.75}$$ (C.III.7)

$$c_t = 1.0$$ (C.III.8)

$$Y_t = c_t Y_t^p$$ (C.III.9)

The salient differences among the three models pertain to the determination of the coefficient of capacity utilization c and the investment rate i. Model I determines c in equations (C.I.8) through (C.I.10), and c is almost always less than 1. Models II and III both set $c = 1$ in equations (C.II.8) and (C.III.8). Models I and II both have the same determination of i:

$$i_t = 3.6699 + 0.01277\, t + 0.27108\, \bar{p}_{t-5} + \varepsilon_{t2} \qquad \text{(C.I.4)} = \text{(C.II.4)}$$

Model III uses a higher value for the intercept coefficient in this relationship:

$$i_t = 6.6699 + 0.01277\, t + 0.27108\, \bar{p}_{t-5} + \varepsilon_{t2} \qquad \text{(C.III.4)}$$

Key numerical results from the simulation experiment are reported in the main text: Chapter 6, Section C.

REFERENCES

Adam, Jan. *Economic Reform in the Soviet Union and Eastern Europe Since the 1960s.* New York: St. Martin's Press, 1989.

Aggar, Ben, ed. *Western Marxism: An Introduction.* Santa Monica, Cal.: Goodyear Pub. Co., 1979.

Aharoni, Yair. *The Evolution and Management of State-Owned Enterprises.* Cambridge, Mass.: Ballinger, 1986.

Ames, Edward. *Soviet Economic Processes.* Homewood, Ill.: Irwin, 1965.

Atkinson, Anthony B. "The Distribution of Wealth and the Individual Life Cycle." *Oxford Economic Papers* 23(2): 239-254, July 1971.

————. *Unequal Shares: Wealth in Britain.* London: Penguin, 1972.

————, ed. *Wealth, Income and Inequality,* second edition. New York: Oxford University Press, 1980.

Atkinson, Anthony B., and A. J. Harrison. *The Distribution of Personal Wealth in Britain.* Cambridge: Cambridge University Press, 1978.

Azariadis, Costas, Kalman J. Cohen, and Alfredo Porcar. "A Partial Utility Approach to the Theory of the Firm." *Southern Economic Journal* 38(4): 485-494, April 1972.

Bailey, Elizabeth E. *Economic Theory of Regulatory Constraint.* Lexington, Mass.: Lexington Books, 1973.

Bailey, Elizabeth E., David R. Graham, and Daniel P. Kaplan. *Deregulating the Airlines.* Cambridge, Mass.: MIT Press, 1985.

Baiman, Stanley. "Agency Research in Managerial Accounting: A Survey." *Journal of Accounting Literature* 1: 154-213, Spring 1982.

Baiman, Stanley, and Joel Demski. "Economically Optimal Performance Evaluation and Control Systems." *Journal of Accounting Research* 18 (Sup.): 184-220, 1980.

Bain, Joe S. *Industrial Organization.* New York: Wiley, 1959.

Balassa, Bela. "The Dynamic Efficiency of the Soviet Economy." *American Economic Review* 54 (Sup.): 490-505, May 1964.

Barlow, Robin, Harvey Brazer, and James Morgan. *Economic Behavior of the Affluent.* Washington, D.C.: Brookings Institution, 1966.

Baumol, William J. *Business Behavior, Value and Growth,* revised edition. New York: Harcourt, Brace and World, 1967.

————, ed. *Public and Private Enterprise in a Mixed Economy.* New York: St. Martin's Press, 1980.

Baumol, William J., and David F. Bradford. "Optimal Departures from Marginal Cost Pricing." *American Economic Review* 60(3): 265-283, June 1970.

Beckwith, Burnham P. *The Economic Theory of a Socialist Economy.* Stanford, Cal.: Stanford University Press, 1949.

————. *Liberal Socialism: The Pure Welfare Economics of a Liberal Socialist Economy.* New York: Exposition Press, 1974.

————. *Liberal Socialism Applied: The Applied Welfare Economics of a Liberal Socialist Economy.* Palo Alto, Cal.: Author, 1978.

Bell, John Fred. *A History of Economic Thought,* second edition. New York: Ronald Press, 1967.

Bennett, John. "Planning Under Market Socialism When Iteration Is Incomplete." *Journal of Comparative Economics* 9(3): 252-266, September 1985.

————. *The Economic Theory of Central Planning.* New York: Basil Blackwell, 1989.

Bergson, Abram. "Socialist Economics." In Howard Ellis, ed., *A Survey of Contemporary Economics,* Philadelphia: Blakiston, 1948.

————. *The Economics of Soviet Planning.* New Haven: Yale University Press, 1964.

————. "Market Socialism Revisited." *Journal of Political Economy* 75(5): 655-673, October 1967.

————. "Optimal Pricing for Public Enterprises." *Quarterly Journal of Economics* 86(4): 519-544, November 1972.

————. *Productivity and the Social System: The USSR and the West.* Cambridge, Mass.: Harvard University Press, 1978.

Bergson, Abram, and Herbert S. Levine, eds. *The Soviet Economy: Toward the Year 2000.* London: George Allen and Unwin, 1983.

Berle, Adolf A. *Power Without Property.* New York: Harcourt Brace, 1959.

Berle, Adolf A., and Gardiner C. Means. *The Modern Corporation and Private Property.* New York: Commerce Clearing House, 1932.

Berliner, Joseph S. *Factory and Manager in the U.S.S.R.* Cambridge, Mass.: Harvard University Press, 1957.

————. "The Static Efficiency of the Soviet Economy." *American Economic Review* 54(2): 480-489, May 1964.

Bernstein, Eduard. *Evolutionary Socialism.* New York: Schocken Books, 1961. Originally published in German in 1899.

Blackburn, Anthony J., and Karl E. Case. *FairModel Student Manual.* Englewood Cliffs, N. J.: Prentice-Hall, 1985.

Blaug, Mark. *Economic Theory in Retrospect,* fourth edition. Cambridge: Cambridge University Press, 1985.

Böhm-Bawerk, Eugen von. *Karl Marx and the Close of His System.* Edited with an introduction by Paul M. Sweezy. New York: Augustus M. Kelley, 1949. Reprinted Philadelpha: Orion Editions, 1984. Originally published in German in 1896.

Borcherding, Thomas E., Werner W. Pommerehne, and Friedrich Schneider. "Comparing the Efficiency of Private and Public Production: The Evidence from Five Countries." *Zeitshrift für Nationalökonomie*, Sup. 2: 127-156, 1982.

Bork, Robert H. *The Antitrust Paradox: A Policy at War with Itself.* New York: Basic Books, 1978.

Bornstein, Morris, ed. *Comparative Economic Systems: Models and Cases*, fifth edition. Homewood, Ill.: Irwin, 1985.

Bornstein, Morris, and Daniel Fusfeld, eds. *The Soviet Economy: A Book of Readings*, fourth edition. Homewood, Ill.: Irwin, 1974.

Bös, Dieter. *Public Enterprise Economics: Theory and Application.* Amsterdam: North-Holland, 1986.

Boskin, Michael J. "Taxation, Saving and the Rate of Interest." *Journal of Political Economy* 86(2): S3-S27, April 1978.

Boudreaux, Kenneth J. "Managerialism and Risk-Return Performance." *Southern Economic Journal* 39(3): 366-373, January 1973.

Bowles, Samuel, and Herbert Gintis. *Schooling in Capitalist America.* New York: Basic Books, 1973.

————. *Democracy and Capitalism: Property, Community, and the Contradictions of Modern Social Thought.* New York: Basic Books, 1986.

Brittain, John A. *The Inheritance of Economic Status.* Washington, D.C.: Brookings Institution, 1977.

————. *Inheritance and the Inequality of Material Wealth.* Washington, D.C.: Brookings Institution, 1978.

Bronfenbrenner, Martin. *Income Distribution Theory.* Chicago: Aldine-Atherton, 1971.

————, ed. *Is the Business Cycle Obsolete?* New York: Wiley, 1969.

Browning, Edgar K., and Jacqueline M. Browning. *Microeconomic Theory and Applications*, second edition. Boston: Little, Brown, 1986.

Browning, Edgar K., and William R. Johnson. "The Trade-Off Between Equality and Efficiency." *Journal of Political Economy* 92(2): 175-203, April 1984.

Burnham, James. *The Managerial Revolution.* New York: John Day, 1941.

Burns, Emile, ed. *The Marxist Reader.* New York: Avenel, 1982.

Carr, E. H., and R. W. Davies. *Foundations of a Planned Economy.* London: Macmillan, 1969.

Carson, Richard L. *Comparative Economic Systems.* New York: Macmillan, 1973.

Cave, Martin, Alistair McAuley, and Judith Thornton, eds. *New Trends in Soviet Economics.* Armonk, N.Y.: M. E. Sharpe, 1982.

Caves, Douglas W., and Laurits R. Christensen. "The Relative Efficiency of Public and Private Firms in a Competitive Environment: The Case of Canadian Railroads." *Journal of Political Economy* 88(5): 958-976, October 1980.

Ciscel, David H. "Determinants of Executive Compensation." *Southern Economic Journal* 40(4): 613-617, April 1974.

Coase, Ronald. "The Problem of Social Cost." *Journal of Law and Economics* 3(1): 1-44, October 1960.

Cole, George D. H. *A History of Socialist Thought*, five volumes. London: Macmillan, 1953-1960.

Cole, John, and Trevor Buck. *Modern Soviet Economic Performance.* New York: Basil Blackwell, 1987.

Comisso, Ellen T. *Workers' Control Under Plan and Market.* New Haven: Yale University Press, 1979.

Conn, David. "Toward a Theory of Optimal Economic Systems." *Journal of Comparative Economics* 1(4): 325-350, December 1977.

Crew, M. A., M. W. Jones-Lee, and C. K. Rowley. "X-Theory Versus Management Discretion Theory." *Southern Economic Journal* 38(2): 173-184, October 1971.

Crew, M. A., and Paul R. Kleindorfer. *Public Utility Economics.* New York: St. Martin's, 1979.

Crosland, C.A.R. *The Future of Socialism.* New York: Schocken, 1963.

Cyert, Richard M., and James G. March. *A Behavioral Theory of the Firm.* Englewood Cliffs, N.J.: Prentice-Hall, 1963.

Davies, David G. "The Efficiency of Public Versus Private Firms: The Case of Australia's Two Airlines." *Journal of Law and Economics* 14(1): 149-165, April 1971.

———. "Property Rights and Economic Efficiency: The Australian Airlines Revisited." *Journal of Law and Economics* 20(1): 223-226, April 1977.

———. "Property Rights and Efficiency in a Regulated Environment: Reply." *Economic Record* 56(153): 186-189, June 1980.

DeAlessi, Louis. "The Economics of Property Rights: A Review of the Evidence." In R. O. Zerbe, Jr., ed., *Research in Law and Economics,* Vol. 2, Greenwich, Conn.: JAI Press, 1980.

Dean, John. *Blind Ambition: The White House Years.* New York: Simon and Schuster, 1976.

Desai, Meghnad. *Marxian Economics.* Totowa, N.J.: Rowman and Littlefield, 1979.

Desai, Padma. *The Soviet Economy in Decline: Problems and Prospects.* New York: Basil Blackwell, 1987.

———. *Perestroika in Perspective.* Princeton, N.J.: Princeton University Press, 1989.

Desai, Padma, and Ricardo Martin. "Efficiency Loss from Resource Misallocation in Soviet Industry." *Quarterly Journal of Economics* 98(3): 441-456, August 1983.

Diamond, Peter, and Michael Rothschild, eds. *Uncertainty in Economics: Readings and Exercises.* New York: Academic Press, 1978.

Dickinson, Henry D. *Economics of Socialism.* London: Oxford University Press, 1939.

Domar, Evsey D. "The Soviet Collective Farm as a Producer Cooperative." *American Economic Review* 56(4): 734-757, September 1966.

———. "On the Optimal Compensation of a Socialist Manager." *Quarterly Journal of Economics* 88(1): 1-18, February 1974.

Drèze, Jacques H., ed. *Allocation Under Uncertainty: Equilibrium and Optimality.*

New York: Wiley, 1974.

Drucker, Peter. *The Unseen Revolution: How Pension Fund Socialism Came to America.* New York: Harper & Row, 1976.

Due, John F., and Ann F. Friedlaender. *Government Finance: Economics of the Public Sector,* sixth edition. Homewood, Ill.: Irwin, 1977.

Duesenberry, James S., Gary Fromm, Lawrence R. Klein, and Edwin Kuh. *The Brookings Quarterly Econometric Model of the United States.* Chicago: Rand McNally, 1965.

Dyker, David A. *The Soviet Economy.* New York: St. Martin's, 1976.

Edgeworth, Francis Y. "The Pure Theory of Taxation, III." *Economic Journal* 7(4): 550-571, December 1897.

Elliott, John E. *Comparative Economic Systems,* second edition. Belmont, Cal.: Wadsworth, 1985.

Erlich, Alexander. *The Soviet Industrialization Debate, 1924-1928.* Cambridge, Mass.: Harvard University Press, 1960.

Estrin, Saul. *Self-Management: Economic Theory and Yugoslav Practice.* Cambridge: Cambridge University Press, 1983.

Evans, Michael K., and Lawrence R. Klein. *The Wharton Econometric Forecasting Model.* Philadelphia: Wharton School, 1967.

Evans, Owen J. "Tax Policy, the Interest Elasticity of Saving, and Capital Accumulation: Numerical Analysis of Theoretical Models." *American Economic Review* 73(3): 398-410, June 1983.

Fair, Ray C. *A Short-Run Forecasting Model of the United States Economy.* Lexington, Mass.: D.C. Heath/Lexington Books, 1971.

Fama, Eugene F. "Efficient Capital Markets: A Review of Theory and Empirical Work." *Journal of Finance* 25(2): 383-417, May 1970.

———. "Agency Problems and the Theory of the Firm." *Journal of Political Economy* 88(2): 288-307, April 1980.

Fama, Eugene F., and Michael C. Jensen. "Separation of Ownership and Control." *Journal of Law and Economics* 26(2): 301-326, June 1983.

Feiwel, George R. "On the Economic Theory of Socialism: Some Reflections on Lange's Contribution." *Kyklos* 25(3): 601-618, 1972.

———. *The Soviet Quest for Economic Efficiency: Issues, Controversies, and Reforms,* revised edition. New York: Praeger, 1972.

Fine, Ben, and Laurence Harris. *Rereading Capital.* New York: Columbia University Press, 1979.

Fisher, Walter D. "Oskar Ryszard Lange, 1904-1965." *Econometrica* 34(4): 733-738, October 1966.

Forsyth, P. J., and R. D. Hocking. "Property Rights and Efficiency in a Regulated Environment: The Case of Australian Airlines." *Economic Record* 56(153): 182-185, June 1980.

Freedman, Robert, ed. *Marx on Economics.* New York: Penguin, 1962.

Friedman, Milton. *Capitalism and Freedom.* Chicago: University of Chicago Press, 1962.

Funkhouser, Richard, and Paul W. MacAvoy. "Sample of Observations on Comparative Prices in Public and Private Enterprises." *Journal of Public Economics* 11(3): 353-368, June 1979.

Furubotn, Eirik, and Svetozar Pejovich. "Property Rights and Economic Theory: A Survey of Recent Literature." *Journal of Economic Literature* 10(4): 1137-1162, December 1972.

————, eds. *The Economics of Property Rights*. Cambridge, Mass.: Ballinger, 1974.

Gardner, H. Stephen. *Comparative Economic Systems*. Chicago: Dryden Press, 1988.

Gisser, Micha, and Paul Jonas. "Soviet Growth in the Absence of Planning: A Hypothetical Alternative." *Journal of Political Economy* 82(2): 333-347, March 1974.

Gordon, Robert A. *Business Leadership in the Large Corporation*. Washington, D.C.: Brookings Institution, 1945.

Granick, David. *Management of the Industrial Firm in the U.S.S.R.* New York: Columbia University Press, 1954.

————. *The Red Executive*. London: Macmillan and Co., 1960.

————. *Job Rights in the Soviet Union: Their Consequences*. New York: Cambridge University Press, 1987.

Greer, Douglas F. *Industrial Organization and Public Policy*, second edition. New York: Macmillan, 1984.

Gregory, Paul R., and Robert C. Stuart. *Soviet Economic Structure and Performance*, second edition. New York: Harper & Row, 1981.

————. *Comparative Economic Systems*, second edition. Boston: Houghton Mifflin, 1985.

Gruchy, Allan G. *Comparative Economic Systems*, second edition. Boston: Houghton Mifflin, 1977.

Hadley, G., and M. C. Kemp. *Variational Methods in Economics*. Amsterdam: North-Holland, 1971.

Halm, George N. *Economic Systems: A Comparative Analysis*. New York: Holt, Rinehart and Winston, 1960.

Harberger, Arnold C. "Monopoly and Resource Allocation." *American Economic Review* 44(Sup.): 77-87, May 1954.

Harbury, Colin D. "Inheritance and the Distribution of Personal Wealth in Britain." *Economic Journal* 72(228): 845-868, 1962.

Harbury, Colin D., and David M. Hitchens. *Inheritance and Wealth Inequality in Britain*. London: George Allen and Unwin, 1979.

Harbury, Colin D., David M. Hitchens, and Patrick C. McMahon. "On the Measurement of Inherited Wealth." *Review of Income and Wealth* 23(3): 309-314, September 1977.

Harbury, Colin D., and Patrick C. McMahon. "Inheritance and the Characteristics of Top Wealth Leavers in Britain." *Economic Journal* 83(331): 810-833, September 1973.

Harrington, Michael. *The Other America: Poverty in the United States.* New York: Macmillan, 1962.

————. *The Twilight of Capitalism.* New York: Basic Books, 1980.

Hayek, Friedrich. "Socialist Calculation: The 'Competitive Solution.'" *Economica* 7 (New Series): 125-149, May 1940.

————. *The Road to Serfdom.* Chicago: University of Chicago Press, 1944.

————. "The Use of Knowledge in Society." *American Economic Review* 35(4): 519-530, September 1945.

————. *The Fatal Conceit: The Errors of Socialism,* edited by W. W. Bartley III. Chicago: University of Chicago Press: 1988.

————, ed. *Collectivist Economic Planning: Critical Studies on the Possibilities of Socialism.* London: George Routledge and Sons, 1935. Reprinted New York: Augustus M. Kelley, 1975. (Hayek's contributions: "The Nature and History of the Problem" and "The Present State of the Debate.")

Heal, Geoffrey M. *The Theory of Economic Planning.* Amsterdam: North-Holland, 1973.

————. "Planning." In Kenneth J. Arrow and Michael Intriligator, eds. *Handbook of Mathematical Economics,* Vol. III, Amsterdam: North-Holland, 1982.

Henderson, James M., and Richard E. Quandt. *Micro-Economic Theory: A Mathematical Approach,* third edition. New York: McGraw-Hill, 1980.

Herber, Bernard P. *Modern Public Finance: The Study of Public Sector Economics,* third edition. Homewood, Ill.: Irwin, 1975.

Hess, James D. *The Economics of Organization.* Amsterdam: North-Holland, 1983.

Hewett, Edward A. *Reforming the Soviet Economy: Equality Versus Efficiency.* Washington, D.C.: Brookings Institution, 1988.

Hindley, Brian. "Separation of Ownership and Control in the Modern Corporation." *Journal of Law and Economics* 13(1): 185-221, April 1970.

Hirshleifer, Jack. *Price Theory and Applications,* fourth edition. Englewood Cliffs, N.J.: Prentice-Hall, 1988.

Hirshleifer, Jack, and John G. Riley. "The Analytics of Uncertainty and Information." *Journal of Economic Literature* 17(4): 1375-1421, December 1979.

Hochman, Harold M., and George E. Peterson, eds. *Redistribution Through Public Choice.* New York: Columbia University Press, 1974.

Hoff, Trygve J. B. *Economic Calculation in the Socialist Society.* London: William Hodge, 1949.

Holesovsky, Vaclav. *Economic Systems: Analysis and Comparison.* New York: McGraw-Hill, 1977.

Hotelling, Harold. "The General Welfare in Relation to the Problems of Taxation and Railway and Utility Rates." *Econometrica* 6(3): 242-269, July 1938.

————. "The Relation of Prices to Marginal Costs in an Optimum System." *Econometrica* 7(1): 151-155, April 1939.

Howe, Irving, ed. *Essential Works of Socialism.* New Haven: Yale University Press, 1976.

Howrey, Philip, and Saul Hymans, "The Measurement and Determination of

Loanable-Funds Saving." *Brookings Papers on Economic Activity* 3: 655-685, 1978.

Hurwicz, Leonid. "Incentive Aspects of Decentralization." In Kenneth J. Arrow and Michael Intriligator, eds., *Handbook of Mathematical Economics*, Vol. III, Amsterdam: North-Holland, 1982.

Hurwicz, Leonid, and Thomas Marschak. "Centralization and Decentralization in Economic Systems." *American Economic Review* 59 (Sup.) 513-537, May 1969.

Hyams, Edward. *The Millenium Postponed: Socialism from Sir Thomas More to Mao Tse-tung.* New York: Taplinger, 1974.

Ireland, Norman J. *The Economics of Labor-Managed Enterprises.* New York: St. Martin's Press, 1982.

Jennergren, L. Peter. "On the Design of Incentives in Business Firms: A Survey of Some Research." *Managerial Science* 26(2): 180-201, February 1980.

Jensen, Michael C., ed. "Symposium on the Market for Corporate Control: The Scientific Evidence." *Journal of Financial Economics* 11(1-4): 1-471, April 1983.

Jensen, Michael C., and William H. Meckling. "Theory of the Firm: Managerial Behavior, Agency Costs and Ownership Structure." *Journal of Financial Economics* 3(4): 305-360, October 1976.

Jensen, Michael C., and Jerold L. Zimmerman, eds. "Symposium on Management Compensation and the Managerial Labor Market." *Journal of Accounting and Economics* 7(1-3): 3-251, April 1985.

Johansen, Leif. *Public Economics.* Chicago: Rand McNally, 1965.

Jones, Anthony. *Perestroika and the Economy: New Thinking in Soviet Economics.* Armonk, N.Y.: M. E. Sharpe, 1989.

Kahn, Alfred E. *The Economics of Regulation: Principles and Institutions,* two volumes. New York: Wiley, 1970.

Kamerschen, David R. "The Influence of Ownership and Control on Profit Rates." *American Economic Review* 58(3): 432-447, June 1968.

Kamien, Morton I., and Nancy L. Schwartz. *Dynamic Optimization: The Calculus of Variations and Optimal Control in Economics and Management.* Amsterdam: North-Holland, 1981.

Kaser, Michael. *Soviet Economics.* New York: McGraw-Hill, 1970.

Katona, George, Charles A. Lininger, and Eva Mueller. *1964 Survey of Consumer Finances.* Ann Arbor: Survey Research Center, University of Michigan, 1965.

Kay, Geoffrey. *The Economic Theory of the Working Class.* New York: St. Martin's Press, 1979.

Kaysen, Carl, and Donald F. Turner. *Antitrust Policy: An Economic and Legal Analysis.* Cambridge, Mass.: Harvard University Press, 1959.

Keane, Simon M. *The Efficient Market Hypothesis and the Implications for Financial Reporting.* London: Gee and Co., 1980.

———. *Stock Market Efficiency: Theory, Evidence and Implications.* New York: Humanities Press, 1983.

Kelf-Cohen, Rolf. *British Nationalization: 1945-1973*. New York: St. Martin's, 1973.

Keynes, John Maynard. *The General Theory of Employment, Interest and Money*. New York: Harcourt, Brace and World, 1936.

Killingsworth, Mark R. *Labor Supply*. Cambridge: Cambridge University Press, 1983.

Kirzner, Israel M. *Competition and Entrepreneurship*. Chicago: University of Chicago Press, 1973.

―――. *Perception, Opportunity and Profit: Studies in the Theory of Entrepreneurship*. Chicago: University of Chicago Press, 1979.

―――. *Discovery and the Capitalist Process*. Chicago: University of Chicago Press, 1985.

Klein, Lawrence R., and Arthur S. Goldberger. *An Econometric Model of the United States, 1929-1952*. Amsterdam: North-Holland, 1955.

Knight, Frank. *Risk, Uncertainty and Profit*. Boston: Houghton Mifflin, 1921.

Kogiku, K. C. *Microeconomic Models*. New York: Harper & Row, 1971.

Kohler, Heinz. *Intermediate Microeconomics: Theory and Applications*, second edition. Glenview, Ill.: Scott, Foresman, 1986.

Kolko, Gabriel. *Wealth and Power in America*. New York: Praeger, 1962.

Kotlikoff, Lawrence J. "Taxation and Savings: A Neoclassical Perspective." *Journal of Economic Literature* 22(4): 1576-1629, December 1984.

Krutogolov, M. A. *Talks on Soviet Democracy*. Moscow: Progress Publishers, 1980.

Laird, Roy. *The Soviet Paradigm*. New York: Free Press, 1970.

Lampman, Robert J. *The Share of the Top Wealth-Holders in National Wealth, 1922-1956*. Princeton, N.J.: Princeton University Press, 1962.

Landauer, Carl. *European Socialism*, two volumes. Berkeley: University of California Press, 1960.

―――. *Contemporary Economic Systems: A Comparative Approach*. Philadelphia: Lippincott, 1964.

Lange, Oskar. "On the Economic Theory of Socialism." *Review of Economic Studies* 4(1): 53-71, October 1936, and 4(2): 123-142, February 1937. Issued in book form with contributions by Benjamin Lippincott, ed., and Fred M. Taylor, Minneapolis: University of Minnesota Press, 1938. Reprinted New York: McGraw-Hill, 1964.

―――. "The Computer and the Market." In C. H. Feinstein, ed., *Socialism, Capitalism and Economic Growth: Essays Presented to Maurice Dobb*, Cambridge: Cambridge University Press, 1967.

―――, ed. *Problems of Political Economy of Socialism*, second edition. New Delhi: People's Publishing House, 1965. First published in 1959 in Poland.

Larner, Robert J. "The 200 Largest Nonfinancial Corporations." *American Economic Review* 56(4): 777-787, September 1966.

―――. *Management Control and the Large Corporation*. New York: Dunellen, 1970.

Lavoie, Don. *Rivalry and Central Planning: The Socialist Calculation Debate Reconsidered*. New York: Cambridge University Press, 1985.

Layard, P. R. G., and A. A. Walters. *Microeconomic Theory*. New York: McGraw-Hill, 1978.

Leeman, Wayne A. *Centralized and Decentralized Economic Systems*. Chicago: Rand McNally, 1977.

————. "On Leland G. Stauber, 'A Proposal for a Democratic Market Economy'." *Journal of Comparative Economics* 2(1): 71-72, March 1978.

Lekachman, Robert. *A History of Economic Ideas*. New York: Harper & Row, 1959.

Lerner, Abba. *The Economics of Control*. New York: Macmillan, 1944.

Lewellen, Wilbur G. *The Ownership Income of Management*. Princeton, N.J.: National Bureau of Economic Research, 1971.

Lewellen, Wilbur G., and Blaine Huntsman. "Managerial Pay and Corporate Performance." *American Economic Review* 60(4): 710-720, September 1970.

Lewis, Ben. *British Planning and Nationalization*. New York: Twentieth Century Fund, 1952.

Liberman, Evsey G. *Economic Methods and the Effectiveness of Production*. White Plains, N.Y.: International Arts and Sciences Press, 1971.

Linz, Susan J., ed. "A Symposium on Reorganization and Reform in the Soviet Economy." *Comparative Economic Studies* 29(4): 1-172, Winter 1987.

Lippmann, Steven A., and John J. McCall. "The Economics of Uncertainty: Selected Topics and Probabilistic Methods." In Kenneth J. Arrow and Michael Intriligator, eds. *Handbook of Mathematical Economics*, Vol. III, Amsterdam: North-Holland, 1982.

Lundberg, Ferdinand. *The Rich and the Super-Rich*. New York: Lyle Stuart, 1968.

Mandel, Ernest. *Marxist Economic Theory*, two volumes. New York: Monthly Review Press, 1970.

Mansfield, Edwin. *Microeconomics: Theory and Application*, fourth edition. New York: W. W. Norton, 1982.

Marchand, Maurice, Pierre Pestieau, and Henry Tulkens, eds. *Performance of Public Enterprise*. Amsterdam: North-Holland, 1984.

Marris, Robin. *The Economic Theory of Managerial Capitalism*. Glencoe, Ill.: Free Press, 1964.

Marris, Robin, and Dennis C. Mueller. "The Corporate Economy: Growth, Competition and the Invisible Hand." *Journal of Economic Literature* 18(1): 32-63, March 1980.

Marris, Robin, and Adrian Wood, eds. *The Corporate Economy: Growth, Competition and Innovative Potential*. Cambridge, Mass.: Harvard University Press, 1971.

Marx, Karl. *Capital: A Critique of Political Economy*, three volumes. New York: International Publishers, 1967. Originally published in German, three volumes, 1867-1894.

McGuire, Joseph W., John S. Y. Chiu, and Alvar O. Elbring. "Executive Incomes, Sales and Profits." *American Economic Review* 52(3): 753-761, September

1962.

Meade, James E. *Efficiency, Inequality and the Ownership of Property*. Cambridge, Mass.: Harvard University Press, 1965.

———. "The Theory of Labour-Managed Firms and Profit Sharing." *Economic Journal* 83(325): 402-428, March 1972.

Meek, Ronald L. *Studies in the Labour Theory of Value*, second edition. New York: Monthly Review Press, 1976. First published in 1956.

Menchik, Paul L. "Inter-Generational Transmission of Inequality: An Empirical Study." *Economica* 46(184): 349-362, November 1979.

———. "The Importance of Material Inheritance: The Financial Link Between Generations." In James D. Smith, ed., *Modeling the Distribution and Intergenerational Transmission of Wealth*, Chicago: University of Chicago Press, 1980.

Milenkovitch, Deborah D. *Plan and Market in Yugoslav Economic Thought*. New Haven: Yale University Press, 1971.

———. "Is Market Socialism Efficient?" In Andrew Zimbalist, ed., *Comparative Economic Systems: An Assessment of Knowledge, Theory and Method*, Boston: Kluwer-Nijhoff, 1984.

Miller, Herman P. *Rich Man, Poor Man*. New York: Thomas Y. Crowell, 1971.

Mills, C. Wright. *The Power Elite*. New York: Oxford University Press, 1956.

Mises, Ludwig von. "Economic Calculation in the Socialist Commonwealth." In Friedrich Hayek, ed., *Collectivist Economic Planning*, London: George Routledge and Sons, 1935. Originally published in German in 1920.

———. *Bureaucracy*. New Haven: Yale University Press, 1943.

———. *Socialism: An Economic and Sociological Analysis*, revised English edition. London: Jonathan Cape, 1951.

———. *The Anti-Capitalist Mentality*. New York: Van Nostrand, 1956.

———. *Human Action: A Treatise on Economics*, third revised edition. Chicago: Henry Regnery, 1966.

Mollenhoff, Clark R. *Game Plan for Disaster: An Ombudsman's Report on the Nixon Years*. New York: Norton, 1976.

Monsen, R. Joseph, John S. Y. Chiu, and David E. Cooley. "The Effect of Separation of Ownership and Control on the Performance of a Large Firm." *Quarterly Journal of Economics* 83(2): 435-451, August 1968.

Morishima, Michio. *Marx's Economics: A Dual Theory of Value and Growth*. Cambridge: Cambridge University Press, 1973.

Murrell, Peter. "The Microeconomic Efficiency Argument for Socialism Revisited: Comment." *Journal of Economic Issues* 15(1): 211-219, March 1981.

———. "Did the Theory of Market Socialism Answer the Challenge of Ludwig von Mises? A Reinterpretation of the Socialist Controversy." *History of Political Economy* 15(1): 92-105, 1983.

———. "Incentives and Income Under Market Socialism." *Journal of Comparative Economics* 8(3): 261-276, September 1984.

Nalebuff, Barry J., and Joseph E. Stiglitz. "Prizes and Incentives: Towards a

General Theory of Compensation and Competition." *Bell Journal of Economics* 14(1): 21-43, Spring 1983.

Nelson, J. R., ed. *Marginal Cost Pricing in Practice*. Englewood Cliffs, N.J.: Prentice-Hall, 1964.

Neuberger, Egon. "The Plan and the Market: The Models of Oskar Lange." *American Economist* 17(2): 153-158, Fall 1973.

Neuberger, Egon, and William J. Duffy. *Comparative Economic Systems: A Decision-Making Approach*. Boston: Allyn and Bacon, 1976.

Neumann, John von, and Oskar Morgenstern. *The Theory of Games and Economic Behavior*, second edition. Princeton, N.J.: Princeton University Press, 1947.

Nicholson, Walter. *Microeconomic Theory: Basic Principles and Extensions*, third edition. Chicago: Dryden Press, 1985.

Nixon, Richard M. *Memoirs*. New York: Grosset and Dunlap, 1978.

Nove, Alec. *The Soviet Economy*. New York: Praeger, 1961.

———. *Efficiency Criteria for Nationalized Industries*. Toronto: University of Toronto Press, 1973.

———. *The Economics of Feasible Socialism*. London: George Allen and Unwin, 1983.

Nutter, G. Warren. "Markets Without Property: A Grand Illusion." In Eirik Furubotn and Svetozar Pejovich, eds., *The Economics of Property Rights*, Cambridge, Mass.: Ballinger, 1974.

Ofer, Gur. "Soviet Economic Growth: 1928-1985." *Journal of Economic Literature* 25(4): 1767-1833, December 1987.

Office of Technology Assessment, U.S. Congress. *The Effects of Nuclear War*. Washington, D.C.: U.S. Government Printing Office, 1979.

Oi, Walter Y., and Elizabeth M. Clayton. "A Peasant's View of a Soviet Collective Farm." *American Economic Review* 58(1): 37-59, March 1968.

Okun, Arthur M. *Equality and Efficiency: The Big Tradeoff*. Washington, D.C.: Brookings Institution, 1975.

Olson, Mancur, and Martin J. Bailey. "Positive Time Preference." *Journal of Political Economy* 89(1): 1-25, February 1981.

Oulton, Nicholas. "Inheritance and the Distribution of Wealth." *Oxford Economic Papers* 28(1): 86-101, March 1976.

Palmer, John. "The Profit Performance Effects of the Separation of Ownership and Control in Large U.S. Industrial Corporations." *Bell Journal of Economics and Management Science* 3(1): 293-303: Spring 1973.

Pegrum, Dudley F. *Public Regulation of Business*, revised edition. Homewood, Ill.: Irwin, 1965.

Peltzman, Sam. "Toward a More General Theory of Regulation." *Journal of Law and Economics* 19(2): 211-240, August 1976.

Perlo, Victor. "'People's Capitalism' and Stock Ownership." *American Economic Review* 48(3): 333-347, June 1958.

Phelps, Edmund. *Golden Rules of Economic Growth: Studies of Efficient and Optimal Growth*. New York: Norton, 1966.

Pickersgill, Gary M., and Joyce E. Pickersgill. *Contemporary Economic Systems: A Comparative View*, second edition. St. Paul, Minn.: West Pub. Co., 1985.

Posner, Richard A. "Theories of Economic Regulation." *Bell Journal of Economics and Management Science* 4(2): 335-358, Fall 1974.

———. *Antitrust Law: An Economic Perspective*. Chicago: University of Chicago Press, 1976.

Projector, Dorothy S., and Gertrude S. Weiss. *Survey of Financial Characteristics of Consumers*. Washington, D.C.: Board of Governors of the Federal Reserve System, 1966.

Pryke, Richard. *Public Enterprise in Practice*. New York: St. Martin's Press, 1971.

———. *The Nationalized Industries: Policies and Performance Since 1968*. Oxford: Martin Robertson, 1981.

Pryor, Frederick L. "The Economics of Production Cooperatives." *Annals of Public and Cooperative Economy* 54(2): 133-173, June 1983.

Radice, H. K. "Control Type, Profitability and Growth in Large Firms: An Empirical Study." *Economic Journal* 81: 547-562, September 1971.

Reekie, W. Duncan. *Markets, Entrepreneurs and Liberty: An Austrian View of Capitalism*. New York: St. Martin's, 1984.

Reid, Graham, and Kevin Allen. *Nationalized Industries*. Harmondsworth, Middlesex: Penguin, 1970.

Rima, Ingrid Hahne. *Development of Economic Analysis*. third edition. Homewood, Ill.: Irwin, 1978.

Roberts, Paul Craig. "On Oskar Lange's Theory of Planning." *Journal of Political Economy* 79(3): 577-583, May-June 1971.

Robinson, Joan. *An Essay on Marxian Economics*, second edition. New York: St. Martin's, 1963. First edition published in 1942.

Robson, William A. *Nationalized Industry and Public Ownership*, second edition. London: Allen and Unwin, 1962.

Roemer, John E. *Analytical Foundations of Marxian Economic Theory*. Cambridge: Cambridge University Press, 1981.

———. *A General Theory of Exploitation and Class*. Cambridge, Mass.: Harvard University Press, 1982.

———. *Free to Lose*. Cambridge, Mass.: Harvard University Press, 1988.

———, ed. *Analytical Marxism*. Cambridge: Cambridge University Press, 1986.

Rose-Ackerman, Susan. "Redistribution Policy and Local Government Behavior, Comment on L. Stauber, 'A Proposal for a Democratic Market Economy'." *Journal of Comparative Economics* 2(1): 73-84, March 1978.

Ruggles, Nancy. "The Welfare Basis of the Marginal Cost Pricing Principle." *Review of Economic Studies* 17(1): 29-46, 1949-1950.

———. "Recent Developments in the Theory of Marginal Cost Pricing." *Review of Economic Studies* 17(2): 107-126, 1949-1950.

Sacks, Stephen R. *Self-Management and Efficiency: Large Corporations in Yugoslavia*. London: Allen and Unwin, 1983.

Sahota, Gian Singh. "Theories of Personal Income Distribution: A Survey." *Journal of Economic Literature* 16(1): 1-55, March 1978.

Salvatore, Dominick. *Microeconomics: Theory and Applications.* New York: Macmillan, 1986.

Samuelson, Paul A. "What Economists Know." In Daniel Lerner, ed., *The Human Meaning of the Social Sciences,* New York: World, 1959.

―――. "Understanding the Marxian Notion of Exploitation: A Summary of the So-Called Transformation Problem." *Journal of Economic Literature* 9(2): 399-431, June 1971.

Sanford, Cedric. *Costs and Benefits of V.A.T.* New York: Heinemann Educational Books, 1981.

Scherer, Frederick M. *Industrial Market Structure and Economic Performance,* second edition. Chicago: Rand McNally, 1980.

Schnitzer, Martin C. *Comparative Economic Systems,* fourth edition. Cincinnati: South-Western Publishing, 1987.

Schroeder, Gertrude E. "The Soviet Economy on a Treadmill of 'Reforms'." In Joint Economic Committee, U.S. Congress, *Soviet Economy in a Time of Change,* Washington, D.C.: U.S. Government Printing Office, 1979.

Schumpeter, Joseph A. *Capitalism, Socialism and Democracy.* New York: Harper & Row, 1947, 1952, 1962.

Schweickart, David. *Capitalism or Worker Control? An Ethical and Economic Appraisal.* New York: Praeger, 1980.

Sen, Amartya S. "Labour Allocation in a Cooperative Enterprise." *Review of Economic Studies* 33(4): 361-371, October 1966.

Sharpe, Myron E., ed. *Planning, Profit and Incentives in the U.S.S.R.,* two volumes. White Plains, N.Y.: International Arts and Sciences Press, 1966.

Sheffrin, Steven M. *Rational Expectations.* Cambridge: Cambridge University Press, 1983.

Shell, Karl, ed. *Essays on the Theory of Optimal Economic Growth.* Cambridge, Mass.: MIT Press, 1967.

Shepherd, William G. *Economic Performance Under Public Ownership.* New Haven: Yale University Press, 1965.

―――. *Public Enterprise: Economic Analysis of Theory and Practice.* Lexington, Mass.: Lexington Books, 1976.

―――. *Public Policies Toward Business,* seventh edition. Homewood, Ill.: Irwin, 1985.

Sherman, Howard. *Radical Political Economy.* New York: Basic Books, 1972.

Smith, Adam. *An Inquiry into the Nature and Causes of the Wealth of Nations,* edited by Edwin Cannan. New York: Modern Library/Random House, 1937. Originally published in 1776.

Smith, Henry. *The Economics of Socialism Reconsidered.* London: Oxford University Press, 1962.

Smith, James D., ed. *The Personal Distribution of Income and Wealth.* New York: National Bureau of Economic Research, 1975.

Smith, James D., and Stephen D. Franklin. "The Concentration of Personal Wealth:

1922-1969." *American Economic Review* 64(2): 162-167, May 1974.

Solberg, Eric J. *Intermediate Microeconomics.* Plano, Tex.: Business Publications, 1982.

Spulber, Nicholas. *The Soviet Economy: Structure, Principles and Problems.* New York: Norton, 1962.

————. "On Some Issues in the Theory of the Socialist Economy." *Kyklos* 25(4): 715-735, 1972.

————, ed. *Foundations of Soviet Strategy for Economic Growth.* Bloomington: Indiana University Press, 1964.

Stauber, Leland G. "The Implications of Market Socialism in the United States." *Polity* 8(1): 38-62, Fall 1975.

————. "A Proposal for a Democratic Market Economy." *Journal of Comparative Economics* 1(3): 235-258, September 1977.

————. "A Democratic Market Economy: A Response." *Journal of Comparative Economics* 2(4): 382-389, December 1978.

————. *A New Program for Democratic Socialism.* Carbondale, Ill.: Four Willows Press, 1987.

Steinherr, Alfred. "The Labor-Managed Firm: A Survey of the Economics Literature." *Annals of Public and Cooperative Economy* 49(2): 129-148, April-June 1978.

Stigler, George. "The Theory of Economic Regulation." *Bell Journal of Economics and Management Science* 2(1): 3-21, Spring 1971.

Sweezy, Paul M. *The Theory of Capitalist Development.* New York: Oxford University Press, 1942.

Taylor, Overton H. *A History of Economic Thought.* New York: McGraw-Hill, 1960.

Thayer, George. *Who Shakes the Money Tree?* New York: Simon and Schuster, 1973.

Thurow, Lester D. *Generating Inequality: Mechanisms of Distribution in the U.S. Economy.* New York: Basic Books, 1975.

Tinbergen, Jan. *Centralization and Decentralization in Economic Policy.* Amsterdam: North-Holland, 1954.

Tullock, Gordon. *Economics of Income Redistribution.* Boston: Kluwer-Nijhoff, 1983.

Vanek, Jaroslav. "Decentralization and Workers' Management: A Theoretical Appraisal." *American Economic Review* 59(5): 1,006-1,014, December 1969.

————. *The General Theory of Labor-Managed Market Economies.* Ithaca, N.Y.: Cornell University Press, 1970.

————. *The Participatory Economy.* Ithaca, N.Y.: Cornell University Press, 1971.

————. *The Labor-Managed Economy: Essays.* Ithaca, N.Y.: Cornell University Press, 1977.

Vaughn, Karen. "Economic Calculation under Socialism: The Austrian Contribution." *Economic Inquiry* 18(4): 535-554, October 1980.

Wachtel, Howard M. *Workers' Management and Workers' Wages in Yugoslavia.*

Ithaca, N.Y.: Cornell University Press, 1973.

Wachtel, Paul. "Inflation and the Saving Behavior of Households: A Survey." In George M. von Furstenberg, ed., *The Government and Capital Formation*, Cambridge, Mass.: Ballinger, 1980.

Walter, James E. *The Investment Process: As Characterized by Leading Life Insurance Companies*. Boston: Division of Research, Graduate School of Business Administration, Harvard University, 1962.

Ward, Benjamin. "The Firm in Illyria: Market Syndicalism." *American Economic Review* 48(3): 566-589, September 1958.

———. *The Socialist Economy: A Study of Organizational Alternatives*. New York: Random House, 1967.

Weber, Warren E. "The Effect of Interest Rates on Aggregate Consumption." *American Economic Review* 60(3): 591-600, September 1970.

———. "Interest Rates, Inflation, and Consumer Expenditures." *American Economic Review* 65(5): 843-858, December 1975.

Wedgwood, Josiah. *The Economics of Inheritance*. London: Routledge and Kegan Paul, 1929.

Weiss, Leonard W. "State Regulation of Public Utilities and Marginal-Cost Pricing." In Leonard Weiss and Michael Klass, eds., *Case Studies in Regulation: Revolution and Reform*, Boston: Little, Brown, 1981.

White, Theodore H. *Breach of Faith: The Fall of Richard Nixon*. New York: Atheneum, 1975.

Wilcox, Clair. *Public Policies Toward Business*, second (revised) edition. Homewood, Ill.: Irwin, 1960.

Wilczynski, J. *Socialist Economic Development and Reforms*. London: Macmillan, 1972.

Wildsmith, J. R. *Managerial Theories of the Firm*. New York: Dunellen, 1973.

Wiles, Peter J.D. *The Political Economy of Communism*. Cambridge, Mass.: Harvard University Press, 1962.

———. *Economic Institutions Compared*. New York: Wiley, 1977.

Williamson, Oliver E. *The Economics of Discretionary Behavior: Managerial Objectives in a Theory of the Firm*. Englewood Cliffs, N.J.: Prentice-Hall, 1964.

———. "The Modern Corporation: Origins, Evolution, Attributes." *Journal of Economic Literature* 19(4): 1537-1568, December 1981.

Wiseman, Jack. "Guidelines for Public Enterprise: A British Experiment." *Southern Economic Journal* 30(1): 39-48, July 1963.

Wolfson, Murray. *A Reappraisal of Marxian Economics*. New York: Columbia University Press, 1968.

Wright, Colin. "Some Evidence on the Interest Elasticity of Consumption." *American Economic Review* 57(4): 850-854, September 1967.

———. "Saving and the Rate of Interest." In Arnold C. Harberger and Martin J. Bailey, eds., *The Taxation of Income from Capital*, Washington, D.C.: Brookings Institution, 1969.

Yanowitch, Murray, comp. *Contemporary Soviet Economics: A Collection of*

Readings from Soviet Sources, two volumes. White Plains, N.Y.: International Arts and Sciences Press, 1969.

Yunker, James A. "The Administrative Costs of Langian Socialism." Ph.D. dissertation, Northwestern University, 1971.

———. "An Appraisal of Langian Market Socialism." *Indian Economic Journal* 20(3): 383-413, January-March 1973.

———. "Capital Management Under Market Socialism." *Review of Social Economy* 32(2): 196-210, October 1974.

———. "A Survey of Market Socialist Forms." *Annals of Public and Cooperative Economy* 46(2): 131-162, April-June 1975.

———. "A World Economic Equalization Program: Results of a Simulation." *Journal of Developing Areas* 10(2): 159-179, January 1976.

———. "On the Potential Efficiency of Market Socialism." *ACES Bulletin* 18(2): 25-52, Summer 1976.

———. "The Social Dividend Under Market Socialism." *Annals of Public and Cooperative Economy* 48(1): 91-133, January-March 1977.

———. "Investment Propensities Under Capitalism and Market Socialism." *Rivista di Scienze Economiche e Commerciali* 25(10): 842-855, October 1978.

———. "The Microeconomic Efficiency Argument for Socialism Revisited." *Journal of Economic Issues* 13(1): 73-112, March 1979.

———. "The Microeconomic Efficiency of Socialism: Reply." *Journal of Economic Issues* 15(1): 220-227, March 1981.

———. "Ideological Harmonization as a Means of Promoting Authentic Detente: A False Hope?" *Co-Existence* 19(2): 158-176, October 1982.

———. "The People's Capitalism Thesis: A Skeptical Evaluation." *ACES Bulletin* 24(4): 1-47, Winter 1982.

———. "Optimal Redistribution with Interdependent Utility Functions: A Simulation Study." *Public Finance* 38(1): 132-155, 1983.

———. "Practical Considerations in Designing a Supernational Federation." *World Futures* 21(3/4): 159-218, 1985.

———. "A Market Socialist Critique of Capitalism's Dynamic Performance." *Journal of Economic Issues* 20(1): 63-86, March 1986.

———. "Would Democracy Survive Under Market Socialism?" *Polity* 18(4): 678-695, Summer 1986.

———. "Is Property Income Unearned? A Survey of Some Relevant Theoretical and Empirical Evidence." Working paper, Center for Business and Economic Research, Western Illinois University, 1987.

———. "Risk-Taking as a Justification for Property Income." *Journal of Comparative Economics* 12(1): 74-88, March 1988.

———. "On the Morality of Capitalism: In Light of the Market Socialist Alternative." *Forum for Social Economics* 17(2): 23-39, Spring 1988.

———. "A New Perspective on Market Socialism." *Comparative Economic Studies* 30(2): 69-116, Summer 1988.

———. "A World Economic Equalization Program: Refinements and Sensitivity

Analysis." *World Development* 16(8): 921-933, August 1988.

————. "Some Empirical Evidence on the Social Welfare Maximization Hypothesis." *Public Finance* 44(1): 110-133, 1989.

————. "Ludwig von Mises on the 'Artificial Market.'" *Comparative Economic Studies* 32(1): 108-140, Spring 1990.

————. "The Equity-Efficiency Tradeoff under Capitalism and Market Socialism." *Eastern Economic Journal* 17(1): 31-44, January 1991.

————. "Relatively Stable Lifetime Consumption as Evidence of Positive Time Preference." *Journal of Post-Keynesian Economics* 14(3), Spring 1992.

————. "New Prospects for East-West Ideological Convergence: A Market Socialist Viewpoint." *Coexistence*, forthcoming 1992.

Yunker, James A., and Timothy Krehbiel. "Investment Analysis by the Individual Investor." *Quarterly Review of Economics and Business* 28(4): 90-101, Winter 1988.

Zeckhauser, Richard. *Principals and Agents.* Boston: Harvard Business School, 1985.

Zimbalist, Andrew, and Howard J. Sherman. *Comparing Economic Systems: A Political-Economic Approach.* Orlando, Fla.: Academic Press, 1984.

SUBJECT INDEX

voting rights (stock), 133

wage and salary income, 135
wages of management and supervision, 133
wasteful competition, 3, 45
Watergate coverup, 253

welfare state/programs, 1, 2, 242
whistle blowing, 251
work ethic, 135
World War I, 78, 200, 288
World War II, 248, 260, 261, 264,
  286, 288
World War III, 26, 260

Name Index

ABOUT THE AUTHOR

JAMES A. YUNKER is Professor of Economics at Western Illinois University, Macomb, Illinois, where he has taught economic theory, econometrics, and comparative economic systems since 1968. Dr. Yunker has authored numerous articles, both in economics and in other disciplines including political science and education, in such journals as *Annals of Public and Cooperative Economy*, *Journal of Economic Issues*, *Comparative Economic Studies*, and *Eastern Economic Journal*.